and

HOW TO AVOID HELL

HELL

The Dogma of Hell, Illustrated by Facts Taken
from Profane and Sacred History

by

Rev. Father F. X. Schouppe, S.J.

plus

HOW TO AVOID HELL

by

Thomas A. Nelson

> *"And other sheep I have, that are not of
> this fold: them also I must bring, and they
> shall hear my voice, and there shall be one
> fold and one shepherd."*
>
> —John 10:16

TAN BOOKS AND PUBLISHERS, INC.
Rockford, Illinois 61105

TAN BOOKS AND PUBLISHERS, INC.
P.O. Box 424
Rockford, Illinois 61105

1989

DEDICATION

This book is dedicated to the Blessed Virgin Mary for the greater honor and glory of God and the salvation of souls. Whatever of good this book contains is due to her inspiration.

ACKNOWLEDGMENTS

Grateful acknowledgment is hereby made to the kind readers who have read and critiqued the manuscript of *How To Avoid Hell*, as well as for their many thoughtful suggestions. Particular mention should be made of those who have read the book for theological correctness. Special thanks must also be given to the editors at TAN for their many helpful suggestions, which have made the material in *How To Avoid Hell* far better than it ever would have been without their help, as well as for their faithful help in checking and rechecking the typescript of the entire book in an effort to make the final version as free from technical errors as possible.

CONTENTS

Contents

Publisher's Preface

The purpose of this book is to help people avoid Hell. Part I of this book was written over 100 years ago by the eminent French theologian, Fr. F. X. Schouppe, S.J. (the author also of *Purgatory—Explained by the Lives and Legends of the Saints*). His little book, though it discusses briefly the dogma of Hell and gives a number of biblical references to it, nonetheless concentrates mainly upon telling actual stories of people who have had religious visions, revelations and experiences of various kinds that exemplify most vividly the reality of Hell. And by this method, the author attempts to bring before the mind of his reader the awesome prospect of Hell and that we should be ever cognizant that Hell truly exists, that it is the just reward of the wicked, and that we never know exactly when it is we shall die (since we have no assurance whatsoever of the length of our days) and that therefore we should always be prepared to render an accounting of our lives.

Because the book was written over a century ago, the author did not have access to two extraordinary revelations about Hell from the 20th century, namely the vision of Hell granted by Our Lady to the three children at Fatima on July 13, 1917 and the revelations about Hell found in the spiritual diaries of Sr. Josefa Menendez (1890-1923), a Spanish nun of the Society of the Sacred Heart who was assigned to the order's convent in Poitiers, France, where she had locutions from Our Lord. (These are described in the famous book *The Way of Divine Love*.) More than likely, Fr. Schouppe would have included these two narrations in his book, had he written after they occurred, and therefore they are included as two appendices to this edition of his book.

Also, it was thought well to add in its entirety the parable of Our Lord about Dives the rich man and Lazarus the beggar found in *Luke* 16, plus to give a little analysis of some of the lessons to be derived from that story. This is done in an effort to bring home something of what must be God's view about warning people regarding the reality and the horror of Hell.

And finally, it was deemed wise to add Part II to this book, entitled "How to Avoid Hell." For admittedly Fr. Schouppe's little book is quite scary and may very well leave many readers with no little trepidation. Therefore, in keeping with the purpose of publishing this book—to help people save their souls—this second part was added with that end in view. After all, Fr. Schouppe was a Catholic, and he wrote this as a Catholic book, *for* Catholics. Being French and writing primarily for the French, he could presume that most of the readership in his day would be Catholic—if not practicing, then fallen-away, but at the very least, knowledgeable about the

Catholic Faith, because France has been a Catholic country since the 5th century, when St. Remigius, bishop of Rheims, baptized Clovis, the King of the Franks, on Christmas Day in 496; and most French people in Fr. Schouppe's time were still ostensibly Catholic. (Even today, over eighty percent of the French still claim to be Catholic, despite the fact that many of them do not practice their faith.)

On the other hand, understanding of the Catholic Faith today is far from universal, especially among English-speaking people, and thus Part II of the book seems all the more necessary. For after reading this book, many people will be interested to know just what a person must do to save his soul. Most people today will not have had that complete training in the Catholic Faith to supply the answer, as did the original readers of Fr. Schouppe's time. Experience points out further that even among English-speaking Catholics today, many, if not indeed *most*, do not really have an adequate knowledge of the *basics* of the Faith. Again, therefore, the need for Part II.

The purpose of this book is not to frighten, but to entreat, to admonish, to warn and to convert. That it *is* frightening cannot be helped—for the very subject of Hell is frightening, as is any discussion about it, insofar as that discussion is honest and factual.

But whenever the topic of Hell comes up, there seems always to be a number of almost "standard objections" that are raised against some aspect or other of this doctrine. For example, scoffers will say with great conviction and boldness, "I don't believe in Hell!" Or they will ask belligerent questions such as the following: "How could an infinitely good God condemn a sinner to an eternity of torment?" Or "How could God condemn someone to Hell for one moment's weakness?" Or another version of the same, "People are too weak to avoid sin; how could God condemn them to Hell for doing what they cannot avoid?" Or "Do you think God would condemn a person to Hell forever for just one mortal sin?" Or, "No one can be so bad as to merit *eternal* punishment!" Or again, "How could anyone be happy in Heaven knowing that a loved one is in Hell?"

Then there are the people who indignantly proclaim: "You should not scare people with all this talk about Hell and eternal suffering!" And again, "Your notion of Hell makes God into some kind of great monster who delights in tormenting people in Hell forever. That's not what I understand by God." And again, "God is a God of love and forgiveness. He doesn't go around scaring people. Why should you?" And then there is the pure invention, "Hell doesn't exist in the *next* world; it is *right here!* Each one of us makes his own hell for himself right here in this world."

And finally, there is the Protestant objection, "You Catholics all think you have to *earn* your salvation, and you fret and fret about whether you are saved or not, when all you have to do is put your trust in the Lord Jesus Christ, accept Him as your personal Saviour and receive the salvation He won *for* you on the Cross, once and for all!''

Let us now consider these ''standard'' objections, asking ourselves from whence they come and what are the answers offered by Catholic writers to refute them.

In the first place, it was the good and gentle Jesus, our divine Lord and Master Himself, who taught about Hell and who spoke to us most often about it. He was quite clear that it lasts forever (''Where their worm dieth not and the fire is not extinguished''—*Mark* 9:47), that it is a place of bitterness, anguish and despair (''there shall be weeping and gnashing of teeth''—*Matt.* 8:12), and that it is to be avoided at all costs (''if thy right eye scandalize thee, pluck it out and cast it from thee. For it is expedient for thee that one of thy members should perish, rather than that thy whole body be cast into hell. And if thy right hand scandalize thee, cut it off, and cast it from thee: for it is expedient for thee that one of thy members should perish, rather than that thy whole body go into hell.''—*Matt.* 5:29-30). The doctrine of Hell comes, therefore, from Our Lord Himself. It is *His* teaching and not the invention of men. It must be added that if we say we believe in the teachings of Jesus Christ and we do not believe in Hell, we deceive ourselves. If one does *not* believe in Hell, he might as well forget completely about believing in Jesus.

As to the scoffers, one can easily see that most of those who raise objections to the doctrine on Hell are not themselves authorities in theology, and often they are the very ones who have the greatest reason to hope that there is no Hell and/or that its torments do not last forever. As Fathers Rumble and Carty have observed, "If we are not afraid of sin, we will be afraid of death. If we are afraid of sin, we will not be afraid of death." (*Radio Replies*, Vol. 3, No. 916). Many of the objections to the doctrine on Hell come from sinners trying to rationalize a bad conscience. In any event, let us consider, one by one, the answers given by Catholic writers to these objections.

Many people simply say, "I don't believe in Hell! I don't care what you say, I don't believe in it, and I am not *going* to believe in it. No one can tell me that an infinitely good God could send someone to eternal damnation—to be punished forever and ever!" The answer to this line of argument is very simple: Because you do not believe in Hell does not mean that it does not exist. People who argue thus about the existence of Hell can be compared to someone who says, "I don't believe in Timbuktu; it's just a mythical place that people refer to in light conversation." However, the fact is that Timbuktu is a real place, a city in Africa on the southern edge of the Sahara Desert. Because a person says he does not believe in something does not mean that thing does not exist. It simply means he does not believe in it—for whatever his opinion is worth. The illogicality of such a position is so obvious it does not need any other refutation. With the case of Hell, however, the matter undoubtedly goes deeper. What the person is really saying underneath his bravado is something more like: "I don't *want* to believe in Hell, because if there is one, I am probably going to go there." Or, "Down deep, I really do believe in Hell, but I have to keep kidding myself (and others) or I just couldn't live with myself because of the sinful way I am living."

As to how God could condemn someone to Hell for a moment's weakness or for just one mortal sin, the answer is that God does not actually condemn the soul but the soul damns itself by disobeying God's law. Also, the Catholic Church does not maintain that *any* individual soul is in Hell, not even Judas, but only that certain sins, that is, mortal sins, will send a soul to Hell if the sinner dies with them on his soul and still unrepented of. For, a mortal sin is a mortal sin, and if a person dies unrepentant of such a sin, the Church teaches that the person committing that sin will go to Hell. Nonetheless, we must remember what God has inspired St. Paul to say in Scripture: "My grace is sufficient for thee: for power is made perfect in infirmity." (*2 Cor.* 12:9). In other words, people *can* overcome their sins—of weakness or whatever else—with the help of God's grace. (Cf. Part II.)

We must remember too the admonition from St. James, "And whosoever shall keep the whole law, but offend in one point, is become guilty of all." (*James* 2:10). And also, "But if the just man turn himself away from his justice, and do iniquity according to all the abominations which the wicked man useth to work, shall he live? all his justices which he hath done, shall not be remembered: in the prevarication, by which he hath prevaricated, and in his sin, which he hath committed, in them he shall die." (*Ezech.* 18:24). And again, "The justice of the just shall not deliver him, in what day soever he shall sin." (*Ezech.* 33:12 *ff.*).

As to a sinner's supposedly not being able to merit *eternal* punishment, we have to consider Him whom the sinner consciously offends and *in what manner it is that he does offend!* God, the Author of all being and the infinite Lawgiver, is the One who is offended, and since God is infinitely just and good, the sin against Him dons the infinite aspect of offending the Infinite Good. Plus, the manner in which the person going to Hell offends is by means of a "mortal sin," i.e., a sin which the person *knows* will kill the life of his soul and cut him off from God forever. For the conditions necessary for a person to commit a mortal sin are these three: 1) The sin the person is going to commit (the thought, word, deed or omission) has to be a *grievous matter* (i.e., something seriously wrong) or at least the person must *think* it is a grievous matter); 2) the person has to *know* it is a mortal sin; and 3) he has to *give full consent of his will to committing it*. A mortal sin is therefore not something a person just casually happens to do (unless a certain type of mortal sin has become habitual with him), but it is a serious evil the person actually *knows* he is committing, and yet goes ahead with and commits anyway, with full consciousness of its seriously wrongful nature and with full consent of his will to do it. Mortal sin is what St. Paul is referring to when he enumerates in *1 Corinthians* 6:9-10 some of the sins which cause a person to lose his soul, for such sins bring death to the soul by killing Sanctifying Grace (which is the life of God, infused into the soul through and at the time of Baptism. Cf. Part II).

As to the objection that Hell really exists right here in this world and not in the next, this is completely refuted by Our Lord, who in Scripture gave us the parable of Dives and Lazarus, wherein He clearly indicates (*Luke* 16:22) that *after they died,* Dives went to Hell and Lazarus "into Abraham's bosom" (a term symbolic of Heaven, though actually Limbo). There is, of course, a certain sense in which it is true that for the sinner Hell already exists in this world, for the sinner always has a bad conscience, which never really stops bothering him, and most often he also encounters all manner of reversals in life—which are none other than warnings sent by God that he is on the path to Hell and that he needs to repent and change his life and do penance for his sins.

"How could anyone be happy in Heaven knowing that a loved one is in Hell?" This is a question that comes up almost invariably in connection with the doctrine of Hell, and it poses a true mystery to our finite minds. The explanation is very simple, but it cannot really satisfy us while we are here on earth and have our extremely limited view of the eternal truths, for there is no way truly to comprehend it now, and there will not be until we see all truth in the Beatific Vision (the direct vision of God in Heaven). Nonetheless, the explanation is simply this, that in Heaven we shall then see the infinite mercy of God in extending His saving grace to each soul, and we shall see, when in Heaven, just why it was that a given soul, *by its own fault*, refused God's grace and thus was lost. Because in God all things are perfect equity—perfect and infinite justice tempered and intermixed with perfect and infinite mercy—we shall see the rightfulness of each damned soul's having lost God for all eternity, and we shall affirm perfectly all of His judgments, even when it includes the eternal perdition of our loved ones.

Actually, what should concern us with regard to the eternal loss of our beloved is that we do everything in our power *now*, while still on this earth, to help insure that they *do* save their souls

And this includes praying for them, offering penances for their conversion (if they are not in God's grace) and admonishing them about their sinful state, urging them to repent and do penance. We can admonish personally, or we can do so by sending someone who is skilled at it and/or who is influential with them, or we can give them something powerful to read that may start them thinking thereby and thus on the road to repentance. Indeed, rather than in some maudlin manner, prejudge God's justice with regard to the possible eternal loss of our loved ones, we need rather to storm Heaven *now* with our prayers on their behalf *while they and we are still alive;* we need to move Heaven and earth by our penances, prayers and admonitions. Then, if we ourselves get to Heaven, we will not have the regretful prospect of learning that one of our loved ones has lost his or her immortal soul, for that person will be there with us for all eternity.

Some critics will argue that we should not scare people with the threat of Hell, that rather it is the love of God that should be used to motivate people to be good. However, the truth of the matter in this regard is actually that *both* motives should be used to induce people to be good. For sometimes, and with some people, the love of God is just not enough of a motive to keep them from committing mortal sin (that type of sin that will condemn a person to Hell) or to get them to repent and change their lives if they are already living in mortal sin. But often the fear of Hell will prevent them from committing a mortal sin, or cause them to repent if they are already living in mortal sin. Consider someone steeped in fornication or adultery. This person knows he is doing wrong, and a very serious wrong. Now the love of God might be preached to him from dawn till dark, but to no avail. Whereas, if it should be brought to his or her attention that "no fornicator, or unclean, or covetous person. . .hath inheritance in the kingdom of Christ and of God" (*Ephesians* 5:5), there is an excellent chance that the fear of Hell will bring that person out of his sin.

St. Paul says, "All scripture, inspired of God, is profitable to teach, to reprove, to correct, to instruct in justice." (*2 Tim.* 3:16). Now Scripture is full of the admonition to sinners to repent. It is full of the mercy of God *to the righteous*. It is full of the disastrous end of the sinner. It is full of *caveats* from Almighty God through His inspired writers to those who break His law. All to what end? Obviously, to warn the sinner of the approach of his eternal perdition. Witness: "The Lord who is just will cut the necks of sinners." (*Ps.* 128:4). "The Lord keepeth all them that love him; but all the wicked he will destroy." (*Ps.* 144:20). "And they said: How doth God know? and is there knowledge in the most High? Behold these are sinners; and yet abounding in the world they have obtained riches. . .I studied that I might know this thing, it is a labour in my sight. . .But indeed for deceits thou hast put it to them: when they were lifted up thou hast cast them down. How are they brought to desolation? they have suddenly ceased to be: they have perished by reason of their iniquity." (*Ps.* 72:11, 12, 16, 18, 19). And the good and gentle Jesus reminds us with these stern words: "Unless you shall do penance, you shall all likewise perish." (*Luke* 13:3).

But added to all the above, *consider the entire tone of Scripture*: It is written with absolute sobriety and seriousness. Whereas it speaks of joy and gladness in many places as being the lot of the just, *it virtually never speaks in a light or joyous manner!* (*The Song of Songs*, and some verses from the *Psalms* might be the only exceptions.) Why not? What is the explanation? Why did not Our Lord Himself come smiling and joyful? No, He was called the "Man of Sorrows." His mission was to warn us of the dire end we face if we do not repent and do penance for our sins.

Indeed, the frightening aspect of Hell causes many to be critical on this score and maintain that we should not scare people by talking about it. But they would have to explain away the fact that Our Lord Himself, the gentle Jesus, did not hesitate to warn people about the reality and the absolute horror of Hell; His admonitions in Scripture are tantamont to saying, *"Do anything you have to; just avoid going to Hell!"* Further, for those critics who are believing Catholics, we have the powerful canon from the Council of Trent, which says, "If anyone says that the fear of Hell, whereby, by grieving for sins, we flee to the mercy of God or abstain from sinning, is a sin or makes sinners worse, let him be anathema." (*Sixth Session, Chapter* XVI, *Canon* 8).

And finally there is the Protestant objection that we not only do not have to *earn* our salvation, but that we *cannot*, that rather it is purely the redeeming grace of Jesus Christ that saves us—if we will only accept Him as our personal Saviour. The answer to this Protestant objection is basically threefold: First, Protestantism, and its teaching of salvation through simply covering over our sins with the merits of Jesus Christ, is the "gift" of Martin Luther (1484-1545), a sixteenth century fallen-away Catholic priest. All Protestants to some degree have to claim him as their spiritual father, since he it was who taught the world to invent new "doctrines" and to violate Christian unity, and all Protestants follow his example in these two ways. We can legitimately ask, "What authority did he have to teach us this new doctrine?" This is not Christ's teaching, and to accept Luther's teaching flies right in the face of St. Paul's admonition: "But though we, or an angel from heaven, preach a gospel to you besides that which we have preached to you, let him be anathema." (*Gal.* 1:8).

Second, this "new" "doctrine" of the Protestants is refuted by the Bible in countless places, e.g., "Not every one that saith to me, Lord, Lord, shall enter into the kingdom of Heaven, but he that doth the will of my Father who is in heaven, he shall enter into the kingdom of heaven.'' (*Matt.* 7:21). "If you love me, keep my commandments." (*Jn.* 14:15). "What shall it profit, my brethren, if a man say he hath faith, but hath not works? Shall faith be able to save him?. . . So faith also, if it have not works, is dead in itself. . . Do you see that by works a man is justified; and not by faith only?" (*James* 2:14, 17, 24). "Wherefore, my dearly beloved. . .with fear and trembling work out your salvation." (*Phil.* 2:12).

In the Protestant's favor, however, it must be added that *purely human works* (good acts performed by a person in the state of mortal sin, as a branch cut off from Christ, the living Vine) will avail a person nothing unto salvation. But when these works are done by a baptized person, in the state of Sanctifying Grace (i.e., with *God's Life* in his soul, as a living branch of Christ, the true vine.—*John* 15:1-6), and offered to God, they then combine with God's grace to form a *supernatural* act or work and can thus contribute to help us gain salvation. Protestants need to meditate long and hard on this teaching of Christ and of the Catholic Church, which they tend to gloss over. They are right about *purely human works* not gaining us salvation, but the *"divinized"* or *"supernaturalized"* human works of the baptized soul in the state of grace do indeed contribute to his salvation. The Bible is very clear on the necessity of good works to obtain salvation; it just does not make the explicitation given above. For that understanding, one must be in the living Christian (i.e., Catholic) Tradition that comes down to us intact from the Apostles. (Cf. Part II for a fuller explanation.)

And the third answer to the Protestant objection about our "earning our salvation" is this: without some kind of *proof* of our love for God, as shown by our sustained good acts (works, actions), where would be the *test* of our love of God? A sixth-grade boy in one of my catechism classes once refuted Protestantism better than anything else, other than Scripture, that I have ever heard or read: When presented with the Protestant teaching about just accepting Christ as one's personal Saviour, he said, "That's too easy!" In other words, there is with this Protestant teaching no room for *a real test*—in Protestantism there is no way for us really to *prove* our love for God, who has said, "If you love me, keep my commandments." (*John* 14:15).

Actually, the concept of "Faith" used by many Protestants today is really the broad sense of the term generally used by St. Paul, which encompasses "belief in the truths God teaches, confidence in His promises, obedience to His commands—all done out of love for Him." In this wider sense of "salvation by faith" one can see that the Protestant view is approaching the Catholic position—although this was not the position of Luther, who actually taught salvation by "Faith alone."

This much said, it would seem wise also to

make several other observations about Hell that have been made by various Catholic writers, this in an attempt to put the subject into better focus for ourselves and to examine the "attitude" of Almighty God with regard to our salvation, as we see it expressed in Sacred Scripture.

In the first place it is impossible for the human mind to comprehend either the true nature or the eternity of Hell, and the reason for this is that our minds simply cannot grasp the infinite. Now there are at least two aspects of the infinite connected to the notion of Hell: The first and more obvious is its eternity, which is "an infinity in time," so to speak. But the human mind, being finite, cannot grasp an unending or infinite duration or experience. (Actually, there is really no "time" in eternity—the next life—, but rather an eternal "now"; nonetheless, for the sake of human understanding, we almost have to think in terms of Hell as being of "unending time.")

And the second infinite dimension of Hell concerns the infinite malice of sin, touched upon above. Theologians explain that, whereas man cannot commit *an infinite sin,* he can and does commit mortal sins, i.e., conscious, willful, grievous sins, and he commits them *against the infinite goodness of God.* He will thereby receive as reward, a type of infinite punishment so to speak, for he has made a fundamental decision which places his will fundamentally against God's will and, should he die with such a sin unrepented on his soul, he will therefore go to Hell, because any element of good-will left in him who dies in this state is destroyed by his fundamental choice for evil, even if only in one regard (one type of sin or even just one mortal sin unrepented). For there exists in his soul a sort of total (or "infinite") absence of good-will or good intention, even if, as said, he sins mortally in only one respect, one type of sin, or just one time. For a mortal sin vitiates or destroys the fruit or value of any remaining good-will left in the mortal sinner. Since we cannot fully conceive such a state of soul, its lying for the most part beyond the realm of our experience, this particular "infinite" aspect of Hell is also for the most part beyond our mental grasp while we are still in this world.

Perhaps many have never thought of the matter of Hell in the following light, but numerous writers have raised this telling point: Without Hell there is no real meaning to morality; *the ultimate Good does not HAVE to be striven for* in order for a person to settle at a given level of *relative* good. Because there is no ultimate evil to be avoided, each person could literally settle in to whatever mix of good and evil in his life that he would be comfortable with. All the moral tone and tenor of life would be removed if the existence of Hell were gone. Together, Heaven and Hell form the framework around our moral choices. All we do is in reference to them. Take away Hell, and the balance to the meaning and value of our actions in this life is totally gone. Actually speaking, it is impossible to think of morality without this "ultimate" framework on the side of evil, because in order for being to exist at all requires Absolute Being to sustain it. And only Absolute Being (God) will satisfy the human mind and heart completely. (The eternal loss of this Absolute Being is what we call "Hell.")

Furthermore, many moral evils pass unrectified in this life; many injustices are not corrected here on earth; and many wrongs are not righted. But those who are the unhappy recipients of the unredressed evil in this world always know "in the back of their minds" that there is a divine equity that will rectify and balance all in the end: "Revenge is mine, and I will repay them in due time." (*Deut.* 32:35).

The ultimate source of good found in all good things is God—the Ultimate Good. The ultimate source of all being is God, the Infinite and Ultimate Being. Now conversely, the absolute and ultimate of evil is the complete absence of any good, if we can think of it in these terms. And that is Hell. From the depositions of saints and privileged souls who have been given a small glimpse of Hell or some special insight into it, all aver that the greatest suffering of Hell by far is the knowledge of the soul that it has lost God *forever* and will forever be without this Infinite Good, this good for which it and all created intellects and wills (human and angelic) were made.

(After our souls leave our bodies, we will see with crystal clarity—unlike now—that God is the only satisfaction for our hearts. And the damned will realize in an instant that they have wasted their lives pursuing sinful temporary goals and pleasures and have lost Him forever. The words of Jesus to Judas will resonate throughout their being, "Friend, whereto art thou come?"—*Matt.* 26:80).

Is Hell a legitimate subject of discussion? Should it be openly discussed? Especially should we tell children about it? The answer to all these questions is a resounding, "Yes!." Hell is a doctrine of the Faith. It was taught openly and quite frequently by Our Lord. He spoke in most forceful terms about it. And as far as children go, knowledge of the reality of Hell helps them, like anyone else, to be good, plus it helps them to gain a very early and healthy maturity. A child well-instructed in the Catholic Faith, and taught also by the good example of his or her parents and elders, will gain a very quick and accurate assessment of the vanity of this world. And it is, incidentally, from just such an accurate and clear-sighted assessment on the part of Catholic young people that flow vocations to the priesthood and religious life. For why else would a young person want to give up his or her life "in the world" and a chance to make a name for himself or herself or have a family and "enjoy life," if it were not for the fact that, when one evaluates fairly the reality of this frail existence of ours, with all its illusive joys and pleasures, he sees that it is actually "vanity of vanities, and all is vanity." (*Ecclesiastes* 1:2). Of what value, for example, are worldly satisfactions, which so very often lead the soul into mortal sin and the risk thereby of eternal damnation? Therefore, the young Catholic, well-instructed in the Faith (which includes having an understanding about the reality of Hell) can say with the Psalmist, "Through thy commandment, thou hast made me wiser than my enemies: for it is ever with me. I have understood more than all my teachers: because thy testimonies are my meditation. I have had understanding above ancients: because I have sought thy commandments . . . By thy commandments I have had understanding: therefore have I hated every way of iniquity." (*Psalm* 118:98-100, 104).

Some will undoubtedly throw up the questions, "How can we be sure that all these stories brought forward by Fr. Schouppe are true?" "How do you know the author is not just making all this up?" The answer to these questions is twofold: First of all, it would not matter one iota if all the stories were complete fabrications and simply invented by the author; for the reality of Hell would still be there, just as gruesome as if his little book had never been written. Sacred Scripture would still be just as sober. Its dire warnings would be just as real. Our Lord would still have taught the ominous reality of Hell. And we would all still have the same problem of trying to be good in order to avoid it.

But secondly, and to answer this question from another direction, the author cites his sources for these stories. Granted he does not add pedantic footnotes, since the book is intended for popular consumption, but nevertheless he cites the sources of his information. And further, there are other stories comparable to the ones he uses; witness Appendix I and Appendix II, which are added because the experiences they describe occurred after he wrote, but which are in the same vein as the rest of his material. And then there are many other comparable stories from the lives of the saints which Fr. Schouppe does not use; he has far from exhausted the supply by what he included in this little book. One such story that comes immediately to mind is that told about St. Dominic (1170-1221), when the latter was preaching a sermon at a funeral for a prominent person in the Cathedral of Notre Dame in Paris. The corpse arose from the coffin and spoke, testifying that the soul had gone to Hell and was lost eternally, leaving the people in the congregation aghast. And then there is the story about St. Anthony of Padua, who, about to give the eulogy at the funeral for a very prominent citizen of that city, astounded the congregation by proclaiming that the man had gone to Hell, and he proceeded to admonish the people to change their ways in order to avoid a similar fate. Georges Panneton in his book *Heaven or Hell* (1955) says that "Cases of this kind, where the deceased themselves have brought intelligence of their fate, are very numerous. Dom Augustin Calmet, the learned Benedictine Father, has written a whole book on the subject, *Apparitions d'esprits* (Ratisbonne, 1855). The advantage of these cases mentioned is that no calm and objective criticism can throw doubt on them. Consequently, the dictum that *'no one has ever returned from the world beyond, to tell us that Hell exists'* is absolutely false. The facts of history which establish the existence of Hell are so numerous and so well authenticated that it would be senseless to dismiss them all as doubtful; this is the opinion expressed in [the article *"Enfer,"* i.e., "Hell" in] the *Dictionnaire de Theologie."* (p. 212).

Often in discussing the subject of Hell, there arises the very thorny question of how many or what percent of people are saved. For this bears directly on the question, *"How hard is it to save one's soul?"* Many people today would have it that just about everyone is being saved, but that judgment is not in agreement with the tone and tenor of the Bible, nor does it reflect the attitude of the Saints. Granted, the Catholic Church has never made a pronouncement on the subject, nor has she ever declared, as mentioned, that any particular person is in Hell. Nonetheless, on this subject we have the very sobering words of Our Lord recorded in St. Matthew: "Enter ye in at the narrow gate: for wide is the gate, and broad is the way that leadeth to destruction, and many there are who go in thereat. How narrow is the gate, and strait is the way that leadeth to life: and few there are that find it!'' (*Matt.* 7:13-14). Also, we have the story of the man who came to the wedding feast without a wedding garment: Our Lord puts the following words into the mouth of the king in that story, ''Bind his hands and feet, and cast him into exterior darkness: there shall be weeping and gnashing of teeth. For many are called but few are chosen.'' (*Matt.* 22:13-14). Then there is St. Peter's exclamation: ''And if the just man shall scarcely be saved, where shall the ungodly and the sinner appear?'' (*1 Peter* 4:18).

The mercy of God is of course infinite and unfathomable, and it is a teaching of the Church that all men are given sufficient grace to save their souls. Therefore, the number of the saved *may* be greater than we might imagine from the Scriptures just cited. Still, when one considers the general state of morality today, when people shamelessly behave in a manner unprecedented since the time of Christ, one can truly question seriously if today there are very many who are saved, especially in light of so many sins being openly committed that have been warned against by St. Paul as meriting eternal perdition: ''Know you not that the unjust shall not possess the kingdom of God? Do not err: neither fornicators, nor idolators, nor adulterers, nor the effeminate, nor liers with mankind, nor thieves, nor covetous, nor drunkards, nor railers, nor extortioners, shall possess the kingdom of God.'' (*1 Cor.* 6:9-10).

Everyone should realize that there are certain sins which, because of their gravity, will condemn a person's soul to Hell—if he should die with them unrepented. Examples of such sins are murder (abortion is murder), fornication, adultery, divorce with remarriage, artificial birth control, homosexual acts, substantial theft, failure to worship God, and many others (see Part II). What we need to realize in regard to these quite common mortal sins is that many supposedly very ''nice'' people often commit these sins and are still accepted in polite society. However, we are not discussing here *man's* law and *man's* custom, but the law of God, by which all will be judged and which He has given all men and women to understand by means of the intellect He created them with (and which He has reinforced by divine Revelation). For God has endowed man with a very powerful mind. After all, we are made in His image and likeness. And we can see and understand basic right from wrong without having gone to school and without someone's having to tell us. Granted our understanding and our conscience become clearer as a result of proper moral education, yet we still understand *a great deal* about our basic moral obligations, even without such an education. And it will not matter, when it comes to our own Particular Judgment, that certain mortal sins in our time were commonly accepted in society; we are going to be judged according to what we knew of God's *eternal* law and how we acted based upon that knowledge. (Yet even on the social and psychological level, if one were to scratch very deeply the surface of these "nice sinners," he would probably find that these so-called "nice" people are not really so very nice at all, but rather that they often are, when examined closely, ugly, selfish and vicious, or at the very least, woefully weak, pusillanimous—lacking resolution—and voluptuous.)

And finally, there are two very important points to remember in any consideration of the terrible reality of Hell: The first is that *it is never too late for anyone to repent and do penance*, and the second is that *God's mercy is boundless* and *it is His will that we all save our souls.*

With regard to the lateness of the hour, St. Paul says, "Behold, *now* is the acceptable time; behold, *now* is the day of salvation." (*2 Cor.* 6:2, emphasis added). In other words, "Don't wait! *Now* is the time to go to work on your salvation." Our Lord, after all, told the parable of the laborers in the vineyard, in order to press home the point that no matter at what time in one's life a person decides to repent, to turn to God, to renounce his sins and to do penance for them, God will reward him also with the eternal happiness of Heaven. As even those who went to work in the vineyard at the eleventh hour received the same wage as those who started at the beginning of the day, so too, those of us who, late in life, renounce our sins and change our lives and make reparation for the wrong we have done can gain the same reward (i.e., Heaven) as those who have always been good. We may not attain the same level of virtue, and our reward in Heaven, therefore, may not be as great as those who have "toiled the whole day," but we will still save our souls and we will still be *perfectly* happy with God and the Saints and angels for all eternity.

Our attitude should never be one of *presumption* on God's grace and mercy, nor should it ever be one of *despair* of receiving His forgiveness. Rather, our attitude should be a golden mean which avoids presumption *and* despair. It should be an attitude of prayer and trust, hope and confidence, joy and fear (a healthy fear of our own weakness and God's greatness, realizing that "The fear of the Lord is the beginning of wisdom."—*Psalm* 110:10).

And finally, we must realize that, no matter how bad our sins might have been, it is nonetheless God's will that we all be saved—*if we will renounce our sins and begin to lead good lives!* There is probably no clearer statement in the Bible that *any sinner* can be saved than those powerful words from the Old Testament prophet Ezechiel: "Is it my will that a sinner should die [lose Sanctifying Grace], saith the Lord God, and not that he should be converted from his ways, and live?...When the wicked turneth himself away from his wickedness, which he hath wrought, and doeth judgment, and justice: he shall save his soul alive. Because he considereth and turneth away himself from all his iniquities which he hath wrought, he shall surely live, and not die. . . Be converted, and do penance for all your iniquities: and iniquity shall not be your ruin. . . For I desire not the death of him that dieth, saith the Lord God, return ye and live." (*Ezechiel* 18:23, 27, 28, 30, 32).

From this it can be seen clearly that no one can rightfully accuse those who openly speak about or teach the doctrine of Hell of conceiving God as some great ogre who delights in tormenting the souls of human beings for all eternity. Scripture proves that just the opposite is the case. The Bible speaks loudly of God's tender and unbounding mercy toward mankind—*if man will be good!* "For I desire not the death of him that dieth, saith the Lord God, return ye and live" (*Ezechiel* 18:32), and again, "For I know the thoughts that I think towards you, saith the Lord, thoughts of peace, and not of affliction" (*Jeremias* 29:11). However, *our being good* is the prerequisite to our receiving God's grace and help in our lives, so that we might lead as nearly as possible a clean and sinless life, and one in conformity with His laws. Knowing this and living in such a manner, we can rely implicitly upon God's mercy and we can call upon Him to exercise it toward us—*and He will*! For He has put into the mouth of King David the following reassuring words, words that should console even the *worst* sinner who ever lived that he too can find forgiveness and salvation:

"The Lord is compassionate and merciful: longsuffering and plenteous in mercy. He will not always be angry: nor will he threaten for ever. He hath not dealt with us according to our sins: nor rewarded us according to our iniquities. For according to the height of the heaven above the earth: he hath strengthened his mercy towards them that fear him. As far as the east is from the west, so far hath he removed our iniquities from us. As a father hath compassion on his children, so hath the Lord compassion on them that fear him: for he knoweth our frame. He remembereth that we are dust: man's days are as grass, as the flower of the field so shall he flourish. For the spirit shall pass in him, and he shall not be: and he shall know his place no more. But the mercy of the Lord is from eternity and unto eternity upon them that fear him: And his justice unto children's children, to such as keep his covenant, and are mindful of his commandments to do them." (Ps. *102:8-18*).

No, dear Reader, the reality of Hell is there, whether we say we believe it or not. It is an eternity of indescribable punishment prepared for those who die in the state of opposition to God's law. It was taught by our divine Saviour with an authority, a simplicity, a power and a force that no mere human being could ever equal.

It is a reality we have to consider at all times and during every day. It is the backdrop to our earthly existence; it is that which gives meaning to our moral actions; it is one of the two alternatives that shall be our lot for all eternity. It will not do to pretend it does not exist, to minimize the totally real possibility that very likely the large majority of people are lost (Cf. *Matt.* 7:13-14 and *1 Peter* 4:18), to think that we can safely defer the time of our conversion (Cf. *2 Cor.* 6:2), that we have our old age in which to repent and "get it all together" before we meet our Creator. It will do no good to rail against those who speak of Hell ("Am I then become your enemy, because I tell you the truth?"—*Gal.* 4:16), to claim Hell does not last forever, to minimize the gravity of our sins, to say to ourselves, "God will understand."

The fact is that *we* understand—however inchoately or deeply within ourselves it may be—*we* understand...that life is deadly serious, that it has ultimate ramifications for eternity, that we are on the road, right now, you and I, to salvation or to perdition. *We* understand that we may *not* have tomorrow to repent, or next year, but that "now is the acceptable time" (*2 Cor.* 6:2), and we should "be about our Father's business," which for us is "cleaning up our act," rectifying our lives, renouncing our sins and turning to a life of prayer, penance and good works. *We* understand that every day, every hour, every minute is a precious gift of God which will never return or ever again be ours to use. Yes, *we* understand a great deal. We know in our heart of hearts that every little inspiration to do good comes from God, that it is meant for our ultimate justification, that it is what Our Lord meant when He said, "Behold, I stand at the gate, and knock. If any man shall hear my voice, and open to me the door, I will come in to him, and will sup with him, and he with me." (*Apoc.* 3:20). In this vein we should remember also His words, "Amen, amen I say to you, he that receiveth whomsoever I send, receiveth me; and he that receiveth me, receiveth him that sent me." (*John* 13:20). And, dear Reader, this book may be that "whomsoever I send" spoken of by Our Lord, as far as *you* are concerned. It may be your final invitation of grace to receive Him who knocks at the gate of every heart, seeking those with whom He can enter in and sup—that He may prove to you the infinite mercy of His Sacred Heart and that His mercy is from "eternity to eternity upon them that fear him." (*Ps.* 102:17).

In such a spirit, then, please read and meditate upon this book, and if you are not already in the state of grace, if you are not living with His heavenly life within you, accept today His knock at your gate and let the Divine Healer of Souls enter in to sup with you, to take up His abode with you, to be with you always. That is the purpose of this book. Take it to heart. Apply its lessons. Turn to God and love Him "with your whole heart, and with your whole soul, and with your whole mind'' (*Matt.* 22:37), and plan to live in unutterable joy and peace together with Him—*forever!*

Thomas A. Nelson, Publisher
October 4, 1988
Feast of St. Francis of Assisi

Part I

HELL

by Fr. F. X. Schouppe, S.J.

Chapter I

THE DOGMA OF HELL

THE DOGMA OF HELL is the most terrible truth of our faith. There *is* a Hell. We are as sure of it as of the existence of God, the existence of the sun. Nothing, in fact, is more clearly revealed than the dogma of Hell, and Jesus Christ proclaims it as many as fifteen times in the Gospel.

Reason comes to the support of revelation; the existence of a Hell is in harmony with the immutable notions of justice engraved in the human heart. Revealed to men from the beginning and conformable to natural reason, this dreadful truth has always been and is still known by all nations not plunged by barbarism into complete ignorance.

Hell never has been denied by heretics, Jews or Mohammedans. The pagans themselves have retained their belief in it, although the errors of paganism may have impaired in their minds the sound notion.

It has been reserved for modern and contemporaneous atheism, carried to the pitch of delirium, to outdo the impiety of all ages by denying the existence of Hell.

There are in our day men who laugh at, ques-

1

tion or openly deny the reality of Hell.

They laugh at Hell. But the universal belief of nations should not be laughed at: a matter affecting the everlasting destiny of man is not laughable; there is no fun when the question is of enduring for eternity the punishment of fire.

They question, or even deny the dogma of Hell; but on a matter of religious dogma, they cannot decide without being competent; they cannot call into doubt, still less deny, a belief so solidly established, without bringing forward irrefragable reasons.

Now, are they who deny the dogma of Hell competent in matters of religion? Or are they not strangers to that branch of the sciences which is called theology? Are they not oftenest ignorant of the very elements of religion, taught in the Catechism?

Whence, then, proceeds the mania of grappling with a religious question which is not within their province? Why such warmth in combatting the belief in Hell? Ah! It is interest that prompts them; they are concerned about the non-existence of Hell, knowing that if there is a Hell, it shall be their portion. These unhappy men wish that there might not be one, and they try to persuade themselves that there is none. In fact, these efforts usually end in a sort of incredulity. At bottom, this belief is only a doubt, but a doubt which unbelievers formulate by a negation.

Accordingly, they say there is no Hell. And upon what reasons do they rest so bold a denial?

All their reasons and arguments may be summed up in the following assertions:

"I do not believe in Hell.

"They who affirm this dogma know nothing about it; the future life is an insoluble problem, an invincible, *perhaps*.

"No one has returned from beyond the grave to testify that there is a Hell."

These are all the proofs, all the theology of the teachers of impiety. Let us examine:

FIRST: *I do not believe in it.* You do not believe in Hell? And there is no Hell because you do not believe in it? Will Hell exist any the less because you do not please to believe in it? Should a thief be so foolish as to deny that there is a prison? Would the prison thereby cease to exist if he did not believe in it? And would the thief not enter it?

SECOND: You say that *the future life is a problem and Hell a "perhaps."* You are deceived; this problem is fully solved by Revelation and left in no uncertainty.

But suppose for a moment that there were an uncertainty, that the existence of eternal torments were only probable, and that it may be said: *"Perhaps there is no Hell."* I ask any man of sound reason, would he not be the silliest of men who, upon such a *perhaps*, should expose himself to the punishment of an everlasting fire?

THIRD: They say that *no one returned from beyond the grave to tell us about Hell.* If it were true that no one has returned, would Hell exist the less? Is it the damned who ought to teach us that there is a Hell? It might as well be said that it is prisoners who ought to inform us that there are prisons. To know that there is a Hell, it is not necessary that the damned should come to tell us; God's word is sufficient for us; God it is who publishes it and informs the world concerning it.

But are you who claim that no dead person has returned to speak of Hell; are you quite sure of it? You say it, you declare it; but you have against you historical, proved, unimpeachable facts. I do not speak here of Jesus Christ, who descended into "Hell," and rose again from the dead; there are other dead persons who returned to life and damned souls who have revealed their everlasting reprobation. Still, whatever may be the historical certainty of this sort of facts, I repeat, it is not upon this ground that we claim to establish the dogma of Hell; that truth is known to us by the infallible word of God; the facts which we adduce serve but to confirm and place it in a clearer light.

Chapter II

THE MANIFESTATIONS OF HELL

As we have just said, the dogma of Hell stands on the infallible word of God; but in His mercy, God, to aid our faith, permits at intervals, the truth of Hell to be manifested in a sensible manner. These manifestations are more frequent than is thought; and when supported by sufficient proofs, they are unassailable facts—which must be admitted like all the other facts of history.

Here is one of these facts. It was juridically proved in the process of the canonization of St. Francis Jerome [1642-1716] and under oath attested to by a large number of eye-witnesses: In the year 1707, St. Francis Jerome was preaching, as was his wont, in the neighborhood of the city of Naples. He was speaking of Hell and the awful chastisements that await obstinate sinners. A brazen courtesan [prostitute] who lived there, troubled by a discourse which aroused her remorse, sought to hinder it by jests and shouts, accompanied by noisy instruments. As she was standing close to the window, the Saint cried out: *"Beware, my daughter, of resisting grace; before eight days God will punish you."* The unhappy creature grew only more boisterous. Eight days elapsed, and the holy preacher happened to be again before the same house. This time she was silent; the windows were shut. The hearers, with dismay on their faces, told the Saint that Catharine (that was the name of the bad woman) had a few hours before died suddenly. *"Died!"* he repeated. *"Well, let her tell us now what she has gained by laughing at Hell. Let us ask her."* He uttered these words in an inspired tone, and everyone expected a miracle. Followed by an immense crowd, he went up to the death chamber, and there, after having prayed for an instant, he uncovered the face of the corpse, and said in a loud voice, *"Catharine, tell us where art thou now."* At this summons, the dead woman lifted her head, while opening her wild eyes; her face borrowed color, her features assumed an expression of horrible despair, and in a mournful voice, she pronounced these words: *"In Hell; I am in Hell."* And immediately, she fell back again into the condition of a corpse.

"I was present at that event," says one of the witnesses who deposed before the Apostolic tribunal, "but I never could convey the impression it produced on me and the bystanders, nor that which I still feel every time I pass that house and look at that window. At the sight of that ill-fated abode, I still hear the pitiful cry resounding: *"In Hell; I am in Hell."* (Father Bach, *Life of St. Francis Jerome.*)

Ratbod, King of the Frisons, who is mentioned in ecclesiastical history in the eighth century, had said to St. Wolfrand that he was not afraid of Hell; that he wished to be there with the kings, his ancestors and most illustrious personages. *"Moreover,"* he added, *"later on, I shall be always able to receive Baptism."* *"Lord,"* answered the Saint, *"do not neglect the grace that is offered to thee. The God who offers the sinner pardon does not promise him tomorrow."* The King did not heed his advice and put off his conversion. A year after, learning the arrival of St. Willibrord, he despatched an officer to him, to invite him to come to the court and confer Baptism on him. The Saint answered that it was too late. *"Your master,"* he said, *"died after your departure. He braved eternal fire; he has fallen into it. I have seen him this night, loaded with fiery chains, in the bottom of the abyss."*

Here is another witness from beyond the grave. History avers that when St. Francis Xavier was at Cangoxima, in Japan, he performed a great number of miracles, of which the most celebrated was the resurrection of a maiden of noble birth. This young damsel died in the flower of her age, and her father, who loved her dearly, believed he would become crazy. Being an idolator, he had no resources in his affliction, and his friends, who came to console him, rendered his grief only the more poignant. Two neophytes [i.e., newly converted Christians] who came to see him before the funeral of her whom he mourned day and night, advised him to seek help from the holy man who was doing such great things, and demand from him with confidence, the life of his daughter. The pagan—persuaded by the neo-phytes that nothing was impossible to the Euro-pean bonze [holy man], and beginning to hope against all human appearances, as is usual with the afflicted, who readily believe whatever com-forts them—went to Father Francis, fell at his feet, and with tears in his eyes, entreated him to bring to life again his only daughter whom he had just lost, adding that it would be to give life to himself.

Xavier, touched by the faith and sorrow of the pagan, went aside with his companion, Fernando, to pray to God. Having come back again after a short time, he said to the afflicted father, *"Go, your daughter is alive!"*

The idolator, who expected that the Saint would come with him to his house and invoke the name of the God of the Christians over his daughter's body, took this speech as a jest and withdrew, dissatisfied. But scarcely had he gone a few steps when he saw one of his servants, who, all beside himself with joy, shouted from a distance that his daughter was alive. Presently, he beheld her approaching. After the first em-braces the daughter related to her father that, as soon as she had expired, two horrible demons pounced upon her and sought to hurl her into a fiery abyss, but that two men, of a venerable and modest appearance, snatched her from the hands of these executioners and restored her life, she being unable to tell how it happened.

The Japanese understood who were these two

men of whom his daughter spoke, and he led her directly to Xavier to return him such thanks as so great a favor deserved. She no sooner saw the Saint with his companion, Fernando, than she exclaimed: *"There are my two deliverers!"* And at the same time, the daughter and the father demanded Baptism.

The servant of God, Bernard Colnago, a religious of the Company of Jesus, died at Catania in the odor of sanctity in the year 1611. We read in his biography that he prepared for the passage by a life full of good works and the constant remembrance of death, so apt to engender a holy life. To keep in mind this salutary remembrance, he preserved in his little cell a skull, which he had placed upon a stand to have it always before his eyes. One day it struck him that perhaps that head had been the abode of a mind rebellious to God, and now the object of His wrath. Accordingly, he begged the Sovereign Judge to enlighten him, and to cause the skull to shake if the spirit that had animated it was burning in Hell. No sooner had he finished his prayer than it shook with a horrible trembling, a palpable sign that it was the skull of a damned soul.

This saintly religious, favored with singular gifts, knew the secret of consciences and sometimes the decrees of God's justice. One day God revealed to him the eternal perdition of a young libertine, who was the apple of his parents' eye. The unfortunate young man, after having rushed

into all sorts of dissipation, was slain by an
enemy. His mother, at the sight of so sad an
end, conceived the liveliest terrors for her son's
everlasting salvation and besought Father
Bernard to tell her in what state his soul was.
Despite her entreaties Father Bernard did not
answer by a single word, sufficiently showing
by his silence that he had nothing consoling to
say. He was more explicit to one of her friends.
This person, inquiring why he did not give an
answer to an afflicted mother, the religious
openly said to him that he was unwilling to increase her affliction, that this young libertine
was damned, and that during his prayer God
had shown him the youth under a hideous and
frightful aspect.

On August 1, 1645, there died in the odor of
sanctity, at the College of Evora, in Portugal, Antony Pereyra, Coadjutor Brother of the Company
of Jesus. His history is perhaps the strangest fur-
nished by the annals of this Society. In 1599, five
years after his entrance into the novitiate, he
was seized by a mortal malady in the Isle of St.
Michael, one of the Azores, and a few moments
after he had received the Last Sacraments, beneath the eyes of the whole community, who
were present at his agony, he seemed to expire,
and became cold like a corpse. The appearance—
almost imperceptible—of a slight throbbing of the
heart alone, prevented his immediate burial. Accordingly, he was left three whole days on his
deathbed, and there were already plain signs of

decomposition in the body, when all of a sudden, on the fourth day, he opened his eyes, breathed and spoke. He was obliged by obedience to account to his superior, Father Louis Pinheyro, all that had passed in him after the last pangs of his agony; and here is the summary of the relation, which he wrote with his own hand: "First, I saw from my death-bed," he says, "my Father, St. Ignatius, accompanied by some of our Fathers in Heaven, who was coming to visit his sick children, seeking those who seemed worthy to be presented to Our Lord. When he was near me, I thought for an instant that he might take me, and my heart leaped with joy; but he soon described to me what I must correct before obtaining so great a favor."

Then, however, by a mysterious dispensation of Providence, the soul of Brother Pereyra was momentarily released from his body, and immediately the sight of a hideous troop of demons, rushing headlong upon him, filled him with dread. But, at the same time, his guardian angel and St. Anthony of Padua, his countryman and patron, put his enemies to flight and invited him in their company to take a momentary glimpse and taste of something of the joys and pains of eternity. "They then, by turns, led me to a place of delights, where they showed me an incomparable crown of glory, but one which I had not yet merited; then, to the brink of the Abysmal Pit, where I beheld souls accursed falling into the everlasting fire, as thick as grains of corn cast beneath an ever-turning millstone. The Infernal Pit was like one of those limekilns in which the flame is smothered for an instant beneath the heap of materials thrown into it, only to fire up again by the fuel with a more frightful violence."

Led thence to the tribunal of the Sovereign Judge, Antony Pereyra heard his sentence to the fire of Purgatory, and nothing here below, he declares, could give an idea of what is suffered there, or of the state of anguish to which the soul is reduced by the desire and postponement of the enjoyment of God and of His blessed presence.

So when, by Our Lord's command, his soul was united again to his body, neither the new tortures of sickness (which, for six entire months, combined with the daily help of iron and fire, caused his flesh, irremediably attacked by the corruption of this first death, to waste away) nor the frightful penances to which (so far as obedience allowed him) he never ceased to subject himself for the forty-six years of his new life, were able to quench his thirst for sufferings and expiation. "All this," he used to say, "is nothing to what the justice and mercy of God have caused me, not only to see, but to endure." Finally, as an authentic seal of so many wonders, Brother Pereyra detailed to his Superior the hidden designs of Providence on the future restoration of the Kingdom of Portugal, at that time still distant nearly half a century. But it

may be fearlessly added that the most unimpeachable testimony to all these prodigies was
the surprising sanctity to which Antony Pereyra
never ceased for a single day to rise.

Chapter III

APPARITIONS OF THE DAMNED

St. Antoninus [1389 - 1459], Archbishop of Florence, relates in his writings a terrible fact which, about the middle of the fifteenth century, spread fright over the whole North of Italy. A young man of good stock, who, at the age of 16 or 17, had had the misfortune of concealing a mortal sin in Confession, and, in that state, of receiving Communion, had put off from week to week and month to month, the painful disclosures of his sacrileges. Tortured by remorse, instead of discovering with simplicity his misfortune, he sought to gain quiet by great penances, but to no purpose. Unable to bear the strain any longer, he entered a monastery; there, at least, he said to himself, I will tell all, and expiate my frightful sins. Unhappily, he was welcomed as a holy young man by his superiors, who knew him by reputation, and his shame again got the better of him. Accordingly, he deferred his confession of this sin to a later period; and a year, two years, three years passed in this deplorable state; he never dared to reveal his misfortune. Finally, sickness seemed to him to afford an easy means of doing it. "Now is the time," he said to himself; "I am going to tell all; I will make a general confession before I die.'' But this time, instead of frankly and fairly declaring his faults, he twisted them so artfully that his confessor was unable to understand him. He hoped to come back again the next day, but an attack of delirium came on, and the unfortunate man died.

The community, who were ignorant of the frightful reality, were full of veneration for the deceased. His body was borne with a certain degree of solemnity into the church of the monastery, and lay exposed in the choir until the next morning when the funeral was to be celebrated.

A few moments before the time fixed for the ceremony, one of the Brothers, sent to toll the bell, saw before him, all of a sudden, the deceased, encompassed by chains that seemed aglow with fire, while something blazing appeared all over his person. Frightened, the poor Brother fell on his knees, with his eyes riveted on the terrifying apparition. Then the damned soul said to him: *Do not pray for me, I am in here for all eternity.*'' And he related the sad story of his false shame and sacrileges. Thereupon, he vanished, leaving in the church a disgusting odor, which spread all over the monastery, as if to prove the truth of all the Brother just saw and heard. Notified at once, the Superiors had the corpse taken away, deeming it unworthy of ecclesiastical burial.

After having cited the preceding example, Monsignor de Segur adds what follows (from *Opuscule on Hell*):

"In our century, three facts of the same kind, more authentic than some others, have come to my knowledge. The first happened almost in my family.

"It was in Russia, at Moscow, a short while before the horrible campaign of 1812. My maternal grandfather, Count Rostopchine, the Military Governor of Moscow, was very intimate with General Count Orloff, celebrated for his bravery, but as godless as he was brave.

"One day, at the close of a supper, Count Orloff and one of his friends, General V., also a disciple of Voltaire, had set to horribly ridiculing religion, especially Hell. *'Yet,'* said Orloff, *'yet if by chance there should be anything the other side of the curtain?' 'Well,'* took up General V., *'whichever of us shall depart first will come to inform the other of it. Is it agreed?' 'An excellent idea,'* replied Count Orloff, and both interchanged very seriously their word of honor not to miss the engagement.

"A few weeks later, one of those great wars which Napoleon had the gift of creating at that time, burst forth. The Russian army began the campaign, and General V. received orders to start out forthwith to take an important command.

"He had left Moscow about two or three weeks, when one morning, at a very early hour, while my grandfather was dressing, his chamber door was rudely pushed open. It was Count Orloff, in dressing gown and slippers, his hair on end, his eyes wild, and pale like a dead man. *'What?*

Orloff, you? At this hour? And in such a costume? What ails you? What has happened?' 'My dear,' replied Count Orloff, *'I believe I am beside myself. I have just seen General V.'* 'Has General V., then, come back?' *'Well, no,'* rejoined Orloff, throwing himself on a sofa, and holding his head between his hands; *'no, he has not come back, and that is what frightens me!'*

"My grandfather did not understand him. He tried to soothe him. *'Relate to me,'* he said to Orloff, *'what has happened to you, and what all this means.'* Then, striving to stifle his emotion, the Count related the following: 'My dear Rostopchine, some time ago, V. and I mutually swore that the first of us who died should come and tell the other if there is anything on the other side of the curtain. Now this morning, scarcely half an hour since, I was calmly lying awake in my bed, not thinking at all of my friend, when all of a sudden, the curtains of my bed were rudely parted, and at two steps from me I saw General V. standing up, pale, with his right hand on his breast, and saying to me: *"What do we do now? There is a Hell, and I am there! What do we do now?"* And he disappeared. I came at once to you. My head is splitting! What a strange thing! I do not know what to think of it.'

"My grandfather calmed him as well as he could. It was no easy matter. He spoke of hallucinations, nightmares; perhaps he was asleep. . .There are many extraordinary unaccountable things. . . and other commonplaces, which constitute the comfort of freethinkers. Then he ordered his carriage, and took Count Orloff back to his hotel.

"Now, ten or twelve days after this strange incident, an army messenger brought my grandfather, among other news, that of the death of General V. The very morning of the day Count Orloff had seen and heard him, the same hour he appeared at Moscow, the unfortunate General, reconnoitering the enemy's position, had been shot through the breast by a bullet and had fallen stark dead."

"There is a Hell, and I am there!" These are the words of one who came back.

Mgr. de Segur relates a second fact, which he regards as alike free from doubt. He had learned it in 1859, of a most honorable priest and superior of an important community. This priest had the particulars of it from a near relation of the lady to whom it had happened. At that time, Christmas Day, 1859, this person was still living and little over forty years.

She chanced to be in London in the winter of 1847-1848. She was a widow, about twenty-nine years old, quite rich and worldly. Among the gallants who frequented her *salon*, there was noticed a young lord, whose attentions compromised her extremely and whose conduct, besides, was anything but edifying!

One evening, or rather one night, for it was close upon midnight, she was reading in her bed some novel, coaxing sleep. One o'clock struck by the clock; she blew out her taper. She was about to fall asleep when, to her great astonishment, she noticed that a strange, wan glimmer of light, which seemed to come from the door of the drawing-room, spread by degrees into her chamber, and increased momentarily. Stupefied at first and not knowing what this meant, she began to get alarmed, when she saw the drawing-room door slowly open and the young lord, the partner of her disorders, enter the room. Before she had time to say a single word, he seized her by the left wrist, and with a hissing voice, syllabled to her in English: *"There is a Hell!"* The pain she felt in her arm was so great that she lost her senses.

When, half an hour after, she came to again, she rang for her chambermaid. The latter, on entering, noticed a keen smell of burning. Approaching her mistress, who could hardly speak, she noticed on her wrist so deep a burn that the bone was laid bare and the flesh almost consumed; this burn was the size of a man's hand. Moreover, she remarked that, from the door of the salon to the bed, and from the bed to that same door, the carpet bore the imprint of a man's steps, which had burned through the stuff. By the directions of her mistress, she opened the drawing-room door; there, more traces were seen on the carpet outside.

The following day, the unhappy lady learned, with a terror easy to be divined, that on that very night, about one o'clock in the morning, her lord had been found dead-drunk under the table, that his servants had carried him to his room, and that there he had died in their arms.

I do not know, added the Superior, whether that terrible lesson converted the unfortunate lady, but what I do know is that she is still alive and that, to conceal from sight the traces of her ominous burn, she wears on the left wrist, like a bracelet, a wide gold band, which she does not take off day or night. I repeat it, I have all these details from her near relation, a serious Christian, in whose word I repose the fullest belief. They are never spoken of, even in the family; and I only confide them to you, suppressing every proper name.

Notwithstanding the disguise beneath which this apparition has been, and must be enveloped, it seems to me impossible, adds Mgr. de Segur, to call into doubt the dreadful authenticity of the details.

Here is a third fact related by the same writer: "In the year 1873," he writes, "a few days before the Assumption, occurred again one of those apparitions from beyond the grave, which so efficaciously confirms the reality of Hell. It was in Rome. A brothel, opened in that city after the Piedmontese invasion, stood near a police station. One of the bad girls who lived there had been wounded in the hand, and it was found necessary to take her to the hospital of Consolation. Whether her blood, vitiated by bad living, had brought on mortification of the wound, or from an unexpected complication, she nonetheless died suddenly during the night. At the same instant, one of her companions, who surely was ignorant of what had happened at the hospital, began to utter shrieks of despair to the point of awaking the inhabitants of the locality, creating a flurry among the wretched creatures of the house, and provoking the intervention of the police. The dead girl of the hospital, surrounded by flames, had appeared to her and said: *'I am damned! And if you do not wish to be like me, leave this place of infamy and return to God.'*

"Nothing could quell the despair of this girl, who, at daybreak, departed, leaving the whole house plunged in a stupor, especially as soon as the death of her companion at the hospital was known.

"Just at this period, the mistress of the place, an exalted Garribaldian and known as such by her brethren and friends, fell sick. She soon sent for a priest to receive the Sacraments. The ecclesiastical authority deputed for this task a worthy prelate, Mgr. Sirolli, the pastor of the parish of Saint-Saviour in Laura. He, fortified by special instructions, presented himself and exacted of the sick woman, before all, in presence of many witnesses, the full and entire retraction of her blasphemies against the Sovereign Pontiff and the discontinuance of the infamous trade she plied. The unhappy creature did so without hesitating, consented to purge her house, then made her confession and received the Holy Viaticum with great sentiments of repentance and humility.

"Feeling that she was dying, she besought the good pastor with tears not to leave her, frightened as she always was by the apparition of that damned girl. Mgr. Sirolli, unable to satisfy her on account of the proprieties which would not permit him to spend the night in such a place, sent to the police for two men, closed up the house and remained until the dying woman had breathed her last.

"Pretty soon, all Rome became acquainted with the details of these tragic occurrences. As ever, the ungodly and lewd ridiculed them, taking good care not to seek for any information about them; the good profited by them, to become still better and more faithful to their duties."

Chapter IV

THE DENIAL OF HELL
IS FOOLISH BRAVADO

There are some miserable men, let us rather say, fools, who in the delirium of their iniquity make bold to declare that they laugh at Hell. They say so, but only with their lips; their consciences protest and give them the lie. Collot de Herbois, famous for his impiety as much as for his sanguinary ferocity, was the chief author of the massacres of Lyons in 1793; he caused the destruction of 1,600 victims. Six years after, in 1799, he was banished to Cayenne, and used to give vent to his infernal rage by blaspheming the holiest things. The least act of religion, the slightest show of Christian piety, became the subject of his jests. Having seen a soldier make the Sign of the Cross, he said to him, *"Imbecile! You still believe in superstition! Do you not know that God, the Holy Virgin, Paradise, Hell, are the inventions of the accursed tribe of priests?"* Shortly after, he fell sick and was seized by violent pains. In an excess of fever he swallowed, at a single draught, a bottle of liquor. His disease increased; he felt as if burned by a fire that was devouring his bowels. He uttered frightful shrieks, called upon God, the Holy Virgin, a priest, to come to his relief. *"Well, indeed,"* said the soldier to him, *"you ask for a priest? You fear Hell, then? You used to curse the priests, make fun of Hell!"* *"Alas!"* he then answered, *"my tongue was lying to my heart."* Pretty soon, he expired, vomiting blood and foam.

The following incident happened in 1837. A young second lieutenant, being in Paris, entered the Church of the Assumption near the Tuileries and saw a priest kneeling near a confessional. As he made religion the habitual subject of his jokes, he wished to go to Confession to while away the time and went into the confessional. "Monsieur l'Abbe," he said, "would you be good enough to hear my confession?" "Willingly, my son; confess unrestrained." "But I must first say that I am a rather unique kind of sinner." "No matter; the Sacrament of Penance has been instituted for all sinners." "But I am not very much of a believer in religious matters." "You believe more than you think." "Believe? I? I am a regular scoffer." The confessor saw with whom he had to deal and that there was some mystification. He replied, smiling: "You are a regular scoffer? Are you, then, making fun of me too?" The pretended penitent smiled in like manner. "Listen," the priest went on, "what you have just done here is not serious. Let us leave confession aside; and, if you please, have a little chat. I like military people very much, and then you have the appearance of a good, amiable youth. Tell me, what is your rank?" "Second lieutenant." "Will you remain a second lieutenant long?" "Two, three, perhaps four years." "And after?" "I shall become a first lieutenant?" "And after?" "I hope to become a captain." "And after?" "Lieutenant colonel?" "How old will you be then?" "Forty to forty-five years." "And after that?" "I shall become a brigadier general." "And after?" "If I rise higher, I shall be general of a division." "And after?" "After! There is nothing more except the Marshal's baton, but my pretensions do not reach so high." "Well and good. But do you not intend to get married?" "Yes, when I shall be a superior officer." "Well! There you are married; a superior officer, a general, perhaps even a French marshal, who knows? And after?" "After? Upon my word, I do not know what will be after."

"See, how strange it is!" said the abbe. Then, in a tone of voice that grew more sober: "You know all that shall happen up to that point, and you do not know what will be after. Well, I know, and I am going to tell you. After, you shall die, be judged, and, if you continue to live as you do, you shall be damned, you shall go and burn in Hell; that is what will be after."

As the second lieutenant, dispirited at this conclusion, seemed anxious to steal away, the abbe said, "One moment, sir. You are a man of honor. So am I. Agree that you have offended me and owe me an apology. It will be simple. For eight days, before retiring to rest, you will say: 'One day I shall die, but I laugh at the idea. After my death I shall be judged, but I laugh at the idea. After my judgment, I shall be damned, but I laugh at the idea. I shall burn forever in Hell, but I laugh at the idea!' That is all. But you are going to give your word of honor not to neglect it, eh?''

More and more wearied, and wishing at any price to extricate himself from this blunder, the second lieutenant made the promise. In the evening, his word being given, he began to carry out his promise. *"I shall die,"* he said. *"I shall be judged."* He had not the courage to add, *"I laugh at the idea."* The week had not passed before he returned to the Church of the Assumption, made his confession seriously and came out of the confessional his face bathed with tears and with joy in his heart.

A young person who had become an unbeliever in consequence of his dissipation kept incessantly shooting sarcasm at religion and making jests of its most awful truths. *"Juliette,"* someone said to her one day, *"this will end badly. God will be tired of your blasphemies, and you shall be punished."* *"Bah,"* she answered insolently, *"it gives me very little trouble. Who has returned from the other world to relate what passes there?"* Less than eight days after, she was found in her room, giving no sign of life, and already cold. As there was no doubt that she was dead, she was put in a coffin and buried. The following day, the gravedigger, digging a new grave beside that of the unhappy Juliette, heard some noise;

it seemed to him that there was a knocking in the adjoining coffin. At once, he put his ear to the ground and in fact heard a smothered voice, crying out: "Help! help!" The authorities were summoned; by their orders, the grave was opened, the coffin taken up and unnailed. The shroud was removed; there was no further doubt, Juliette had been buried alive. Her hair, her shroud were in disorder, and her face was streaming with blood. While they were releasing her and feeling her heart to be assured that it was still beating, she heaved a sigh, like a person for a long time deprived of air; then she opened her eyes, made an effort to lift herself up, and said: *"My God, I thank Thee."* Afterward, when she had got her senses well back and, by the aid of some food, recovered her strength, she added: *"When I regained consciousness in the grave and recognized the frightful reality of my burial, when after having uttered shrieks, I endeavored to break my coffin, and struck my forehead against the boards, I saw that all was useless; death appeared to me with all its horrors; it was less the bodily than the eternal death that frightened me. I saw I was going to be damned. My God, I had but too well deserved it! Then I prayed, I shouted for help, I lost consciousness again, until I awoke above ground. Oh, the goodness of my God!"* she said, again shedding tears. *"I had despised the truths of Faith; Thou hast punished me, but in Thy mercy, I am converted and repentant."*

They who deny Hell will be forced to admit it soon; but alas! it will be too late. Father Nieremberg, in his work *The Difference between Time and Eternity,* speaks of an unfortunate sinner, who, as the result of his evil ways, had lost the Faith. His virtuous wife exhorted him to return to God and reminded him of Hell, but he would answer obstinately: *"There is no Hell."* One day his wife found him dead, and strange circumstance, he held in his hand a mysterious paper on which in large characters was traced this terrifying avowal: *"I now know that there is a Hell!"*

Chapter V

THE AWAKING OF THE UNGODLY SOUL IN HELL

Unhappy sinners who are lulled to rest by the illusions of the world and who live as if there were no Hell will be suddenly stripped of their illusions by the most frightful of catastrophes. From the midst of their pleasures they shall fall into the Pit of Torments.

The disaster of the Cafe Kivoto supplies an image of the catastrophe still more terrible which awaits them sooner or later.

The Kivoto was a theatrical cafe at Smyrna, built upon piles in the sea. The extremely stout stakes that kept the house above the waves—water and time-eaten—had lost their solid contents. It was on February 11, 1873, at 10 p.m. Two hundred persons had assembled to witness a comic spectacle. They were amusing themselves when all at once a frightful crash was heard. At the same moment everything gave way and was turned topsy-turvy; the house, with the theater and spectators, was pitched forward and swallowed up in the sea. What an awful surprise for those amusement amateurs! But a more tragic surprise awaits the worldling! A day will come when, from the center of his pleasures, he shall all of a sudden behold himself cast headlong into a sea of sulphur and fire.

On the night of March 31-April 1, 1873, a stately and magnificent steamship, the *Atlantic*, foundered on the Canadian banks near Halifax. The number on board, passengers and crew, reached 950, of whom 700 were lost in this shipwreck. Most of them were wrapped in sleep when the vessel, striking some rocks, sank almost instantaneously. Swallowed up by the sea in the middle of their repose, they awoke in the waters and were suffocated before being able to account for the terrible accident which had just happened. Frightful awaking! But more frightful by far will be the awaking of the atheist when he shall see himself suddenly engulfed in Hell.

On December 28, 1879, there occurred the Tay Bridge accident. The train from London to Edinburgh crosses the Tay, near Dundee, over an iron bridge half a league long. A dreadful storm, which had swelled the waves and broken the bridge during the day, ended by sweeping away several arches, despite the iron cross-bars and piers. These arches, when falling, left an empty space, which was not perceived in the darkness. At 7:30 p.m., the express train out from Edinburgh thundered along, carrying a hundred travellers; it mounted the fatal bridge, and soon, coming on the empty space, was hurled into the waves. Not a cry was heard; in the twinkling of an eye, the victims were in the depths below. What a surprise! What a sudden change! But what will it be when the sinner shall see himself, in the twinkling of an eye, in the pit of Hell?

Chapter VI

TRUTH OF HELL

This is how the Son of God speaks to us of Hell:

"Woe to the world because of scandals. For it must needs be that scandals come: but nevertheless woe to that man by whom scandal cometh.

"And if thy hand, or thy foot scandalize thee, cut it off and cast it from thee. It is better for thee to go into life maimed or lame, than having two hands or two feet to be cast into everlasting fire.

"And if thy eye scandalize thee, pluck it out, and cast it from thee. It is better for thee, having one eye to enter into life, than having two eyes to be cast into hell fire." (*Matt.* 18:7-9; compare 5:29-30).

✠

"And fear ye not them that kill the body, and are not able to kill the soul: but rather fear him that can destroy both soul and body in hell." (*Matt.* 10:28).

"The rich man also died: and he was buried in hell.

"And lifting up his eyes when he was in torments, he saw Abraham afar off, and Lazarus in his bosom.

"And he cried, and said, Father Abraham, have mercy on me, and send Lazarus, that he may dip the tip of his finger in water to cool my tongue: for I am tormented in this flame." (*Luke* 16:22-24).

✠

"Then he shall say to them also that shall be on his left hand: Depart from me, you cursed, into everlasting fire which was prepared for the devil and his angels." (*Matt.* 25:41).

✠

"And I say to you that many shall come from the east and the west, and shall sit down with Abraham, and Isaac, and Jacob in the Kingdom of heaven.

"But the children of the kingdom shall be cast out into the exterior darkness: there shall be weeping and gnashing of teeth." (*Matt.* 8:11-12).

✠

"The King went in to see the guests: and he saw there a man who had not on a wedding garment.

"And he saith to him: Friend, how camest thou in hither not having on a wedding garment? But he was silent.

"Then the King said to the waiters: Bind his

hands and feet, and cast him into the exterior darkness: there shall be weeping and gnashing of teeth." (*Matt.* 22:11-13).

✠

"The unprofitable servant cast ye out into the exterior darkness. There shall be weeping and gnashing of teeth." (*Matt.* 25:30).

✠

"But I say to you, that whosoever is angry with his brother, shall be in danger of the judgment. And whosoever shall say to his brother, Raca, shall be in danger of the council. And whosoever shall say, Thou fool, shall be in danger of hell fire." (*Matt.* 5:22).

✠

"The Son of man shall send his angels, and they shall gather out of his kingdom all scandals, and them that work iniquity:

"And shall cast them into the furnace of fire: there shall be weeping and gnashing of teeth." (*Matt.* 13:41-42).

✠

"And if thy hand scandalize thee, cut it off: it is better for thee to enter into life, maimed, than having two hands to go into hell, into unquenchable fire.

"Where their worm dieth not, and the fire is not extinguished.

"And if thy foot scandalize thee, cut it off. It is better for thee to enter lame into life everlasting than having two feet, to be cast into the hell of unquenchable fire.

"Where their worm dieth not, and the fire is not extinguished.

"And if thy eye scandalize thee, pluck it out. It is better for thee with one eye to enter into the kingdom of God, than, having two eyes to be cast into the hell of fire.

"Where their worm dieth not, and the fire is not extinguished." (*Mark* 9:42-47).

✠

"Every tree that bringeth not forth good fruit, shall be cut down, and shall be cast into the fire." (*Matt.* 7:19).

✠

"I am the vine; you the branches; he that abideth in me, and I in him, the same beareth much fruit: for without me you can do nothing.

"If any one abide not in me, he shall be cast forth as a branch, and shall wither, and they shall gather him up, and cast him into the fire, and he burneth." (*John* 15:5,6).

✠

"But Jesus turning to them, said: Daughters of Jerusalem, weep not over me; but weep for yourselves, and for your children.

"For behold, the days shall come, wherein they

will say: Blessed are the barren, and the wombs that have not borne, and the paps that have not given suck.

"Then shall they begin to say to the mountains: Fall upon us; and to the hills: Cover us.

"For if in the green wood they do these things, what shall be done in the dry?" (*Luke* 23:28, 30-31). That is to say, what will sinners be, destined, like the dry wood, to be burned.

✠

"For now the axe is laid to the root of the trees. Every tree therefore that doth not yield good fruit, shall be cut down and cast into the fire.

"I indeed baptize you in water unto penance, but he that shall come after me, is mightier than I, whose shoes I am not worthy to bear, he shall baptize you in the Holy Ghost and fire.

"Whose fan is in his hand and he will thoroughly cleanse his floor and gather his wheat into the barn; but the chaff he will burn with unquenchable fire." (*Matt.* 3:10-12). Words of St. John the Baptist.

✠

"And the beast was taken, and with him the false prophet, who wrought signs before him, wherewith he seduced them who received the character of the beast, and who adored his image. These two were cast alive into the pool of fire, burning with brimstone." (*Apoc.* 19:20).

Where they were tormented day and night, for ever and ever.

"And whosoever was not found written in the book of life, was cast into the pool of fire." (*Apoc.* 20:15).

To doubt about Hell is to doubt the infallible word of God; it is to give ear to the speech of libertines rather than to the infallible teachings of the Church. The Church teaches that there is a Hell; a libertine tells you that there is not; and should you prefer to believe a libertine? An honorable Roman, Emilius Scaurus, was accused by a certain Varus, a man without word or honor. Being obliged to prove his innocence, Scaurus addressed the people in this short speech: *"Romans, you know Varus, and you know me; now, Varus says I am guilty of the crime charged against me, and I protest that I am not guilty. Varus says yes, I say no; whom will you believe?"* The people applauded, and the accuser was confounded.

Natural reason confirms the dogma of Hell. An atheist was boasting that he did not believe in Hell. Among his hearers, there was a sensible young man, modest, but who thought that he ought to shut the silly speaker's mouth. He put him a single question: *"Sir,"* he said, *"the kings of the earth have prisons to punish their refractory subjects; how can God, the King of the Universe, be without a prison for those who outrage*

His majesty?" The sinner had not a word to answer. The appeal was presented to the light of his own reason, which proclaims that, if kings have prisons, God must have a Hell.

The atheist who denies Hell is like the thief who should deny the prison. A thief was threatened with sentence to prison. The foolish fellow replied: *"There is no court, there is no prison."* He was speaking thus when an officer of justice put his hand on his shoulder and dragged him before the judge. This is an image of the atheist who is foolish enough to deny Hell. A day will come when, taken unawares by divine justice, he shall see himself dashed headlong into the Pit which he stubbornly denied, and he shall be forced to acknowledge the terrible reality of Hell.

The atheist who denies Hell is like the African ostrich. That stupid bird, when chased by hunters, plunges its head into the sand and, standing still, believes it is secure from danger because it does not see the enemy. But soon the piercing arrow comes to undeceive it. Thus absorbed, sunk in earthly things, the sinner is persuaded that he has nothing to fear from Hell, until the day when death strikes him and shows him, by a sad experience, how deceived he has been.

The truth of Hell is so clearly revealed that heresy has never denied it. Protestants, who have demolished almost all dogmas, have not dared to touch this dogma. This fact suggested to a Catholic lady this witty answer. Anxiously importuned by two Protestant ministers to pass over into the camp of the Reformation, she replied, *"Gentlemen, you have indeed achieved a fine reformation. You have suppressed fasting, Confession, Purgatory. Unfortunately, you have kept Hell; put Hell away, and I shall be one of you."* Yes, Messrs. Freethinkers, remove Hell, and *then* ask us to be yours. But know that an *"I do not believe in it"* is not sufficient to do away with it.

Is it not the most inconceivable folly to rely on a *"perhaps"* at the risk of falling into Hell? Two atheists went one day into an anchorite's [hermit's] cell. At the sight of his instruments of penance, they asked him why he was leading so mortified a life. *"To deserve paradise,"* he replied. *"Good Father,"* they said, smiling, *"you would be nicely caught if there is nothing after death!"* *"Gentlemen,"* rejoined the holy man, as he looked at them with compassion, *"you will be quite otherwise if there is!"*

A young man belonging to a Catholic family in Holland, as a consequence of imprudent reading, had the misfortune to lose the treasure of faith and to fall into a state of complete indifference. It was a subject of the bitterest grief for his parents, especially his pious mother. In vain did this "other Monica" give him the most solid lectures; in vain did she admonish him with tears to come back to God; her unhappy son was deaf and insensible. Yet at last, to satisfy his mother, he was pleased to consent to spend a few days in a religious house, there to follow the exercises of a retreat, or rather, as he put it, to rest a few days and smoke tobacco, an enjoyment he loved. So he listened with a distracted mind to the instructions given to those making the retreat and speedily after began again to smoke without thinking further of what he had heard. The instruction on Hell, to which he seemed to listen to like the rest, came on, but being back again in his little cell, while he was taking his smoke as usual, a reflection arose in his mind in spite of himself: *"If, however, it should be true,"* he said to himself, *"that there is a Hell! If there be one, clearly it shall be for me! And in reality, do I know myself that there is not a Hell? I am obliged to acknowledge that I have no certainty in this behalf; the whole basis of my thinking is only a perhaps. Now, to run the risk of burning for eternity on a perhaps, frankly speaking, as a matter of extravagance, would be to go beyond bounds. If there are some who have such courage, I have not sufficiently lost my senses to imitate them."* Thereupon, he began to pray; grace penetrated his soul; his doubts vanished; and he rose up, converted.

A pious author relates the history of the tragic punishment that befell an ungodly scoffer of Hell. This was a man of quality whom the author, through respect for his family, does not name; he designates him by the fictitious name of Leontius. This unfortunate man made it a boast to brave Heaven and Hell, which he treated as chimerical superstitions. One day, when a feast was about to be celebrated at his castle, he took a walk, accompanied by a friend, and wished to go through the cemetery. Chancing to stumble against a skull lying on the ground, he kicked it aside with profane, blasphemous words: *"Out of my way,"* he said, *"rotten bones, worthless remains of what is no more."* His companion, who did not share in his sentiments, ventured to say to him that he did *"wrong to use this language. The remains of the dead,"* he added, *"must be respected on account of their souls, which are always alive, and which will assume their bodies again on the day of the Resurrection."* Leontius answered by this challenge, spoken to the skull: *"If the spirit that animated thee still exists, let it come and tell me some news about the other world. I invite it for this very evening to my banquet."* Evening came; he was at table with numerous friends and telling his adventure of the cemetery, while repeating his profanations, when all at once, a great noise was made, and almost at the same time a horrible ghost appeared in the dining room and spread fright among the guests. Leontius, especially, losing all his audacity, was pale, trembling, out of his wits. He wanted to flee; the spectre did not give him time, but sprang upon him with the swiftness of lightning, and smashed his head to pieces against the wainscot. A day will come when the pride of the ungodly shall be dashed down and their heads broken by the Judge of the living and the dead: *"The Lord shall judge among nations, he shall fill ruins; he shall crush the heads in the land of many."* (*Ps.* 109:6).

Here is another fact almost contemporaneous and related by a trustworthy author: Two young men, whose names, through respect for their families, must remain secret, but whom I shall call Eugene and Alexander, old schoolmates and college friends, met again later in life after a long separation. Eugene, having stayed at home, used to occupy himself with works of charity, according to the spirit of the Society of St. Vincent de Paul, of which he was a member. Alexander had entered the army and obtained the rank of colonel, but unhappily, there lost every spark of religion. Having procured a leave of absence of a few days, he had returned to his family and wished to see Eugene. The interview happened on a Sunday. After they had chatted together for a time, Eugene said, *"Alexander, it is time to leave you."* *"Where do you wish to go? It cannot be there is anything pressing?"* *"I am going first after the business of salvation; then I must attend a benevolent reunion."* *"Poor Eugene; I see it; you still believe in Paradise and Hell. 'Tis all a chimera, superstition, fanaticism."* *"Dear Alexander, do not speak so; you, like me, learned that the dogmas of faith rest on unexceptionable facts."* *"Chimeras, I tell you, which I believe no longer. If there be a Hell, I am willing to go there today. Come with me to the theater."* *"Dear friend, use your liberty, but do not brave God's justice."* Eugene spoke to a deaf man, who was unwilling to heed salutary advice. He left him with a sore heart. That very day, in the evening, Eugene was already in bed, when he was awakened. *"Quick,"* they said to him, *"rise, go to Alexander's; he has just been brought back from the theater, seized by a frightful pain."* Eugene ran there, and found him tossed by violent convulsions, with foam in his mouth and rolling his wild eyes. As soon as he saw Eugene, he shouted, *"You say there is a Hell; you say truly there is a Hell, and I am going there; I am there already; I feel its tortures and fury."*

In vain did Eugene try to calm him; the unhappy man answered only by yells and blasphemies. In the transports of his rage, he tore with his teeth the flesh off his arms and cast the bleeding fragments at Eugene, his mother, and sisters. It was in this paroxysm of agony that he expired. His mother died of grief, his two sisters entered religion, and Eugene also quitted the world; owner of a brilliant fortune, he forsook all to consecrate himself to God and avoid Hell.

Chapter VII

PAINS OF HELL

What predominates in the words of Scripture when it exhibits to us the pains of Hell is the terrible torture of the fire. The Scriptures call Hell a "pool of sulphur and fire," the "gehenna of fire," the "eternal fire," a "fiery furnace where the fire shall never be extinguished." But this fire, kindled by divine justice, will possess an activity incomparably superior to that of all the furnaces, all the fires, of this world. Alas! Do we understand how it shall be possible to bear it? How it will be necessary to dwell in it as in an everlasting habitation? *"Which of you,"* demands the Prophet, *"can dwell with devouring fire? Which of you shall bear everlasting burnings?"* (*Isaias* 33:14).

In 1604, in the city of Brussels, there occurred the celebrated apparition of a damned soul, attested by Blessed Richard of St. Ann, of the Order of St. Francis, who suffered martyrdom at Nagasaki, in Japan, on September 10, 1622, and who was beatified by Pius IX in 1868. Blessed Richard related the fact to a theologian of the Spanish Inquisition, Father Alphonsus of Andrada, of the Company of Jesus; he, in turn, communicated it to Adrian Lyroeus, who has

inserted it in his *Trisagium Marianum,* Book
III. Saint Alphonsus Liguori, who cites the same
fact in his *Glories of Mary,* has made Blessed
Richard one of the two actors in this frightful
drama; he [Bl. Richard] was only a witness, like
many others who were living at Brussels, but
the impression he experienced was so lively that
it became the determining cause of his entrance
into the Seraphic Order.

This is how the occurrence is related, after
authentic documents in the *Annals of Franciscan Missions,* for the years 1866-67.

It was not without a terrible, though merciful
interposition of God's justice, that Blessed
Richard was brought to demand the habit of St.
Francis. It was in 1604. There were at Brussels,
where Richard was at that time, two young students who, instead of applying themselves to
study, thought only of how to live in pleasure
and dissipation. One night, among others, when
they had gone to indulge in sin in a house of
ill-fame, one of the two left the place after some
time, leaving his miserable companion behind
him.

Having reached home, he was about to lie down
in bed, when he remembered that he had not
recited that day the few *Hail Marys* which he
had the habit of saying every day in honor of
the Holy Virgin. As he was overpowered by sleep,
it was troublesome for him; however, he made
an effort and said them, although without devotion; then he went to bed. In his first sleep he

heard all of a sudden, a rude knocking at the door; and immediately afterward he saw before him his companion, disfigured and hideous. "Who are you?" he said to him. "What? Don't you know me?" replied the unhappy youth. "But how are you so changed? You look like a devil?" "Ah, pity me; I am damned!" "How is that?" "Well, know that upon leaving that accursed house a devil sprang upon me and strangled me. My body has remained in the middle of the street, and my soul is in Hell. Know, moreover, that the same chastisement awaited you, but the Virgin preserved you from it, thanks to your practice of reciting every day a few *Hail Marys* in her honor. Happy are you if you know how to profit by this information, which the Mother of God gives you through me."

While finishing these words, the damned soul partly opened his garment, allowed the flames and serpents that were tormenting him to be seen, and vanished. Then the young man, melting into tears, threw himself on his face on the floor to thank the Holy Virgin Mary, his deliverer. Now, while he was praying in this manner and reflecting upon what he ought to do to change his life, he heard the Matins bell ring at the Convent of Our Fathers.

That very moment he cried out, "There it is that God calls me to do penance." The next day, indeed, at a very early hour, he went to the convent and begged the Father Guardian to receive him. The Father, who was aware of his bad

life, having presented difficulties at first, the
young student, shedding a torrent of tears,
related to him all that had taken place. And
really, two religious, having repaired to the street
indicated, found the corpse of the wretched
youth, black as a coal. Then the postulant was
admitted among the Brothers, whom he edified
by a life altogether devoted to penance.

Such is the terrible fact which struck dismay
and fright into many souls and which induced
Blessed Richard also to consecrate himself entirely to God in the same Order into which the
young student, so wonderfully protected by Mary,
had just been received.

The following fact is related by Father Martin
Del Rio, from the *Annals of the Company of
Jesus*. It is an apparition that occurred in 1590
and was vouched for by trustworthy witnesses:
Not far from Lima, dwelt a Christian lady who
had three maid-servants, one of whom, called
Martha, was a young Indian of about sixteen
years. Martha was a Christian, but little by little she grew cool in the devotion she had at
first displayed, became negligent in her prayers,
and light, coquettish, and wanton in her con-
versations. Having fallen dangerously ill, she
received the Last Sacraments. After this serious ceremony, during which she had evinced
very little piety, she said, smiling to her two
fellow servants, that in the confession she had
just made she had taken good care not to tell
all her sins to the priest. Frightened by this

language, the girls reported it to their mistress, who by dint of exhortations and threats, obtained from the sick girl a sign of repentance and the promise to make a sincere and Christian confession. Martha confessed then, over again, and died shortly afterward.

Scarcely had she breathed her last, when her corpse emitted an extraordinary and intolerable stench. They were obliged to remove it from the house to a shed. The dog in the courtyard, usually a quiet animal, howled piteously, as if he were undergoing torture. After the interment, the lady, according to custom, was dining in the garden in the open air, when a heavy stone fell suddenly onto the center of the table with a horrible crash and caused all the table settings to bounce, but without breaking any article. One of the servants, having occupied the room in which Martha had died, was awakened by frightful noises; all the furniture seemed to be moved by an invisible force and thrown to the floor.

We understand how the servant did not continue to occupy that room; her companion ventured to take her place, but the same scenes were renewed. Then they agreed to spend the night together there. This time they distinctly heard Martha's voice, and soon that wretched girl appeared before them in the most horrible state, and all on fire. She said that by God's command she had come to reveal her condition to them, that she was damned for her sins of impurity and for the sacrilegious confessions she had continued to make until death. She added, *"Tell what I have just revealed to you, that others may profit by my misfortune."* At these words she uttered a despairing cry and disappeared.

The fire of Hell is a real fire, a fire that burns like this world's fire, although it is infinitely more active. Must not there be a real fire in Hell, seeing that there is a real fire in Purgatory? *"It is the same fire,"* says St. Augustine, *"that tortures the damned and purifies the elect."* A number of indisputable facts demonstrates the reality of the fire in the place of expiation. This is what Mgr. de Segur relates:

"In the year 1870, in the month of April," he writes, "I saw, or at least, touched at Foligno, near Assisi, in Italy, one of those frightful imprints of fire, caused sometimes by souls that appear and prove that the fire of the other life is a real fire. On November 4, 1859, there died of a stroke of apoplexy, at the Convent of the Tertiary Franciscans of Foligno, a good Sister named Theresa Gesta, who had been many years mistress of novices and at the same time in charge of the poor little clothesroom of the monastery. She was born at Corsa in Bastia in 1797, and she entered the monastery February, 1826. It need not be said that she was well prepared for death.

"Twelve days afterward on the 6th of November, a sister named Anna Felicia, who replaced her in her office, went up to the wardrobe and was about to enter when she heard moans which seemed to come from the interior of this room. Somewhat alarmed, she hastened to open the door; no one was there. But new moans resounded, so clearly articulated that, despite her usual courage, she felt seized by fear. *'Jesus, Mary!'* she exclaimed, *'what is this?'* She had not finished when she heard a plaintive voice, accompanied by this mournful sigh: *'Oh, my God, how I suffer!'* (*'Oh! Dio che peno tanto.'*) The shocked sister recognized at once the voice of poor Sister Theresa. Then the whole hall was filled with a dense smoke, and the ghost of Sister Theresa appeared, moving toward the door, while gliding along by the wall. Having almost reached the door, she exclaimed forcibly: *'This is a sign of the mercy of God.'* And saying that, she struck the highest panel of the door, leaving hollowed in the charred wood a most perfect stamp of her right hand; then she disappeared.

"Sister Anna Felicia had remained half dead with fear. All confused, she began to cry out and call for help. One of her companions hastened to her, then another, then the whole community; they pressed eagerly around her, and they were all astonished at finding a smell of burnt wood. Sister Anna Felicia told them what had just taken place and showed them the terrible stamp on the door. They immediately recognized the shape of Sister Theresa's hand, which was remarkably small. Alarmed, they took flight, ran to the choir, began to pray, spent the night praying and doing penances for the deceased, and the next day all received Communion for her.

"The news spread abroad, and the different communities of the city joined their prayers to those of the Franciscans. The next day following, November 18, Sister Anna Felicia, having retired to her cell to go to bed, heard herself called by her name and recognized perfectly the voice of Sister Theresa. At the same instant an all-resplendent sphere of light appeared before her, lighting up the cell as if at noonday, and she heard Sister Theresa, who, with a joyous, triumphant voice, uttered these words: *'I died on Friday, the day of the Passion, and behold, on a Friday I depart for glory! Be brave in carrying the Cross; be courageous in suffering; love poverty.'* Then, adding affectionately, *'Adieu, Adieu, Adieu!'* she became transfigured into a thin, white, dazzling cloud; she flew away to Heaven and vanished.

"A canonical inquest was immediately held by the Bishop of Foligno and the magistrates of the city. On November 23, in the presence of a great number of witnesses, the grave of Sister Theresa was opened and the stamp burned into the door was found exactly to correspond with the hand of the deceased. The result was an official judgment that established the perfect certainty and authenticity of what we have just narrated. The door with the burned mark is preserved with veneration in the Convent. The Mother Abbess, a witness of this fact, deigned to show it to me herself.''

St. Peter Damian speaks of a worldling who lived only for amusement and pleasure. To no purpose was he advised to think of his soul; to no purpose was he warned that, by following the life of the wicked rich man, he should reach the same end; he continued his guilty life unto death. He had scarcely ceased to live when an anchorite [a hermit] knew of his damnation. He saw him in the midst of a fiery pool; it was an immense pool like a sea, in which a great number of people, howling with despair, were plunged. They were striving to gain the shore, but it was guarded by pitiless dragons and demons, who prevented them from coming near it, and hurled them far back into that ocean of flames.

Nicholas of Nice, speaking of the fire of Hell, says that nothing on earth could give an idea of it. If, he adds, all the trees of the forests were cut down, piled up into a vast heap and set on fire, this terrible pile would not be a spark of Hell.

Vincent of Beauvais, in the twenty-fifth book of his history, narrates the following fact, which he says happened in the year 1090: Two young libertines, whether seriously or through mockery, had made a mutual promise: whichever of the two died first would come and tell the other in what state he was. So one died, and God permitted him to appear to his companion. He was in a horrible state and seemed to be the prey of cruel sufferings, which consumed him like a burning fever and covered him with sweat. He wiped his forehead with his hand and let a drop of his sweat fall onto his friend's arm, while saying to him: *"That is the sweat of Hell; you shall carry the mark of it till death."* That infernal sweat burned the arm of the living man, and penetrated his flesh with unheard-of pains. He profited by this awful information and retired to a monastery.

Peter, the venerable Abbot of Cluny, tells an incident of the same kind. A dying man persisted in sin and was about to die impenitent. Burned by fever and tortured by thirst, he asked for some cold water to cool himself. God permitted, thanks to prayers offered for this wretched man, two infernal spirits to appear to him under a visible form. They bore a goblet containing a liquid, a drop of which they threw on the sick man's hand, saying: *"This is the cold water used for cooling Hell!"* The infernal liquid went through and through the hand, burning the flesh and bones. The attendants saw with astonishment this terrible phenomenon, as well as the convulsions of the sinner, who twisted and turned in his unspeakable sufferings. If the cold water of Hell burns like that, what will the boiling water and blazing sulphur do?

In 1870, the city of New York witnessed a conflagration, the circumstances of which offered an image of Hell. The Barnum menagerie became the prey of flames. It was stocked with tigers, lions and other wild beasts. All these animals were burned alive in their iron cages, the bars of which grew to a white heat. As the fire and the heat became more intense, the beasts became more enraged. With extreme violence they sprang at the bars of their prisons, and fell back like inert heaps, only to leap again at the insuperable obstacle which held them captive. The awful roars of the lions, the screams of the tigers, the howls of all the animals, which betrayed supreme despair, were blended together and formed a frightful chorus, bringing to mind what the damned must hear resounding in Hell. But the sounds of this terrible concert grew weaker and weaker, until the lion having uttered his last roar, the silence of death succeeded the most doleful din.

Fancy in these shining iron cages, not animals, but men, and men who, instead of dying in the fire, continue to live in it, as if their bodies were harder than iron; this would be an image of Hell, but an imperfect one, for all of that.

On Friday, February 18, 1881, there was a carnival ball given at Munich by the young artist-painters. They were numerous and masked, some as monks, priests, comical pilgrims, carrying grotesque-looking beads, and making a parody of religious usages; others like Esquimaux, covered with tow, pitch and hemp. A cigar, imprudently lighted, set fire to one of these inflammable costumes. The unfortunate person, seeing himself in flames, rushed headlong among his companions; in a minute all these tow and pitch garments were on fire. Twelve of the dancers, like living torches, ran about crazy, unable to receive help. They flung themselves onto one another, roamed around uttering mournful wails, rushed blazing into all the corners of the hall, spreading around a disgusting odor. Soon three of them were only charred corpses. Nine others died shortly after; thirteen were transported to the hospital. Among these last was Joseph Schonertzer; he expired when skillful hands were proceeding with the first bandaging. The skin peeled off his breast and arms; it came off partly in rolls, leaving the living flesh bare, scorched also by the fire. This dreadful death was regarded, not without reason, as a chastisement of the Divine Justice, which these unhappy young people had provoked by their excesses of impiety and dissipation. It presents at the same time an image of Hell, but with two great differences: it is far less cruel, and it lasts only a short time.

On March 24, 1881, another catastrophe threw the city of Nice into a state of fright and dismay: the municipal theater became a prey to flames. This theater had doors exceedingly narrow and absolutely insufficient for passage in case of a great rush. On March 24, a brilliant presentation, which had drawn numerous spectators, was given. The curtain had just risen for the first act when, at the expiration of a few minutes, there was an explosion among the footlights; all at once the flames were seen to issue from the frail boards and gain the stage. The shouts, *"Fire! fire!"* came from all parts of the theater, and the panic became general, especially when new explosions were heard.

The orchestra and the stage were in complete darkness. Only the glimmer of the great fire, which was rapidly spreading, revealed to the gaze a few unfortunate actresses crossing the stage, crazy, wild with terror, and seeking an outlet, which the flames barred against them. The audience in the galleries, with a frenzied violence, rushed headlong down the winding stairs to the corridors.

The women, the children, were trampled under foot. Only shouts of terror and despair were heard, the shouts of all those human beings, who were struggling to save their lives and who felt themselves dying, suffocated by the smoke, or ground beneath the feet of their neighbors.

When the firemen, soldiers and marines could penetrate the interior, the spectacle was horrible. There was a pile of corpses, black, hideous, some almost entirely reduced to cinders. These were the bodies of the unfortunate spectators, who rushed down, all at once, by the narrow stairways. Men, women and children, hanging on to one another, had rolled into this place. What poignant, frightful dramas must have been enacted during these few supreme minutes, when safety was possible no more.

At three in the morning, 63 corpses were borne to the Church of St. Francis of Paola. They were half burned. The anguish of the most harrowing agonies might be detected in their faces and postures.

What will it be in Hell? There also, all outlet is closed in the midst of the great fire; there too, is the anguish of direct agony; but there death does not come to end it. Were these unhappy people ready to die? Alas! It is not to the theater that we go to prepare for death! Is it not to be feared that this place may have literally been the gate of Hell for them? Ah! If the grilled, charred victims had known that this fate awaited them, would they not have foregone a pleasure which must cost them so dearly? Your guilty pleasures, worldlings, will cost you dearer, and you do not renounce them.

An omen still more frightful, the burning of the *Ring Theater*, at Vienna, happened on December 8, 1881. Offenbach's *Contes d'Hoffman* [*Stories of Hoffman*] were going to be represented. This piece, which was to be played for the first time, had drawn quite a throng of spectators; their number exceeded 1,500. At seven in the evening, just when the performance was about to begin, fire burst forth, and a cry of alarm threw fright into the assemblage, fright which became frenzy when the flames were seen to shoot forward, stretch out, and swiftly invade the vast enclosure. In the twinkling of an eye, this hall, packed with people, was found to be all on fire and changed into a genuine hell. To describe the tumult, the cries of distress, despair, rage, would be impossible. The wretched people rushed toward the narrow exits, were upset, and crushed, one by the other, or by the fiery timbers that toppled over their heads. Others, in the gallery, crushed their way to the windows to jump into the street. They were seen from the outside, clinging to one another, and forming as if human bunches of grapes, suspended a moment, then letting go, and trusting to the empty space, to escape the terrible element of fire.

But the great number were imprisoned within. A thousand men, women, children, abandoned in the midst of the flames, died the most horrible death, burned alive, charred, reduced to cinders. In the sweepings, all that was found of them was their charred bones. However, all were not so completely consumed, and many corpses were only half-burned. An enormous heap was discovered, with arms entwined together, grappling with one another, and betraying the supreme struggle in which they had expired. It was recognized with horror that in this furnace there had been a desperate combat among the fugitives; these unfortunate people had jostled their way, seized, knocked down furiously everyone to gain an exit, which they were not to find. They were forced to undergo the pain [of fire] and to die there.

This is of course only a very weak image of Hell. There the damned are tortured by fire, an everlasting fire, but do not die.

On the occasion of the dreadful catastrophe of the Ring Theater, an estimate of the theaters burned during the previous century was made; the figure rose to several hundred. Is there not a lesson of Providence here, upholding the warnings which the Church does not cease to give the faithful? Since the contemporary theater is generally a school of irreligion and immorality, a hotbed of corruption for nations, do not the continual great fires point out sufficiently that these edifices, given up to fire, are for souls the gates of Hell?

The sight of a soul that falls into Hell is of itself alone an incomparable pain. St. Margaret Mary, as her history relates, beheld the apparition of one of her sisters in religion, recently deceased. That sister implored her prayers and suffrages; she was suffering cruelly in Purgatory. *"See,"* she said to St. Margaret, *"the bed I lie on, where I am enduring intolerable pains."* I saw that bed, writes the Saint, and it still makes me shudder; it was bristling with sharp and fiery spikes which entered the flesh. The deceased added that she was suffering this torture for her sloth and negligence in observing the rule. *"This is not all,"* she said again; *"my heart is torn in my bosom to punish my murmurs against my superiors; my tongue is eaten by worms for my words contrary to charity and my breaches of silence. But all this is a small matter in comparison with another pain which God made me experience; although it did not last long, it was more painful to me than all my sufferings."* The Saint, having desired to know what this dire pain was, she replied, *"God showed me one of my near female relatives who had died in a state of mortal sin sentenced by the Supreme Judge and dashed into Hell. That sight caused me a fright, horror, pain that no tongue could communicate."*

Surius, in the *Life of St. Lydwine*, relates that, in an ecstasy, this servant of God saw an abyss, the wide opening of which was bordered with flowers, and the great depth of which, when the eye pierced it, chilled with terror. There issued from it an indescribable noise, a frightful mixture of yells, blasphemies, tumult, ringing blows. Her Angel Guardian told her that it was the abode of the damned, and he wanted to show her the torments they suffer. *"Alas!"* she replied, *"I could not bear the sight of them. How could I, as the mere noise of these despairing yells caused me an unbearable horror?"*

If the damned suffered no other pain in Hell than to remain there always, without motion, without changing place or position, that alone would be an insupportable torment. A wealthy voluptuary, loaded down with crimes and dreading Hell, did not have the courage either to break off with his evil habits or to expiate his sins by penance. He had recourse to St. Lydwine, who at that time was edifying the world by her patience, and begged her to do penance for him. *"Willingly,"* she replied. *"I will offer my sufferings for you on condition that for the space of one night you keep the same position in your bed, without changing sides, budging [or] stir-*

ring." He readily consented. But, having lain down in bed, he had scarcely rested half an hour when he felt uncomfortable and wished to move. Nevertheless, he did not do it and remained immovable, but the discomfort went on increasing, so much so that at the end of an hour it seemed intolerable to him. Then a salutary reflection sprang up in his mind: *"If it is such a torture,"* he said to himself, *"to remain without motion upon a comfortable bed for the space of one night, what would it be, if I were bound down on a bed of fire for the space of a century, of an eternity? And do I fear to redeem such a punishment by a little penance?"*

St. Christina, a virgin, justly surnamed "The Admirable," born at St. Trond in 1150, after her death came to life again and lived afterward for forty-two years, enduring unheard of sufferings for the relief of the souls in Purgatory and the conversion of sinners.

After a youth spent in innocence, patience and humility, Christina died in the odor of sanctity at the age of 32 years (1182). Her body was borne to the Church of Notre Dame, in which her obsequies were to be celebrated, and it was placed in the middle of the nave, after the manner of that period, in an open coffin. The great throng of people who were present were praying devoutly, when at the time of the *Agnus Dei,* the deceased lifted herself up in her coffin, and a few seconds after, with the lightness of a bird, shot up toward the dome and sat calmly on a cornice. At this sight the whole congregation took to flight in a panic; the eldest sister of Christina alone stayed in the church with the priest, who finished the Sacrifice. As soon as he came down from the altar, having ascertained what had happened, he commanded Christina to descend. She obeyed instantly, came down softly, as if her body had no weight, and calmly returned home with her sister.

There, being questioned by her friends and relations, she spoke to them thusly: "When I had given my last sigh, my soul, gone out of my body, found itself surrounded by a troop of angels, who bore it to a dark and frightful place in which there was an innumerable multitude of human souls. There I saw pains and torments which no tongue could express. Among those who were enduring them I noticed many whom I had known on earth. At the sight of their cruel sufferings, I was penetrated with the liveliest compassion, and I asked my guides what this place was. I scarcely doubted that it was Hell, but they replied that it was Purgatory.

"Afterward, they showed me the tortures of the damned: there I saw, also, a few unhappy creatures I had once known.

"Then the angels bore me to the heights of Heaven, before the eternal throne of God. The look, full of love, with which the Most High greeted me, filled my soul with an unspeakable joy. I felt that for all eternity I should enjoy His Blessed Presence. Answering my thoughts, the

Lord said to me: 'Yes, My daughter, you will be eternally with Me, but for the moment, I leave you the choice either to enjoy beatitude from now on, or to return again to earth, there to suffer in a mortal body the pains of the immortal souls [in Purgatory], these pains, however, being unable to cause any damage to your body. By these sufferings you will deliver the souls that have inspired you with so lively a pity, and you will contribute powerfully to the conversion and sanctification of the living. When you shall have filled up the time of this mission, you shall return here again and enter into the possession of My kingdom.'

"Such was the choice of God proposed to me. I did not hesitate; I chose the part of charity; and God, visibly satisfied with my choice, commanded the angels to bring me to earth.

"My friends," added the Saint, "be not astonished at the excess of the wonders which you shall see wrought in my person. They will be the work of God, who does what He pleases, and who acts in everything by designs often hidden, but always adorable."

Upon hearing these words, it may well be understood that the hearers were struck with a holy dread; they looked at Christina with astonishment and trembled at the thought of the sufferings which this woman, returned to life, was going to endure. Indeed, from that moment on, quite different from what she had been before her death, Christina seemed to be a soul from

Purgatory in a mortal body. Her life was nothing more than a tissue of unheard-of marvels and sufferings.

She abandoned human society and lived habitually in solitude. After having assisted in the morning at Mass—at which she often approached the Holy Table—she was observed fleeing to the woods and wild places, there to spend days and nights in prayer. Endowed with the gift of agility, she flew from one place to another with the speed of lightning, darted to the tops of trees, the roofs of houses, the towers of churches and castles. Often passersby would see her resting on the branches of a tree, then taking flight and disappearing at their approach.

Using no shelter, she lived like the birds of the woods, exposed to all the hardships of the weather, even in the most severe season. Her dress was modest, but excessively coarse and poor. She ate, like animals, what she found in the streets. If she saw a fire lighted, she would plunge her hands or feet into it, or if she could, her whole body altogether, and would endure as long as possible this torture. She used to watch for the opportunity of entering glowing furnaces, red-hot limekilns, to sink as deeply as she could into hot boilers. In winter, she spent the night in the icy water of the rivers; at times she would allow herself to be borne by the current upon mill-wheels, cling to them, suffering herself to be dragged by the machine which struck and broke her against obstacles. Another ingenuity of her passion for torments was to tease packs of dogs so as to be bitten and torn by these animals. At times she rolled in the bushes and thorns until she was covered with blood.

These are some of the means by which she tortured her body; and wonderful circumstance, but conformable to the promise which God had made to her, as soon as she emerged from her torture, she retained no wound of it; her body was untouched and without the least lesion.

This life of sufferings served for the edification of a countless multitude of the faithful who were witnesses of it for the space of forty-two years during which the Saint still lived. She also converted a great number of sinners and finally went to enjoy the glory of the elect in the year 1224.

If such mortification makes us shudder, what are we to think of the tortures of the other life? *"There,"* says the author of the *Imitation, "one hour in torment will be more terrible than a hundred years spent here below in the most rigorous penance."* (Book 1, Chap. 24).

The history of Japan speaks of the horrible abysses of Mount Ungen, situated not far from Nagasaki. Its lofty summit is divided into three craters, the intervals between which form frightful pits; forth from these shoot momentarily into the air eddies of flames, corroding waters and burning mud, which carry such stinking exhalations with them that these abysses pass in the country for the sewers of Hell. All the animals shun them with horror, and the very birds do not fly with impunity over them, however high they soar. The tyrant, Bungondono, the Prince of Ximbara, resolved to dash the Christians head-foremost into these frightful chasms. Let the frightful agony they must suffer there be imagined! It was an agony to which death was not to come and put an end, for the consolation of dying was not left to them. Before they were suffocated, they were carefully drawn out to let them regain their breath. Then, soaked as they were by the sulphurous waters, the bodies of the martyrs were covered with frightful pus sacs and were soon but one wound; all their flesh dropped into putrefaction. In this condition they were abandoned like corpses, cast into the common sewer. Are these torments the torments of Hell? They are only a shadow of them.

The same Bungondono devised unheard of tortures to combat Christianity in Japan. One day, seven Christians were led before him; they displayed great joy to suffer for the name of Jesus Christ. At this sight, inflamed with rage, the tyrant caused seven ditches to be dug, in which seven crosses were erected; he had the martyrs bound to them and ordered their limbs to be sawed with sharp-edged canes and at the same time salt thrown into their wounds. This torture was executed with a cruel slowness; it lasted five whole days. By an abominable use of the art destined for the preservation of men, the physicians had cordials taken to the martyrs to prolong their sufferings. Is this one of the tortures of Hell? It is only a shadow of them.

At the time of the inroads of the Calvinists into Holland in the 16th century, those sectaries, having seized at Maestricht some priests of the Company of Jesus, resolved to practice all the cruelty of their fanatical hatred upon them. After having overwhelmed them with contempt and outrages, they put round their necks iron collars provided with knives and sharp spikes, [they] encircled their arms and legs with similar rings, then seated them on seats bristling with nails so that the martyrs could neither rest nor move without pain. Then they surrounded them with flames, to burn them slowly. What torture! If the sufferers remained motionless, they were burned; if they moved, they were torn by the spikes and knives. The servants of God triumphed by the help of grace over all this barbarity; it is true, nevertheless, that their torments were atrocious. Now, are these the torments of Hell? They are but the shadow of them.

Antiquity has preserved the names of three tyrants: Mezentius, Actiolinus and Phalaris. The first, *Mezentius*, it is said, chained his victims to corpses and left them in that revolting state until the infection and putrid inhalations of the dead killed the living. *Actiolinus* had such frightful dungeons that the condemned used to ask as a favor to be strangled, not to enter them. This grace would be denied; they were lowered with ropes into these stinking caves, there to be buried alive in putrefaction. *Phalaris* used to shut up his victims in a brazen bull, which he then surrounded with flames to burn them in this manner, while alive. All these pains are horrible, but they are only a shadow of the pains of Hell.

The Romans punished parricides [i.e., those who murdered their fathers] by a special kind of torture. The guilty person was tied up in a sack with serpents, and thus cast into the depth of the sea; a feeble image of the torture reserved for those who are guilty of parricide toward God.

We shudder when reading in history the description of the frightful torments which the assassin of William, Prince of Orange, had to endure. His body was lacerated by iron rods.

Sharp spikes were driven into his flesh; then he was exposed to the action of a slow fire, which caused him inexpressible pains, and, just as he was on the point of expiring, after his hands had been burned with a red iron, he was torn asunder by horses. That unhappy man committed an enormous crime, but he attacked only a mortal prince. What will not be the chastisement of one who has assailed the King of Kings?

According to certain historians, the Emperor Zeno, a prince as impious as he was dissolute, died by a most tragic death. On the night of April 9, 491, after an excess at table, he fell into so violent a coma that he was believed to be dead, and he was hurriedly buried in the imperial burial vault. There, having regained consciousness, he called in vain for his servants and his guards; no one answered his shouts; he beheld himself in darkness, shut up with the dead on all sides, meeting only cold walls and iron doors. Then giving way to all the transports of rage and despair, he dashed himself against his surroundings and broke his skull against the walls. It was in this terrible state that his corpse was discovered. What a horrible situation for that prince, buried alive! Is that the situation of the reprobate?

Hell is the sink of the world and the receptacle of all the moral filth of humanity. There, impurity, intemperance, blasphemy, pride, injustice and all the vices which are like the rottenness of souls, are found heaped up. To this moral filth a corporal stench is added more insupportable than all the stenches of hospitals and corpses. If the body of a damned person, says St. Bonaventure, were deposited on the earth, that of itself alone would be sufficient to make the earth uninhabitable; it would fill it with its infection, as a corpse that might be left to rot in a house would infect it all the way through.

A man at Lyons had gone into a burial vault in which a corpse lately buried was found wholly putrefied. Scarcely had he gone down when he fell dead. The poisonous exhalations caught him so violently that he was suffocated.

Sulpicius Severus narrates in the life of St. Martin of Tours, that toward the end of the Saint's life the demon came to tempt him under a visible form. The spirit of lies appeared before him with royal magnificence, a crown of gold on his head, and said he was the King of Glory, Christ, the Son of God. The holy bishop recognized the tempter under these appearances of human grandeur and chased him away with contempt. Proud Satan was confounded; he disappeared, but for his revenge, he left the holy man's room filled with a stench which did not allow him to remain there any more.

The Fathers of the Company of Jesus had, during the lifetime of St. Ignatius, established a residence near the sanctuary of Our Lady of Loretto. Jealous of the good they were doing among souls, the devil declared war upon them, and God permitted him to trouble them by visible apparitions. The whole house was infested by malign spirits, who sometimes frightened the religious, sometimes ill-used them, sometimes even sought by seductive illusions to induce them to enter the world again. One of these perfidious tempters, repulsed by a religious and obliged to leave his cell, withdrew, saying: *"Ah! my counsels are not pleasing to you; see, then, if my breath will be more agreeable to you."* At these words he opened a horrible mouth, and blew so fetid a breath into his face that the religious believed himself choked. The cell, infected by that infernal breath, was uninhabitable for several days.

Another torture of Hell is the horrible society of the devils and the damned. There are some wretched sinners who, seeing plainly that they

are walking toward Hell, are comforted by saying, *"I shall not be there alone!"* Sad consolation! It is that of the convicts sentenced to wear
irons together in the galleys. Still it is intelligible
how a convict finds a certain life in the company of his kind. Alas! It will not be thus in Hell,
in which the damned will be mutual executioners.
"There," says St. Thomas, *"the associates of his
wretchedness, far from alleviating the lot of the
damned soul, will make it more intolerable for
him."* (*Suppl.* 9, 86, A. 1). The society of even
those persons who on earth were their best
friends is insupportable to the damned in Hell.
They would esteem themselves happy to have
tigers and lions for companions, rather than their
relatives, brothers, or their own parents.

Do you wish to see the poverty of Hell and
the privations that are suffered there by those
who made the goods of this world their god? Consider the wicked rich man of the Gospel. Accustomed during his life to eat delicate meats
served in silver utensils, to drink exquisite wines
in goblets of gold, to wear purple and fine linen,
having become an inhabitant of Hell, he found
himself brought down to the last extremity of
need. He who refused poor Lazarus the crumbs
from his table, was obliged to beg in his turn.
He asks, not delicacies, but a drop of cold water,
which he will be happy to receive from a leper's
finger. Now, this drop of water is refused to him.
Has not the Saviour said: *"Woe to you that are
rich, for you have your consolation. Woe to you*

that are filled, for you shall hunger." (*Luke* 6:25).

"There is no light," writes St. Teresa (*Autobiography*, Chapter 25), "in the eternal pit, only darkness of the deepest dye; and yet, O mystery! although no light shines, all that can be most painful to the sight is perceived. Among those objects which torture the eyes of the damned, the most frightful are the demons, who reveal themselves in all their hideousness. St. Bernard speaks of a religious who, being in his cell, uttered all of a sudden frightful cries, which attracted the community. He was found beside himself and uttering only these sorrowful words: *"Accursed be the day I entered religion!"* Terrified and troubled by this curse, the cause of which they did not understand, his brethren questioned and encouraged him and spoke to him of confidence in God. Soon, being quieted, he replied, *"No, no, it is not the religious life that I should curse. On the contrary, blessed be the day I became a religious! My brethren, do not be astonished at seeing my mind disturbed. Two devils have appeared to me; their horrible appearance has put me out of my senses. What monstrosity! Ah! Rather all torments than again to endure the sight of them!"*

A holy priest was exorcising a demoniac, and he asked the demon what pains he was suffering in Hell. *"An eternal fire,"* he answered, *"an eternal malediction, an eternal rage, and a frightful despair at being never able to gaze upon*

Him who created me." "What would you do to have the happiness of seeing God?" "To see Him but for one moment, I should willingly consent to endure my torments for 10,000 years. But vain desires! I shall suffer forever and never see Him!"

On a like occasion, the exorcist inquired of the demon what was his greatest pain in Hell. He replied with an accent of indescribable despair: *"Always, always! Never, never!"*

One day, a holy soul was meditating upon Hell, and considering the eternity of the pains, the frightful *"always. . . never,"* she was thrown into complete confusion by it, because she was unable to reconcile this immeasurable severity with the divine goodness and other perfections. *"Lord,"* she said, *"I submit to Thy judgments, but do not push the rigors of Thy justice too far." "Do you understand,"* was the answer, *"what sin is? To sin is to say to God, I will not serve Thee! I despise Thy law, I laugh at Thy threats!" "I understand, Lord, that sin is an outrage to Thy Majesty." "Well, measure, if you can, the greatness of this outrage." "Lord, this outrage is infinite, since it attacks infinite Majesty." "Must it not, then, be punished by an infinite chastisement? Now, as the punishment could not be infinite in its intensity, justice demands that it be so at least in its duration. Accordingly, it is the divine justice that wills the eternity of the pains: the terrible 'always,' the terrible 'never.' The damned themselves will be obliged to render homage to this justice and cry out in the midst of their torments: 'Thou art just, O Lord, and thy judgments are equitable.'"* (*Ps.* 118: 137).

St. John Damascene relates, in the life of St. Josaphat, that this young prince, being one day exposed to violent temptations, prayed to God with tears to be delivered from them. His prayer was graciously heard; he was caught up in an ecstasy, and he beheld himself led to a dark place, full of horror, confusion, and frightful spectres. There was a pool of sulphur and fire in which were plunged innumerable wretches, a prey to devouring flames. Amid the despairing howls and shouts, he heard a heavenly voice, which uttered these words: *"Here it is that sin receives its punishment; here it is that a moment's pleasure is punished by an eternity of torments."* This vision filled him with new strength and enabled him to triumph over all the assaults of the enemy.

The most bitter regret of the damned will be, says St. Thomas, to be damned for "nothing," while they might have so easily obtained everlasting happiness.

Jonathan was condemned to death for having eaten a little honey, against the prohibition of Saul. In his misfortune he said, while moaning, *"Alas! I did but taste a little honey...and behold I must die!"* (*1 Kings* 14:43).

More bitter will be the regrets of the damned when they shall see that, for a "honeycomb," for a fleeting enjoyment, they have incurred everlasting death.

King Lysimachus, besieged by the Scythians, who had cut off all the springs, beheld himself reduced to the last extremity by lack of water. Yielding to the cravings of his thirst, he surrendered to the enemy, who left him only his life safe. Then a cup of water was given him to quench his thirst. When he had drunk it, he said, *"Oh, how quickly has the pleasure passed for which I have lost my throne and my liberty!"* It is in this manner that the damned will speak, but with far more bitterness: Oh, how quickly passed the guilty pleasure for which I forfeited an eternal crown and happiness!

Esau returned faint from the chase, and seeing Jacob, who was cooking lentils, he sold him his birthright for a dish of the pottage. *"And so taking bread and the pottage of lentils,"* says the Scripture, *"he ate and drank, and then went his way, making little account of having sold his birthright."* But when the time came to receive his inheritance, when he saw the large portion given to his brother and the small portion that was left to him, *"He was filled with consternation, and uttered a great cry."* Then, having sought in vain to better his lot, he yielded to the bitterest regrets and filled the air with his doleful cries; they were less cries than roars. *"Irrugit clamore magno."* ("He roared out, with a great cry.") (*Gen.* 25, 27:34). What will be the cries of the damned when they shall see that they have sold their heavenly inheritance for less than ''a dish of pottage''—when they shall see that for a trifle they have sold everlasting benefits and incurred everlasting torments?

The prophet Jeremias had warned Sedecias, King of Juda, of the future that awaited him; he had spoken to him on behalf of God. *"Behold life, and behold death; if you observe my words, you shall remain quiet on your throne; if you trample them under foot I will deliver you into the hands of the King of Babylon."* (*Jerem.* 29:39). Sedecias paid no attention to these warnings of God, and soon the chastisements foretold fell upon him; he was delivered to Nebuchadnezzar, blinded, loaded with chains and thrown into the prison of Babylon. Then, what were not his regrets, his grief, at the remembrance of the words of Jeremias? A weak image of the tardy regrets, the cruel sorrows that devour the damned.

They weep for the time they lost in vain amusements and in forgetfulness of their salvation. *"One hour,"* they say, *"would have given us what an eternity could give us back no more!"* Father Nieremberg relates that a servant of God, finding himself in a secluded place into which no other man had ventured, heard mournful wails, which could proceed only from a supernatural cause. He demanded, then, who were the authors of these piteous cries and what they meant. Then a sad voice replied to him: *"We are the damned. Let it be known that we are deploring in Hell the time lost, the precious time which we wasted on earth in vanities and crime. Ah! One hour would have given us what an eternity could restore to us no more."*

Chapter VIII

A SALUTARY FEAR OF HELL

We ought to believe in Hell, because we may fall into it. Alas! It is very easy to be damned, and the damned are very numerous. St. Teresa compares them to the flakes of snow which fall in the dreary days of winter. The servant of God, Anthony Pereyra, in a very authentic vision with which he was favored (See pages 10-13), saw the souls of sinners descending into the pit like corn beneath the millstones, like stones cast in heaps into a huge limekiln. God showed one day before a large multitude that they fall into it as the dead leaves in autumn fall from the trees under the breath of the wind. The venerable Father Anthony Baldinucci, a celebrated missionary of the Company of Jesus, who died in the odor of sanctity in the year 1717, was preaching in the open air because the church could not contain the faithful who came in crowds to hear him. Speaking of Hell, he said, *"My brethren, would you know how great is the number of those who are damned? Look at that tree."* All eyes were turned to a tree that was there, covered with leaves. At the same moment a gust of wind, rising, shook all the branches of the tree and caused the leaves to fall so plentifully that there remained only a certain number of them, thinly scattered and easy to count. *"See,"* went on the man of God, *"what souls are lost, and what souls are saved. Take your precautions to be among the latter."*

Father Nieremberg speaks of a bishop, who by a special permission of God, received a visit from an unhappy sinner who had died impenitent a short time before. Addressing the prelate, this damned soul demanded *if there were men still on earth.* As the bishop seemed astonished at this question, the lost soul added: *"Since I have been in that melancholy abode, I have seen such a prodigious multitude arrive that I am at a loss to conceive that there are men still on earth."* This speech recalls that of the Saviour in the Gospel: *"Enter ye in at the narrow gate; for wide is the gate, and broad is the way that leadeth to destruction, and many there are who go in thereat. How narrow is the gate and strait is the way that leadeth to life: and few there are that find it!"* (*Matt.* 7:13-14).

To avoid Hell, it is necessary to avoid the road to it and to destroy the cause of damnation, that is, sin, under all its forms. Men permit themselves to be allured to their ruin by different bonds of iniquity, sometimes by one, sometimes by another. There are many who die in their sins because they are deprived of the Last Sacraments, and among those who receive them, there are not a few who are lost because they lack sincerity in the accusation of their sins. Here is an incident which we read in the *Annals of Paraguay*, during the year 1640. In the Reduction [Jesuit mission plantation] of the Assumption, a woman died who had left a son of about twenty years. This young man beheld his mother appear to him in the most frightful condition. She told him *that she was damned for not having made a sincere Confession, and that many others were damned like her for having concealed their sins in Confession. "And you,"* she added, *"do profit by the example of your unfortunate mother."*

Father Nieremberg mentions also another damned person who revealed the cause of his damnation. A young man was leading an apparently Christian life, but he had an enemy whom he hated, and while frequenting the Sacraments, he all the while harbored in his heart sentiments of ill-will and revenge, which Jesus Christ commands to be discarded. After his death, he appeared to his father and told him *that he was damned for not having forgiven his enemy,* after which he exclaimed with an accent of unutterable sorrow: *"Ah! If all the stars in Heaven were so many tongues of fire, they could not express what torments I endure!"*

Let us listen again to the same author. An unhappy man who had the habit of taking pleasure in immodest thoughts fell sick and received the Last Sacraments. The next day his confessor, going to visit him again, saw him on the road coming to meet him. *"Go no further,"* he said to him, *"I am dead and damned." "How?"*

demanded the priest. *"Did you not make a good confession of your sins?"* *"Yes, I made a good confession, but afterwards the devil represented to me sinful pleasures and asked me whether in case of a cure I should not return again to my pleasures? I consented to these evil suggestions, and at the same moment death surprised me."* Then, opening his garment, he showed the fire that was devouring him and disappeared.

We read also in Father Nieremberg that a noble lady, who was exceedingly pious, asked God to make known to her what displeased His Divine Majesty most in persons of her sex. The Lord vouchsafed in a miraculous manner to hear her. He opened under her eyes the Eternal Abyss. There she saw a woman a prey to cruel torments and in her recognized one of her friends, a short time before deceased. This sight caused her as much astonishment as grief: the person whom she saw damned did not seem to her to have lived badly. Then that unhappy soul said to her: *"It is true that I practiced religion, but I was a slave of vanity. Ruled by the passion to please, I was not afraid to adopt indecent fashions to attract attention, and I kindled the fire of impurity in more than one heart. Ah! If Christian women knew how much immodesty in dress displeases God!"* At the same moment, this unhappy soul was pierced by two fiery lances, and plunged into a caldron of liquid lead.

Thomas of Cantimpre, a learned religious of the Order of St. Dominic, relates that there was at Brussels an unhappy sinner, the slave of intemperance and the other vices which it foments. He had a friend, the companion of his dissipation, to whom he was greatly attached. A sudden death put an end to his disorders. His sorrowful companion, after having accompanied him to the grave, had returned home and was alone in his chamber, when he heard moans underground. Frightened at first and not knowing what to do, he ventured at length to ask *who it was that he heard moaning. "It is I, your companion, whose body you attended to the grave. Alas! My soul is buried in Hell."* Then, uttering a cry, or rather a dreadful roar, he added, *"Woe to me! The abyss has swallowed me, and the pit has closed its mouth upon me."*

Louis of Granada speaks of a young woman whose damnation had no other source than vanity and the desire to please. She led a regular life, but her passion to attract attention by the charm of her beauty was the moving cause of her whole conduct. Having fallen sick, she died, having received all the Sacraments. While her confessor was praying for her soul, she appeared to him, saying that she was damned and that the cause of her damnation was vanity. *"I sought,"* she added, *"only to please the eyes of men. This passion caused me to commit a multitude of sins; it prevented me from receiving the Sacraments well, and it has led me to everlasting torments."*

A usurer had two sons who followed the evil

example of their father. One of the two, touched by God, forsook his guilty profession and retired to the desert. Before setting out, he exhorted his father and brother with tears to think, like him, of the salvation of their souls. It was to no purpose; they persevered in sin and died in a state of impenitence. God permitted the solitary to know their unhappy condition. In an ecstacy he saw himself on a high mountain at the foot of which was a sea of fire from which arose confused cries, like a tempest. Soon, in the midst of these burning waves, he perceived his father and brother, furiously raging against each other, mutually upbraiding and cursing each other and holding this dreadful dialogue: *"I curse thee, detestable son! It is for thee that I did injustice and lost my soul." "I curse thee, unworthy father, who ruined me by thy bad example." "I curse thee, foolish son, who joined thy father in his sins." "I curse thee, the author of my life, who reared me up for damnation!"* Behold how wicked parents and wicked children will eternally rend one another by reciprocal maledictions. (*Lives of the Fathers of the Desert*).

Chapter IX

THE THOUGHT OF HELL

St. Dositheus, who lived in the eleventh century, was brought up as a page at the Court of Constantinople and at first led a life altogether worldly, in a profound ignorance of the truths of faith. As he had heard a great deal about Jerusalem, he visited it out of a motive of curiosity. There it was that God's mercy was awaiting him. To touch him, it made use of a picture placed in a church representing the pains of Hell. Miserable souls were seen there in despair, plunged in a sea of fire, in which horrible monsters were tormenting them and making game of their tortures. Struck by these terrible scenes, Dositheus demanded the explanation of them from an unknown person who was there. *"It is Hell,"* answered this person; *"they are the pains of the damned." "How long will these pains last? Why are they damned? Might I myself fall into such a terrible state of woe? What must I do to be safe from Hell?"* Such were the questions that Dositheus by turns proposed to the person who was instructing him. He was impressed by the answers to such a degree that he quit the world that very hour to go and live in seclusion. He entered a monastery in which, thanks to the thought of Hell, which he had always before his eyes, and to the wise direction of the Abbot whom he found there, he made rapid progress in the ways of God.

Whoever thinks of Hell will not fall into it because in the time of temptation this thought will retain him in his duty. St. Martinian had lived twenty-five years in solitude when God allowed his fidelity to be put to a violent test. A perfidious woman, the courtesan Zoe, came to solicit him to sin. She was disguised as a mendicant, and taking advantage of a rain storm, knocked at the cell of Martinian, begging shelter from him. The holy anchorite could not refuse it in these circumstances. He let the stranger in and having lighted a fire, invited her to dry her garments. But soon the unfortunate woman, casting off the borrowed rags she wore, appeared to the eyes of Martinian in a most brilliant dress and with all her fascinating charms. The servant of God, in the presence of a most dreadful danger, remembered Hell, and drawing near the fire, which was blazing on the hearth, he took off his shoes and plunged both feet into the fire. The pain drew cries from him, but he said to his soul, *"Alas! My soul, if thou canst not bear so weak a fire, how wilt thou be able to bear the fire of Hell?"* The temptation was overcome, and Zoe was converted. Such was the salutary effect of the thought of Hell.

Another recluse, assailed by a violent temptation and afraid of being conquered, lighted his lamp. Then, to be penetrated vividly with the thought of Hell, he put his fingers into the flame and let them burn there with inexpressible sufferings. *"Since thou dost wish,"* he said, addressing himself, *"to sin and accept Hell, which will be the punishment of thy sin, try first if thou shalt have the courage to support the pain of an everlasting fire."*

It is related that St. Philip Neri received one day a visit from a man who was leading a sinful life. Imbued with the most unfriendly feelings toward the Saint, this visitor addressed him with the most unjust reproaches and heaped insults upon him. His anger was such that he was incapable of listening to reason. Then St. Philip made him draw near the chimney, and pointing out the place where the fire was made, he said, *"Look at this fireplace."* The sinner looked, but instead of a fireplace, he saw a pit all on fire, in the bottom of which he recognized a place that was destined for him. Seized with fright, this furious sinner grew calm, suddenly recognized the evil state of his soul, and changed his life.

In 1815 the young Louis Francis de Beauvais died at the College of St. Acheul near Amiens. He was only 14 years old, but he was ripe for Heaven, so innocent and holy had been his life. Such solid virtue in so tender a youth was due to the thought of Hell. One day, while still quite a child, he was seated at his mother's side before a warm fire. *"Mamma,"* he asked her, *"could* *the fire of Hell be as hot as this?"* "Alas, my child, this fire is nothing in comparison to Hell!" "Well, if I should fall into it?"* he rejoined with fright. *"Hell,"* said his mother, *"is only for sinners. If you keep away from sin, you have nothing to fear."* This idea was engraved in the heart of Louis Francis; it was the source of his sorrow of sin and of his holy life.

In 1540 Blessed Peter Lefevre, one of the first companions of St. Ignatius of Loyola, returning from Parma to Rome, while following the way from Florence to Siena, was overcome by nightfall in the midst of a country infested by robbers and brigands. He had recourse, as was his wont, to his Angel-Guardian, and perceived pretty soon a house, at which he asked hospitality. It was in the month of October; the weather was cold and rainy. The people who dwelt at the manor, seeing that the traveller was a priest, welcomed him with respect and kindness, offered him refreshments, and invited him to draw near the fire to dry his clothes. While he was seated near the hearth and speaking with his hosts of the things of God, a noise of hurried steps was heard, then violent rappings at the door, and behold, men armed to the teeth dashed into the house. It was a band of brigands. They were sixteen and demanded noisily that all the provisions in store should be given to them; then, having ranged themselves round a table, they set to drinking and eating amid rude songs and immodest conversation. Blessed Peter Lefevre was not taken aback; he remained seated, calm, pensive, his eyes fixed on the fire. The leader of the bandits asked him what he was doing there. The man of God did not reply at first. *"You do not answer,"* remarked the brigand. *"Are you deaf? Are you dumb?"* *"No,"* he replied then, *"but a thought occupies my mind."* *"What is this great thought? Tell us. What are you thinking of?"* *"I am thinking,"* he said, in a calm, grave tone, *"that the joy of sinners is very sad; this fire brings to my mind that of Hell, which they shall not be able to escape if they do not hasten to return sincerely to God."* These words were spoken with a force and unction that struck these savage men with respect. They said not a word more, and the servant of God took advantage of their attention to speak to them of the danger they ran of falling into the hands of human justice, and still more, into those of God's justice; then he touched on the security of a good conscience and the mercy of God, of whom he spoke in language so touching that he caused them to melt into tears and demand forgiveness of their sins. He encouraged them and prepared them so well that the whole sixteen made their confessions to him that night.

The thought of Hell fortifies the weakest. Two [early] Christians, Domnina and Theomilla, were brought before the [Roman] prefect Lysias, who gave them notice of the order to renounce the Faith in order to adore idols. They absolutely refused. Then Lysias had a funeral pyre lighted and the altar to the false gods set up. *"Choose,"* he said to them, *"either to burn incense on the altar of our gods or to be yourselves burned in the flames of this pyre."* They replied, without hesitating a moment: *"We fear not this burning pile, which will be soon extinguished; the fire we do fear is that of Hell, which never goes out. Not to fall into it, we detest your idols and we adore Jesus Christ."* They underwent martyrdom in the year 235.

Caesarius relates that a wicked man, for whom many prayers had been offered, fell sick and died. As he was going to be buried, he came back to life again, and rose up full of strength, but seized with an exceeding alarm. Interrogated concerning what had happened to him, he answered, *"God has just granted me a signal favor; He showed me Hell, an immense ocean of fire, into which I was about to be plunged for my sins. A delay was accorded to me that I might redeem my sins by penance."* Thenceforth, this sinner was changed into a different man. He thought no more of anything save of expiating his sins by his tears, fasts and prayers. He used to walk barefooted on brambles and thorns; he lived on bread and water only and gave to the poor whatever he earned by his labor. When people would prevail upon him to moderate his austerities, he would reply, *"I have seen Hell; I know that too much cannot be done to avoid it. Ah, Hell! If all the trees and all the forests were heaped up in a vast pile and set on fire, I should prefer to remain in that burning*

*fire to the end of the world rather than endure
for only one hour the fire of Hell."*

The Venerable Bede speaks of a rich inhabitant of Northumberland, whom the sight of Hell changed after a like fashion into a new man. He was called Trithelmus, and he led a worldly life, pretty much like that of the wicked rich man of the Gospel. God, by an exceptional mercy, granted him a vision, in which He showed him the eternal pains of the damned. Having come back to himself again, Trithelmus confessed all his sins, distributed all his wealth to the poor, and went into a monastery, where he put no bounds to his austerities and penances. In winter he stood in the freezing water; in summer he endured the burden of heat and toil; he practiced vigorous fasts and continued his mortifications to the last stage of decay. When he was spoken to about diminishing his penances, he would reply, *"If you had seen, like me, the pains of Hell, you would talk otherwise." "But how can you keep up such severe mortifications?" "I count them as nothing beside the pains of Hell, which I have deserved by my sins."*

Mgr. de Segur narrates a rather singular fact which happened at the Military School of St. Cyr in the last years of the Restoration. The Abbé Rigolot, the almoner of the institution, was preaching a retreat to the pupils who assembled every evening in the chapel before retiring to the dormitory.

A certain evening when the worthy almoner

had spoken on Hell, the exercises being finished, he was retiring, with a small candlestick in his hand, to his room, which was situated in a wing reserved for the officers. Just as he opened his door, he heard himself called by someone who was following him up the staircase. It was an old captain with a gray moustache and by no means elegant appearance. *"Pardon, Monsieur Almoner,"* he said in a slightly ironical tone of voice, *"you have just given us a very fine sermon on Hell; only you forgot to tell us whether, in the fire of Hell, we should be grilled or roasted or boiled. Could you tell me?"* The almoner seeing whom he had to deal with, looked at him straight in the eye and putting the candlestick under his nose, quietly replied, *"You shall see this, Captain!"* and he shut his door, unable to refrain from laughing somewhat at the silly, baffled expression on the face of the poor captain.

He thought of it no more, but from that time forth he fancied that the captain used to take to his heels from him, as far as possible. The Revolution of July came on. The military almonery was abolished, that of St. Cyr like the rest. The Abbé Rigolot was nominated by the Archbishop of Paris to another position not less honorable.

Twenty years after, the venerable priest was one evening in a drawing room in which there was a numerous gathering, when he saw coming toward him an old man with a white moustache, who asked him if he were not the Abbé Rigolot, at one time almoner of St. Cyr. And upon his affirmative reply, the old soldier said with emotion, *"O Monsieur Almoner, permit me to clasp your hand and express all my gratitude to you: you saved me." "I? And how so?" "Well! You do not know me! Do you remember one evening when a captain, an instructor of the school, having proposed to you, after the close of a sermon on Hell, an exceedingly ridiculous question, you answered him while putting your candlestick under his nose, 'You will see this, Captain?' I am that captain. Fancy, that from that time, your speech pursued me everywhere, as well as the thought that I might be burned in Hell. I struggled for ten years, but at last I was forced to surrender: I have been to my confession; I have become a Christian, a Christian in the military fashion, that is to say, like a soldier. It is to you I owe this happiness, and I am very glad to meet you, to be able to tell you so."*

Father de Bussy, of the Company of Jesus, gave at the beginning of this century, in a certain large city of the South, an important mission, which roused the whole population. It was in the heart of winter; Christmas Day was at hand, and it was very cold. In the room in which the Father was receiving the men, there was a stove with a good fire.

One day the Father saw a young man coming to him who had been recommended to him on account of his dissipation and open parade of impiety. Father de Bussy soon saw there was nothing to be done with him. *"Come here, my good friend,"* he said pleasantly; *"I do not hear the confessions of people in spite of themselves. Stay; sit down there, and let us have a little chat while warming ourselves."* He opened the stove, and noticed that the wood was going soon to be burned up.

"Before sitting down, pray bring me one or two logs," he said to the young man. The latter, somewhat astonished, did, nevertheless, what the Father asked. *"Now,"* the latter added, *"put it in the stove for me; there, very far down in the bottom."* And, as the other was getting the wood into the door of the stove, Father de Bussy, all at once, took his arm, and plunged it into the bottom of the stove. The young man uttered a shout and sprang backward. *"Ah me!"* he shouted. *"Are you crazy? You were going to burn me?"* *"What ails you, my dear man?"* remarked the Father calmly; *"should you not get accustomed to it? In Hell, where you shall go if you continue your present course of life, it will not be merely the tips of the fingers that shall be burned by the fire, but your whole body, and this little fire is nothing to the other one. Come, come, my good friend, be brave; you must get accustomed to everything burning."*

The young libertine went away in a thoughtful mood. He was reflecting indeed; he did reflect so well that he was not slow in coming back again to the missionary, who helped him to get rid of his faults and enter anew on the good path.

I affirm, adds Mgr. de Segur, that of a thousand, ten thousand men who live far from God, and therefore on the way to Hell, there would not be one, perhaps, who could resist the test of fire. There would not be one who should be so crazy as to accept this bargain: During the year, you may yield to all your passions, gratify all your whims, on the condition of spending *one day,* only one day, or even *one hour,* in fire. I repeat, not a single person would accept the bargain. Will you have a proof of it? Listen to the history of the three sons of an old usurer.

A father of a family who grew rich only by doing wrongs had fallen dangerously ill. He knew that the final stages of death had already set in, and nevertheless he could not decide to make restitution. *"If I make restitution,"* he said, *"what will become of my children?"*

His confessor, a man of sagacity, had recourse to a singular stratagem to save this poor soul. He told him that if he wished to be cured, he was about to give him an extremely simple, but costly remedy. *"Should it cost a thousand, two thousand, even ten thousand francs, what odds?"* answered the old man briskly. *"What is it?"* *"It consists in pouring the melted fat of a living person on the dying parts. It does not need much. If you find anyone willing, for ten thousand francs, to suffer one hand to be burned for less than a quarter of an hour, that will be enough."*

"Alas!" said the poor man, sighing, *"I am very much afraid I can find no such person."* *"I will*

help you," said the priest quietly. *"Summon your eldest son; he loves you; he is to be your heir; say to him, 'My dear son, you can save your old father's life if you consent to allow one hand to be burned only for a small quarter of an hour.' If he refuses, make the proposal to the second, pledging yourself to make him your heir at the expense of his elder brother. If he refuses in his turn, the third will no doubt accept."*

The proposition was made successively to the three brothers, who, one after the other, rejected it with a shudder. Then the father said to them: *"What! To save my life, an instant's pain alarms you? And I, to procure your comfort, would go to Hell—to be burned eternally! Indeed, I should be quite mad."* And he hastened to restore all he owed without regard to what should become of his children. He was quite right, and so were his three sons. To suffer a hand to be burned, a short quarter of an hour, even to save a father's life, is a sacrifice above human strength.

In 1844, again writes Mgr. de Segur, I was acquainted at the Seminary of St. Sulpice at Issy, near Paris, with an extremely distinguished professor of science, and a man whose humility and mortification were admired by everyone. Before becoming a priest, the Abbé Pinault had been one of the most eminent professors of the Polytechnic School. In the seminary he made the course of physics and chemistry. One day, during an experiment, the fire somehow caught the phosphorus he was manipulating and in a moment his hand was wrapped in flames. Assisted by his pupils, the poor professor tried to no purpose to put out the fire that was eating into his flesh. In a few minutes his hand was but a shapeless, shining mass; the nails had disappeared. Overcome by the excess of pain, the unfortunate professor lost consciousness. His hand and arm were plunged into a pail of cold water to try to assuage a little of the violence of this martyrdom. All day and all night he uttered but one cry, an irresistible and heartrending cry; and when, now and then, he could utter a few words, he would say and say again to the three or four seminarians who were waiting on him: *"O my children! my children! Do not go to Hell! Do not go to Hell!"*

A brother, named John Baptist, was living at the time of St. Ignatius at the profession-house in Rome. He was remarkable for the spirit of fervor and mortification which he derived from the thought of Hell. As he filled the humble office of cook, the fire, which he had incessantly under his eyes, reminded him of the fire of divine justice, which shall torment eternally the impious in Hell, and caused him to conceive a great horror for sin which merits such horrible chastisements. One day, when profoundly absorbed by these thoughts, he yielded to the grief which his sins caused him; he was seized by an attack of indiscreet fervor; he plunged his hand into the fire and there left it burning. The odor which arose from it was smelled by the Father who exercised the office of minister of the house. He came into the kitchen and asked what was the matter. The brother could not conceal the excess of his pain, acknowledged his fault, and falling at his knees, humbly begged his pardon. St. Ignatius was informed of the matter; he was told that this brother had just deprived himself of the use of his hand and had become incapable of doing his work. The Saint considered his fault more worthy of compassion than punishment. He set to prayer and spent a part of the night in it, as was his custom. The next morning the brother's hand was cured and as sound as if it had not been injured. God manifested by this miracle that, if this fervent religious had done an inconsiderate act, the motive that prompted him to do it—that is, the fear of Hell—was agreeable to Him.

St. Teresa had seen the place that was prepared for her in Hell, and the remembrance gave her strength to bear the severest trials. This is how she speaks, in the 32nd chapter of her autobiography: "Being one day in prayer, in an instant I found myself, without knowing how, carried body and soul into Hell. I understood that God wished to make me see the place I should have occupied had I not changed my life. No words can give the least idea of such suffering—it is beyond comprehension. I felt in my soul a devouring fire, and my body was, at the same time, a prey to intolerable pains. I had endured cruel sufferings during my lifetime, but all that I had suffered was nothing when compared to what I experienced then. What filled up the measure was the prospect that they should be unending and unalleviated. The tortures of the body, however cruel they might have been, were nothing in their turn beside the anguish of the soul. While I felt myself burned, and as if hacked into a thousand pieces, I was suffering all the agonies of death, all the horrors of despair. There was not a particle of hope, of consolation, in this frightful sojourn. There was a pestiferous odor, by which one was continually suffocated. There was no light, only darkness of the sombrest hue; and yet, O prodigy! though there was no light shining, whatever is most distressing to the sight is seen. In short, all I had heard said of the pains of Hell, all I had read of it in books was nothing beside the reality. There was the same difference as between a lifeless portrait and a living person. Ah! the hottest fire in this world is such a trifling thing! It is like a painted fire compared to that fire which burns the damned in Hell. Almost ten years have passed since that vision, and I am still seized with such a fright in describing it that my blood is frozen in my veins. Amid trials and sufferings I call up this remembrance, and it gives me strength to bear all.''

The wonderful conversion of an obstinate Protestant lady, which created quite a sensation in America, was owing to the thought of Hell. This person was none other than the wife of General X., one of the ablest generals of the Northern army in the war of 1860. Here are the particulars of this conversion, as Monsignor Fitzpatrick, Bishop of Boston, related them at St. Michael's College at Brussels, in November, 1862.

General X., first a Protestant, had had the happiness of hearing a simple, clear explanation of the Catholic religion. It was sufficient for this upright and noble man to make him see the truth and embrace Catholicism with all his heart. From that time, full of faith and fervor, he devoted himself, not only to living as a true Catholic, but also to procuring for other Protestants the grace of conversion. In a short time he won over twenty officers and wrote a book destined to furnish instruction for soldiers. We can well understand that he had not forgotten his wife, who was a Protestant, but he had the grief of seeing all the efforts of his zeal fail in this direction. Meanwhile, God permitted Madame X. to be attacked by an illness which reduced her to the last extremity. The General, after having exhausted to no purpose all the resources of faith and charity, seeing the sick woman on the point of dying in her obstinacy, recurred to a last means. He called in four Irishwomen whom he had in his service, and, with tears in his eyes, said to them: *"My friends, you know my wife is a Protestant and that she is unwilling to hear the Catholic religion spoken of. She is going to die in her obstinacy and fall into Hell. I shudder at the thought of such a misfortune; it must be absolutely prevented if it is possible. Let us pray, then, to the Holy Virgin and do violence to her merciful heart.''* Thereupon, the General drew forth his beads, and began to pray on his knees; the poor attendants did as much, and the whole five continued to pray for one hour. Then the general went to the bed of the invalid and discovered her in a sort of coma, out of her senses, without consciousness. At the end of some time, returning to herself and looking at her husband, she said to him in a very intelligible voice: *"Call a Catholic priest.''* The General believed at first that she was delirious and made her repeat what she desired. *"I beg,''* she said, *"for a Catholic priest without delay.'' "But my dear, you would not have one.'' "Ah! General, I am entirely changed. God has shown me Hell and the place that awaited me in the eternal fire if I did not become a Catholic.''* So the sick woman had the happiness of returning to the bosom of the Church. She even recovered her health and lived afterward as a fervent Catholic. Such was the narrative of the venerable Bishop of Boston; he had these details from General X.'s own mouth.

THE END OF FR. SCHOUPPE'S
ORIGINAL BOOK

Appendix I

SR. JOSEFA MENENDEZ'
DESCRIPTION OF HELL

The following material is quoted verbatim from the Appendix to The Way of Divine Love *of Sr. Josefa Menendez [1890-1923], a book subtitled* The Message of the Sacred Heart to the World, *which first appeared in 1938 in French in an abbreviated form under the title* Un Appel â l'Amour *(in English,* Christ's Appeal for Love, *which is still in print at this time, as is* The Way of Divine Love*). The complete edition, from which this Appendix is taken, appeared a few years later, and was quickly translated into numerous languages and spread throughout the world. Sr. Josefa was a Spanish nun of the Society of the Sacred Heart and lived only four years as a religious, at the convent of Les Feuillants in Poitiers, France, where she died at the age of 33. The Way of Divine Love consists largely of her notebooks, in which she wrote down under obedience from Our Lord the revelations of His Sacred Heart, plus portions of her biography. This material was composed after Fr. Schouppe wrote his book on Hell, but is appended to his book because it is similar to what he has included in his book and exemplifies still further the points he is trying to emphasize.*

Sister Josefa wrote with great reticence on this subject. She did it only to conform to Our Blessed Lord's wishes, Our Lady having told her on October 25, 1922: ''Everything that Jesus allows you to see and to suffer of the torments of Hell, is...that you may make it known to your Mothers. So forget yourself entirely, and think only of the glory of the Heart of Jesus and the salvation of souls.''

...She repeatedly dwelt on the greatest torment of Hell, namely, the soul's inability to love.

One of these damned souls cried out: ''This is my torture...that I want to love and cannot; there is nothing left me but hatred and despair. If one of us could so much as make a single act of love...this would no longer be Hell.... But we cannot, we live on hatred and malevolence...'' (March 23, 1922).

Another of these unfortunates said: ''The greatest of our torments here is that we are not able to love Him whom we are bound to hate. Oh! how we hunger for love, we are consumed with desire of it, but it is too late.... You too will feel this same devouring hunger, but you will only be able to hate, to abhor, and to long for the loss of souls...nothing else do we care for now!'' (March 26, 1922).

The following passage was written by obedience, though it was extremely repugnant to Josefa's humility:

''Every day now, when I am dragged down to Hell and the devil orders them to torture me, they answer: 'We cannot, for her members have undergone torture for *Him*...' (then they blasphemously name Our Blessed Lord)...then he orders them to give me a draught of sulphur ...and again the reply is: 'She has voluntarily deprived herself of drink...' 'Try to find some part of her body to which she has given satisfaction and pleasure.'

"I have also noted that when they shackle me to take me down to Hell, they never can bind me where I have worn instruments of penance. I write all this simply out of obedience." (April 1, 1922).

She records, too, the accusations made against themselves by these unhappy souls: "Some yell because of the martyrdom of their hands. Perhaps they were thieves, for they say: 'Where is our loot now?.... Cursed hands.... Why did I want to possess what did not belong to me...and what in any case I could keep only for a few days...?'

"Others curse their tongues, their eyes...whatever was the occasion of their sin.... 'Now, O body, you are paying the price of the delights you granted yourself! ...and you did it of your own free will...'" (April 2, 1922). [That is, illegitimate delights].

"It seemed to me that the majority accused themselves of sins of impurity, of stealing, of unjust trading; and that most of the damned are in Hell for these sins." (April 6, 1922).

"I saw many worldly people fall into Hell, and no words can render their horrible and terrifying cries: 'Damned forever.... I deceived myself; I am lost.... I am here forever.... There is no remedy possible...a curse on me...'

"Some accused people, others circumstances,

and all execrated the occasions of their damnation.'' (September 1922).

''Today, I saw a vast number of people fall into the fiery pit...they seemed to be worldlings and a demon cried vociferously: 'The world is ripe for me.... I know that the best way to get hold of souls is to rouse their desire for enjoyment.... Put *me* first...*me* before the rest...no humility for *me*! but let me enjoy myself.... This sort of thing assures victory to me...and they tumble headlong into Hell.''' (October 4, 1922).

''I heard a demon, from whom a soul had escaped, forced to confess his powerlessness. 'Confound it all...how do so many manage to escape me? They were mine' (and he rattled off their sins)...'I work hard enough, yet they slip through my fingers...Someone must be suffering and repairing for them.''' (January 15, 1923). [''Repairing,'' that is, ''making reparation'' for them].

''Tonight,'' wrote Josefa, ''I did not go down into Hell, but was transported to a place where all was obscure, but in the center was a red smoldering fire. They had laid me flat and so bound me that I could not make the slightest movement. Around me were seven or eight people; their black bodies were unclothed, and I could see them only by the reflections of the fire. They were seated and were talking together.

''One said: 'We'll have to be very careful not to be found out, for we might easily be discovered.'

"The devil answered: 'Insinuate yourselves by inducing carelessness in them...but keep in the background, so that you are not found out...by degrees they will become callous, and you will be able to incline them to evil. Tempt these others to ambition, to self-interest, to acquiring wealth without working, whether it be lawful or not. Excite some to sensuality and love of pleasure. Let vice blind them....' (Here they used obscene words).

"'As to the remainder...get in through the heart...you know the inclinations of their hearts ...make them love...love passionately...work thoroughly...take no rest...have no pity; the world must go to damnation...and these souls must not be allowed to escape me.'

"From time to time Satan's satellites answered: 'We are your slaves...we shall labor unceasingly, and in spite of the many who war against us, we shall work night and day. We know your power!'

"They all spoke together and he whom I took to be Satan used words full of horror. In the distance I could hear a clamor as of feasting, the clinking of glasses...and he cried: 'Let them cram themselves with food! It will make it all the easier for us...Let them get on with their banqueting. Love of pleasure is the door through which you will reach them....'

"He added such horrible things that they can neither be written nor said. Then, as if engulfed in a whirl of smoke, they vanished." (February 3, 1923).

"The evil one was bewailing the escape of a

soul: 'Fill her soul with fear, drive her to despair. All will be lost if she puts her trust in the mercy of that...' (here they used blasphemous words about Our Lord). 'I am lost; but no, drive her to despair; do not leave her for an instant; above all, make her despair.'

"Then Hell re-echoed with frenzied cries, and when finally the devil cast me out of the abyss, he went on threatening me. Among other things he said: 'Is it possible that such weaklings have more power than I, who am mighty.... I must conceal my presence, work in the dark; any corner will do from which to tempt them...close to an ear...in the leaves of a book...under a bed...some pay no attention to me, but I shall talk and talk...and by dint of suggestion, something will remain.... Yes, I must hide in unsuspected places.'" (February 7, 8, 1923).

Josefa, on her return from Hell, noted the following: "I saw several souls fall into Hell, and among them was a child of fifteen, cursing her parents for not having taught her to fear God nor that there was a Hell. Her life had been a short one, she said, but full of sin, for she had given in to all that her body and passions demanded in the way of satisfaction. Especially she had read bad books." (March 22, 1923).

Again, she wrote: "...Souls were cursing the vocation they had received, but not followed ...the vocation they had lost, because they were unwilling to live a hidden and mortified life..." (March 18, 1922).

"On one occasion when I was in Hell, I saw a great many priests, religious and nuns, cursing their vows, their order, their Superiors and everything that could have given them the light and the grace they had lost. . . .

"I saw, too, some prelates. One accused himself of having used the goods belonging to the Church illicitly. . ." (September 28, 1922).

"Priests were calling down maledictions on their tongues which had consecrated, on their fingers that had held Our Lord's Sacred Body, on the absolution they had given while they were losing their own souls and on the occasion through which they had fallen into Hell." (April 6, 1922).

"One priest said: 'I ate poison, for I used money that was not my own. . .the money given me for Masses which I did not offer.'

"Another said he belonged to a secret society which had betrayed the Church and religion, and he had been bribed to connive at terrible profanations and sacrileges.

"Yet another said that he was damned for assisting at profane plays, after which he ought not to have said Mass. . .and that he had spent about seven years thus."

Josefa noted that the greater number of religious plunged into hell-fire were there for abominable sins against Chastity. . .and for sins against the vow of Poverty. . .for the unauthorized use of the goods of the Community. . .for passions against charity (jealousy, antipathies, hatred, etc.), for tepidity and relaxation; also for comforts they had allowed themselves and which had led to graver sins...for bad confessions through human respect and want of sincerity and courage, etc.

Here, finally, is the full text of Josefa's notes on "the hell of consecrated souls." (Biography: Ch. VII—September 4, 1922).

"The meditation of the day was on the Particular Judgment of religious souls. I could not free my mind of the thought of it, in spite of the oppression which I felt. Suddenly, I felt myself bound and overwhelmed by a crushing weight, so that in an instant I saw more clearly than ever before how stupendous is the sanctity of God and His detestation of sin.

"I saw in a flash my whole life since my first confession to this day. All was vividly present to me: my sins, the graces I had received, the day I entered religion, my clothing as a novice, my first vows, my spiritual readings, and times of prayer, the advice given me, and all the helps of religious life. Impossible to describe the confusion and shame a soul feels at that moment, when it realizes: 'All is lost, and I am damned forever.'"

As in her former descents into Hell, Josefa never accused herself of any specific sin that might have led to such a calamity. Our Lord meant her only to feel what the consequences would have been, if she had merited such a punishment. She wrote:

"Instantly I found myself in Hell, but not dragged there as before. The soul precipitates itself there, as if to hide from God in order to be free to hate and curse Him.

"My soul fell into abysmal depths, the bottom of which cannot be seen, for it is immense... At once, I heard other souls jeering and rejoicing at seeing me share their torments. It was martyrdom enough to hear the terrible imprecations on all sides, but what can be compared to the thirst to curse that seizes on a soul, and the more one curses, the more one wants to. Never had I felt the like before. Formerly my soul had been oppressed with grief at hearing these horrible blasphemies, though unable to produce even one act of love. But today it was otherwise.

"I saw Hell as always before, the long dark corridors, the cavities, the flames.... I heard the same execrations and imprecations, for—and of this I have already written before—although no corporeal forms are visible, the torments are felt as if they were present, and souls recognize each other. Some called out, 'Hullo! *you* here? And are you like us? We were free to take those vows or not...but now!...' and they cursed their vows.

"Then I was pushed into one of those fiery cavities and pressed, as it were, between burning planks, and sharp nails and red-hot irons seemed to be piercing my flesh."

Here Josefa repeated the multiple tortures from which no single member of the body is excluded:

"I felt as if they were endeavoring to pull out my tongue, but could not. This torture reduced me to such agony that my very eyes seemed to be starting out of their sockets. I think this was because of the fire which burns, burns. . .not a finger-nail escapes terrifying torments, and all the time one cannot move even a finger to gain some relief, nor change posture, for the body seems flattened out and [yet] doubled in two.

"Sounds of confusion and blasphemy cease not for an instant. A sickening stench asphyxiates and corrupts everything, it is like the burning of putrified flesh, mingled with tar and sulphur . . .a mixture to which nothing on earth can be compared.

"All this I felt as before, and although those tortures were terrific, they would be bearable if the soul were at peace. But it suffers indescribably. Until now, when I went down into Hell, I thought that I had been damned for abandoning religious life. But this time it was different. I bore a special mark, a sign that I was a religious, a soul who had known and loved God, and there were others who bore the same sign. I cannot say how I recognized it, perhaps because of the specially insulting manner in which the evil spirits and other damned souls treated them. There were many priests there, too. This particular suffering I am unable to explain. It was quite different from what I had experienced at other times, for if the souls of those who lived in the world suffer terribly, infinitely worse are the torments of religious. Unceasingly the three words, Poverty, Chastity and Obedience, are imprinted on the soul with poignant remorse.

"*Poverty:* You were free and you promised! Why, then, did you seek that comfort? Why hold on to that object which did not belong to you? Why did you give that pleasure to your body? Why allow yourself to dispose of the property of the Community? Did you not know that you no longer had the right to possess anything whatsoever, that you had freely renounced the use of those things?. . .Why did you murmur when anything was wanting to you or when you fancied yourself less well treated than others? Why?

"*Chastity:* You yourself vowed it freely and with full knowledge of its implications. . .you bound yourself. . .you willed it. . .and how have you observed it? That being so, why did you not remain where it would have been lawful for you to grant yourself pleasures and enjoyment?

"And the tortured soul responds: 'Yes, I vowed it, I was free. . . . I could have not taken the vow, but I took it and I was free. . . .' What words can express the martyrdom of such remorse," wrote Josefa, "and all the time the jibes and insults of other damned souls continue.

"*Obedience:* Did you not fully engage yourself to obey your Rule and your Superiors? Why, then, did you pass judgment on the orders that were given you? Why did you disobey the Rule? Why did you dispense yourself from common life? Remember how sweet was the Rule. . .and you would not keep it. . .and now,'' vociferate satanic voices, ''you will have to obey us not for a day or a year, or a century, but forever and ever, for all eternity. . . . It is your own doing. . .you were free.

''The soul constantly recalls how she had chosen her God for her Spouse, and that once she loved Him above all things. . .that for Him she had renounced the most legitimate pleasures and all she held dearest on earth, that in the beginning of her religious life she had felt all the purity, sweetness and strength of this divine love, and that for an inordinate passion. . .now she must eternally hate the God who had chosen her to love Him.

''This forced hatred is a thirst that consumes her. . .no past joys can afford her the slightest relief.

''One of her greatest torments is shame,'' added Josefa. ''It seems to her that all the damned surrounding her continually taunt her by saying: 'That we should be lost who never had the helps that you enjoyed is not surprising. . .but you. . . what did you lack? You who lived in the palace of the King. . .who feasted at the board of the elect.'

''All I have written,'' she concluded, ''is but a shadow of what the soul suffers, for no words can express such dire torments.'' (September 4, 1922).

Appendix II

THE CHILDREN OF FATIMA
SEE HELL

The following passages are excerpted from a small booklet entitled The Forgotten Secret of Fatima and The Silent Apostolate *by Msgr. Joseph A. Cirrincione (TAN, 1988). The six apparitions of Our Lady at Fatima on the 13th of each month from May through October, 1917 constitute the greatest approved Marian apparition ever and were witnessed by three young children, ages 6, 7, and 9. Msgr. Cirrincione quotes the exact words of Sr. Lucy, one of the three visionaries at Fatima, who at this time (1988) is still living and is a Carmelite nun at the Convent of Our Lady at Coimbra, Portugal. The paragraphs he quotes are taken from* Fatima in Lucia's Own Words, *1977, page 104. Fatima occurred after Fr. Schouppe wrote his book on Hell, and the vision of Hell witnessed by the three children is given here because it too exemplifies the points Fr. Schouppe is trying in this book to bring home to his readers' minds.*

As Sister Lucy writes in the Prologue of her Fourth Memoir, she was asked by her Bishop to write *another* account of the very same thing [i.e., the vision of Hell, seen by the three children at Fatima], leaving out nothing that could be revealed. She begins by writing:

"I shall begin, then, my new task, and thus fulfill the commands received from Your Excellency as well as the desires of Rev. Dr.

113

Galamba. With the exception of that part of the Secret which I am not permitted to reveal at present, I shall say everything. I shall not knowingly omit anything, though I suppose I may forget just a few small details of minor importance."

After writing about the apparitions of the angel that occurred three times and of the first two apparitions of Our Lady, in May and June of 1917, she takes up once again the matter of the Secret revealed by Our Lady in the apparition of July, 1917. After a few preliminary remarks, she writes:

"And she [Our Lady] continued:

"'Sacrifice yourselves for sinners, and say many times, especially whenever you make some sacrifice: O Jesus, it is for love of You, for the conversion of sinners, and in reparation for the sins committed against the Immaculate Heart of Mary.'

"As Our Lady spoke these last words, she opened her hands once more, as she had done during the two previous months. The rays of light seemed to penetrate the earth, and we saw, as it were, a sea of fire. Plunged in this fire were demons and souls in human form, like transparent burning embers, all blackened or burnished bronze, floating about in the conflagration, now raised into the air by the flames that issued from within themselves together with great clouds of smoke, now falling back on every side like sparks in huge fires, without weight or equilibrium, amid shrieks and groans of pain and despair, which horrified us and made us tremble with fear. (It must have been this sight which caused me to cry out, as people say they heard me). The demons could be distinguished by their terrifying and repellent likeness to frightful and unknown animals, black and transparent like burning coals. Terrified and as if to plead for succor, we looked up at Our Lady, who said to us, so kindly and so sadly:

"'You have seen Hell where the souls of poor sinners go. To save them, God wishes to establish in the world devotion to my Immaculate Heart. If what I say to you is done, many souls will be saved and there will be peace. The war is going to end [i.e., World War I]; but if people do not cease offending God, a worse one will break out during the pontificate of Pius XI. When you see a night illumined by an unknown light, know that this is the great sign given you by God that He is about to punish the world for its crimes by means of war, famine, and persecutions of the Church and of the Holy Father.

"'To prevent this, I shall come to ask for the consecration of Russia to my Immaculate Heart, and the Communion of Reparation on the First Saturdays. If my requests are heeded, Russia will be converted, and there will be peace; if not, she will spread her errors throughout the world, causing wars and persecutions of the Church. The good will be martyred, the Holy Father will have much to suffer, various nations will be annihilated. In the end, my Immaculate Heart will triumph. The Holy Father will consecrate Russia to me, and she will be converted, and a period of peace will be granted to the world." (*Pages VII-IX*).

Appendix III

THE PARABLE OF DIVES AND LAZARUS WITH A COMMENTARY

The following passage of Scripture is taken from St. Luke's Gospel, Chapter 16, Verses 19-31. It tells the story of Dives, the rich man, who dined sumptuously, and Lazarus, the beggar outside his gate, who desired for food only some remnants that fell from the rich man's table. Because this story told by Our Lord is replete with spiritual lessons for us, a short explanation of the parable is also given.

19 "There was a certain rich man, who was clothed in purple and fine linen; and feasted sumptuously every day. 20 And there was a certain beggar, named Lazarus, who lay at his gate, full of sores. 21 Desiring to be filled with the crumbs that fell from the rich man's table, and no one did give him; moreover the dogs came, and licked his sores. 22 And it came to pass, that the beggar died, and was carried by the angels into Abraham's bosom. And the rich man also died: and he was buried in hell. 23 And lifting up his eyes when he was in torments, he saw Abraham afar off, and Lazarus in his bosom: 24 And he cried, and said: Father Abraham, have mercy on me, and send Lazarus, that he may dip the tip of his finger in water, to cool my tongue:

for I am tormented in this flame. ²⁵ And Abraham said to him: Son, remember that thou didst receive good things in thy lifetime, and likewise Lazarus evil things, but now he is comforted; and thou art tormented. ²⁶ And besides all this, between us and you, there is fixed a great chaos: so that they who would pass from hence to you, cannot, nor from thence come hither. ²⁷ And he said: Then, father, I beseech thee, that thou wouldst send him to my father's house, for I have five brethren, ²⁸ that he may testify unto them, lest they also come into this place of torments. ²⁹ And Abraham said to him: They have Moses and the prophets; let them hear them. ³⁰ But he said: No, father Abraham: but if one went to them from the dead, they will do penance. ³¹ And he said to him: If they hear not Moses and the prophets, neither will they believe, if one rise again from the dead.''

—Luke 16:19-31

In this parable, Dives, the rich man, is surprised (as all sinners will be) to realize the horrors and the eternity of Hell and that he has freely gone there. Longing for just a modicum of relief, he asks Abraham to send Lazarus, the beggar whom he despised during life, to touch his tongue with only a drop of water. But even such small relief is not granted to those sinners who land in Hell.

Next, Dives requests that at least Abraham send Lazarus to his father's house, where he has five ''brethren'' or relatives, that they might be warned about the existence of Hell and the likelihood that they will go there. But this request too is denied; Abraham reminds Dives that the people on earth "have Moses and the prophets," that is, Scripture or God's Inspired Word, to warn them and instruct them about Hell.

Yet Dives still insists that Lazarus be sent to them to warn them, saying, "But if one went to them from the dead, they will do penance." (*Verse 30*). Then does Our Lord put into the mouth of Abraham the ominous words, "If they hear not Moses and the prophets, neither will they believe, if one rise again from the dead." (*Verse 31*).

What is Our Lord trying to tell us in this parable? Many things, of course, nor can we presume to plumb the entire meaning or instruction packed into this story, but the main lessons would seem to be the following:

1) The rich man goes to Hell for not having succored the poor and hungry—for not having followed the coporal work of mercy "To feed the hungry." This falls into line with the reasons Our Lord elicits why souls at the Last Judgment are condemned to Hell: "Lord, when did we see thee hungry, or thirsty, or a stranger, or naked, or sick, or in prison, and did not minister to thee? Then he shall answer them, saying: Amen I say to you, as long as you did it not to one of these least, neither did you do it to me. And these shall go into everlasting punishment; but the just, into

life everlasting.'' (*Matt.* 25:44-46).

2) However, the principal reason for quoting the above parable from *Luke* is to highlight what would appear to be God's attitude about how we are to be warned concerning the reality and the eternity and the unbelievable sufferings of Hell. As the parable says, we ''have Moses and the prophets'' to warn us, that is to say, we have Sacred Scripture, God's Inspired Word, to be our guide. What more do we need, especially in light of the fact that, with the New Testament also to serve to warn us, we have more than adequate knowledge that Hell exists and that to avoid it we must adhere strictly to the moral law (the moral law as our unaided intellect sees and understands it and also the moral law as we are assisted in understanding it from the Bible and Catholic Tradition).

This parable of Our Lord is saying in effect, ''What good would it do to send someone back from Hell to warn others, if they do not heed the Scriptures'' (''Moses and the prophets''), which are most explicit about the reality of Hell and the eternal import of our moral actions. ''How long,'' the parable seems to be saying, ''would people on earth listen to this person who came back from Hell?''

Would they listen to him for a year, or for a month, or for a week? Realistically, it would probably be news for only a day or two, and after that a relative few would still be interested for somewhat longer. But then the exigencies of this life would interrupt the attention of those who need to be warned, and they would begin to be distracted and even to doubt the person who had come to warn them, and probably they would end by mocking him, and if he made a real pest of himself, by imprisoning him, or even killing him, as they did with Our Lord.

No, it would not work very well to have someone come back to us who is in Hell. People would not listen. But suppose a second and a third, and a fourth were to return. Would that make a difference? No. The effect would be even less with each succeeding one.

Therefore, it can easily be seen, from this line of reasoning, that God does not send us people from Hell to warn us and to go about among mankind preaching the reality of Hell.

In general, the ''frightening'' silence from the ''other side of the veil'' is far more sobering and much more effective in gaining our attention. For the mortal sinner knows that he is not on the path to Heaven and that if he would save his soul, he must change his ways.

At the very most, and seemingly in contradiction to the words of the above parable, God gives ''little'' glimpses to a soul here or one there, at one time or another in history, that there is a Hell and that the souls in Hell suffer incomprehensible pains. Such is the sort of episode Fr. Schouppe has recorded in his little book of stories. But these do not constitute someone's returning from Hell to go among people, preach-

ing to them about the reality of Hell. And even
these instances, considering the hundreds and
hundreds of millions of souls that have lived on
this earth, are very, very rare indeed. Yes, a book
was issued in 1855 entitled *Apparitions d'esprits*,
which shows that there have been "numerous"
such events such as Fr. Schouppe records—
enough indeed to confirm to the minds of believing people the reality of Hell, and that souls
there *are* lost for all eternity—but yet, as mentioned, the number of such incidents is minis-
cule compared to the number of souls who have
lived. Still this type of phenomenon constitutes
yet another type of warning that Almighty God
has permitted, in His infinite mercy, to help
people avoid Hell.

God, of course, *has* sent Someone from the
other world, namely His divine Son, who con-
descended to become man that He might warn
us even further (in addition to "Moses and the
prophets") about the reality of Hell, and just
what life is all about, from the eternal perspective. But do we human beings heed even the Son
of God made man? Some do; but most today, it
would seem, do not!

Yet God has gone two steps further to warn
us about the reality of Hell and the dangers of
falling into it. He has given us His church to be
a *constant* reminder to us about the reality of
Hell and the possibility of going there; plus, He
has sent us certain of His saints and holy people
to whom He has given visions of Hell and spe-

cial insights into its nature and reality. As the Reverend Father Garrigou-Lagrange says in his book *Life Everlasting*, "Further, Our Lord deigns frequently to give privileged souls a higher knowledge of Hell, by contemplation, or by vision, imaginary or intellectual, in order to carry them on to greater hatred of sin, to growth in charity, to more burning zeal for the salvation of souls. It is sufficient here to recall the visions. Like St. Teresa, many saints were thus illumined by contrast, on the infinite greatness of God and the value of eternal life." (*Page 135*).

To reiterate, God *has* warned us about Hell. And He has warned us sufficiently. In fact He has almost gone overboard, so to speak, to warn us. In the first place, He has made us in His image and likeness, with a powerful mind that comprehends good and evil, without any other assistance. And we know, therefore, deep within ourselves that there is an eternal import to our moral actions. Then He has given us Sacred Scripture, which He has inspired, such that there is no other book even remotely to be compared to it for understanding about the meaning and value of life and the rewards and punishments that are to follow—that is to say, He has given us "Moses and the prophets." And, as if this were not enough, He has sent us His only-begotten Son, to teach us and to redeem us. He has given us, besides, His Church, spread throughout the entire world and teaching all nations. Plus, He has enlightened certain of His saints who have been given special insights into the reality of Hell. And beyond all this, He has allowed certain apparitions of damned souls, or manifestations of the realitiy of Hell, to individual people at various times and places, to reinforce belief in the reality of Hell.

To warn us about Hell, then, we have our unaided reason, Sacred Scripture, Our Lord Himself, the Church, certain of the Saints and holy people, and periodic apparitions and manifestations to various individuals. Are these six enough? For some, yes. For others, no. There is yet a seventh type of warning that God uses, namely, *chastisement!* Both Scripture and the saints agree that if there is hope to save a sinner, God will send him chastisements: "For whom the Lord loveth, he chastiseth; and he scourgeth every son whom he receiveth." (*Hebrews* 12:6). "O how good and sweet is thy spirit, O Lord, in all things! And therefore thou chastisest them that err, by little and little: and admonishest them, and speakest to them, concerning the things wherein they offend: that leaving their wickedness, they may believe in thee, O Lord." (*Wisdom* 12:1-2).

Many saints aver that if a mortal sinner is prospering and doing well and living relatively free of troubles, he has been abandoned by Almighty God and that God is allowing him some pleasures while in this life, because that person is going to spend eternity in Hell.

Yes, God has warned us. God does warn us.

God is warning us at all times about the reality of Hell. Besides Sacred Scripture, the admonitions and example of Our Lord (who went to His horrible death on the Cross to show us the seriousness of sin), the constant teachings of the Church, the revelations to holy people, and periodic extraordinary apparitions and manifestations, we have our conscience and the chastisements of God to remind us of the dangers of falling into Hell. With regard to our conscience, which is the voice of Truth speaking within us, Our Lord says in Scripture, "Behold, I stand at the gate, and knock. If any man shall hear my voice, and open to me the door, I will come in to him, and will sup with him, and he with me." (*Apoc.* 3:20).

However there is a problem with conscience which we should be aware of, namely, that it can be blunted and dulled by our sins, especially by our mortal sins, so that the perception we have of the seriousness of our sins is not accurate and therefore our conscience in this respect does not bother us enough when we commit repeated mortal sins (those sins which are serious enough to send us to Hell). And the problem with God's chastisement in our lives is that we often think these events "just happened accidentally," forgetting that Almighty God has control of all things at all times and that nothing happens without His sending it or at least permitting it.

To understand about Hell, therefore, we need to think about it, to read about it, to meditate on it, to consider our lives and all the wicked and contemptible things we might have done, and then to renounce our sins and discontinue them, on the one hand, and make reparation for them, on the other hand, by doing penance. Scripture, in many places, calls for penance to repair for our sins. "But unless you shall do penance, you shall all likewise perish." (*Luke* 13:3). "And God indeed having winked at the times of this ignorance, now declareth unto men, that all should everywhere do penance." (*Acts* 17:30).

Unlike Dives, the rich man of Our Lord's parable, *there is still time for us who are still alive to do penance for our sins.* We still have life, and if we will turn from our sins, we can still save ourselves. God wills that we do, and He will help us: "Is it my will that a sinner should die, saith the Lord God, and not that he should be converted from his ways, and live?" (*Ezechiel* 18:23). Let us choose God, and His law and His justice, while there is still time!

Part II

HOW TO AVOID HELL

by Thomas A. Nelson

Chapter I

INTRODUCTION

Just what is it that we have to do to avoid Hell? We have seen earlier (cf. the Publisher's Preface) that God says, "I think...thoughts of peace, and not of affliction." (*Jer.* 29:11). And, "For I desire not the death of the sinner, saith the Lord God, but that he be converted and live." (*Ezech.* 18:32). Also, we have heard God speak through the Psalmist, saying, "The mercy of the Lord is from eternity and unto eternity upon them that fear him." (*Ps.* 102:17). In other words, God did not create anyone to go to Hell, but it is His will and His tender mercy that everyone be saved and spend an eternity of joy with Him and all the saints and angels.

Just what is it, therefore, that we have to do to save our souls? That is the ultimate question of life, for if we fail to save our souls and attain Heaven, what will life have been worth? Our Lord said, "It were better for him, if that man had not been born." (*Matt.* 26:24). And, "What doth it profit a man, if he gain the whole world, and suffer the loss of his own soul? Or what exchange shall a man give for his soul?" (*Matt.* 16:26). These are the immortal words of our Divine Saviour, ever reminding us about what is truly important in life.

In the 10th chapter of St. Mark we read of a certain rich man who ran up to Our Lord and, kneeling before Him, asked: "Good Master, what shall I do that I may receive life everlasting? And Jesus said to him . . .Thou knowest the commandments: Do not commit adultery, do not kill, do not steal, bear not false witness, do no fraud, honour thy father and mother." (*Mark* 10:17-19). It is quite obvious from the context of this passage that Jesus meant that the man should keep *all* the Commandments and that those He enumerated were intended only to reflect some of the more important ones and that the Commandments are not confined to these six, but rather embrace many others as well.

For we hear Him in the Sermon on the Mount mentioning a number of things that a person must do and avoid in order to gain eternal life, for example: "But I say to you, that whosoever is angry with his brother, shall be in danger of the judgment. . . And whosoever shall say, Thou fool, shall be in danger of hell fire." (*Matt.* 5:22). "But I say to you, that whosoever shall look on a woman to lust after her, hath already committed adultery with her in his heart." (*Matt.* 5:22). "But I say to you, that whosoever shall put away his wife, excepting for the cause of fornication, maketh her to commit adultery: and he that shall marry her that is put away, committeth adultery." (*Matt.* 5:32). "But let your speech be yea, yea: no, no: and that which is over and above these, is of evil." (*Matt.* 5:37). "Judge not, that you may not be judged." (*Matt.* 7:11). "All things therefore whatsoever you would that men should do to you, do you also to them. For this is the law and the prophets." (*Matt.* 7:12).

Then we read in the words of Our Lord other very sobering reminders: "Unless your justice abound more than that of the scribes and Pharisees, you shall not enter into the kingdom of heaven." (*Matt.* 5:20). "It is easier for a camel to pass through the eye of a needle, than for a rich man to enter the kingdom of God." (*Mark* 10:25). "I would thou wert cold, or hot. But because thou art lukewarm, and neither cold, nor hot, I will begin to vomit thee out of my mouth." (*Apoc.* 3:15-16). "Be you therefore perfect, as also your heavenly Father is perfect." (*Matt.* 5:48). "Then he shall say to them also that shall be on his left hand: Depart from me, you cursed, into everlasting fire which was prepared for the devil and his angels. For I was hungry, and you gave me not to eat: I was thirsty and you gave me not to drink. I was a stranger, and you took me not in: naked, and you covered me not: sick and in prison, and you did not visit me. Then they also shall answer him, saying: Lord, when did we see thee hungry, or thirsty, or a stranger, or naked, or sick, or in prison, and did not minister to thee? Then he shall answer them, saying: Amen I say to you, as long as you did it not to one of these least, neither did you do it to me." (*Matt.* 25:41-45).

Other powerful quotations from Scripture could be brought forward to support the thesis that it is not just the Ten Commandments of God that Our Lord was referring to when He told the rich young man described in *Mark* 10:19, ''Thou knowest the commandments. . .'' But the passages cited above are sufficient to prove that there is more to saving one's soul than simply obeying *literally and only just what the Ten Commandments command or forbid.* The Bible is filled with injunctions and warnings of what we are to do and to avoid in order to please God and to save our souls. However, the problem with using the Bible as a moral guide is that it is very large, its subject matter is scrambled, it can be very confusing and it is often translated in different ways. The Bible almost begs of someone to codify it, break it down, make it easier, create from it a handbook so that the average person can quickly and easily understand just what it is that he must do and not do in order to avoid Hell and attain Heaven.

Knowing this, Our Lord has provided for us that very instrument to make understanding of our moral obligations easier. He has instituted a Church, a Church which, in its broadest definition, is none other than *He Himself*, in the Person of His Mystical Body, a Church projected in space and time, an institution that is to last for all time and provide a beacon to the world, a light in the darkness, a holy temple wherein all those who go searching for Him—like Mary and

Joseph when the child Jesus was lost—will find Him there, just as Mary and Joseph did, a Church that will teach mankind *with authority* so that people will have a sure and certain guide to follow in working out their salvation. That Church He founded on the Apostles, and especially upon Peter, to whom He gave supreme authority over His Church and upon whom He founded it when He said: "Thou art Peter; and upon this rock I will build my church, and the gates of hell shall not prevail against it. And I will give to thee the keys of the kingdom of heaven. And whatsoever thou shalt bind upon earth, it shall be bound also in heaven: and whatsoever thou shalt loose on earth, it shall be loosed also in heaven." (*Matt.* 16:18-19). It was this Church to which He was referring when He said to the Apostles, "You are the salt of the earth" (*Matt.* 5:13), and "A city seated on a mountain cannot be hid." (*Matt.* 5:14). To His Apostles He also said, "He that heareth you, heareth me; and he that despiseth you, despiseth me; and he that despiseth me, despiseth him that sent me." (*Luke* 10:16). Further, in speaking with Pilate, Our Lord proclaimed, "Every one that is of the truth, heareth my voice." (*John* 18:37). And He promised them, moreover, "Behold, I am with you all days, even to the consummation of the world" (*Matt.* 28:20), and "I will not leave you orphans." (*John* 14:18).

Now what is this Church that Our Lord was referring to? Is it visible today? How can we recognize it? What are its marks? Is there really a one, true Church that actually represents Christ in this world, that really teaches His doctrine, pure and unalloyed? If so, where is it to be found? How can the searcher after truth actually find it?

Let us prescind for a moment from answering these questions and step back to ask some even more fundamental questions, as long as we are trying to establish the criteria of our belief: How do we know that Jesus Christ is the Redeemer promised to Adam and Eve, our first parents, in the Garden of Eden? How do we know that His revelation is from God? And how do we know that He is Himself God?

In answer to these questions, it can be stated, *first*, that Our Lord Jesus Christ was prophesied by many of the Prophets of the Old Testament, and His life and works fulfilled these prophecies to the letter. The *second* criterion is that Jesus worked an untold number of miracles, all of which testify to His being the Redeemer. And the *third* is that no man ever spoke like He did, for "his speech was with power." (*Luke* 4:32). His words went right to the heart of those who heard Him, and people could recognize the truth of what He preached. *Fourth*, there was His entirely sinless life, something impossible to an ordinary human being; moreover, it was a life lived without any pomp or wealth or circumstance; no one, for example, has ever criticized Our Lord for being born into easy circumstances or for living "high." *Fifth*, He *said* He was God: "I and the Father are one." (*John* 10:30). "Amen, amen, I say to you, before Abraham was made, I am." (*John* 8:58). "Again the high priest asked him, and said to him: Art thou the Christ the son of the blessed God? And Jesus said to him: I am. And you shall see the Son of man sitting on the right hand of the power of God, and coming with the clouds of heaven." (*Mark* 14:61-62). *Sixth*, there was His incredible, bitter Passion and His death upon the Cross, all of which He underwent willingly and without resisting, as a lamb led to the slaughter. It is probable that no one ever died a more horrible death, physically speaking, and certainly no one ever did from the psychological and emotional standpoint, for Christ was human perfection itself, and His senses and awareness of pain could not have been surpassed; plus, the fact of His Godhead and His perfect innocence made the humiliation of His death, suffered at the hands of His own subjects—people whom He was supporting in their very existence while they were torturing and murdering Him—a supreme degradation and a supreme act of sacrifice. In this regard we must remember His words to the Jews recorded in *John* 10: "No man taketh it [My life] away from me; but I lay it down of myself, and I have power to lay it down: and I have power to take it up again." (*John* 10.18). *Seventh*, to crown all His miracles, He rose from the dead and spent 40 days thereafter appearing to various of His Apostles and disciples, to the number of about 500, many of whom lived for decades afterwards and were a universal testimony to His Resurrection. *Eighth*, before the very eyes of His Apostles, He ascended into Heaven from Mt. Olivet with the promise that He would return again as He had gone.

And, as if all this proof were not enough, *ninth*, He sent His Apostles, only 12 men, out into the entire world with the commission: "Go ye into the whole world, and preach the gospel to every creature. He that believeth and is baptized, shall be saved: but he that believeth not shall be condemned." (*Mark* 16:15-16). Now the Apostles took this commission of Our Lord absolutely seriously and went out into the entire known world and in fact made disciples from among all nations, and, *tenth*, as a witness of the truth of what they taught the people, every one of the Apostles, to a man, suffered martyrdom for the truth of what he preached. (St. John the Evangelist was cast into a cauldron of boiling oil, but miraculously, he did not die, nor was he injured. The fact that he willingly underwent what would normally be a martyrdom enables us to assert that *all* the Apostles gave their lives as a testimony to the truth of their witness.)

As an *eleventh* proof of the divinity of Christ and the divine mission He gave to His Church, there is the literally miraculous, rapid spread of Christianity during the Roman era, despite terrible persecution—10 major persecutions by the year 304 A.D., which claimed an untold number of lives. *Twelfth*, these persecutions of the Church fulfilled His prophecy: "If they have persecuted me, they will also persecute you." (*John* 5:20). Yet, Christ's Church survived all these persecutions to emerge in the early fourth century as the official religion of the Roman Empire. And *thirteenth* and finally, His Church went on from there to spread throughout the entire world and into all nations, and has come down, in uninterrupted succession, to our own time, all while teaching exactly the same faith and having exactly the same worship—plus, affecting human society so profoundly that all of history dates from the birth of Christ, and all nations, whether they realize it or not, whether they accept Christ or not, imitate the Christian concept of the proper human life as the ideal or normative way for mankind to live.

And what is that Church which Jesus Christ founded except the Roman Catholic Church? And what is that religion which He established except Roman Catholicism?

How did it come to be at Rome? The answer is really very simple: St. Peter first set up his apostolic see, or bishopric, at the major city of Antioch, in what is now southwestern Turkey, but later he moved it to Rome, the capital of the Roman Empire. It was there he established the central government of the Church of Jesus Christ, it was there that it took root, and it was there that it flourished. Also, it was there that he was martyred, as were almost all of the 30 Popes of the first three centuries of Christianity. (Including St. Peter, there have been 266 Popes who have ruled the Roman Catholic Church from the beginning until our time—1988.)

And that Church has flourished to become easily the largest church or religion in the world, having over 900 million members (a conservative projection from the latest figures of 1986). The Catholic Church is larger than all non-Catholic Christian denominations taken together —in fact, approximately twice as large. (Some claim the Catholic Church is three times as large as all Protestant Christianity. However, there are no formal figures to prove this claim.) There is a Catholic archbishop in virtually every major city of the world, and a Catholic bishop in virtually every provincial capital throughout the world.

Further, the Catholic Church is a *true government*. Granted its affairs are "not of this world," but insofar as it has structure and has to deal with real people, set laws for their conduct, own property and conduct its affairs in the world, it is to that extent a real government, the size and complexity of which would astound most people. The Vatican (or central) government of the Catholic Church alone is comprised of a Secretary of State, 9 Congregations or cabinet-type special agencies, 3 "Offices" or specialized service agencies, and 3 Tribunals or courts. Its central government employs some 4,000 people and is a larger bureaucracy than the central government of many countries. Plus, it has ambassadors or nuncios in virtually every nation of the world.

Indeed, it is this visible Church, located with its headquarters at Rome and spread throughout the entire world, which is the Church that Christ has established. And it is this Church that He was referring to when He told the Apostles, "You are the light of the world. A city seated on a mountain cannot be hid." (*Matt.* 5:14).

Now, we digress to explain all this about the Roman Catholic Church only because it has bearing upon how we are to avoid Hell and attain Heaven. This present book will undoubtedly be read by people of every imaginable religious persuasion, most of whom accept the Bible as the true word of God. (People accept the Bible or God's word largely because of the interior evidence. The tone, manner, subject and sublimity of the Bible speak louder than words that it was not written by man alone.)

At this point, having presented numerous passages of Scripture indicating that there are many things a person must do and avoid in order to attain salvation, and having presented Fr. Schouppe's book with its very frightening stories of real-life experiences concerning Hell and those who have gone there, we think we would be terribly remiss if we were not also to give a short, albeit a detailed explanation of what it is a person must do and what he must avoid in order not to go to Hell. What good would it do to scare people with the grim realities of Hell and then not help them by showing them how to avoid going there.

Today most people in Western society are either of no religious persuasion, are non-Catholic Christians, or are Catholic. Generally those with no religion do not know what Christ taught about salvation, and non-Catholic Christians do not have the true Christian dispensation or Tradition and therefore the correct teachings of Christ. Moreover, most Catholics today who were born after approximately 1955-1960 do not possess a thorough knowledge of the Catholic Faith (due to what is commonly called the "present confusion in the Church"). Thus, there is all the more reason for and the need of this present explanation.

Our Lord sent the Apostles out into the world with the commission, "Preach the gospel to every creature. He that believeth and is baptized, shall be saved: but he that believeth not shall be condemned." (*Matt.* 15:15-16). Notice that there is no word here, or anywhere else in Scripture, to the effect that the Apostles were to go forth and *write. . .write the Bible,* and have it copied and distributed everywhere. Rather, they were to *preach* and *teach*—which they did. The canon (or authoritative listing) of authentic books of the Bible was not absolutely settled until the Catholic Church's Council of Trent (1545-1563), and printing did not come into common use until the 1440's.

But even the Council of Trent merely defined what was already the traditional list of the books of the Bible that the Catholic (i.e., the Christian) Church had always accepted, even from the times of the Apostles. The earliest formal and approved list of the books of the Bible that we have record of comes from the African Synod (regional Church council) of Hippo in 393, which list was reconfirmed at the African Synod of Carthage in 397, to which the great Father and Doctor of the Church, St. Augustine, signed his name, along with 43 other African bishops. The latter synod added to the list the following statement: "But let the Church beyond the sea [i.e., Rome] be consulted about confirming the canon." Pope St. Innocent I (401-417) approved this list as canonical (i.e., official) in a letter to Exsuperius of Toulouse (France). Plus, a decretal attributed to Pope Gelasius I (492-496), giving this same list, was embodied in the medieval Code of Canon Law (Catholic Church Law). Therefore, the list of 73 books which the Catholic Church proclaims to be the true books of the Bible is the same list of 73 books that go back to early Christian times.

Most of the Christians who were proselytized during the first 14 centuries of our era, therefore, were converted through *preaching* and *teaching*. Now the body of knowledge from which they were evangelized by the Catholic

Church is called the *Tradition* of the Church. *Tradition* is understood by the Catholic Church as one of the two great sources of the deposit of Faith (the knowledge we have of Christ's message) along with the *Bible*, which is the other. Tradition is actually more complete than the Bible, contains teachings which may not be found in the Bible or which may be only hinted at in the Bible, and actually *includes* the Bible and much of how the Bible should be interpreted. A Scriptural reference to this fact is contained in St. Paul's second letter to the Thessalonians, wherein he states, "Therefore, brethren, stand fast; and hold the *traditions* which you have learned, whether by *word*, or by our epistle." (*2 Thess.* 2:14, emphasis added). There is a similar passage which reads: "And we charge you, brethren, in the name of Our Lord Jesus Christ, that you withdraw yourselves from every brother walking disorderly, and not according to the *tradition* which they have received of us." (*2 Thess.* 3:6, emphasis added). And finally St. John says, "But there are also many other things which Jesus did; which, if they were written every one, the world itself, I think, would not be able to contain the books that should be written." (*Jn.* 21:25). Therefore, not all that Christ did, and presumably not all that He *said*, was recorded in writing.

In our present century, when the searcher after truth embarks upon finding the True Church of God, he can discover that Church and determine its authenticity as the true Church of God by what the Catholic Church calls the Four Marks of the Church: That is, that Christ's Church is 1) One, 2) Holy, 3) Catholic (or Universal), and 4) Apostolic. These four marks cannot be explained by natural causes, and they are found in no organization on earth other than the Roman Catholic Church. The explanation of these Marks is as follows:

1. *One*: Christ's Church has one head, the Pope; one government, still located at Rome, where St. Peter established it; one method of worship (the Holy Sacrifice of the Mass); one set of doctrines believed by all who are Catholic; and finally, all this unity has continued throughout all the centuries since the time of Christ. For example, in the Catholic Church we still refer to and use the writings of the great saints and spiritual doctors who have written throughout all the centuries. It was this very unity which St. Paul referred to when he wrote to the Ephesians that they should be "Careful to keep the *unity* of the Spirit in the bond of peace. *One* body and *one* Spirit; as you are called in *one* hope of your calling. *One* Lord, *one* faith, *one* baptism. *One* God and Father of all, who is above all, and through all, and in us all." (*Eph.* 4:3-6, emphasis added). No institution of merely human origin and organization could possibly have achieved this sort of oneness or unity which the Catholic Church has always displayed throughout the world. Such unity and solidarity can come only from God.

2. *Holy*: The Catholic Church is holy in its Founder, Jesus Christ, who is both God and man. It is holy in its doctrines, which are none other than the doctrines Christ Himself taught and which are found in Sacred Scripture. It is holy in its members, that is to say, it produces holy people, saints, in every age. The Catholic Church never maintains that *all* its members are holy; indeed, some are great sinners. But those who follow the holy doctrines and pious practices of the Church arrive at virtue, and in many cases at great sanctity.

3. *Catholic* (or *Universal*): The Roman Catholic Church alone can truly be said to be spread throughout the entire world. Of the world's largest religions, Hinduism is confined mainly to India; Buddhism to India and Indo-China; Shintoism to Japan; Islam to the Arab world, Iran, India, Pakistan, Afghanistan, and Turkey; and of the various non-Catholic Christian denominations, these too are peculiar to only a few countries: The Anglicans are confined mainly to the English-speaking world, the Lutherans to northern Europe and the U.S.A., the Baptists basically to the same, and so forth. But the Catholic Church is found virtually *everywhere*, and in most places in great force and everywhere with high organization. Even the Eskimos of northern Alaska have their own Catholic bishop, and during the Middle Ages when the Norsemen were still Catholic, their colony on Greenland had some 13 consecutive bishops before it was wiped out.

Our Lord decreed that His Church was to be *for all* people, not just for those in the local area: "...You shall be witnesses unto me...even to the uttermost part of the earth." (*Acts* 1:8). "Go ye into the *whole* world, and preach the gospel to *every* creature." (*Mark* 16:15, emphasis added). "Going therefore, teach ye all nations...and behold I am with you all days, even to the consummation of the world." (*Matt.* 28:19-20). It is in this sense that the Roman Catholic Church is called Catholic or universal—i.e., it is to be spread everywhere—and in fact it is!

But in another sense, and in the sense which gave the Church the name "Catholic," it is *Catholic* or *universal* in that it teaches *all* the truths revealed by Christ, and not just *some* of them, as the various Christian denominations do. The name "Catholic" comes from the very first century and is attributed to St. Ignatius (d. 107), the third bishop of Antioch, who in reply to those who believed only part of what Christ taught, answered the question as to what he believed by using the Greek word *"katholikos,"* "all"— "I believe *all* that Christ taught!" Thus the name "Catholic" was coined from virtually the very beginning of the history of the Church.

4. *Apostolic:* The Roman Catholic Church traces her origin back to the Apostles themselves. She has a record not only of all 266 of the Roman Pontiffs back to St. Peter himself, but she traces the existence of the bishoprics of many cities to Apostolic times, and she reveres as great saints

many bishops of the first centuries (every bishop is a successor of one of the 12 Apostles): St. Augustine of Hippo (354-430), St. Ambrose of Milan (340-397), St. Irenaeus of Lyons (125-203), St. Ignatius of Antioch (d. 107), to mention only a few. Moreover, the Catholic Church still uses and refers to the writings of the Great Fathers and Doctors of the Church from earliest times, e.g., St. Basil the Great (329-379), St. Augustine (354-430), St. Jerome (342-420), St. John Chrysostom (347-407), St. Ignatius of Antioch (d. 107), St. Ambrose of Milan (340-397), St. Caesarius of Arles (470-543), St. Gregory the Great (540-604), St. Gregory of Nyssa (330-395), and many, many others.

Beyond these proofs of her Apostolic ancestry, she also reveres the memory of early saints (mostly martyrs for the Christian faith) who go back even to the first century, the century of Our Lord Himself and of the Apostles. In the traditional Roman Canon of the Mass, said every day at Catholic altars throughout the world, the Church commemorates the Blessed Virgin Mary, the Apostles, several early popes, and some early martyrs. Hear in her own words how the Catholic Church prays every day just before the words of Consecration: ''Being in holy fellowship, we reverently bring to mind, firstly the glorious Mary, ever Virgin, Mother of our God and Lord Jesus Christ, and then Thy Blessed Apostles and martyrs, Peter and Paul, Andrew, James, John, Thomas, James, Philip, Bartholomew, Matthew,

Simon and Jude [all Apostles], Linus [second pope], Cletus [third pope], Clement [fourth pope], Sixtus [eighth pope], Cornelius, Cyprian, Lawrence [deacon in Rome under Pope Sixtus], Chrysogonus, John and Paul, Cosmas and Damian, and all Thy saints. . .'' And then after the words of Consecration the Church prays: ''To us, also, Thy sinful servants, who hope in the multitude of Thy mercies, be pleased to grant some place and fellowship with Thy holy Apostles and martyrs: with John, Stephen, Matthias, Barnabas, Ignatius, Alexander, Marcellinus, Peter, Felicity, Perpetua, Agatha, Lucy, Agnes, Cecilia, Anastasia and with all Thy saints.'' These saints either were Apostles or lived during or close to Apostolic times.

In and around the city of Rome itself are the four Great Basilicas: St. Mary Major, St. John Lateran, St. Paul Outside-the-Walls and St. Lawrence Outside-the-Walls (all of which date from the 4th century). The visitor to Rome does not have to believe words in a book, claiming the Apostolic antiquity of the Church; he can see in these buildings themselves, concrete, standing testimonials to the truth of the Church's claim that she proceeds from the Apostles and was established by Jesus Christ Himself, who said to St. Peter, ''And I say to thee: That thou art Peter; and upon this rock I will build my church, and the gates of hell shall not prevail against it.'' (*Matt.* 16:18). And as if these were not indications enough, the greatest basilica of the

Roman Catholic Church, located in the diocese, or the See (or Seat) of St. Peter himself, is called by no other name than St. Peter's. And wonder of wonders, whose tomb should be discovered there (starting) in 1939 in the subterranean caverns beneath this great basilica but that of St. Peter himself, the Great Fisherman, the Prince of the Apostles, the first Roman Catholic Pontiff, and the Rock (*"petra"* in Greek means "rock") upon which Christ founded His Church and against which the "Gates of Hell," as He foretold, will not prevail. And there today stands Christ's Church, the Roman Catholic Church, nearly two thousand years later, the "city seated on a mountain [which] cannot be hid." (*Matt.* 5:14). Indeed, the evidence that the Roman Catholic Church is the true Church of Christ is too palpable to be mistaken!

What bearing, again, does all this have upon how we are to avoid Hell? Every bearing in the world! For it is only in the Catholic Church that we find the complete doctrine of Christ; it is only in the Catholic Church that we find a simplified, easily understood, comprehensive, and workable codification of the true Christian way of life, that life which corresponds completely with what we find taught in the Bible. It is only in the Catholic Church, also, that we find the Body and Blood of Jesus Christ in the Sacrament of the Eucharist—without which Our Lord said we would have no life in us. (*John* 6:54).

It is only the Catholic Church that maintains it has the actual Body and Blood, the Real Presence of Jesus Christ, in its tabernacles and on its altars. It is only the Catholic Church which provides its members with this "Bread of Heaven," spoken of by Our Lord in that famous passage from St. John: "I am the bread of life. Your fathers did eat manna in the desert, and are dead. This is the bread which cometh down from heaven; that if any man eat of it, he may not die. I am the living bread which came down from heaven. If any man eat of this bread, he shall live for ever; and the bread that I will give, is my flesh, for the life of the world...Amen, amen I say unto you: Except you eat the flesh of the Son of man, and drink his blood, you shall not have life in you. He that eateth my flesh, and drinketh my blood, hath everlasting life: and I will raise him up in the last day. For my flesh is meat indeed: and my blood is drink indeed. He that eateth my flesh, and drinketh my blood, abideth in me, and I in him. As the living Father hath sent me, and I live by the Father; so he that eateth me, the same also shall live by me. This is the bread that came down from heaven. Not as your fathers did eat manna, and are dead. He that eateth this bread, shall live for ever." (*John* 6:48-52, 54-59).

There is no doubt that Jesus meant these words quite literally, for He stated the case in this passage in a long and complete manner, expressing Himself in several different ways, and since "many of his disciples went back, and walked no more with him" (*John* 6:67) because of these words—and He gave no indication that they had misinterpreted His words in the slightest—we can see that He truly meant them literally, rather than in some figurative sense, as is maintained by those who say, for example, that by this passage He meant the "Word of God," Scripture, which we are supposed to "eat up," or again, that Jesus becomes spiritually present to us *only* when we *receive* Him and to the extent that we believe.

No, from everything said in *John* 6, it has to be concluded that He meant His *real* flesh and blood, the Body and Blood of Christ. Now, only the Catholic Church maintains it has the True Body and Blood of Christ—in the Sacrament of the Eucharist.

(The Greek and Russian Orthodox Churches, covering basically Eastern Europe and the Northern part of Asia, still have the Eucharistic Body and Blood of Jesus Christ according to the official teaching of the Roman Catholic Church. For these two groups still have true and valid priests and bishops, still possess the full deposit of the Faith and are "Catholic" in every respect, except that they do not accept the leadership and authority of the Pope in Rome over the entire Church of Jesus Christ. For this reason they are called "schismatic," i.e., separated or cut off from the Catholic Church. But in every other respect they are Catholic, and for purposes of referring to the sacramental or Real Presence of Christ in the Eucharist, they are understood for our purposes to be included in the term Catholic, though the Roman Catholic Church actually refers to them as the "Orthodox" Churches.)

There is a famous saying in the Catholic Church that goes, "Outside the Church there is no salvation." This saying simply expresses in different words Our Lord's meaning when He said: "He that believeth and is baptized, shall be saved: but he that believeth not shall be condemned." (*Mark* 16:16). Now the Catholic Church teaches—in connection with this doctrine that there is no salvation outside the Church—that there exists a "baptism of desire" and a "baptism of blood." "Baptism of Desire" is the term used to describe the baptism one receives who is not baptized with water (sacramental Baptism), but who nevertheless (through grace from God) desires and determines within his or her heart to fulfill all that God requires for salvation—and, of course, at the same time leads a life which is free of mortal sin and has "perfect contrition" (which includes pure love of God, cf. Ch. VII) for any mortal sins he may have committed. Such a person will be able to save his soul, for such a person is said to have received "Baptism of Desire"; implicit in Baptism of Desire is the condition that, if the person knew that the Catholic Church is the One True Church established by God, he would join it. Having received God's life (Sanctifying Grace) in his soul through Baptism of Desire, he will be saved if he stays in the state of grace by avoiding all mortal sin until death; or, if he falls into mortal sin, by repenting in the way God requires. (Cf. Chapter VII).

"Baptism of Blood" is the term used for the "baptism" received by an unbaptized person who dies for or sacrifices his life in testimony of the truth of Christianity, professing in his own blood his faith in Christ.

Despite these two possibilities for salvation (i.e., Baptism of Desire and Baptism of Blood) for those not officially (i.e., sacramentally) baptized as Catholics, it nonetheless remains necessary for salvation that one join the Catholic Church if he comes to the knowledge that the Catholic Church is the Church which Christ has founded and which He expects everyone to join in order to be saved. And if a person even *suspects* that the Catholic Church might be the Church which God has founded, that person is duty-bound to investigate its claims to determine whether or not they are true. If he suspects it is God's true Church and fails to investigate it to be certain, he is liable for his own damnation. If he investigates and finds them true, but fails to join, he is again liable for his own damnation. If he investigates but cannot see that they are true, because he did not receive the grace of conversion from Almighty God, he may still be able to save his soul—if he has true Baptism of Desire and leads a life free from mortal sin.

Why is it necessary to be a Catholic in order

to be saved? There are two main reasons: *First:* It is only in the Catholic Church that there exists the complete truth revealed by Christ and faithfully taught by the Popes, the successors of St. Peter, and by those bishops (successors of the Apostles) who are in union with the Pope. Without this truth, a person simply *does not know the way to God: he does not know what he must* BELIEVE *and what he must* DO *in order to be saved.* Our Lord proclaimed this truth when He said, ''I am the way, and the truth, and the life. No man cometh to the Father, but by me.'' (*John* 14:6). *Without an accurate assessment of the job of attaining our salvation, how shall any of us know how to go about the task of saving our souls?* If we are not properly apprised of the way, of the difficulties that are entailed along the way and of the means necessary for our successful journey, how shall we ever expect to arrive? A man in San Francisco may as well set out for Chicago by traveling west on a bicycle. Both his direction and his means of transportation will be wrong, and he will simply not be successful.

The *second*, and (if we could speak of it in these terms) more important reason it is necessary to be a Catholic in order to achieve salvation is that without the grace of God, a) to bring the *life of God* to our souls (Sanctifying Grace) and b) to *help* us to do good in our day-to-day actions (actual grace), we can do nothing good in the supernatural (heavenly) order (i.e., nothing spiritually alive which is of value for salvation and heavenly reward). Our Lord has given us a number of statements that express this truth; for example: "Without me you can do nothing." (*John* 15:5). And, "Except you eat the flesh of the Son of man, and drink his blood, you shall not have life in you." (*John* 6:54). The Catholic Church possesses all seven of the Sacraments instituted by Our Lord. These are outward signs instituted by Christ to give grace to our souls. *Without the means of these God-given channels to supply grace to our souls, we cannot enter upon the life of Sanctifying Grace,* which is none other than the life of God within us and which God requires of us for our salvation (this takes the Sacrament of *Baptism*), *nor can we so surely live and persevere in Sanctifying Grace during our life once we have received it in Baptism.* Human frailty being what it is, one can almost say that without the assistance of the Sacraments of the Church to help us avoid mortal sin and keep the law of God, there is virtually a moral certainty that we cannot do so.

This explanation of the twofold need for the Catholic Church for salvation is both a common-sense approach and one in keeping with the words of Our Lord found in the Bible. In order to know what one must believe and do to be saved, and in order to receive the Sacraments, one needs to join the Church founded by Christ, the Church which has a divine origin and which possesses the divine authority to teach in Christ's name.

What gives the teaching of the Catholic Church a particular power and claim to authority is the fact that her uninterrupted history of unity of doctrine, moral precepts, worship, and government goes right back to St. Peter himself, the first Pope, who was commissioned by Jesus Christ Himself; the fact that she teaches this same doctrine throughout the world, in all places, that her teachings correspond to those of the Bible; and the fact that some 900 million people (in 1988) accept (at least in principle) the very strict, unified, disciplined, exact Catholic belief and practice (though, of course, not all live up to her ideals). All this represents a phenomenon beyond the capability of any strictly human organization to produce. But the Roman Catholic Church is not just a human organization. It is also a *divine* organization that is comprised of human beings. For the Catholic Church maintains that she is none other than the Mystical Body of Christ in the world, mentioned by St. Paul in the Scriptures (*Colossians* 1:18, *1 Corinthians* 12:20-27, *Ephesians* 5:30, *Romans* 12:4-5, and *1 Corinthians* 6:15), and that the Holy Spirit guides and protects her through the ages of time and safeguards the truth of her doctrine throughout the entire world. No other church even attempts to make this claim or a claim even remotely similar.

Now just what is it that the Catholic Church teaches with regard to avoiding Hell and gaining Heaven? It is nothing other than what is found in the Bible, what we saw was admonished by Our Lord Himself in the passages quoted above. However, there is considerably more involved in salvation than what is contained in those random ideas we quoted in the few scriptural verses earlier, and it is much better codified by the Catholic Church than what one finds in the Bible: this is due to the fact that the Catholic Church and her Tradition go right back to Christ Himself, who taught her these things in the person of the Apostles, and due also to the fact the Church has had nearly 2,000 years of history, under the protection and guidance of the Holy Spirit, to digest the message of Christ and to capsulize, organize and break it down into its most understandable terms. Moreover, she has the *authority* from Christ to do this, who said, "Going therefore, teach ye all nations; baptizing them in the name of the Father, and of the Son, and of the Holy Ghost. Teaching them to observe all things whatsoever I have commanded you: and behold I am with you all days, even to the consummation of the world." (*Matt.* 28:19-20).

In general, this codification of belief and morality is what the Catholic Church has called "the Catechism," and this is what she teaches all her members, be they Catholic school children learning their lessons for the first time, or adult prospective converts. Without a knowledge of the Catechism, a person simply cannot become a Catholic. For the Catechism contains all the basic beliefs given to us by Jesus Christ, an explanation of the Sacraments, an explanation of the Commandments (what they are and what they require of us), and in general an explanation of what constitutes the Christian way of life.

To begin with, the Catechism teaches that man's nature, though essentially good, was vitiated (or harmed) by the Original Sin committed by our first parents. This Original Sin, besides having lost for man the Life of Sanctifying Grace (the divine life of God which He now imparts to our souls in Baptism, and which Adam and Eve possessed before the Fall), and having introduced death and suffering and ignorance into the world, has also left man inclined toward evil; man is not fundamentally evil in his nature, but he has a propensity, or a "leaning," toward evil, which includes a darkness of the intellect and a weakness of the will, with an inclination to make self the center and god of his life. To overcome Original Sin, Christ instituted the Sacrament of Baptism, which washes away Original Sin and gains back for us Sanctifying Grace, making us holy and pleasing to God. However, many of the *after-effects* of Original Sin are still within us (sickness, suffering, death, darkness of the intellect and weakness of the will, etc.). Baptism does not take these away, and because we are still inclined toward evil and have a free will, we can still commit sin—*and we do!*

Now the sin which *we* commit is called *actual sin*—the sin of our own acts. Actual sin, moreover, is categorized by the Church into *mortal sin* and *venial sin*. A mortal sin is a sin deadly to the soul; it drives out the life of Sanctifying Grace won for us by Baptism, separating us from God and depriving us of His friendship. Mortal sin is a grave offense against the law of God, one that we realize is a grave offense, and yet one that we fully decide to commit anyway, with full consent of our free will. If one commits such a sin and dies unrepentant with it upon his soul, he will go to Hell. *Venial sin* is a less serious offense against the law of God, one which does not lose for us Sanctifying Grace. However, the danger of venial sin, especially *willful* venial sin—that is, venial sin committed with the full knowledge that it *is* against the law of God and with full consent of our will—is that it can and often will lead us into committing mortal sin. (Sinning tends to grow, both in number and in magnitude.)

Although Scripture does not use the terms *mortal sin* and *venial sin*, it does in fact make this same distinction, though one must almost know this distinction before he can see that the Scriptural writers are indeed making it.

For biblical examples of *mortal sin* (that sin which causes death to the soul and eternal perdition in Hell), let us consider the following verses from St. Paul and from the *Apocalypse*: ''Being filled with all iniquity, malice, fornication, avarice, wickedness, full of envy, murder, contention, deceit, malignity, whisperers, detractors, hateful to God, contumelious, proud, haughty, inventors of evil things, disobedient to parents, foolish, dissolute, without affection, without fidelity, without mercy. Who, having known the justice of God, did not understand that they who do such things, are worthy of death; and not only they that do them, but they also that consent to them that do them." (*Rom.* 1:29-32). "Know you not that the unjust shall not possess the kingdom of God? Do not err: neither fornicators, nor idolaters, nor adulterers, nor the effeminate, nor liers with mankind, nor thieves, nor covetous, nor drunkards, nor railers, nor extortioners, shall possess the kingdom of God." (*1 Cor.* 6:9-10). "Now the works of the flesh are manifest, which are fornication, uncleanness, immodesty, luxury, idolatry, witchcrafts, enmities, contentions, emulations, wraths, quarrels, dissensions, sects, envies, murders, drunkenness, revellings, and such like. Of the which I foretell you, as I have foretold to you, that they who do such things shall not obtain the kingdom of God." (*Gal.* 5:19-21). "For know you this and understand, that no fornicator, or unclean, or covetous person (which is a serving of idols), hath inheritance in the kingdom of Christ and of God." (*Eph.* 5:5). "Mortify therefore your members which are upon the earth; fornication, uncleanness, lust, evil concupiscence, and covetousness, which is the service of idols. For which things the wrath of God cometh upon the children of unbelief." (*Col.* 3:5-6). "But the fearful, and unbelieving, and the abominable, and murderers, and whore-mongers, and sorcerers, and idolaters, and all liars, they shall have their portion in the pool burning with fire and brimstone, which is the second death." (*Apoc.* 21:8).

As examples of *venial sin*, on the other hand, let us ponder the following passages: "For a just man shall fall seven times and shall rise again: but the wicked shall fall down into evil." (*Proverbs* 24:16). "For there is no just man upon earth, that doth good, and sinneth not." (*Ecclesiastes* 7:21). "But I say unto you, that every idle word that men shall speak, they shall render an account for it in the day of judgment." (*Matt.* 12:36). "For in many things we all offend. If any man offend not in word, the same is a perfect man." (*James* 3:2). "If we say that we have no sin, we deceive ourselves, and the truth is not in us." (*1 John* 1:8).

It will be noted that the passage from *Proverbs* says the *"just"* man; now if he is "just," he is pleasing to God and in God's grace. *Yet,* the passage says he shall fall (commit venial sin) seven times and rise again. *Ecclesiastes* says "no just man...sinneth not." Now if he is "just," he is in God's grace, but if he commits *mortal* sin, he is not just; therefore, he must be committing a less serious sin than mortal sin—and this is what the Catholic Church calls "venial sin." The passage from *Matthew* says that we shall have to render an account for "every idle word" in the day of judgment; is it reasonable for God to condemn a soul to Hell for all eternity for so small a sin as an idle word? Therefore, this type of sin must be a "venial sin," as the Catholic Church terms it. And finally, the passage from St. John's epistle indicates that we *all* have sin within us. If there is no differentiation between serious (mortal) sins and lesser (venial) sins, then no one would be worthy of salvation (despite the Sanctifying Grace one received from the Sacrament of Baptism, despite one's being therefore an adopted "child of God," and despite the good works one has done while in this "State of Grace") which is an absurd position. Therefore, the Bible does in fact distinguish between mortal and venial sin, but simply not in those exact terms.

Some examples of *obvious* mortal sin are murder, abortion, fornication, adultery, and larger thefts (usually those which equal a day's wage—or more—of the person from whom one steals). But there are other mortal sins as well, sins which are very commonly committed, such as rejecting the gift of supernatural Faith, apostasy (abandoning the Faith), heresy (refusing to accept all the truths of the Faith), agnosticism (maintaining one does not or cannot know in the face of obvious truth), "divorce" without a sufficiently serious reason, "remarriage" after "divorce," artificial birth control, purposefully missing Mass (for Catholics) on Sundays and/or holydays of obligation without sufficiently grave reason, and others as well.

The general catalog of sins is the Ten Commandments of God, as given by God to Moses on Mount Sinai (*Exodus* 1:17 and *Deuteronomy* 5:6-21) during the time the Israelites were on their journey from Egypt to the Promised Land. This group of commandments is sometimes called the Decalogue—"deca" in Greek means "ten," and "logos" means "word."

For the sake of completion in explaining how to avoid Hell, it is imperative at this point to list the Ten Commandments of God and to give an explanation of each one, for today there are relatively few people well-instructed in the True Faith, and many readers of this book may either not know these Commandments of God completely or they may not understand all that is covered by them. (The Ten Commandments are basically general statements covering broad categories of activity.) It is hoped the instructed Catholic will indulge us here while we present a statement of the Ten Commandments of God and give a brief enumeration, according to the teachings of the Catholic Church, of many of the sins covered by each of these Commandments. We will cover numerous points which many Catholics will recall from their catechism days. The reader should understand, moreover, that the following list of the sins covered by the Ten Commandments is not at all to be considered complete, but rather it is only a list of some of the more common sins.

Chapter II

THE TEN COMMANDMENTS

Further to what has just been said in the preceding chapter regarding mortal and venial sin, the reader should well note as he proceeds through this chapter on the Ten Commandments and the various groups of sins covered by each specific Commandment, that not all sins discussed in this chapter are mortal sins. Some are mortal (such as murder, adultery, larger thefts) and some are venial. The purpose of this chapter is simply *to list many of the types of sin* that Catholic moralists generally include under the individual precepts of the Ten Commandments. Later, in Chapter 9, the "common mortal sins" committed today are mentioned and discussed in detail.

When speaking of mortal and venial sin, the Catholic Church is very careful not to make definite pronouncements on most types of sin as to whether they are mortal or venial because the seriousness of sins can vary, based upon either the circumstances surrounding the sin or the person's awareness of the degree of its sinfulness. These two factors can change so dramatically that in some cases there is a mortal sin, in others there is a venial sin, and in still others there is no sin at all. For example, a poor person with many children to feed may over a period of time steal a substantial amount of food from a truck farmer because it is the only place near enough from which to obtain food and because the owner will not give it to him; the alternative would be the possible sickness or death of his children. In this case there would probably not even be so much as a slight venial sin, though the person would be duty-bound to pay for the food taken if he ever could.

But the Church *does say* that with regard to some sins the matter is *always* mortally sinful. These sins include sins directly against God (against the First Commandment) and sins of impurity (against the Sixth and Ninth Commandments). The Church does teach that, so long as the three determining factors for mortal sin are present—namely, 1) a serious matter (or a matter considered to be serious by the sinner), 2) sufficient reflection and 3) full consent of the will—then sins against God (blasphemy, rejecting the gift of Faith or purposely not becoming a Catholic when one knows this is what God wants of all people, apostasy, heresy, agnosticism, schism) and all sins of impurity (cf. below under the Sixth and Ninth Commandments, and also Chapter IX) are in themselves *always* mortally sinful, as are willful murder, suicide, abortion, artificial birth control and operations intended to cause sterility (e.g., tubal ligation, vasectomy). Such sins are always mortally sinful, given the presence of the other two factors needed to constitute a mortal sin.

Other sins can be mortal sins at some times and venial sins at other times, or no sin at all, depending on the circumstances. A good example would be lying. If the lie involves a serious matter, it would be mortally sinful; if it does not, it would be venially sinful; if the person asking has no right to know, it would be no sin at all, but rather, what is called a *mental reservation* (cf. the Eighth Commandment below).

Using just this last example for consideration, we can quickly see that with certain lies— because they at least rather serious—*it may be impossible to determine* whether they are mortally sinful or only venially sinful. This is one reason why the Catholic Church has pronounced that no one knows *for certain* whether he be in the state of grace or in the state of mortal sin, which is nothing more than a reinforcement of that same truth expounded in Sacred Scripture where the Bible says, "And yet man knoweth not whether he be worthy of love, or hatred." (*Ecclesiastes* 9:1). Therefore, the true Catholic lives his life in *great* humility, not knowing for certain whether he is basically pleasing to God (i.e., in the state of Sanctifying Grace) or not— whether he is basically corresponding to God's grace as he should, or not. It is for this reason that St. Paul tells us, "With fear and trembling work out your salvation" (*Philippians* 2:12), that is, with great reverence and care. Our Lord has told us, "Be you therefore perfect, as also your heavenly Father is perfect" (*Matt.* 5:48), as a norm for which we are to strive all our lives. Therefore, we should strive to eliminate both mortal *and* venial sin from our lives. For anyone who enters Heaven will have to be perfect, because nothing can enter there that has *any* imperfection whatever. The Catholic Church teaches that we will have to eliminate our imperfections in this world and/or in Purgatory before we will be admitted into Paradise. It is for this reason obviously that Scripture repeatedly calls for perfection in the Saints, for example, "Thou shalt be perfect, and without spot before the Lord thy God." (*Deut.* 18:13).

1. *I am the Lord thy God; thou shalt not have strange gods before Me.* Under this Commandment we are forbidden to worship gods other than the one true God who created all things. At the coming of Christ, many nations (such as the Greeks, Romans, and Egyptians) worshipped a multiplicity of gods. People today, for the most part, do not have trouble with temptations to worship such false gods, but we do indeed have trouble with this Commandment, for there is a sense in which it is of all the Commandments the one broken most often.

In general, under the First Commandment we are required to worship God *as He has revealed that we are to worship Him.* Any other form of worship, if we realize this fact, is a form of idolatry, in the sense that it is the worship of God in a *false* manner, a manner of man's own choosing, rather than the way God has prescribed, and therefore it is idolatry to the extent that man is really worshipping himself as a "false god" before the one true God. (In other words, man is worshipping in *his* way instead of in God's way.) Moreover, we are obliged to seek His face, that is, to seek Him out and learn for ourselves what it is that He requires of us.

The Catholic Church has always maintained quite openly that it is the one, true, revealed religion of God, and that it is in the Catholic Church that all men are meant by Almighty God to worship Him, and in the manner which He has shown to His Church that He wants to be worshipped. Anyone who suspects the Catholic Church is the True Religion and who fails to take up this challenge and investigate its claims to be the True Faith revealed by God will be held accountable by Almighty God for not joining His Church and receiving Baptism, which imparts the life of God Himself (Sanctifying Grace) to the soul, as well as for any sins he might have avoided had he accepted the challenge, made the requisite investigation and embraced the Faith of Christ, which has been entrusted to the Catholic Church.

Sins against the theological virtues of Faith and Hope come under the First Commandment. Sins against the virtue of Faith include refusal to believe all that Christ has taught, preferring rather to pick and choose what we wish to believe (heresy). It also includes doubting the Faith and not searching out the truth, preferring to rely on what we *think* is the truth about some element of the Faith, or about the entire Faith, rather than inquire of someone knowledgeable and have our questions intelligently answered. It includes leaving the Faith for another "religion," or just abandoning belief in the True Faith entirely (apostasy). It includes also the sin of *schism,* which a Catholic commits by separating himself from the rightful leadership of the Pope, the Vicar of Christ, over the entire body of Christians.

Sins against the Theological Virtue of Hope are presumption and despair. We sin by *presumption* when we *presume* before we sin that God will give us the necessary graces to repent, or when we *presume* we will be able to renounce our sins at a later date, or when we *presume* that our sins are not as bad as in fact they are. We sin by *despair* when we think that God could never forgive us because our sins are so bad, or that we simply cannot save our souls, or that God does not want to help us save our souls, or that He will *not* help us save our souls.

Still another way of offending against the First Commandment is through spiritualism, séances, witchcraft, Ouija boards, or anything else that calls upon occult spirits to intervene in our lives with messages and "help." For, in so doing, we are giving to creatures (the evil spirits) that honor we are obliged to give to God alone. Akin to calling up spirits is placing credence in and basing our actions upon readings from tarot cards, palmistry, tea leaves, astrology, phrenology and so forth. Many of these things—such as witchcraft, spiritualism and astrology—are expressly forbidden in the Bible.

Further to the above, there is a definite, albeit broad sense in which *every time we sin, we violate the First Commandment of God* because we have thereby put a created thing and/or our own will above or before the law of God. And in that sense, we have placed an "idol" or a "strange god" before the one true God. Going beyond even this, *anything* to which we give undue time or attention or money, *to the extent that it tends to detract from our God-given duties in life,* is a false god placed before the one true God. For a student, it might be his grades, slavishly sought for at the price of really learning. For a professor, it might be his erudition, bought at the price of worshipping God. For an athlete, it might be his physique or prowess, overly developed at the price of study or work or worship. For the businessman, it might be his success, purchased at the price of his wife and family's overall welfare. For a housewife, it might be the preening of her home at the cost of not sufficiently supporting the Church or being able to send her children to a Catholic school. For a young woman, it might be her beauty or her figure or her hair, pampered at the cost to her, for example, of her prayers or her education. For the young man, it might be his automobile, if he gives it undue time and attention, which might draw him away from his education or other duties in life. Scripture puts into the mouth of our Creator the sobering words, "For the worship of abominable idols is the cause, and the beginning and end of all evil." (*Wisdom* 14:27).

2. *Thou shalt not take the name of the Lord thy God in vain.* Under this Commandment is forbidden all insincere and irreverent use of the name of God. Whenever we use God's name, it must be with respect. Under the Second Commandment Catholic theologians generally distinguish among *cursing, swearing, profanity* and *vulgarity.* 1) *Cursing* amounts to willing that some person or thing be damned to Hell, and if we really mean it in the case of a person, it would be a mortal sin. 2) *Swearing* is the calling of God to witness to the truth of what we are saying; it takes the form of an oath that we swear to, as when giving witness in court, and it should never be done lightly, but always for a serious reason. 3) *Profanity* is the irreverent or insincere use of the name of God; unless done with vehemence, forethought and full consent of the will, it is considered to be a venial sin. 4) *Vulgarity* is the use of gross, impolite, or socially unacceptable terms or expressions and includes the words "damn" and "Hell." Vulgarity is generally considered by Catholic theologians to be no sin at all. (Often when one uses vulgar-

ity, it is in anger; the anger would then be the sin, not the vulgarity.) However, the danger of habitually using vulgar language is that it could lead one gradually—or in the excitement of the moment—to use God's name in vain. In the *spirit* of the Commandment, therefore, we should always employ our faculty of speech with respect and honor and avoid vulgar language altogether, realizing that we are made in the image and likeness of God, and that God created us and all things simply by speaking His word, by His mere command. Even when we human beings speak, things happen. When a mother says, "Time to go to bed," things happen; the children go to bed. When a businessman tells his staff, "We will take a four-day weekend over Thanksgiving holiday," the company is off on the Friday after Thanksgiving, and that is that. When a man and woman stand before the altar of God and say, "I do," they are married. Speech is a Godlike faculty, and it really should not be abused in *any* way, if we are to please God. Our Lord has said, "But let your speach be yea, yea: no, no: and that which is over and above these, is of evil." (*Matt.* 5:37). (Various writers have claimed, as have some Catholic saints and the recipients of certain *private* revelations, that there is an intrinsic sacredness to the name of God, of Jesus Christ, etc. St. Bernardine of Seina even says, "God and His name are one." No one would use his mother's name as an expletive; why then should we use God's?)

Perjury, or lying under oath, is a particularly serious sin against the Second Commandment since by taking an oath we call God to witness the truth of what we say—and then we insult Him by lying. (Perjury is also an offense against the Eighth Commandment, which forbids lying.)

Blasphemy ("any word of malediction, reproach or contumely pronounced against God"—Suarez) is probably the ultimate misuse of the power of speech, for with blasphemy we thereby insult the infinite majesty of God by our cursing against Him, by our railing at Him, or by any deprecatory language we might hurl at Him in our anger and frustration. Blasphemy is considered to be a sin against Faith, and is primarily a sin against the First Commandment, but by violating the use of our faculty of speech it also violates the Second Commandment as well.

3. *Remember thou keep holy the Lord's Day.* For Catholics, this entails attending and participating in the Holy Sacrifice of the Mass on Sundays, and for all people it requires worshipping God in a special manner during that day, as well as refraining from unnecessary work or business activities that would detract from the sacred character of the day. Sundays should be spent in resting, visiting relatives and the sick, saying extra prayers, doing spiritual reading, spending time with one's family and engaging in moderate recreation.

The Commandment definitely forbids unnecessary shopping on Sundays, even if those are the days on which stores have the best sales! (We might do well to imagine ourselves, for a moment, telling Almighty God on Judgment Day, before the entire heavenly court, that we consistently violated the Third Commandment of God by shopping on Sunday *because that was the day they always had the good sales!*) For one thereby forces another person to violate God's law on Sunday by working, plus the shopper himself violates the sanctity of Sunday by engaging in a mundane, work-type activity for which there is ample time during the other six days of the week. This Commandment definitely forbids a businessman's making his employees work on Sundays if the business conducted is not crucial to the smooth functioning of society, such as keeping a gas station or a restaurant open on a super highway.

4. *Honor thy father and thy mother.* Under this Commandment we are required always to honor and respect the people who brought us into this world. Often this Commandment is thought to require only obedience by young children toward their parents. But there is indeed more to our obligations under the Fourth Commandment than that. By the Fourth Commandment, we are required to obey our parents when we are in our minority (through approximately 18 to 21 years of age) and thereafter to honor and respect them for the rest of our lives, which includes caring

for them when they are old. St. Paul says, "But if any man have not care of his own, and especially of those of his house, he hath denied the faith, and is worse than an infidel." (*1 Tim.* 5:8).

In a broad and general sense, the Fourth Commandment also requires us to obey all lawful superiors and all lawful authority. When we are young, it is required toward our teachers and all who are put in authority over us, just as if they were our parents. (Both civil law and Church law use a Latin term, *in loco parentis,* "in place of the parent," to signify the principle involved.) In general, we must at every age of life obey all lawful authority and all laws of our city, state and nation, insofar as it is not immoral to do so.

5. *Thou shalt not kill.* Even Our Lord, in *Mark* 10:19, specifically includes the prohibition against killing as one of the Commandments that must be obeyed if we are to attain eternal life. (Therefore, murder presumably is not so impossible to commit—especially today, with abortion being so common.) Now the Church teaches that there is a number of allied sins forbidden by this Commandment (by reason, presumably, of their connection with the final act of murder). And they include quarrelling, arguing, fighting, anger and hatred. They also include suicide (taking one's own life), which of course is also murder; as well as abortion, which is a particularly heinous murder—so wicked, in fact, that the Catholic Church in America has reserved this sin to the

local bishop for forgiveness. Before abortion was legalized and became so common, a Catholic confessing this sin to a priest could not normally receive absolution from the priest (unless the priest had received in advance the special faculty—i.e., permission and authority—to grant forgiveness) until and unless the priest referred the case to the bishop. With the sin of abortion-murder being so common today, it is usually the case that most bishops grant their priests in advance the special "faculty" of absolving this sin without referring the case specifically to him, though it is still considered a sin "reserved" to the bishop for absolution. Now the reason for the terribly serious nature of abortion-murder is that the life of a totally innocent and defenseless human being is being snuffed out, but more particularly, because that person does not have a chance to be baptized and go to Heaven, to be happy with God for eternity. Further, the sin of abortion involves at least two people—and often three, four or more—namely, the mother and the abortionist, plus "nurses" and other attendants. Often too, it also involves the father of the child aborted—the mother's paramour or husband—and sometimes the parents of the mother, who have pressured her to have the abortion. Further, abortion-murder is a sin against society, because it robs society of a new member. Too, it places a terrible and virtually unerasable sense of guilt on the offending mother, a guilt that will often haunt her the rest of her life.

What many may not realize is that in keeping with not killing or injuring the body, the Fifth Commandment also forbids self-mutilation of all kinds, which includes vasectomy and tubal ligation for strictly birth-control purposes. "You are not your own," says St. Paul, but "you are bought with a great price." (*1 Cor.* 6:20). (These forms of birth control are generally considered to fall under the 6th Commandment of God as well.)

The underlying principle behind not killing or doing one's self or another any bodily harm is that God has made us and God will take us when it is our time. Our vessels (bodies) are to be considered sacred and to be possessed in dignity and with integrity. After all, each one of us receives only one body, and it is in this body that we must move about and function and work out our salvation during our entire lives.

Many may not realize that using illegal drugs for the thrill they give violates the principles of the Fifth Commandment, for these drugs are very powerful stimulants or depressants and are very addictive. Stimulants force the blood and nervous systems of the body to work unduly hard in an effort to eliminate them. During this "stimulation" period, the person feels a euphoria due to his system's being "charged up." The subsequent let-down, however, leaves the body exhausted and in dire need of recuperation and rebuilding. When more drugs are then used, the second "high" is not so high, and the following low is even lower. With continued drug use, the poor body starts to lose its overall vitality and to struggle vainly to regain a state of normalcy. Sometimes, when drug addicts finally quit their bad habit, they no longer have the sharpness of mind and determination of will that they formerly enjoyed, and their overall physical vigor does not return to what it was prior to their addiction. (The thought of this possibility is not, of course, reason to continue in a drug habit. Continuance in a drug habit generally only leads still further downward; and the earlier one quits, the better off he will be when he returns to a non-drug situation.) Anyone, therefore, who takes illegal drugs just for the thrill they give, knowing their harmful effects upon the body, sins against the Fifth Commandment in that he is to a great degree destroying his body, this unique and priceless gift of God, the "vessel" in which he is to work out his eternal salvation. (It is not a valid excuse to say, "I am only harming myself," or "My life is my own business." For even if it were possible not to harm others by using drugs, it remains true that God gave us our lives and our bodies, both of which are to be built up and used for constructive ends. We should consider the parable of the servants who were given the talents by their master to be used for trading and increase. The Divine Master will require a strict account of every one of us for the use we made of these priceless treasures.)

A person who drinks alcoholic beverages to excess also violates the Fifth Commandment be-

cause, by willfully consenting to put himself in
a state of alcoholic intoxication, he has implicitly
consented temporarily to abdicate at least partially the full use of his reason and his will. This
is gravely sinful because there is no way to know
what foolish or dangerous actions he may perform in this condition. Man is made in the image
and likeness of God, and it is in his reason and
free will that man most resembles his Creator,
and it is these faculties that distinguish him from
the animals. A person is always guilty, at least
to a very great extent, for whatever he does
while intoxicated because of his own free decision beforehand to become intoxicated. He
thereby assumes the guilt of whatever he will
do while under the influence of drink.

6. *Thou shalt not commit adultery.* Adultery
is illicit but "natural" sexual relations between
a man and a woman who are not married to each
other and when at least one of the persons is
married to someone else. If neither is married,
the illicit act is called fornication. In the Bible,
adultery and fornication are both spoken of as
grave sins, which will cause one to lose his soul.
Though the Sixth Commandment does not specifically mention fornication, it is included by
implication, as are all sins of impurity, which are
all always mortally sinful when fully consented
to. St. Paul uses the word *porneia*, which is sometimes translated as "fornication," but which
really means "sexual looseness." Fornication, as

a term, is often used by Sacred Scripture to symbolize sin in general. Thus we have proof that this sin is particularly displeasing to Almighty God and that presumably it is quite common.

Male or female, we are all born with sexuality, and it is a faculty we have to control during a time roughly from puberty until death. It is usually *easily* awakened in a man, being triggered very quickly by sight or by thought, and oftentimes simply by the "humors" of the body itself; and in a woman, once she becomes "sexually active," can be very hard to contain. The Catholic Church teaches that sins against the Sixth Commandment, when purposely willful, are always mortal sins, because the matter (the act in itself) is always grievous (i.e., serious or mortally sinful). Now the sexual act never begins full-blown, but rather is preceded by "foreplay," or at least by looks, words or desires. But inasmuch as all such preceding thoughts, looks, words, kisses, touches, etc. lead up to the final sexual act, they too are all likewise mortally sinful—because of what they can lead to, and as soon as a person willfully agrees to them. (Intimate kisses and touches, in particular, are *always* mortally sinful for the unmarried. Cf. Ch. IX.) If one could separate the foreplay from the final act, the case might be different, but because the preceding activity is linked, as in a chain, with the culminating act, all such activity is not only a sin, but a mortal sin. (Nor can anyone excuse himself by saying he will not go all the way, for inevitably such will happen, even to the strongest-willed person. God has created us that way.)

Sins against the Sixth Commandment are called impurity or unchastity, and no other sin blinds the correct moral understanding of a human being so completely as this sin. Even the immortal Homer comments to this effect in his writings. There is a twofold blindness to impurity: The first is that the person about to commit the sin is overwhelmed by the desire to commit it and is blinded thereby to its seriously wrongful nature, but also it is a sin that very easily becomes habitual, and thereby, secondly, the person quickly loses the deep sense of guilt that usually accompanies it initially. (In other words, he becomes blinded.) A young woman, for example, is usually appalled at what she has done when she first engages in illicit sexual activity and loses her virginity, but often it is not long afterwards that she returns to the same sin and, in a matter of only a few times, is given over completely to it.

Rationalization soon sets in for those who engage in adultery or fornication. They say that God understands and ask how can one avoid it since it is "natural." (That is, it springs from a natural drive and often from love.) True. . .God understands our weakness and forgives us if we are truly sorry, and it *is* "natural" (though avoidable with God's grace and the practice of virtue). But the Commandment still says, "Thou shalt not commit adultery." Why?

The reason why this sin is so serious is that sex is the faculty which God, in His infinite wisdom, has endowed us with in order to provide for the birth of new people. *Now human beings are immortal creatures with an eternal destiny of either Heaven or Hell, depending on how they behave—which in turn depends in large part on how they are taught and how they are formed in youth.* But people enter the world as helpless babes and need nurturing, protection and help until approximately 18 to 21 years of age, plus advice, counsel, good example and various types of help all the rest of their lives. It is for this reason that Almighty God has wrapped up the sexual faculty in human love and the psychological fulfillment of the parents and has placed it within marriage. Before this faculty is permitted to be used lawfully, it is necessary for the two parties to make a lifetime commitment to each other in the form of public marriage vows, so that the children born of their union—the immortal souls whom they help bring into this world—will have the necessary assistance throughout *all* their lives, that they may be reared and educated when young, and guided and counseled when adults. The Bible says, "Bastard slips shall not take deep root, nor any fast foundation." (*Wis.* 4:3). And "The children of adulterers shall not come to perfection, and the seed of the unlawful bed shall be rooted out." (*Wis.* 3:16). Yes, sex is natural. Man is weak. And

God understands. But still, "Thou shalt not commit adultery" is what the Commandment says, and for plenteous good reasons.

Those who would overcome or avoid sins of impurity must not fight them head on, as with other sins, say the great Catholic spiritual writers, but rather, they should *flee* from them. For being "natural" to mankind, sexual sins, if a person simply tries to resist them where he knows that there is danger, will easily overcome his resistance and plunge him into sin. If one has great difficulty in being pure, there is the advice of St. Paul, "But if they do not contain themselves, let them marry. For it is better to marry than to be burnt." (*1 Cor.* 7:9). Natural use of the sexual faculty within marriage is, of course, in accord with God's law; it is part of a sacred vocation, is intended by God to be a beautiful experience, and can be a meritorious act if engaged in with the proper dispositions. But adultery, fornication and the other sexual sins are not licit, and they profane the sacredness of the sexual faculty. "No fornicator, or unclean, or covetous person (which is a serving of idols) hath inheritance in the kingdom of Christ and of God." (*Eph.* 5:5).

Many young boys and young men, especially, fall into the sin of masturbation (called "self-abuse") and often cannot seem to shake it. Masturbation too is a mortal sin, according to the moral teaching of the Catholic Church. Because it is so common and often so hard to correct, many want to excuse this sin and say that it is not seriously wrong (a mortal sin), or even that it is no sin at all. But that is not at all the Church's teaching on this subject! Although our intellects may not be able to discern completely why this sin is mortal, let us, in the interest of examining the matter, consider the following points: Masturbation is a gross misuse of the sexual faculty, making sexual pleasure an end in itself and frustrating the purpose for which God created this faculty. The person who commits masturbation robs himself for the time being of his vital sexual drive and thereby and for that time is not oriented properly toward a member of the opposite sex, and thereby toward the procreation of children, for he is satisfied sexually to an extent and for a time. Masturbation is much easier for a young man, for example, than courtship, and possibly courtship might not occur if the young man in question never overcomes this sin. Moreover, there exists a universal instinct in mankind which judges that this act is shameful and impure.

However, despite whatever *reasons* we might adduce to demonstrate the wrongfulness of masturbation (or any sin for that matter), we should always remember that God, through the teaching authority of the Church which He founded to teach all mankind, has condemned this act as a mortal sin. Though we cannot with our limited understanding entirely plumb the depths of God's mysteries, as built into our nature, we may therefore not understand *all* the reasons why masturbation is a mortal sin, but it is. Although other reasons why masturbation is seriously wrong could be brought forward, let it at least be said in regard to this sin that St. Thomas Aquinas (considered to be the greatest Catholic theologian ever) ranked it a worse sin than fornication, for it is an unnatural act; whereas, fornication is not.

Then there is the sin of homosexuality (sex between persons of the same sex—*homo* is Greek for "same"), which also, generically, includes lesbianism (sex between women—which derives its name from the Island of Lesbos off Greece, from which the famous ancient Greek poetess Sappho came, who was a sexual deviate). Homosexuality is one of the four sins which the Bible says "cry to heaven for vengeance" (*Gen.* 18:20-21; *Rom.* 1:26-32) and is classed thereby with murder (*Gen.* 4:10), defrauding the laborer of his hire (*James* 5:4), and oppression of the poor (*Exod.* 2:23). Homosexual acts, needless to say, are always mortally sinful, and terribly so, because they are completely against nature. When first committed, they have to be entered into, as it were, almost by force against one's better judgment and understanding. One has to *pervert* his very intelligence and every right sentiment within himself in order to commit these sins, for which reason such people are called "perverts." Under the Old Testament law homosexuals were to be put to death, and in the history of the Kingdoms of Juda and Israel in the Old Testament the Kingdoms always suffered decline and every sort of malady when this sin (called "effeminacy" by the Bible) gained ascendancy. This sin violates the individual's nature, as created by Almighty God, and is a sin against society, for it deprives society of new members; plus, like a cancer, it tends to grow, because such a sinful person is not checked by the bounds of reason and morality and goes from partner to partner, ever widening the circle of those corrupted by his vice. Homosexuals give the excuse that this is just the way they are, that they were "born this way"; they see this sinful proclivity as their basic sexual orientation; and to some degree, with some individuals, this may be true, due to their physio-psychological make-up; but for many homosexuals, the truth is that they are oriented that way because they have done what they have done. *And even were their claim true*, that they are oriented that way by nature, still the only lawful sexual activity open to mankind is that between a man and woman who are properly married to each other in the eyes of God and who perform the natural sexual act in a manner wherein the man climaxes within the woman in a way that will allow a child to be conceived. The non-married *all* must be sexually continent (inactive); *that is God's law*, and this extends to homosexual activity as well. The homosexual tendency of such people is just one more of the illicit human impulses that man must avoid— and, with the help of God's grace, *can* avoid.

A married couple, the Church teaches, can do whatever they want sexually, so long as the man climaxes in the woman in the natural way, and with the possible conception of a child left entirely open. Nonetheless, even properly married people may have a preference for some sort of sexual activity which is not natural and licit; such preferences do not thereby mean these actions are all right; rather, even married people must avoid such acts. So too with homosexuals, who may indeed prefer their activity to the natural sexual act; this does not mean, however, that their activity is all right, that it is natural or that they have a right to it; it only means that *they like it, they prefer it!* (Simply having homosexual inclinations, of course, is not sinful in itself; but *engaging* in these shameful sexual acts is a very serious sin.)

Granted that sex is a powerful force and one that can easily be misused, and granted that the misuse can become habitual and can often "take over" in one's life, nonetheless, sexual activities *can* be curbed, channeled, and even curtailed altogether. As Our Lord said to St. Paul, "My grace is sufficient for thee: for power is made perfect in infirmity." (*2 Cor.* 12:9). If the married person must behave properly in marriage, in order to observe God's law, and if the single person must remain continent, why then cannot and must not the homosexually-oriented person refrain from his or her particular sexual preference, knowing it violates the law of God in a manner that will surely send him to Hell. "I can't help it" or "That's just the way I am" will not pass at the Judgment when Christ will separate the wicked from the good.

Finally, we come to considering the sexual sins of imagination. These too are mortally sinful when purposefully and knowingly given in to. Here we must distinguish among three elements connected to impurity of thought: 1) the *temptation*, which takes the form of an image (or phatasm, to use the technical word), which pops into the mind and which is no sin at all because it arises involuntarily; 2) *toying with the temptation*, rather than getting rid of it, which can be a mortal sin if the person recognizes the danger and fully consents to it, because it is leaving oneself in the near occasion of a mortal sin; and 3) *willfully taking pleasure in the impure thought* which suggests itself to the mind, which is always a mortal sin. One must immediately drive away temptations to impure thoughts because giving in to them is always a mortal sin and even toying with them can be.

Filthy T.V. talk shows these days often feature people who call this simply "fantasizing," but Our Lord said, "Whosoever shall look on a woman to lust after her, hath already committed adultery with her in his heart." (*Matt.* 5:28). With the constant presentation of immodestly dressed women on T.V., in the movies and in advertising, men especially have to be on their guard against this sin. As with all sins against purity, sexual sins of the imagination are to be overcome by calling *immediately* on the Blessed Mother of God, Mary most holy, to help us, and also by driving such thoughts from our minds *immediately* when they first present themselves, rather than waiting till they have grown and are powerful. (It is easier to root out a seedling than a tree.) Prayer, frequent Confession and the frequent reception of Holy Communion are also essential, as is daily recitation of the Holy Rosary. One must really *attack* temptations against impure thoughts with these holy tools and precautions and not temporize with such temptations *even to the slightest degree*, or he runs the very likely risk of falling into mortal sins of impurity. Where these expedients to overcoming impure thoughts are swiftly, resolutely and sincerely employed, this vice, as well as all sexual sins, cannot long remain.

Scoffers will likely think that all this discussion of the evils of sexual sins is sheer prudery, but they should consider that their consciences, though blunted perhaps by years of sins against purity, still function well enough to remind them that sexual sins are wrong, grievously wrong; they need to ponder within themselves the thought of spending their eternity in Hell, regretting forever their illicit sinful pleasures and wishing for someone from Heaven to come and relieve them, just a little, from their eternal torment, as Dives wished Lazarus to do. Then it will be too late. But now it is not.

And those who think that impurity is just one more of the many sins to be avoided, like cursing and stealing and all the rest, should pause to consider this sobering fact, that the Saints say impurity is the sin that leads to Hell most of the people who go there. St. Alphonsus Liguori—himself one of the greatest Doctors of the Catholic Church—tells us that the great Fathers and Doctors of the Church are unanimous in their opinion that most by far of the people who go to Hell go there because of this type of sin. No, impurity is not just "one more" of the sins we must overcome. For most people, it is *the* sin, especially today in our libertine society.

And sex is all the more dangerous because it *is* "natural," it is a drive within us, it is powerful, it can be triggered quite easily, it wells up within us spontaneously in the form of concupiscence, it involves our need for psychological fulfillment with and in the person of another individual (love), we can step off into it gradually, it is being promoted by the agents of the devil through their domination of the mass media, it impinges upon us in immodesty of dress, it is accepted by our corrupted society as "really not too bad, not bad at all" or "not anything to get upset about," and it is prevalent everywhere and in all sorts of forms. Under the best of circumstances a person has always to be vigilant and on his guard against falling into some form or other of sins of impurity. Today, how-

ever, a person oftentimes has to be positively heroic in order to remain virtuous. But as Our Lord
has told us through the writing of St. Paul, ''My
grace is sufficient for thee.'' (*2 Cor.* 12:9).

Impurity is a sin for which we cannot make
any accommodation in our lives. If we are not
properly married, no form of sexual activity is
allowed to us. And if we are properly married,
the only such activity allowed is the natural sexual activity between a man and wife that is allowed to culminate, if God is willing, in the
conception of a child. (The Church teaches
through her moral theologians that any foreplay
is allowable to a properly married couple, so long
as the man culminates in the woman in the natural way.)

Extra consideration has been given to this Commandment due to the fact that it claims so many
souls for Hell. For impurity is common, is always
mortally sinful (if fully consented to) and is easily habit-forming.

7. *Thou shalt not steal.* Virtually everyone acknowledges the wrongfulness of stealing. Civil
society considers it a serious crime. But yet there
are forms of stealing that many people engage
in without, it would seem, sufficient consideration that it *is* stealing, or of the price they will
pay. For they *will* pay, both in this life—by their
guilty conscience and likely too at the hands of
God, who chastises sinners to wake them up—
and they will pay in the next life, if they do not

make proper restitution here on earth.

Let us consider some of the more subtle forms of stealing: Probably the most common is that of not putting in an honest day's work for the pay one receives. What every worker should realize is that when he contracts with the employer to work for so much per hour or per week, etc., he is duty-bound to live up to that agreement, and put in work for the time he is hired, even if he thinks his wage is not fair. On the other side of the coin, there is the employer: if he takes advantage of employees and fails to pay them sufficiently well, he is in effect stealing from them. Too, there is the case of the businessman who fails to produce a product equal in quality to that which he has agreed to or has advertised; such a one is in effect stealing from those he sells to. Or again, it is stealing if he fails to sell the exact quantity that he says he is selling. Again, if a person buys on credit and fails to pay the bill, or buys without really and realistically being able to pay the bill, he is in effect stealing. Or if he delays paying the bill so long that he is taking undue advantage of his vendors, the same is true. Then there is the employee who steals things from the company he works for; for example, the product they sell, the shipping materials they use, tools, postage, the telephone (especially using it for long-distance calls), use of the vehicles, etc.

Another common form of stealing is willful damage to rental property. With so many people having to rent their living quarters today, this type of stealing can be very common. And it is often a mortal sin because it involves damage that usually is quite expensive to repair.

Two other sins covered by the Seventh Commandment of God are slander and detraction. Both constitute sins of stealing another's good reputation. *Slander* is saying something bad about another that is untrue; slander also violates the Eighth Commandment, because it is a lie. *Detraction* is the telling of something true about an individual which detracts from his character in the estimation of those who hear the story. Sometimes it is necessary for the management personnel of a company to discuss the shortcomings of their employees or for the faculty of a school to discuss the students or for parents to discuss the faults and problems of their children. But even in these cases, such discussion must be kept strictly to the purpose of the discussion and among themselves. Any other such unfavorable talk would constitute a sin.

Another form of stealing involves dating, where one of the parties is not serious about the relationship and is just keeping company with the other ''for the fun of it'' or to have someone to go with, while the other person is in love and serious about the relationship. Even if the party who is not serious were to tell this to the one in love, it is not really just and fair to continue dating that person, for he or she is simply taking advantage of the emotional vulnerability of the other, and the longer the relationship goes on, the worse the parting is going to be for the one who is truly in love.

In general, it is important for people to be most circumspect about violating the Seventh Commandment because, as mentioned, stealing can take numerous and subtle forms. Many students, for example, think that it is not stealing to cheat in school; whereas, it most surely is. It means taking something that does not belong to us—in this case, the correct answers, and the honor that attends being right. But the principal person the cheating student is stealing from is actually himself. For he has a duty to learn what is being taught in order to round out his education. Failure to do so will leave a void in his education, and that perhaps for the rest of his life. His higher grades won at the price of cheating also steals from the student, who won higher grades honestly, the full honor of his achievement. But society also suffers injustice because the cheater goes forth to assume a place in society as one with "such and such" an education when he really does not have that education at all. Further, he steals from everyone else because he is now a person that much less capable than he should be or could have been.

There are indeed other subtle forms of stealing too numerous to list here in so short an analysis. Each person really needs to evaluate his own life and examine his conscience to determine in what way he may be breaking the Seventh Commandment by depriving another of his just due, even if this means without actually and physically stealing some *thing* from him.

8. *Thou shalt not bear false witness against thy neighbor.* "To bear witness" means to tell the truth, to testify by one's words to the truth of a matter. "To bear false witness" means to lie. Everyone acknowledges that lying is wrong—very wrong—even though they may not understand why in a way whereby they can clearly express just what *is* so very wrong about lying. But a little analysis will reveal to us that telling the truth is the very fabric of our social lives: We simply *have* to communicate honestly with one another in order to function together. When a person lies, he breaks down the necessary links we have with one another. When we cannot trust someone, it imposes a great burden on us; therefore, no one likes a liar. And no one trusts a liar. Human beings find lying one of the most detestable sins. We want to get the liar out of our sight and out of our lives. It is for these reasons that good parents are so insistent to teach their children not to lie. (In this regard we ought to look upon ourselves—when we commit sin—from the eyes or perspective of Almighty God, who gave us the intelligence to discern right from wrong, and we should realize that, with every sin we consciously commit, we are lying to ourselves and trying to lie to God!)

Upon the seriousness of the matter will depend the seriousness of the sin of lying. If the matter is grave, a person who knowingly and willfully lies will commit a mortal sin. If the matter is slight the sin will be venial. But lying in general is a sin we all recognize to be a sin—even when in the slightest matter—and it is one we should strive never ever to commit. For it completely violates the integrity of our minds, and thereby and to whatever extent we lie, we open ourselves to any and every sin we are tempted to, for when we can lie to others, we will surely be able to lie to ourselves about the wrongfulness of our other sins. And unless we lie to ourselves first, we cannot really commit any sin, for our minds see the truth—God created them to—and when we sin, we act consciously against the truth, telling ourselves either that the sin is *not* a sin or it is really not so bad as we know it is. Probably it is this deep-seated realization within us all about the social and moral ramifications with regard to lying that causes us to react so immediately and so adversely to lying when we encounter it in another.

Under the Eighth Commandment are also included a number of other sins in addition to lying. These are slander (sometimes called calumny), detraction, strict mental reservation, rash judgment, rash suspicion, contumely and revealing secrets. These are either lying themselves or related to lying and are covered under the Eighth Commandment because they are related to our communication with others.

Slander (or calumny) is a particular type of

lie; it is the telling of something false about another person which thereby harms his or her reputation. Slander not only violates the Eighth Commandment, in that it is lying, it violates also the Seventh Commandment because it is stealing.

Detraction is the unnecessary telling of something which is true but which is bad about another or injurious to his good reputation. Strictly speaking, perhaps, detraction is not really lying, but rather stealing, and thereby really violates the Seventh Commandment more than the Eighth. But it is included under the Eighth Commandment because it relates to speech and is a cousin to slander. Detraction is a sin against justice because it robs a person of his good name, which is more valuable than his money or his goods.

A mental reservation is the holding back ("in reserve") a part of what one is saying so that the person hearing may not be able to understand what was really meant, based upon what was said. For example, if an executive in a company receives a call, his secretary may without sin tell the caller that Mr. Jones is "not in," or that "he is in conference" and cannot be disturbed; whereas, the fact is that Mr. Jones is present but does not wish to be disturbed. What the secretary is really saying to the caller is something like, "Mr. Jones is not in *to you. . . at this time.*" Or, "Mr. Jones is in conference with the people who have written him letters." This is legitimate because otherwise Jones might get nothing done all day due to disruption from phone calls, and thereby his business might be ruined.

Also, the caller does not actually have a *right* to speak with Mr. Jones or to know what he is doing, and the caller can figure out that "not in" means "not available to speak with *you*"; in fact, this is one of the standard accepted meanings of the term "not in." A mental reservation which contains some clue to its true meaning is called a *broad* mental reservation and is not sinful if the person asking does not strictly speaking have a right to know. However, if the mental reservation is *strict*, i.e., without any clue to its meaning, it would be a sin because it would be equivalent to a lie, and we do not under any circumstances possess the right to lie. An example of a strict mental reservation would be if someone asked another if he were planning to attend a party and that person answered yes, but really meant that he planned to attend it in thought only.

Rash Judgment is the forming of an opinion or decision about someone's supposed sin based upon insufficient information or reason, either as to the deed itself or the circumstances surrounding it. Although probably better placed under the Fifth Commandment, it is related to lying because it has the same effect in one's mind as if he had heard a lie. Rash judgment with regard to another is a sin because it detracts from his good name or reputation in the mind of the person judging.

Rash Suspicion is a sin of entertaining a suspicion about another without good reason. We should form the habit of presuming the best when a person's reputation is in doubt—unless we are a parent, teacher, supervisor, etc. and have an obligation to correct the person if necessary. Persons in authority should be prudently suspicious and watchful of problems that need to be corrected.

Contumely is any form of communication *in the presence of another* that detracts from that person's honor, respect or reputation. This can be in the form of speaking outright lies or degrading truths, making snide remarks, giving sarcastic looks or gestures, engaging in malicious caricatures, mimicry, etc. A contumelious person shows contempt for another by these various means, right to the person's face and often in the company of others.

Revealing secrets is a sin against the Eighth Commandment in that one thereby divulges truths he has no right to utter. A person may be bound to a secret in several different ways— by voluntarily promising not to tell it, by being pledged in advance not to tell it, by not being able to tell it because of the circumstances attendant to receiving the information (as a priest in Confession, a doctor with his patient or a lawyer with his client). We may not morally steal secret information by eavesdropping, bribery, trickery, threats, prying into files or correspondence, etc. And once we have obtained secret information, we are morally bound not to reveal it.

Whenever we deceive another in any way, we are lying. As with stealing, there are subtle forms of lying that we may not be so conscious of. For example, we can lie without using words—when we communicate by gestures or in any other manner. We can also lie by the impression we give, as when we seem to show approval of another's wrong speech or actions by not openly expressing our disapproval.

And on the other side of the coin, in speaking and communicating with others, we are just as often the *recipients* of information: when it pertains to the defects of character of another, we must take great care not to continue to listen to a conversation, or we should speak or show our disapproval of it; and we should not entertain a rash suspicion or form an unfounded judgment.

9. *Thou shalt not covet thy neighbor's wife.* In general, we are forbidden under the Ninth Commandment to *think* or *desire* what we are forbidden to do under the Sixth Commandment. Coveting one's neighbor's wife includes also, by implication, of course, coveting one's neighbor's husband. In today's society this is a particularly difficult commandment to keep, for most people have a vocation to be married, and all people gain a definite psychological fulfillment from

members of the opposite sex. In the world today, with divorce so very common, it is not at all unusual for a man or woman to be young and "divorced" and ready and willing to "marry" again. Where the "former" spouse usually does not care, and where society condones "remarriage" after "divorce," it takes heroic virtue on the part of those who wish to be good to resist the temptation to desire someone who is really still married, especially when the spouse of that other person has already gone and does not care in the least, having possibly even taken up with or "married" someone else. Yet to desire such a "divorced" person is still to "covet" one's neighbor's wife.

An additional word, and one of encouragement, must be said in regard to people being eligible to marry after "divorce": In today's society, many of the marriages that have been entered into are likely to be invalid, that is, not really marriages at all, due to a defective intention on the part of one or both of the "marriage" partners (but not because of problems that came later). In particular, and as a common example of defective intention, many people today "marry" with the idea they can always get a divorce if it does not work out; however, if either or both parties do not intend the union to be permanent, they are not really married to begin with because they did not truly enter into a marriage, which requires a commitment for life. Thus, the "divorced" party from such a "marriage" will actually never have been married at all. Also, many people "marry" those who are "divorced" (i.e., still truly married in the eyes of God, though having a piece of paper from the court saying they are single); therefore, the single partner to such an arrangement has never really been married because marriage can only be contracted between unmarried persons. If, therefore, one should become interested in a "divorced" person, it is imperative to discover *right from the start* whether that person was ever actually married or not, and the only truly competent judges in these matters are Catholic priests, who are the only people properly trained in the theology of marriage; they also have a special grace received from the Sacrament of Holy Orders (whereby they become priests), which helps them discern the truth in such pastoral matters. Moreover, only the Catholic Church has the authority to pronounce on the validity or invalidity of a marriage; individual priests, however, have no power to render an *official* judgment in a marriage case on behalf of the Catholic Church. This right belongs only to the Church herself, which employs an official "Marriage Tribunal" or Court to render this type of decision.

Because marriage is a complex contract between the consenting man and woman, only a person who is competently trained in the theology of marriage can really give sound advice in regard to the possible eligibility for marriage of those who were "married" before. But for the person who wants to be good and to act according to God's law, it is essential to determine the truth about the marriageability of a prospective spouse right from the start, before emotional involvement sets in and the single person finds himself or herself in a dead-end relationship with a person who is still actually married. (Just practical wisdom would warn that the other party may indeed not be the best person, even under ideal and legitimate circumstances, for us to marry, but rather may represent a test from Almighty God to prove whether or not we love Him. If we can resist the temptation, there is a great likelihood that, as a blessing from Almighty God for having followed His law, a different and much better choice of mate will be presented to us, a spouse with whom we will be able to live in peace of conscience and with whom we will be much happier.)

Under the Ninth Commandment, Catholic moralists generally also include, as stated above, all *desires* to commit unchaste acts, that is, desires to commit all acts forbidden under the Sixth Commandment. Any conscious and willful pleasure taken in thoughts of unchaste acts (i.e., immoral sexual acts) is itself a mortal sin. This was Our Lord's meaning when He said, "But I say to you, that whosoever shall look on a woman to lust after her, hath already committed adultery with her in his heart." (*Matt.* 5:28). Some may ask what harm *just thinking* about these things will do. But it is obvious that entertaining unchaste desires corrupts the heart of a person and leads him to violate the law of God interiorly, which is where all sin stems from anyway.

10. *Thou shalt not covet thy neighbor's goods.* The Tenth Commandment forbids wanting what the Seventh Commandment forbids taking. In other words, not only may we not take what does not belong to us, we may not even *want* it. In today's society, where mass production puts virtually every product within the reach of anyone who has the money to buy it, the Tenth Commandment is not so hard to keep. Nonetheless, when it comes to art objects, pets, handmade goods, houses, and/or anything that is one-of-a-kind, we have to restrain our desire for what belongs to another. Under the Tenth Commandment, moralists often add that we are forbidden to envy the success, wealth, beauty, health, talents, etc. of our neighbor, for this is none other than desiring what he or she has.

Chapter III

THE PRECEPTS OF THE CHURCH

Besides the Ten Commandments of God, Catholics are obliged to observe the Precepts of the Catholic Church. These are laws which have been made by the official teaching and law-giving authority of the Catholic Church—called the "Magisterium" of the Church—and are given to us through the authority vested by Our Lord Himself in St. Peter and his successors to loose and to bind (*Matt.* 18:18), that is, to make laws for the welfare of souls in order to help them to attain their eternal salvation. Traditionally, there are Six Precepts of the Church, and they are the following:

1. *To assist at Mass on all Sundays and Holydays of Obligation.* A Holyday of Obligation is a specially designated feastday which is to be treated by Catholics the same as a Sunday, examples of which are Christmas Day, December 25, and the Feast of the Circumcision, now called the Solemnity of Our Lady, January 1. (Both of these, incidentally, are also legal holidays in most Christian countries.) On Holydays of Obligation, Catholics are obliged to attend Mass under pain of mortal sin, just as on Sunday, and also to re-

frain from their regular work and shopping, as far as they are able. Also, extra prayers should be said on these days, and one should do extra spiritual reading, rest, visit the sick, etc., the same as on Sunday. The purpose of Holydays of Obligation is to commemorate in a public and special way important events in the history of our salvation, in order to keep before our minds the essential truths of our Holy Religion. (Obviously, in our secular society, which does not recognize these special holydays, it is difficult for Catholics to observe them as perfectly as they can observe Sundays, but the ideal is to treat them the same as Sundays, as far as this is practicable.)

2. *To fast and abstain on the days appointed.* On certain days of the year (Ash Wednesday, Good Friday, and all the Fridays of Lent) Catholics age 14 and over are obliged to abstain from meat, as was formerly the case on all Fridays; and on certain other days (now only Ash Wednesday and Good Friday) Catholics between the ages of 21 and 59 are required to ''fast.'' (Illness, grave inconvenience and heavy manual labor are typical valid reasons that excuse a person from this obligation.) Fasting according to the Catholic method consists of eating only one full meal per day, sufficient to maintain one's strength, and at which meal only a person may eat meat; plus two smaller meatless meals, which together may not equal the third. No food may

be taken between meals (though drinking liquids between meals is allowed). This may not appear to be much of a fast, but if voluntarily undertaken during Lent, a period of about six weeks, or during Advent, about four weeks, it amounts to a demanding penitential practice. For after about the third day, the effects of the fast take hold and a person often throughout the day feels hunger pangs. Our Lord said, "Unless you shall do penance, you shall all likewise perish." (*Luke* 13:3). Now it is for this reason that the Catholic Church in her wisdom has required of her members, fasting and abstaining. (Although the law of Friday abstinence has been changed, it has not actually been removed altogether, as many of the uninformed may believe. In honor of Christ's death on a Friday, Catholics are still obliged on every Friday of the year to refrain from eating meat foods, OR to perform some other act of penance or respect in honor of Christ's great sacrifice for us on that day.)

3. *To confess our sins at least once a year.* We all sin, and by this Precept of the Church Catholics are required, at least once a year, if they have a mortal sin to confess, to go to the Sacrament of Penance (or Confession) and confess their sins with sincere sorrow. The reader will recall the exclamation of St. Peter, "If the just man shall scarcely be saved, where shall the ungodly and the sinner appear?" (*1 Peter* 4:18). In the Sacrament of Penance (Confession)

Catholics receive the forgiveness of God through the absolution of the priest, His representative. Moreover, they are aided to overcome their sins by sacramental grace bestowed by God through the Sacrament, and oftentimes by the good advice they receive from the priest in Confession.

To receive sacramental forgiveness of our sins in Confession we must 1) have a sincere sorrow for all our mortal sins (at the minimum) which includes a firm resolve to avoid all sin in the future (or at least all mortal sin), 2) confess at least all our mortal sins (their kind and number) to the priest, 3) receive the absolution (forgiveness) which he gives us, and 4) perform the penance that he gives.

The first step toward overcoming any bad habit or practice is for the person to admit that he has the problem. And on the practical level, that is one of the main functions the Sacrament of Confession fills. Some habitual sins, such as sins of impurity or profanity, can be overcome only with the aid of frequent Confession, combined with frequent Communion, ardent and continual and consistent prayer (especially the Rosary), and appealing to the Blessed Virgin Mary for special assistance. If even the worst sinner were honestly to maintain such a spiritual routine, there is no doubt he would overcome whatever sins have taken hold of him, and he would begin to make steady advancement in virtue. The key to it all is *frequent* Confession and Communion. The Church *requires* Confession only once a year, and then actually only if the person has committed a mortal sin, but because we can never be 100% certain we are in the state of grace, i.e., free from mortal sin, and also because Confession purifies our souls of venial sin and gives us special graces to avoid our own particular sins, it is good to go to Confession often. Many of the Saints went several times a week and some even every day! St. Alphonsus Liguori (1696-1787), a great Doctor of the Church, wrote in *A Christian's Rule of Life* that if you are serious about saving your soul, you will go to Confession often, *"at least* every week, and oftener if possible, with the advice of your spiritual director." (*Rules for a Good Life*, emphasis added.)

4. *To receive Holy Communion during the Easter Time.* Here again, the Church requires Catholics to receive Communion, that is, the Body and Blood of Jesus Christ, only once a year, and that (according to the traditional norm and) preferrably during the Easter Time. (In the U.S.A., this is from the first Sunday of Lent to Trinity Sunday, i.e., the Sunday after Pentecost, inclusive, though now, any other time during the year is considered to fulfill the obligation.) But the Church urges her members to receive often, even daily if they can. Why? We have seen the answer above. Our Lord said, "Except you eat the flesh of the Son of man, and drink his blood, you shall not have life in you." (*John* 6:54). "He that eateth my flesh, and drinketh my blood,

hath everlasting life: and I will raise him up in the last day.'' (*John* 6:55). Many books have been written by holy writers exclaiming upon the love which God must bear toward us that would cause Him to give us such a gift as the Blessed Eucharist. Yet many there are who scoff at this great Sacrament. On the Day of Judgment, unfortunately for them, when the scales will fall from their eyes and they will perceive with clarity the reasons behind this sublime mystery of Christ's Body and Blood, it will be too late then for them to take advantage of it. How God must love us to want to be closer than close to us, and to place Himself so intimately at our disposal that we might ask of Him whatsoever we will, which He has promised to give us! ''Ask, and it shall be given you: seek, and you shall find: knock, and it shall be opened to you.'' (*Matt.* 7:7). Also, ''Whatsoever you shall ask the Father in my name, that will I do.'' (*John* 14:13).

According to Catholic doctrine, everyone who is saved is saved only through the Sacrifice of Christ on the Cross. And the Holy Sacrifice of the Mass, celebrated by Catholic priests on Catholic altars throughout the world, and found only in the Catholic Church, is none other than the unbloody but true *re-presentation* or *re-enactment* of that unique sacrifice of Christ on the Cross. It is by means of the Sacrifice of the Cross that all men who achieve salvation are saved, and it is by means of the Sacrifice of the Mass (which is the same as the Sacrifice of the

Cross, though offered in an unbloody manner) that all graces come into the world to us, and all our prayers ascend to God and are found acceptable to Him, insofar as God accepts them. Once a person grasps the nature of what the Mass is and the role it plays in our salvation, then the Catholic Church's precept of obligatory Mass attendance on Sundays and Holydays of Obligation comes into clear focus, for the God-Man, Jesus Christ, is there at the Mass, in His Body, Blood, Soul and Divinity, who said, "Without me you can do nothing" (*John* 15:5), and "Except you eat the flesh of the Son of man, and drink his blood, you shall not have life in you." (*John* 6:54). This Precept of the Church simply makes plain to us our utter dependency upon Christ for our salvation, a fact the Church realizes and wishes to make clear to her spiritual children.

5. *To contribute to the support of the Church.* The rationale behind this Precept of the Church is found in Our Lord's words, "He that is not with me, is against me: and he that gathereth not with me, scattereth." (*Matt.* 12:30). Also, "Make unto you friends of the mammon of iniquity." (*Luke* 16:9). ("Mammon of iniquity" means your money.) And, "No man can serve two masters. For either he will hate the one, and love the other: or he will sustain the one, and despise the other. You cannot serve God and mammon." (*Matt.* 6:24). In contributing to the support of the Catholic Church, the Catholic is helping

to build up the very instrument of salvation for all men which has been given to us by God Himself. Contributing to the support of God's holy Religion makes us partakers in the job of the salvation of souls. By contributing to the support of the Catholic Church, we are thereby helping "gather" with Our Lord; we are using our money to make friends in Heaven; we are serving God, rather than mammon ("riches").

6. *To observe the laws of the Church concerning marriage.* The principal law of the Catholic Church concerning marriage, and the one all Catholics are to observe, is that Catholics who wish to be married must be married before a duly authorized priest and two witnesses. The Catholic Church is so adamant about this requirement that she has made it a law binding upon her members that unless Catholics are married before a priest and two witnesses (even if they have received a proper dispensation from the Church to have their marriage celebrated in a place other than a Catholic church), they are not even married at all in the eyes of God. (Remember Our Lord's words: "Whatsoever you shall bind upon earth, shall be bound also in heaven..." —*Matt.* 18:18).

We are dealing here with God's Religion, the True Faith, not something created by man. And the laws of the Church are all concerned with helping us save our souls. Now why would the Church be so demanding about how its members marry? After all, it is even Catholic thology that the two people getting married confer the Sacrament of Matrimony upon each other; the priest does not actually marry them. The primary role of the priest is to be the official witness representing Christ and His Church. Moreover, it is also his role to see that the couple understand their obligations in marriage, that the ceremony is properly conducted and that all requirements for a valid marriage are present. Therefore, why is the Catholic Church so adamant about a priest being present at the weddings of Catholics? Why is she so strict in this regard? The answer to these questions is very simple: Marriage is a complex contract between two people, and one which entails a number of essential elements, any one of which being missing, a ''marriage'' is no marriage at all. And to avoid any possibility of this complex contract's being invalid (that is, null and void), the Church in her wisdom has required that a Catholic priest guide and advise and instruct the couple about the nature of marriage and their rights and duties in and by their marriage—toward God, toward each other and toward their prospective children.

Let us consider briefly some of the things that could invalidate a marriage contract: 1) One of the parties might not be sure he or she should contract this marriage, but ''marries'' anyway, thinking, ''If it doesn't work out, I can always get a divorce.'' With the idea or disposition in the mind of even one of the partners in marriage that he or she can terminate the marriage by divorce, there is no marriage at all, for marriage by its nature is indissoluble; it is to last as long as both parties to the marriage are alive. 2) One of the people contracting the supposed marriage might say to himself or herself, "I am not going to have any children." If this is the case, again, there is no marriage. For the primary purpose or end of marriage is the procreation and raising of children. 3) A person may have the following intention: "I will marry you, but I want it understood this will be an 'open' marriage; I still intend to have other sexual partners." This condition violates the exclusivity of marriage and thus renders the marriage invalid; when they marry, people pledge themselves to each other *alone*. 4) If one of the parties to the marriage intends to and does in fact refuse the other party the right of ever having sexual relations, without the other person's express consent, there would be no marriage. For to contract a marriage, two steps must be taken: a) there must be a public ceremony at which marriage vows are exchanged, and b) there must occur the consummation of the marriage—marital, i.e., sexual relations between the two. (Technically speaking, a marriage where only the ceremony has taken place and not the consummation—sexual relations—is still a marriage as long as both the parties to the marriage freely agree to such an arrangement. Such was the case with the Blessed Virgin Mary and St. Joseph. But if only one partner intends the marriage to be of this sort, the marriage is said to be unconsummated and therefore could be declared void. Even civil law recognizes this type of invalidating circumstance.) 5) One of the parties to a marriage might be "divorced" from a previous valid marriage. Such a person is not eligible to marry again and thus a marriage with such a person would be invalid.

There are priests who get doctoral degrees in theology with specialization in marriage theology alone. Marriage cases can become very complicated and involved, and can perplex the minds of even the best theologian experts on marriage. In the interest of avoiding, right from the start, any potential problems to a marriage, the Catholic Church, in her wisdom and under the guidance of the Holy Spirit, simply says to her members in her Sixth Precept: "Observe the laws of the Church concerning marriage." If all people, Catholic and non-Catholic alike, would come to the Catholic Church and let her guide them through the complex contract of marriage, and would do what she requires of her own members, there would be far fewer invalid marriages and far less marital grief than we see today.

Married life is considered by the Church to be a foretaste of Heaven. It is a great and beautiful thing. Scripture says: "With three things my spirit is pleased, which are approved before God and men: The concord of brethren, and the love of neighbors, and *man and wife that agree well together*." (*Ecclesiasticus* 25:1-2, emphasis added).

And, "For this cause shall a man leave father and mother, and shall cleave to his wife." (*Matt.* 19:5). But it takes care to contract a marriage correctly, lest the couple fail to effect a valid marriage and end up living in fornication.

Chapter IV

THE ROLE OF GRACE

At this point in our discussion of how to avoid Hell, it is imperative to discuss the matter of grace. We have touched upon this subject earlier in discussing the Catechism and the different types of sin. In Catholic theology the tract on grace is very simple in its outline, but very difficult to comprehend; in fact, it is the most difficult part of theology, dealing as it does with the spiritual interactions between God and the human soul.

Basically, there are two kinds of grace, *Sanctifying Grace* and *Actual Grace*. Now *Sanctifying Grace* is none other than a sharing in the very "LIFE" of God Himself, which He imparts to us at Baptism, and which increases with the good acts we perform while in that state. To be in the state of grace is to be a "living branch" on the vine which is Christ, and to be capable of "bearing much fruit." (*John* 15:1-6). But we lose Sanctifying Grace any time that we commit a mortal sin—that is, an act we know is grievously wrong (or at least which we think is grievously wrong) and which we do anyway with full knowledge of the mind and complete consent of the will. But Sanctifying Grace can be gained back by the sinner's making an act of perfect contrition (cf. the prayer and the explanation of perfect contrition in Chapter VII, following) and/or by going to Sacramental Confession and confessing the sin to the priest with sincere sorrow.

The other kind of grace is *Actual Grace*, which is a transitory (or "passing") supernatural "HELP" from God "which enlightens our minds and strengthens our wills to do good and avoid evil" in our daily actions.

First, let us consider *Sanctifying Grace*. Sanctifying Grace is absolutely necessary to salvation because it is the supernatural life of God Himself, and only possession of this supernatural life will enable us to attain to the supernatural happiness of Heaven, where this same supernatural or divine life abounds in the souls of all the angels and Saints. In the Bible, especially in the writings of St. John, the word *"life"* means Sanctifying Grace, and *"light"* means the knowledge of God and the truths of salvation which we possess by *faith*. St. John tells us in the opening chapter of his Gospel, "In him [Christ] was *life*, and the *life* was the *light* of men. And the *light* shineth in the darkness, and the darkness did not comprehend it...That was the true *light*, which enlighteneth every man that cometh into the world...But as many as received him, he gave them power to be made the sons of God, to them that believe in his name...For the law was given by Moses; *grace* and truth came by Jesus Christ." (*John* 1:4, 5, 9, 12, 17, emphasis added in this and the following quotes). "He it is that baptizeth with the Holy Ghost [i.e., imparts to the baptized person a sharing in the life of God]. And I [St. John the Baptist speaking] saw and I gave testimony, that this is the Son of God." (*John* 1:33-34). "For as the Father raiseth up the dead, and giveth *life*: so the Son also giveth *life* to whom he will." (*John* 5:21). "Amen, amen I say unto you, that he who heareth my word, and believeth him that sent me, hath *life* everlasting; and cometh not into judgment, but is passed from death to *life*." (*John* 5:24). "Amen, amen I say unto you, that the hour cometh, and now is, when the dead [i.e., the spiritually dead, those in mortal sin] shall hear the voice of the Son of God, and they that hear shall *live*." (*John* 5:25). "For as the Father hath *life* in himself, so he hath given to the Son also to have *life* in himself." (*John* 5:26). "And you [i.e., the leaders of the Jews] will not come to me that you may have *life*." (*John* 5:40). "Then Jesus said to them: Amen, amen I say to you; Moses gave you not bread from heaven, but my Father giveth you true bread from heaven. For the bread of God is that which cometh down from heaven, and giveth *life* to the world . . . And Jesus said to them: I am the bread of *life*: he that cometh to me shall not hunger: and he that believeth in me shall never thirst . . . And this is the will of my Father that sent me: that every one who seeth the Son, and believeth in him, may have *life* everlasting, and I will raise him up in the last day. . . Amen, amen I say unto you: he that believeth in me, hath everlasting *life*. I am the bread of *life*. . .This is the bread which cometh down from heaven; that if any man eat of it, he may not die. I am the *living* bread which came down from heaven. If any man eat of this bread, he shall *live* for ever; and the bread that I will give, is my flesh, for the *life* of the world. . .Amen, amen I say unto you: Except you eat the flesh of the Son of man, and drink his blood, you shall not have *life* in you. He that eateth my flesh, and drinketh my blood, hath everlasting *life*: and I will raise him up in the last day. For my flesh is meat indeed: and my blood is drink indeed. He that eateth my flesh, and drinketh my blood, abideth in me, and I in him. As the *living* Father hath sent me, and I *live* by the Father; so he that eateth me, the same also shall *live* by me. This is the bread that came down from heaven. Not as your fathers did eat manna, and are dead. He that eateth this bread shall *live* for ever. . .It is the spirit that *quickeneth* [i.e., gives life]: the flesh profiteth nothing. The words that I have spoken to you, are *spirit* and *life*.'' (*John* 6:32-33, 35, 40, 47-48, 50-52, 54-59, 64, emphasis added).

From these passages of St. John's Gospel, we see how forceful Our Lord was in maintaining that the *life* that is in Him came from the heavenly Father, and that He, Jesus, wishes to communicate this *life* to us, and moreover, that this *life* is the *light* of the world, the *light* whereby we are helped to see and understand what it is that we have to do to save our souls—what we have to do to avoid Hell and attain Heaven. And we see that this *life of God* is communicated from the Father to the Son, who became man as Jesus Christ, and from Jesus Christ to us. Further, we see from the above passages that this *life of God*, which Jesus receives from the Father (in the ongoing act of the Blessed Trinity), He gives to us through Baptism and increases it in us in and through the Sacrament of His Body and Blood (called the Holy Eucharist by the Catholic Church). It can be seen from these passages quoted above, moreover, that unless a person have this *life from Christ*, he will not live eternally with Christ—he will not have everlasting life, and he will not go to Heaven. But receiving this *life of God* requires the instruments or channels of the Catholic Sacraments of Baptism and Holy Communion (the Holy Eucharist). Now it is only in the Catholic Church that one can be *absolutely certain* he receives Baptism (because of the certainty of the intention of the person baptizing and the correctness of the words used to administer the Sacrament), and it is only in the Catholic Church that one receives the True Body and Blood of Jesus Christ in Holy Communion.

From these passages, we see further that receiving the *life of Christ* results from believing in Christ and receiving Baptism, which fact will recall to our minds the commission Our Lord gave to the Apostles: "Go ye forth into the whole world, and preach the gospel to every creature. He that believeth and is baptized, shall be saved: but he that believeth not shall be condemned." (*Mark* 16:15-16).

But Jesus goes on in St. John's Gospel to link His *life* with the "*light*" whereby His followers see the truth and understand what they must do. Let us review some more of the passages from St. John that occur later in that Gospel which demonstrate still further the emphasis placed on Our Lord's being the source of true (supernatural) life. Here one can easily see a continuation of the idea found in *John* 1:4 that "In him was *life*, and the *life* was the *light* of men." (Emphasis added.)

"Again therefore, Jesus spoke to them, saying: I am the *light* of the world: he that followeth me, walketh not in darkness, but shall have the *light* of *life*." (*John* 8:12). "Then Jesus said to those Jews, who believed him: If you continue in my word, you shall be my disciples indeed. And you shall know the truth, and the truth shall make you free." (*John* 8:31-32). From these words, we see that the followers of Christ, if they will do all that Christ commands and requires, will have spiritual understanding, and that if they will live by His word, they will know the truth and the truth shall make them free. (A far cry from the way this passage is usually misquoted and misinterpreted—namely, "Know ye the truth and the truth shall make you free.")

Then we hear Jesus proclaim, "Amen, amen I say to you: If any man keep my word, he shall not see death for ever." (*John* 8:51). In Chapter 9 of St. John's Gospel, we hear Our Lord say, "As long as I am in the world, I am the *light* of the world." (*John* 9:5). And again, "I am come that they may have *life*, and may have it more abundantly." (*John* 10:10).

Then there are in Chapter 11 of St. John some seemingly convoluted statements by Our Lord, statements which might appear at first sight to be mistranslations. But in light of all the other passages throughout the Gospel of St. John regarding *Christ's life* being the *light* and *life* of this world and the *light* and *life* of all His true followers, they make eminent sense, especially in view of there being still more and similar passages further along in St. John's Gospel.

Our Lord says in *John* 11, "If a man walk in the day, he stumbleth not, because he seeth the *light* of this world: But if he walk in the night, he stumbleth, because the *light* is not in him." (*John* 11:9-10, emphasis added). "I am the resurrection and the *life*: he that believeth in me, although he be dead, shall live: And every one that *liveth*, and believeth in me, shall not die for ever." (*John* 11:25-26, emphasis added).

In Chapter 9 of St. John, there is a description of how Our Lord cures a man born blind, who becomes thereafter a reproof to the unbelieving leaders of the Jews; He then also converts him. This cure is a symbol of the healing of our spiritual blindness: as the blind man is cured of his physical blindness and then is converted and thus cured of his spiritual blindness, so we are to be cured by Our Lord of our spiritual blindness. So too, in Chapter 11, immediately after Jesus speaks about being the *light of the world* and the resurrection and the *life*, He raises Lazarus from the dead, who had died four days earlier. The symbolism of this miracle (also in Chapter 11) is that Christ, by giving us His *divine life*, which the Catholic Church calls *"Sanctifying Grace,"* not only heals us of our spiritual blindness, but that He calls us back from our spiritual death—all if we believe in Him, are baptized and continue in His word.

In Chapter 12 of St. John, Jesus continues the theme of His being the *light* of this world when He says, "Yet a little while, the *light* is among you. Walk whilst you have the *light*, that the darkness overtake you not. And he that walketh in darkness, knoweth not whither he goeth. Whilst you have the *light*, believe in the *light*, that you may be the children of *light*." (*John* 12:35-36, emphasis added). And again, "I am come a *light* into the world; that whosoever believeth in me, may not remain in darkness." (*John* 12:46, emphasis added). At the Last Supper, Our Lord told the Apostles, "I am the way, and the truth, and the *life*. No man cometh to the Father, but by me." (*John* 14:6, emphasis added).

And finally, Our Lord says, "Yet a little while: and the world seeth me no more. But you see me: because I *live*, and you shall *live*." (*John* 14:19, emphasis added).

What do all these quotations from the Bible tell us about *Sanctifying Grace?* Actually, they tell us a great deal. For they are Scripture's way of expressing exactly what the Catholic Church teaches, though in somewhat different terms. What the Catholic Church calls "Sanctifying Grace" can best be described as "the life of God Himself imparted to the human soul," that the soul may be holy and pleasing to God and therefore attain Heaven when the person dies.

According to the teaching of the Catholic Church, only a person in the state of grace (i.e., having Sanctifying Grace in his soul) can gain supernatural merit, that is, merit which has a divine value and which will help him to save his soul and earn a higher place in Heaven when he dies. The Church teaches that Sanctifying Grace is a free gift of God, which man cannot earn or acquire on his own. Since it is the *life of God*, only God can give it; man cannot on his own earn it or "buy" it or take it. *Once a person has Sanctifying Grace in his soul, however, his good actions then don a supernatural character.* By his prayers and good actions he merits an *increase* of Sanctifying Grace, and if he dies in this "state of grace," as the Catholic Church calls it, he will be able to enter into eternal life itself, for he is a "living branch" on the "True Vine," which is Christ. Without Sanctifying Grace, we can still perform good acts, but these are good acts of the strictly *natural* (human) order only; they are not *supernaturalized* acts, as when we are in the state of Sanctifying Grace, and therefore they are not meritorious for our salvation. In one sense, they are wasted, as far as eternal salvation goes—though a person should still perform such acts as "stepping stones," so to speak, to returning to the state of grace through repentance.

(If Protestants would only understand this part of the Catholic theology of grace, they would cease to claim that Catholics believe they are saved by "works," meaning, "merely human works." For the "works" [good deeds] of a person in the state of Sanctifying Grace are now no longer mere "human works" [works of the natural man], but they are *divinized* works [works of the super-naturalized man, an adopted son of God].)

If through mortal sin a person loses Sanctifying Grace, whatever good he does in that condition will not help him merit Heaven, nor will it earn him a higher place in Heaven when he dies. Before he will gain back Sanctifying Grace and once again be in a state of soul whereby he can gain supernatural merit for his good actions, he must first at least make an act of perfect contrition (see Chapter VII) or he must go to Sacramental Confession.

Not enough can ever be said about the importance of Sanctifying Grace in our souls. For with it in our soul when we die, we will be saved, and without it we will not. From the many passages cited above, taken from the Gospel of St. John (who is called the "Theologian" among the four Evangelists), we can see the importance of possessing this *life* which Our Lord gives us. Without it we are spiritually dead; with it, we truly live. Witness the passage from St. John quoted earlier, "Amen, amen I say unto you, that the hour cometh, and now is, when the dead shall hear the voice of the Son of God, and they that hear shall *live.*" (*John* 5:25). Now it is obvious that the *physically* dead cannot possibly hear; therefore, it was the *spiritually* dead that Our Lord was referring to; that is, to those who have either never been baptized and had Original Sin removed from their souls, or to those who are living in a state of mortal sin subsequent to having been baptized. In any event, it is a person's belief in the word of God, i.e., the teachings of Jesus Christ, combined with the Sacrament of Baptism, that brings to his soul the divine life called Sanctifying Grace. The entire discussion in St. John's Gospel about *"life"* and *"light,"* how Christ is the *life* and the *light* for all men, is not accidental; one might go so far as to say that this subject is the predominant theme of St. John's Gospel; therefore, this *"life"* and *"light"* are essential to man—if he is to be saved. Now the *"life"* spoken of by Our Lord in St. John's Gospel is none other than what the Catholic Church calls Sanctifying Grace, "the supernatural life of the soul," which is given to us by God in the Sacrament of Baptism—and which is restored to us by the priest's absolution in the Sacrament of Penance (Confession), if we have had the misfortune to lose Sanctifying Grace by committing mortal sin. (The *"light"* Our Lord refers to is the knowledge of supernatural things that comes with, is inspired by and develops from supernatural Faith.)

The second kind of grace is called "actual grace." As explained briefly above, *actual grace* is "a supernatural HELP from God which enlightens our mind and strengthens our will to do good and avoid evil." It is called "actual" grace because we need it to perform supernaturally good "acts" and to avoid committing evil ones (sin). Now it is a doctrine of the Catholic Faith that man cannot on his own, *without the help of God through the agency of actual grace*, do anything good on the supernatural level, i.e., anything which will gain him merit for Heaven. (Of course, to do anything good on the supernatural level, a person must first be in the state of *Sanctifying* Grace.) Each supernaturally good thing we do must be prompted by actual grace from God, or we would not be able to do it.

In this regard, let us recall certain famous passages of the Bible which mention and explain this doctrine: First of all, there are Our Lord's words, "For without me, you can do nothing." (*John* 15:5). Then St. Paul states the matter powerfully and succinctly when he says, "For it is God who worketh in you, both to will and to accomplish, according to his good will." (*Phil.* 2:13). And again, St. Paul says, "But by the grace of God, I am what I am; and his grace in me hath not been void, but I have labored more abundantly than all they: *yet not I, but the grace of God with me.*" (*1 Cor.* 15:10, emphasis added). And further, St. Paul states, "I can do all things in him who strengtheneth me." (*Phil.* 4:13). Again, we read in *2 Corinthians*, "Not that we are sufficient to think any thing of ourselves, as of ourselves: but our sufficiency is from God." (*2 Cor.* 3:5). Also, "No man can say the Lord Jesus, but by the Holy Ghost." (*1 Cor.* 12:3). (*Rom.* 11:35). And finally, there is the famous passage, "My grace is sufficient for thee." (*2 Cor.* 12:9).

From all the above Scriptural quotations, we can see that God continues to prompt us with His supernatural *help* to do good and to avoid evil. Now this supernatural *help* that prompts and enables us to perform individual good actions we call Actual Grace—the *help* of God to do each and every specific good act that will contribute to our gaining salvation and avoiding Hell.

To reiterate, *Sanctifying Grace* is "LIFE," a sharing in the supernatural life of God which God imparts to our soul at Baptism; also, this grace is increased by our reception of the Body and Blood of Jesus Christ in the Sacrament of the Holy Eucharist, as well as by prayer and good works. *Actual Grace*, on the other hand, is "HELP," the transitory supernatural assistance of Almighty God which enables us to do good acts and avoid evil ones. With regard to the workings of both types of grace, Sanctifying Grace and Actual Grace, it becomes difficult for the mind of man to understand exactly what role it is that man plays in his supernaturally meritorious deeds, and therefore in his salvation. But the entire tenor of Scripture is that *man* must do good and obey the commandments in order to be saved, and therefore that *man* also has an essential role in his own salvation. Man exercises his part in his salvation by using his free will either to accept or to reject God's grace. Plus, the Catholic Church has solemnly proclaimed in the Council of Trent:

"If anyone says that the good works of the one justified are in such manner the gifts of God that they are not also the good merits of him justified; or that the one justified by the good works that he performs by the grace of God and the merit of Jesus Christ, whose living member he is, does not truly merit an increase of grace, eternal life, and in case he dies in grace, the attainment of eternal life itself and also an increase of glory, let him be anathema [i.e., 'excommunicated']." (Council of Trent, Sixth Session, Canon 32.)

That person who thinks he can avoid Hell and gain Heaven on his own merits is sadly mistaken. We need God's assistance to make this possible,

first with the gift of Sanctifying Grace and then
with the help of the actual graces He sends us
to enable us to do good and avoid sin in our daily
lives. As we can see from the Scriptural quotations cited above, when we believe and are baptized and when we thereafter follow what Christ
has taught, then we "walk in the day" (understand or see the spiritual truth), and we "stumble not" (i.e., we avoid sin) because we see "the
light of this world" (Jesus Christ, the Redeemer
of all mankind, and the truth He taught about
how to save our souls). (Cf. *John* 11:9). But if
we do not believe and receive instruction and
are not baptized, then we are as one who walks
in the night and who stumbles because the light
(of spiritual understanding from Christ) is not
in us. (Cf. *John* 11:10).

Chapter V

VIRTUE AND VICE

Man is a creature of habit. No one will deny this who thinks of it for a minute. We sit, for example, at the same place at the table in our homes. We tend to do the same things each Tuesday night or Saturday morning or Wednesday afternoon. We frequent the same restaurants, eat the same foods, watch the same T.V. programs, play the same sports, smoke the same brand of cigarettes, drink the same brand of beer or pop, go through basically the same routines again and again, day after day, week after week, month after month, year after year. . .often for the whole of our lives.

Moralists describe *virtue* as simply "a good habit" and *vice* as "a bad habit." Our good habits are virtues. Our sins, when they become habitual, are vices. And the sins we tend to commit are for the most part habitual sins. *That is something very important to realize about sin if we are going to combat it successfully.* A person can sometimes slip into a sin on a one-time basis, or occasionally, but when the pattern of one's sins is closely examined, it will usually be found that by far the greater number of our sins are those we repeat—our habitual sins, our *vices.* Yes, our sins are like all our actions: they are almost always habitual, and insofar as they are habitual, they are vices.

It is mortal sin that sends us to Hell (if we die unrepentant with it still on our soul), and sins of various kinds (whether mortal or venial) tend to be habitual; for our sins quickly become repeated actions. Knowing this, therefore, we have to ask ourselves, "What must one do to overcome his bad or sinful habits?" The answer is easy. First of all, we have to *pray* for the grace to overcome our sins. Second, we have to give ourselves sufficient good reason why we *want* to overcome our sinful habits. Third, we have to avoid the near occasions of our sins. (A "near occasion" of sin is any person, place or thing that is likely to lead us into sin. Often we know what these are from past experience. If we tell ourselves, for instance, "I'll still watch this T.V. show, but I just won't let myself get drawn into sinful thoughts like I usually do," then we are not serious about avoiding sin.) Fourth, we have to *find those ways* that have been successful for other people in overcoming our particular type of sinful habit. And fifth, *we then have to supplant our sins with good habits, or virtues.* For creatures of habit we are and creatures of habit we shall always be. To convert ourselves from habits of sin (vice) to good habits (virtue) we have to follow the simple procedures outlined above.

The Catholic Church has nearly 2,000 years'

experience dealing with the various sinful habits of mankind, and in her wisdom she can give specialized help to those who struggle against the dominance of any particular sin. In the first place, when trying to overcome an habitual sin, we must never become discouraged if we fall into the sin again and again. In such a case, we should think of our sin in terms of its being an ingrained habit (like smoking) and one that we have to root out thoroughly, entailing perhaps long hard work on our part. Then we shall realize that it may take time, and that there may be some relapses; but if we set our minds to the task resolutely and determine to rise each time we fall, we shall eventually be successful, especially if we employ all the proven techniques which have helped others to be successful in the past. If we go to Hell, it will most likely be because of our *habitual* sins; it will be because we failed to see that our sins for the most part *are* habits and *because we never really came to grips with them.*

Any particular sin is avoidable, for Our Lord told St. Paul, "My grace is sufficient for thee." (*2 Cor.* 12:9). We must first *want* to avoid the sin; then we must *pray* to avoid it; and finally we must *use the grace* God gives us to avoid it. Here again, the role of frequent Confession and Communion cannot be overemphasized. They are essential to overcoming our habitual sins—our vices.

Chapter VI

THE SEVEN CAPITAL SINS

Catholics are taught in their Catechism that they must constantly be on guard and war against the "Seven Capital Sins." These sins are *pride, covetousness, lust, anger, gluttony, envy* and *sloth*. Actually, they are not sins in themselves, unless and until we consent to them, but very definitely *they are the conditions or inclinations within us from which sin arises*. They are propensities to sin which reveal themselves in particular sinful acts. (Cf. *Catholic Encyclopedia*). They are both the "roots of sin within us and the sins we commit most often"; they are the dispositions of our fallen nature, tainted by the Original Sin of our first parents, and they ultimately lead us into every manner of sin we commit. They are at the "head" of our sins, and thus they are called "capital" in that they are the chief sins we commit and the chief sources from which all sin arises. (*Caput* means "head" in Latin.) They are, as it were, seven types of inclination to sin within us, seven distinct weaknesses of our poor mortal frame, and the seven types of sin we most often commit.

Knowing that we humans have within ourselves these seven evil dispositions or inclinations as part of our very being, and knowing that these are the seven chief sins people commit, Catholics are better prepared to war against their sinful nature and the fruits of these "Capital Sins," which fruits are the various "actual sins" we commit and which stem from the Seven Capital Sins. Capital Sins, to state it another way, are the seven chief sins we commit because we have seven chief weaknesses or evil inclinations within our nature to go against God's law.

1. *Pride* is the first Capital Sin because it is actually the cause of all sin. It is defined as "excessive love of one's own excellence," and it involves an implicit denial of the fact that everything we have or have accomplished comes from God. Thus, it involves a denial of the truth. "Never suffer pride to reign in thy mind, or in thy words: for from it all perdition took its beginning." (*Tobias* 4:14). In reality, all the Capital Sins can be reduced to *inordinate self-love*, or pride, i.e., putting one's self and one's evil inclinations, one's own sinful will and desires, before the will of God. Inordinate, prideful selfishness is what we must constantly war against if we would free ourselves of sin.

Pride might well be considered the *greatest* sin because it is the height of self-love, and it is directly opposed to submission to God. It is the sin of Lucifer and the fallen angels and of Adam and Eve. It is the disposition we must have in our souls and it is the sin we must commit first before we can commit *any* other sin. Therefore it is listed first. Scripture says, "Pride goeth before destruction: and the spirit is lifted up before a fall." (*Prov.* 16:18). By this is meant that the sinner thinks he is strong and can resist temptation, but in reality he is weak and cannot (without caution and the grace of God), and therefore he does not avoid the "near occasions of sin" or seek God's grace to avoid sin, and consequently he falls.

One of the great dangers of pride is that it blinds our intellect to the truth of matters. Moreover, pride can take many forms; for example, we manifest pride by being self-centered, overbearing, critical of others, inconsiderate, self-pitying, presumptuous, inordinately ambitious, oversensitive, resentful, grudging, suspicious, hostile, self-complacent, vain, disobedient, insubordinate, indignant, haughty, arrogant, conceited, and so forth. The manifestations of pride can be very subtle and extremely varied, such as self-pity—which is nothing more than an indication we have a false and exalted opinion of ourselves—but all such manifestations come down to one common denominator, an inaccurate and inflated opinion of ourselves and our own worth.

To overcome pride, we must practice the virtue of humility, which is mainly the virtue of seeing ourselves as we actually are, realizing that even the greatest individual is little more than a worm in comparison to God, who is infinite, and that it is God who maintains us in existence at every instant. (Were He to remove His power from supporting our existence, we would immediately cease to be.) Our Lord favors the humble, for He has said in the Sermon on the Mount, "Blessed are the poor in spirit [the humble]: for theirs is the kingdom of heaven." (*Matt.* 5:3). This is the very first Beatitude. And the virtue of humility is the hallmark of every saint. Why are the humble so pleasing to God? They are the ones who see clearly, who see both themselves and other things as they really are. St. Teresa of Avila said, "Humility is walking in the truth." The humble person knows that the good in us and the good we do come from God; whereas, the evil that we do comes from ourselves. Knowing this protects a person from pride. To practice humility, we should say extra prayers and practice patience, forebearance, charity, kindness, meekness, submission, abandonment to God and conformity to His will, sympathy, modesty, acceptance of humiliations, etc.

2. *Covetousness* (avarice or greed) is an inordinate love of worldly goods and material things. In many respects covetousness is distrust of God's providence, and it is placing love of money and things before the love of God and our neighbor. Paradoxically, one need not be rich to be covetous, for covetousness is a condition of the heart. Actually, some very wealthy people are just the opposite of covetous, and some poor ones are paragons of this Capital Sin.

Covetous people are generally hardhearted toward the poor, stingy in sharing what they have, slow to pay what they owe, unwilling to lend, and distraught at their losses. The covetous person generally has little or no time for God and the affairs of his soul. He is like the seed of the parable that fell among thorns, which was "choked with the cares and riches and pleasures of this life, and yield[ed] no fruit." (*Luke* 8:14).

In order to fight covetousness or avarice, we have to practice generosity and mercy toward the poor and less fortunate, spend only a moderate amount upon ourselves, perhaps practice (if our state in life will allow it) taking no notice of how much money we have with us or exactly what is in our bank account, set aside a predetermined and substantial portion of our earnings for charity each time we receive our income, and take this portion for God and His poor "*off the top*" of what we earn, rather than taking care of all our other obligations first and then seeing what we have left (if anything) to give to God's Church and to charity. (Many with small means make the great mistake of giving to God "off the bottom" of their earnings, i.e., they take care first of all their other obligations and then see if there is anything left for charity, and as a result, they never seem to have enough for God, *or* for themselves; whereas, those who give to charity *first* and *generously*, always seem to have enough for their needs, plus some left over besides. Scripture says, "And you shall give the first fruits of your meats to the priest, that he may return a blessing on thy house."—*Ezech.* 44:30).

3. *Lust* is the desire to express our sexual promptings in an illicit way. The only morally correct expression of our sexual faculty is within marriage, between husband and wife, and that only in a manner that does not preclude conception of children, that is, when sexual relations are performed in the natural manner, without use of artificial birth control, and which under normal circumstances could lead to the conception of a child. Any other type of sexual activity is sinful, and in the study of morality it is called *impurity*, whether it be in thought, word or action. As mentioned in the discussion of the Sixth Commandment of God, impurity tends to blind the sinner to the implications of what he or she is doing. Those who engage in fornication, for example, defile themselves, stimulate their sexual appetite (which will not long be satisfied), and run the risk of procreating a child whom they usually are not ready or willing or able to support and who will be hurt by their action the rest of his life. But such a sinner is blind to all this and is impelled by his or her lust to achieve satisfaction at any price. St. Paul says of sins of impurity, "Let it not so much as be named among you." (*Eph.* 5:3). We can commit sins of lust in the mind, with the eyes, by touch, with pictures, by ourselves, with others, even in marriage (if the desire or action is not

properly oriented). Because our sexual nature is part of ourselves and with us at all times, it is something that we must continually battle in order to keep in check. As mentioned earlier, sins of impurity (lust) are considered by the great theologians and Doctors of the Church to cause the loss of more souls than any other form of sin.

The way to achieve purity is through modesty in dress, modesty of the eyes, modesty in our speech, modesty in not listening to lewd stories, modesty in our thoughts, great care in our entertainment (television, movies, plays, books, magazines, pictures, night clubs, the beach, etc.), precaution in not being alone too long with a member of the opposite sex, absolutely avoiding impure people, having recourse continually to prayer to possess the virtue of purity, especially invoking the aid of the Blessed Mother and St. Joseph, being *constant* in our prayers, frequenting the Sacraments, being constant and unrelenting in our determination to avoid or overcome all impurity at whatever price, resorting to prayer *immediately* upon being tempted, and always having a complete distrust of our strength in resisting temptations against purity, knowing that sexual activity is "natural" to mankind and that it is gratifying to our nature to give in to this vice.

Because sins of impurity are all mortal sins, and because the near occasion of sins of impurity will almost inevitably lead us to commit them, it is imperative to avoid the near occasion of sins of impurity. Almost always, placing ourselves in the near occasion of sins of impurity (i.e., those persons, places, or things which have led us into sins of impurity before and/or which are a strong temptation to us) is itself going to be a mortal sin. Therefore, whether it means turning off the T.V. or leaving a movie early, whether it means avoiding the company of certain people or not picking up a particular magazine, whether it means discontinuing an otherwise fascinating book or getting up and doing something different to interrupt an impure train of thought, we should realize that, when confronted by temptations to sins of lust or impurity, we should always act *swiftly* to get ourselves out of the near occasion of these sins. If we do so, we will avoid these sins; if we do not, we shall commit them. As Scriptures say, "He that loveth danger shall perish in it." (*Ecclesiasticus* 3:27).

4. *Anger* is a passion of the soul that wells up within us and stems from an offense, real or imagined, that makes us want to get even with the offender. There is a "righteous anger," which arises from seeing the law of God broken by someone who should be observing it, such as a mother becoming angry with her child who is purposely naughty, or even being angry when *we* have been wrongly and/or unjustly treated. Such anger is not a sin, so long as it is directed at an evil rather than a person and so long as it is kept in proportion to the offense and is not allowed to eventuate in sinful action. Righteous

indignation or anger is what St. Paul referred to when he said, "Be angry, and sin not." (*Eph.* 4:26). Our Lord displayed such anger when He cast the money changers out of the Temple. One might say that righteous indignation is a reasoned and measured response equal to an obvious offense against God's justice and His laws. Such anger is *not* what is referred to under this Capital Sin—though it is very easy for just anger to develop into unjust anger, something we must be careful to avoid.

The Capital Sin of Anger, however, is something quite different, being an inordinate, unreasoned, passionate response to something or someone whom we perceive to have offended us or who may have in fact offended us. Anger is a passion and must be subject to the higher faculties of our soul—the intellect and will and must not be allowed to overrule them. Becoming angry, initially, is not a sin, because it is largely an automatic reaction, but *harboring* or cultivating or nurturing or "feeding" the anger inside us and/or consenting to let it burst out is what is a sin, and can possibly be a very dangerous and serious one. Moreover, our own expressed anger usually generates a sinful response from others, and often this will lead to further action—undoubtedly improper and sinful action. Anger which is harbored can also develop into hatred, quarelling, fighting, a desire for revenge, and even murder. Thus, the sin of anger, not curtailed and suppressed, can be a serious sin both in itself and because it can lead us to hatred and to other sinful actions, actions which in turn can have terribly serious consequences for ourselves and others.

To overcome our propensity to anger, we must cultivate calmness within our souls, humility and an acceptance of God's will in our daily lives. It is good to make a practice of providing a place of peace within ourselves to which we can retreat and take a step backwards when we are tempted to the sin of anger. In this interior retreat we can take an objective look at what is prompting us to anger and then put off any decision to act till later, when we are calmer and can consider an appropriate, reasoned and measured form of response. "Revenge is mine, I will repay, saith the Lord." (*Romans* 12:19).

When tempted to anger, we can think of Our dear Lady, Mary the Mother of God, and how sweet and peaceful she was and of St. Joseph, her spouse, who was so quiet and calm that we do not even have a record of any of his words, either in the Bible or anywhere else. We can thereafter recommend our problem to God and ask Him to help us adopt the correct response, to have the right attitude and to behave toward those who are offending us in the way He wants us to.

5. *Envy* is distress of soul at the success or prosperity of another, and from it flow anger, hatred, calumny, detraction, persecution, jeal-

ousy, contempt, uncharitableness, malice, back-
biting, ill-will, etc. Envy is a sin against charity.
It proceeds from pride, whereby we desire to be
something we are not or whereby we think that
we are (or deserve to be) better than we are.
The American philosopher-poet Emerson has observed, "Envy is ignorance," and it *is*, to the
extent that we do not see accurately just what
we are and to the extent that we find displeasure because of the talents, successes and
prosperity of others; when we envy another, we
do not see that what is important is not to be
jealous of or copy that person but that *we should
perfect ourselves* and let matters thereafter take
their own course. The envious person fails to realize that all things which happen to us either come
directly *from* God or are at least *allowed* by Him
for our correction and our greater good. Therefore, envy is also, in a very real sense, a sin
against the justice and love of God, who has made
us as we are and who has sent us what we have.

To fight envy, we should daily meditate on this
truth, that God ultimately sends or allows all
things that we have or that happen to us, and
that He does this for our true best interest. Further, we should develop the habit of seeing in
another's talents and well-being the beneficent
action of God toward all His creatures, for without the many and varied talents within different people, how would society find that overall
balance of abilities that allows it to function har-
moniously. Too, we should meditate upon the

Mystical Body of Christ, of which all true Christians are members and to which all mankind is called. We should try to see that each person's talents and possessions are in a real sense a gift from God to the entire world, if that person will just use them for God's work and for His greater honor and glory. Prayer, abandonment to God's will and the active practice of charity, in time, will completely dissolve our inclination to envy, but we have to give ourselves over completely to seeing things from God's perspective and to being conformed and resigned to His holy will. (This approach is admirably brought out in the life of St. Gertrude. This saint had the laudable habit of praising God for the graces He gave to others. One day He revealed to her that every time she did this, He bestowed on her graces equal to those for which she had praised Him. Thus He revealed a beautiful system whereby everybody wins and nobody loses—and envy doesn't have a chance.)

6. *Gluttony* is inordinate eating or drinking or other consumption, just for the sheer pleasure of it, rather than primarily as an attempt to nourish our body—the reason for which God has attached pleasure to eating and drinking. Gluttony is a very easy sin to fall into because our appetite for food and drink often persists even after we have eaten enough. The great Napoleon observed that he could never eat too little, but it was very easy to eat too much. St. Augustine,

also, has commented on the difficulty of not eating too much, because there is often a very fine line between enough and too much. If, when eating, we always leave ourselves a little on the hungry side, we will never fall into this sin. Also, so long as we do not have ulcers, diabetes, or some other illness which requires frequent small meals, if we practice the penance of not eating between meals, we will keep our minds off the pleasure of food and drink and more on the need of food and drink for the nourishing of our bodies.

Drunkenness is included in the vice of gluttony, for drunkenness comes from overconsumption of alcoholic beverages. Drunkenness, or intoxication, is likewise a very easy sin to fall into because alcoholic beverages often do not trigger a strong response from the body that says, "I have had enough," as do other foods and beverages. Often one cannot drink even water in the quantities he can drink beer, wine and some other alcoholic drinks. Thus, it is easy to drink intoxicating beverages to excess. But alcohol taken in excess dulls the intellect, weakens the will and lowers our inhibitions. Therefore the dire consequences of overindulging in alcohol are all the forms of irrational, reckless and sinful behavior that the drunkard will engage in, most notably reckless driving, fits of anger and fighting, sins of impurity, failure to get to work, dissipation of one's money (especially if one has dependents who have a right to be supported by that money), damage to property and so forth.

The person who becomes intoxicated is guilty of all the evil things he does while under the influence of alcohol—to the extent that he knows what the effects of the alcohol will be before he even starts to drink. Catholic morality even teaches that the person who foresees that he is getting drunk and may do certain sinful acts as a result, and nonetheless continues to drink, is then guilty of those sins, even if he actually does not do them.

A drunken person is guilty of the reckless deeds he does when drunk because they stem from his lack of control over himself, which in turn stems from his drinking too much, which in its turn stems from a conscious and willful decision on his part to keep drinking when he knows he has had enough. The drunkard's degree of guilt may be lessened when he does something wrong while under the influence of alcohol because 1) he does not fully will to do the deed, or 2) he probably would not have done it had he not been intoxicated, and/or 3) he did not realize what his drinking would lead to. But a very major degree of guilt remains, nonetheless, for whatever one does while intoxicated. And those who know that any drinking usually leads them to drunkenness will commit a mortal sin by drinking at all, since they thereby put themselves in the near occasion of the mortal sin of drunkenness.

In addition to all the above in regard to drunkenness, overindulgence in alcoholic drink and/or steady "drinking" can lead to alcoholism, which is a particular problem in itself. There is hardly anyone in our society who does not realize how serious a problem alcoholism is. Therefore, anyone who finds himself being drawn into an addiction to alcohol is duty-bound to take *immediate* and *drastic* measures to curtail dramatically or completely halt his drinking. Anything less—if a person realizes how serious this problem is once one becomes addicted—would be a mortal sin. Once a person *is* an alcoholic, the level of guilt for falling back into the sin of drunkenness would be mitigated somewhat by the addiction—yet it may not be, if the addicted person knows that professional help (i.e., help from an Alcoholics-Anonymous type organization) is the only proved and successful method of overcoming alcoholism, and still that person refuses to obtain this type of help.

Though most people may not realize it, *smoking* can be a form of gluttony, if it is an inordinate use of tobacco. Smokers tend to keep smoking even when they have really had enough. This overindulgence in smoking can prove extremely harmful to their health over a prolonged period. And from this overindulgence arises the guilt of smoking. The smoker should realize that smoking lowers his vitality in general and makes him more susceptible to illness and that it has the long-term effect of contributing to cancer and emphysema (among other diseases and debilities), both in himself and in those who must breathe the air he pollutes by his smoking. With all that is known today about the evil side-effects of smoking, it is difficult to imagine that smoking is not at least a venial sin, though perhaps a "small" one, even for those whose health is not seriously affected by this practice.

To combat gluttony, we should realize that the pleasures connected to eating and drinking are not ends in themselves but the *means* to an end (the nourishing of our bodies), and that as we must strive for temperance in all our actions, we should especially strive for it in eating and drinking. Also, we have the assurance from Our Lord that "Unless you shall do penance, you shall all likewise perish." (*Luke* 13:3). In curtailing our eating and drinking, we can practice a very good and effective type of penance. Moreover, we should realize that this type of penance will contribute to a greater strength of will, to our own greater vitality and to better health. Through the example and admonition of Our Lord and the Apostles, we are called upon to spiritualize everything we do: "Whether you eat or drink, or whatsoever else you do, do all to the glory of God." (*1 Cor.* 10:31).

7. *Sloth* is actually spiritual laziness, though most will think of it as bodily laziness. But in as much as all human activity comes from the will (a spiritual faculty), sloth will be easily seen to be a spiritual ill. Among the Seven Capital Sins, *sloth (in one sense at least) is considered*

*to be the most dangerous because sloth leads us
to reject the graces and inspirations of the Holy
Spirit and disinclines us to do those things necessary for our salvation.*

Sloth can adopt the form of voluptuousness,
ease, tepidity, lukewarmness, and indifference
in God's service. By slothfulness our wills become weaker and weaker, and we end up unable to resist other sins. Sloth can hide behind
activity, even great or feverish activity, for the
things we are doing may be activities we *like*
to do, which are done in place of what we *ought*
to be doing. "Escapism" is often nothing other
than sloth.

We should realize that Our Lord, in the parable of the talents given to three servants (a talent was a large sum of money), took away the
one talent given to the servant who did not develop it into more, and condemned him and called
him a wicked servant, and gave his one talent
to the servant who had been given ten talents
and had already doubled his master's money.
(*Matt.* 25:14-28). What Our Lord is saying by this
parable is that God expects a return on His in-
vestment in us; He expects us to grow and develop ourselves. But sloth counteracts God's
intent and frustrates His grace in us. For by sloth,
we give back nothing new to God; whereas, we
should have gained something by the use of the
abilities and graces He has given us to help us
do good. If we did not exercise our bodies, they
would become useless; if we did not use our

minds, they would become inactive and unimaginative; and if we do not motivate our souls, especially our wills, we will become spiritually inactive (slothful) and neglect all those things we must do to attain our eternal salvation.

To combat the sin of sloth, we should apprise ourselves accurately about the task of our salvation and about the ease of losing our souls eternally. This will provide a true and "automatic" motivation, so to speak. Then, we should pray fervently to overcome this evil inclination, asking the Holy Spirit to help us with His heavenly graces and inspirations. We should stir up our souls to increased activity in the service of God, take care that we perform all the duties of our state in life, regulate and perhaps reduce our time for ease and entertainment, say extra prayers, and set up a regular program of physical exercise, mental stimulation (a reading program, for example) and prayer; and then we should stick to our program, even advancing our activities in all these areas. All the while, we should remember Our Lord's words, "My Father worketh until now; and I work." (*John* 5:17). If God "works," then it is a Godlike quality in us to work. Now work is opposed to sloth. By diligent work and prayer, therefore, we will overcome this "most dangerous" of all vices.

A word here must be said about legitimate relaxation and recreation. A person needs a certain amount of rest, relaxation and recreation *every day, every week, every month* or so, and *every year.* Our Lord Himself said, "Sufficient for the day is the evil thereof." (*Matt.* 6:34). In other words, when the day is done, it is done, and we should take it easy so that we can recuperate and refresh ourselves and be ready for the next day. Too, each week, generally on Saturday, we need to back off a little from work and then we need to rest completely from our work on Sunday in order to be ready for the next week. Also, every month or so, we should take an extra day off—as occurs with our national holidays and the Catholic holydays—in order to give ourselves a little extra time to refresh our minds and our bodies and be that much more able to work when we resume our normal activities. Plus, ideally, every year we should take off from our work one to three weeks or so for a vacation—depending on our needs, our financial means and our ability to be away from work—and at this time let our minds and hearts completely rebuild and gain a new orientation on life. (Obviously parents of young children usually cannot take a vacation from their families, but they can often change their family routines in small ways, if they do not have the financial means to travel, such as to constitute a form of vacation right at home.)

The human frame is simply not able to go and go and go. We should take the counsel of older, more experienced people in this regard and employ periodic times off to rebuild our energies. It is not only *not* a sin of sloth to take legitimate recreation each day, week, month and year, but failure to observe these periodic rest times will only hurt us in the long run, and impair the proper fulfillment of our duties. Proper relaxation and recreation, quite opposed to sloth, do not constitute a sin, but a virtue. However, it is the *overuse* of these that amounts to a form of sloth and that would be a sin.

St. Paul compares Christians to athletes and to soldiers, both of whom must train and work diligently to be ready for the contest. We must be spiritual athletes and spiritual soldiers in order to lead the true Christian life, and we will thereby not have to worry about violating God's law by the sin of sloth, for we will thereby be actively and steadily engaged in doing God's work, such as He has given it to us to do.

In review, the Seven Capital Sins are the seven chief sins we commit (if we give in to them), and they are the seven basic weaknesses of our human nature, whereby we are *inclined* or prone to sin. They are the seven principal sins we commit and also the seven roots from which all sin flows. As weaknesses, they are our sevenfold inclination to evil, inherited from our first parents through Original Sin. To achieve anything great, even in the natural order (athletics, education, work, etc.), we have to overcome (at least to some extent) these seven propensities to evil, or else our efforts to achieve even in the natural realm will be alloyed with the corruption of sin, and we will fail, or at least come short of the mark we otherwise could have achieved had we overcome them.

Agnostics, atheists and freethinkers may jeer at the entire notion of Original Sin and the Seven Capital Sins, but whatever even they achieve in the physical or intellectual realms can be attributed only to the degree that they have curtailed these seven evil inclinations within themselves, which the Catholic Church describes as the Seven Capital Sins.

But when it comes to the *supernatural order* (avoiding Hell and gaining Heaven), we must overcome them *absolutely*, for nothing imperfect will enter Heaven. Having unrepented serious sins (mortal sins) on our souls when we die—or even just one—will send us to Hell; having sins on our souls which are not grievous but yet which are still sins (venial sins) will cause us to go to Purgatory, as will any spiritual debt we have still outstanding when we die (spiritual debts due to mortal and venial sins already forgiven but not made up for by our penances and good works). In Purgatory we will be purified by involuntary suffering until all of the debts incurred by our sins and still owed to God's justice shall have been paid. Therefore, in the supernatural order we must overcome *totally* the Seven Capital Sins (the seven chief sins we commit and our seven propensities to evil) to the extent that we no longer sin even venially—before we will be eligible to enter Heaven as soon as we die. Anything short of overcoming them completely will result in our having to go to Purgatory to make up for what we did not achieve in this life.

Chapter VII

PERFECT AND IMPERFECT CONTRITION

We all commit sin. The Bible says that even the just man falls seven times a day (*Proverbs* 24:16), meaning that he commits at least "small" sins. Therefore, once we have committed sin, how do we go about gaining God's forgiveness? Just what must we do to insure that we are back in God's grace? We all know, deep within us, what we have to do. We have to be sorry for our sins, without reserve, and beg God's forgiveness for them. But there is something more involved in being certain we are gaining that forgiveness.

First of all, to gain God's forgiveness for our sins, our sorrow must be 1) interior, 2) supernatural, 3) supreme, and 4) universal. Our sorrow is *interior* when it comes from our heart, genuinely, and not merely from a wish to be forgiven and without really taking the necessary steps to gain that forgiveness. (This does not mean that our sorrow has to be *emotionally* "felt," for emotions can vary. It simply has to be genuine and sincere.) Our sorrow must be *supernatural*, that is, aided by God's grace and arising from motives that spring from Faith, and not merely from natural motives, such as fear of getting caught and punished. Our sorrow must be *supreme*, that is, we must hate sin above every other evil and be willing to endure any suffering rather than offend God in the future (at least by mortal sin); in other words, we must have a firm purpose of amendment. And finally, our sorrow must be *universal*, that is, it must include sorrow for every mortal sin we have ever committed; and for the future, we must firmly renounce at least all mortal sin.

The Catechism distinguishes between two kinds of contrition (sorrow for sin), "perfect contrition" and "imperfect contrition." *Perfect Contrition* is sorrow for sin because sin offends God, whom we love above all things for His own sake. And *Imperfect Contrition* is sorrow for our sins because they are hateful in themselves or because we fear God's punishment (especially, going to Hell).

Now, every Catholic knows that for us to be forgiven mortal sin and receive Sanctifying Grace back into our souls *without* the Sacrament of Penance (Confession), *it is necessary that our contrition be "perfect contrition"* (and if we are Catholic and therefore have access to the Sacrament of Penance, we must also intend to go to Confession as soon as possible). But even if (with God's help) a Catholic can achieve perfect contrition for his mortal sins, this is not sufficient in itself to enable him to receive Holy Communion worthily; first he must go to the Sacrament of Penance (Confession) and receive absolution (sacramental forgiveness) from God through the priest. However, if a person commits a mortal sin and can achieve in his heart only imperfect contrition (sorrow because the sins are bad in themselves or sorrow out of fear of God's punishment), yet if that person goes to Sacramental Confession and receives absolution from the priest, this type of contrition—*in combination with the Sacrament of Confession*—suffices for forgiveness of even mortal sins; the repentant sinner thereby returns to the state of grace and may thereafter receive Holy Communion.

Catholics are taught to cultivate *perfect contrition* for their sins, so that between the time they might have the misfortune to commit a mortal sin and the time they can go to Confession to a priest, they can have nonetheless obtained forgiveness from God, so that should they die before going to the Sacrament of Confession, they will still save their souls. Contrition for our sins is both a gift of God (which He loves to give) and an act of the human will; therefore, as part of our daily prayers we should ask God for the gift of contrition for our sins, and particularly perfect contrition, so that should we fall into mortal sin, we will have this precious gift from God, plus the habit within our will to ask for forgiveness. In order to cultivate the sorrow for sin called "perfect contrition," the Church has traditionally taught her spiritual children a prayer called "The Act of Contrition," and it goes like this in its traditional form:

The Act of Contrition

"O my God, I am heartily sorry for having offended Thee, and I detest all my sins because I dread the loss of Heaven and the pains of Hell, but most of all because they offend Thee, my God, Who art all good and deserving of all my love. I firmly resolve, with the help of Thy grace, to confess my sins, to do penance and to amend my life. Amen."

If a person will say this prayer often, especially each night before retiring, and whenever he or she may have had the misfortune to commit a mortal sin, and if the person will truly mean what he or she is saying, then that person will be cultivating the sorrow for sin called "perfect contrition," which, of its own, is sufficient to enable one to obtain God's forgiveness of mortal sin and to return to the state of grace and save his or her soul, even without going to Sacramental Confession. (It should be noted that perfect contrition may contain an admixture of motives of imperfect contrition and yet still be perfect contrition. Thus, a person would still have perfect contrition even if, in addition to his sorrow for sin because it has offended God, he also was sorry because he feared going to Hell.)

To the best of my knowledge, it is only Catholics who are taught this thorough and exact type of sorrow for sins. Non-Catholics may achieve it, by a genuine movement of their minds, hearts, and wills, under the promptings of the grace of

God, to renounce sin once and for all because
they love God above all things and because sin
is infinitely hateful to Him, but do they really
know that they are fulfilling all the requirements
for that sorrow for sin called "perfect contrition"—which alone will enable them to be with
God should they die after having committed mortal sin? On the basis of probability alone, the
likelihood does not seem too good. Even a Catholic cannot be *absolutely sure* his contrition is
really perfect contrition because it is always difficult for us human beings to be certain about
our motivation, which applies to contrition as
well.

But at least the Catholic knows for sure what
are the requirements for perfect contrition, and
moreover, he has available to him the Sacrament
of Confession, instituted by Christ to grant God's
forgiveness for certain and also to give special
graces to the penitent. Plus, the priest sitting
in the tribunal seat of the confessional is a trained
expert in moral theology, a "doctor of the law,"
so to speak, and can help the penitent to achieve
the proper sorrow for his sins through whatever
explanation and advice he deems is needed to
instruct him.

Non-Catholics might deride the idea of Confession, but over and above its primary purpose
of being God's instrument for forgiving sins, it
does wonders for the soul. For with Confession
a person makes a thorough examination of conscience before going to the Sacrament, adopts

a spirit of contrition for his sins, tells all his mortal sins, and usually all the venial sins he can think of as well; then he comes away with the certain knowledge that he has received God's forgiveness, along with His special graces attached to this Sacrament that will help him overcome his sins in the future. The combination of Confession followed by sincere and worthy Holy Communion places the individual squarely back in God's grace and on the road to Heaven. And the resultant peace of soul that the person achieves is simply not of this world! It is that peace of which Our Lord spoke when He said, "Peace I leave with you, my peace I give unto you: not as the world giveth, do I give unto you. Let not your heart be troubled, nor let it be afraid." (*John* 14:27).

Non-Catholics may go to expensive psychiatrists in an effort to achieve that interior peace which any Catholic can receive for free just by going to Confession, and the person who visits a psychiatrist usually comes away not much better off than when he started; the reason is that generally he has not come to grips with his own sins, accused himself of them, decided firmly never again to commit these sins, and asked God's forgiveness. Sacramental Confession, which automatically requires sincere contrition for our sins and a firm purpose of amendment never to commit them again, brings a balm to the soul that, if the world knew of it, would cause a wide path to be beaten to the door of every Catholic Church.

Chapter VIII

THE CORPORAL AND SPIRITUAL WORKS OF MERCY

In Sacred Scripture we find a number of attempts to summarize the whole Christian way of life in a sentence or two. One of the most famous ones is to be found in the Epistle of St. James, where we read, "Religion clean and undefiled before God and the Father is this: to visit the fatherless and widows in their tribulation: and to keep one's self unspotted from this world." (*James* 1:27). Again, in St. John, we read, "If you love me, keep my commandments." (*John* 14:15). But undoubtedly the best summary of all of the entire Christian way of life is contained in the Two Great Commandments, for these embody in essence the whole law of God: "Thou shalt love the lord thy God with thy whole heart, and with thy whole soul, and with thy whole mind...And...thy neighbour as thyself." (*Dt.* 6:5; *Matt.* 22:37, 39). Along this same line, St. John observes, "If any man say, I love God and hateth his brother; he is a liar. For he that loveth not his brother, whom he seeth, how can he love God, whom he seeth not." (*1 Jn.* 4:20). And then we have Our Lord's own words, which He said He would speak at the Last Judgment: "For I was hungry, and you gave me to eat; I was thirsty, and you gave me to drink; I was a stranger, and you took me in: naked, and you covered me: I was in prison, and you came to see me. . . Amen I say to you, as long as you did it to one of these my least brethren, you did it to me." (*Matt.* 25: 35-37, 40).

The Catholic Catechism sums up our obligation to show our love of God by the love we show our neighbor in what are called by the Catholic Church the Corporal and Spiritual Works of Mercy. There are seven Corporal (bodily) and seven Spiritual Works of Mercy:

The Corporal Works of Mercy

1. To feed the hungry.
2. To give drink to the thirsty.
3. To clothe the naked.
4. To visit the imprisoned.
5. To shelter the homeless.
6. To visit the sick.
7. To bury the dead.

The Spiritual Works of Mercy

1. To admonish the sinner.
2. To instruct the ignorant.
3. To counsel the doubtful.
4. To comfort the sorrowful.
5. To bear wrongs patiently.
6. To forgive all injuries.
7. To pray for the living and the dead.

The Corporal Works of Mercy

1. *To feed the hungry.* Despite the modern welfare state's being firmly in place in many countries and despite its assuming many corporal works of mercy, there are still people in our society who are actually going hungry. The "street people" are the most famous, but there are others besides (the elderly, the mentally disturbed, abused and neglected children, illegal aliens etc.)—people who, for one reason or another, are without enough to eat. Then there are the so-called "Third World" countries. According to a report given in 1988 by one of the UNESCO agencies to the BBC in England, there are approximately one thousand children dying each day in Africa alone, mostly from malnutrition. As Our Lord told us, "The poor you have always with you." (*Matt.* 26:11). If we think, because poor and hungry people are not right under our noses (as the beggar Lazarus was with the rich man Dives) we thereby no longer have an obligation "to feed the hungry," we are sadly mistaken and we need to think again of the ending of this parable and make a conscious effort to search out the hungry and help them to the extent that our means will allow.

2. *To give drink to the thirsty.* Today the second Corporal Work of Mercy is basically covered under the first. In the days when private wells were the primary source of water, anyone traveling, even for a short distance, be he rich or poor

night indeed have had to beg for water to drink. And in more primitive societies, this would still be the case, and therefore, "To give drink to the thirsty" is still a common work of mercy. In modern, more developed countries, there are generally drinking fountains in most public places, but it is not so everywhere, and giving drink to the thirsty remains even today a simple but great act of charity, because it fulfills for everyone an essential bodily need.

3. *To clothe the naked.* There are of course many applications of this work of mercy other than actually giving some clothing we own to someone who knocks at the door. Today, in almost every country, there are charitable agencies that collect used and unneeded clothing to give to the poor or to sell to them at only nominal prices. In the better-off countries of the world, most people have older clothing hanging in their closets or on their clothes racks that either no longer fit or which they no longer use. If these will be given to the proper relief agencies, they can end up being used by those truly in need, and we shall to a great extent have fulfilled our obligation under this Work of Mercy "to clothe the naked." Especially during winter in the colder climates is this work of particular merit. A warm but unused coat in our attic will do far more good for our soul when given to a charitable agency than it ever would for our body by providing an "extra" coat if we ever need it—because of the supernatural merit it will earn for us.

4. *To visit the imprisoned.* Few people think about prisoners. Many people have the cavalier attitude that prisoners deserve whatever they get, forgetting that even prisoners are people too and that Our Lord Himself was once held prisoner—and He Innocence Itself. Even though we personally may not know anyone in prison, we can still send them good Catholic books through the prison chaplains to help inspire and encourage them and to help them truly reform their lives, get themselves turned around again and put their souls in proper order in the eyes of God, that when they are released, they will all the better have the motivation to lead a holy life on the outside, become solid citizens once more, and in the end save their souls. Prisoners are the "forgotten souls" in our society. We may think, because we do not personally know anyone in prison, that we have no obligation to those who are there, but yet we do, and we can fulfill it, at least partially, by the means mentioned above and also by prayer and by supporting those who make it their apostolate to come to the corporal and spiritual assistance of prisoners.

5. *To shelter the homeless.* Times come in nearly everyone's life when he has a chance to take in someone who is in need of a place to stay. At the very least, we should help these poor people by arranging for them to be accommodated somewhere until they can get themselves situated again. Here too, by contributing to relief agencies that help the homeless, we can ourselves

oin in this great work of mercy. We should always remember the passage from *Isaias*, "Deal thy bread to the hungry, *and bring the needy and harbourless into thy house:* when thou shalt see one naked, cover him, and despise not thy own flesh." (*Isaias* 58:7, emphasis added).

6. *To visit the sick.* In everyone's life there are ample opportunities to perform this work of mercy, for everyone knows people who become old or ill and are either hospitalized, placed in nursing homes, or forced to remain home because of illness. Often, nothing brightens the day of a sick person more than a visit from someone he or she knows and/or loves. In comparison to God, we are all helpless little creatures, and our visiting those who are sick and incapacitated is a Godlike act of kindness and mercy toward those who are incapable of helping themselves to any great degree or of getting out into society. Though we should be motivated primarily by spiritual motives, it would be well to remember in this regard that possibly we too shall live to become old, and perhaps we too shall lose our health. How we shall long to have someone visit us as we should have visited the less fortunate when we were in full possession of our strength. When or if sickness should ever come to us (and God forbid it does), surely the good Lord will remember our many kindnesses toward the sick and send visitors to us in our own time of need.

7. *To bury the dead.* Seldom if ever shall we be called upon (peace remaining in our society)

actually to dig a hole in the ground to bury the dead. But what is meant by this work of mercy, for most of us, is to assist at and take part in the funeral services and subsequent gatherings when those we know die. Nothing will bring back the departed, but our presence and our caring for those who grieve for the loss of their loved ones will bolster the spirits of those who are left. And we should remember that our financial assistance to the family of the departed is always deeply appreciated at the time of death, because there are always "hidden" expenses connected with death and burial. But the most good by far that we can do at the time of death is to pray for the soul of the departed, have Masses offered for him and offer plenary indulgences for the repose of his soul. (One plenary indulgence, of course, is sufficient, but because of our own disposition, we do not know for certain if it is acceptable by God. Also, we never know for certain if God will allow a given plenary indulgence to be granted to the specific person we offer it for.) The family members of the deceased should be informed of our efforts in this regard, that they may be consoled about their loved one. People without the Faith think that there is nothing we can do for those who have died, but that is not at all true. For we can continue to remember them in our prayers and Masses and gain indulgences for their relief from the sufferings of Purgatory. (Seventh Spiritual Work of Mercy).

Since this list is merely a codification by the Teaching Church of our charitable obligations, and since it was compiled before the advent of publicly condoned abortion, it should probably include something like "To protect the endangered," in order to cover abortion and euthanasia. During the era when the Moslems systematically enslaved Christian captives, this list included, "To ransom the captive." This work of mercy has been dropped from the list because it no longer applies to a common need.

The Spiritual Works of Mercy

1. *To admonish the sinner.* We read in *Ezechiel:* "If, when I say to the wicked, Thou shalt surely die: thou declare it not to him, nor speak to him, that he may be converted from his wicked way, and live: the same wicked man shall die in his iniquity, but I will require his blood at thy hand. But if thou give warning to the wicked, and he be not converted from his wickedness, and from his evil way: he indeed shall die in his iniquity, but thou hast delivered thy soul." (*Ezechiel* 3:18-19). So heavy is our obligation to admonish the sinner, that Scripture says if we do not do so, we will be held accountable for not having warned him. But if we do admonish him and he does not repent, then we have fulfilled our obligation. We have under this first Spiritual Work of Mercy, therefore, a great obligation toward those we know, if we see them doing something

seriously wrong, to admonish them to renounce their sin and return to a good life.

Catholic theologians generally give three conditions that qualify our obligation to admonish the sinner: 1) We are morally certain that a mortal sin is involved; 2) we have reasonable hope of success; and 3) we can do so without grave inconvenience to ourselves. There is still a further qualification that must be kept in mind, namely, *an obligation in justice* versus *an obligation in charity* to admonish the sinner. Those in authority—such as parents, teachers, priests, bishops, religious superiors, etc.—have an obligation in justice to admonish those under their authority, even if it causes a grave inconvenience to them. We all have an obligation in charity to admonish whomever we see doing or advocating the doing of something seriously (mortally) sinful. (This obligation to admonish the sinner, both in justice and in charity, also extends to lesser—i.e., venial—offenses, and not just to mortal sins.)

We should realize in all of this that to admonish the sinner does not mean putting oneself up on a pedestal, and thus possibly succumbing to pride. Moreover, before one incurs the obligation to admonish another, he must himself come to a knowledge of the truths of Holy Faith. Obviously, a person cannot admonish another to follow a course of action that he himself does not know about or is not sure of. But as we come more and more to understand exactly what the

Faith teaches, the more we are obliged to practice this work of mercy. As stated above, to those in authority—bishops, priests, parents, etc.—it is a particularly heavy moral obligation. To those, who by special grace, have deep insight into and understanding of morality it is also a heavy obligation. But even for the average person, there is a serious obligation to testify to the truth insofar as he knows it. "Everyone therefore that shall confess me before men, I will also confess him before my Father who is in heaven. But he that shall deny me before men, I will also deny him before my Father who is in heaven." (*Matt.* 10:32-33). Our remaining silent in the face of someone's publicly committing or espousing sin, especially mortal sin, can be tantamount to denying Christ. For by our silence, we are assenting to the person's sin.

There are other proofs from Scripture testifying to our obligations in this regard; one further example should suffice. Our Lord proclaimed: "I am come to cast fire on the earth: and what will I, but that it be kindled?. . .Think ye, that I have come to give peace on earth? I tell you, no; but separation. For there shall be from henceforth five in one house divided: three against two, and two against three. The father shall be divided against the son, and the son against his father, the mother against the daughter, and the daughter against the mother, the mother in law against her daughter in law, and the daughter in law against her mother in law." (*Luke* 12:49, 51-53).

Moral truths embraced with the supernatural gift of Christ's Faith demand testimony before others of our commitment to His truth. Normally, we should let our actions speak for what we believe in, but where the question concerns a serious public sin or a public avowal of a serious sin, we are bound, if we know better, either in justice or in charity (depending on our position), to speak up. Where the issue is the salvation of a person's soul, there is no room for compromise. This factor in Catholicism is indeed the stuff of martyrs for the Faith. St. John the Baptist was decapitated for just such a stand.

2. *To instruct the ignorant.* Parents in particular have the obligation of constantly instructing their children. Failure to do so is a sin. Of course, too, parents must provide for their children's formal education, but also, and most importantly, they must see to their religious instruction, which they should reinforce by their own good example. So great is this obligation of parents that Scripture says, "It is better to die without children, than to leave ungodly children." (*Ecclesiasticus* 16:4). Nor does there seem to be any better example in matters religious than to see the father of the family faithfully fulfilling his religious obligations, for there is an element in human fatherhood akin to the Fatherhood of God over all creation; and when a father gives this good example to his family, the effect on his wife and children is out of all proportion to the effort he makes.

Today, more than ever, there is a dearth of true spiritual understanding. And whereas most people are not able actually to instruct others, and for the most part, these others would not take the time to hear instruction if it were offered, yet by giving good Catholic books, we can fulfill this obligation better perhaps than in any other way. For a book is always there; it is impersonal; it can be read and reread; it can be taken to work; it can be read a little at a time; it is generally a thorough treatment of the subject matter; and it is often the culmination of a wise person's entire life and thinking and learning. Who could rival St. Alphonsus Liguori, for example, for sheer impact upon the mind and heart of his readers, and this great Doctor's works are still generally available in inexpensive editions.

3. *To counsel the doubtful.* Oftentimes people become confused about what their obligations are to Almighty God, and it is a great work of charity to help them understand them. Here again, good Catholic books play an important role, but there is nothing so reassuring as a committed and confident Catholic to give advice and counsel, a Catholic in the state of grace and who knows and loves his or her religion. This is due to that Catholic's being instructed in the truths of God's holy Religion and his being in the state of grace, i.e., having God's own life dwelling within his soul. (Although one cannot judge whether a person is in the state of grace, there are many indications that a person is—because

the goodness of a person is manifest in his bearing and demeanor, and communicates itself to others.) Today, with the religious and moral chaos that is reigning virtually everywhere, the Third Spiritual Work of Mercy is especially needed. In particular, more and more people are just about to be or are in the process of seriously entangling their lives in bad (invalid) marriages and all sorts of sins against the Sixth and Ninth Commandments of God. Particularly common is the practice of artificial birth control, which most non-Catholics today, and unfortunately many uninformed Catholics too, think is virtually a God-given right. Little do they realize that it is so heinous a mortal sin in the eyes of God that He slew Onan in the Old Testament (*Gen.* 38:1-10) as a punishment for practicing this abomination. (Moreover, many people do not realize that they are actually causing early abortions by the use of birth control pills (and the IUD), since these pills often and sometimes always work by ridding the woman's body of the already-conceived child in its very early stages.)

Many people today are "married" to divorced partners or are about to "contract" such a "marriage." It is only right to advise them of their obligation not to try to contract such a union, reminding them of Our Lord's words, "He that shall marry her that is put away committeth adultery." (*Matt.* 5:2). And, "Neither fornicators, nor idolaters, nor adulterers shall possess the kingdom of heaven." (*1 Cor.* 6:9-10).

4. *To comfort the sorrowful.* The Catholic religion calls this world a "vale of tears." For there is no earthly joy, however great, that is not alloyed with some sorrow or privation or limitation, and we all encounter some of our fellow human beings who are, from time to time, sad about or grieving over something. It is a great act of charity, therefore, just to hear them out in such times of grief, to commiserate with them in their sadness and to try to bring them cheer and relieve their sorrow. Because of the absence of True Religion in the lives of so many people, those who are distressed should be advised and encouraged and admonished not to resort to drugs or alcohol and definitely not to commit suicide (a practice which has increased drastically in our society in the past two decades). Scripture says, "For it is thou, O Lord, that hast power of life and death." (*Wis.* 16:13).

5. *To bear wrongs patiently.* Probably no one passes through life without having someone falsely accuse him or injure him unjustly in some way or other. The Bible says, "A mild answer breaketh wrath." (*Prov.* 15:1). When we handle such wrongs in a patient and Christlike way, we show to others that our religion really means something to us. And there is nothing so powerful with which to reproach the wrongdoer as a quiet word or the absence of retaliation in the face of injustice. Our Divine Lord has told us, "If one strike thee on thy right cheek, turn to him also the other." (*Matt.* 5:39). Indeed, there

is no greater reproof to the sinner or the unjust than not to avenge his injustice.

6. *To forgive all injuries.* Here again, there is no one who has not at some time or other been injured by his fellow man, but Our Lord has told us, "Blessed are they that suffer persecution for justice' sake: for theirs is the kingdom of heaven." (*Matt.* 5:10). Also, "Whosoever is angry with his brother shall be in danger of the judgment." (*Matt.* 5:22). And again, "So also shall my heavenly Father do to you [deliver the person to the torturers until he has paid all of his debt], if you forgive not every one his brother from your hearts." (*Matt.* 18:35). And in the Our Father we pray to be forgiven by God "as we forgive those who trespass against us."

What we need to remember whenever someone wrongs us is that Almighty God has *sent* this misfortune to us. We know that God, being infinitely good, cannot be the *cause* of moral evil (sin). Yet He definitely has *willed to permit* this misfortune to come to us at the hands of others; therefore, it has come to us, *at least by God's permission,* in order for us to learn some lesson that God sees we need to learn, or to help us grow in virtue or be purified. Whenever we view our misfortunes at the hands of others in this light, we cannot help but realize we must forgive those who injure us because we can see our neighbor as only the *immediate cause* of our trouble, but Almighty God as the One who actually permits the sad lesson to occur which we have had to undergo. To reiterate, we are not saying here that God sends us moral evil (injustice, sin); being infinitely good, He cannot be the author of moral evil. However, He most definitely does will to *allow* something bad to happen at the hands of others for our correction or our ultimate good.

7. *To pray for the living and the dead.* Whenever we see problems besetting our friends, neighbors and loved ones, we can help ameliorate their problems by our prayers. The poet has penned the immortal words, "More things are wrought by prayer than this world dreams." God answers prayer when it is sincerely and perseveringly offered by a person in the state of grace; there is no doubt about it. "For the continual prayer of a just man availeth much." (*James* 5:16). The Bible contains many passages admonishing us to pray and instructing us how to pray. God would not have inspired the writers of the various books of the Bible to give us these admonitions if prayer were not powerful to effect change. One of the greatest consolations we can give those with problems is to tell them we will be praying for them. Not only will they benefit by our prayers, they will also be consoled by the *knowledge* that we are praying.

When it comes to praying for those who have died, the great spiritual writer Father Frederick Faber tells us there is no greater charity, in fact, than praying for the "Poor Souls in Purgatory," as Catholics call them. Father Faber says that this work constitutes the highest charity we can perform and the summation of all charity. In God's eyes, according to Father Faber, it is the most pleasing charity we can do.

How many people can be said to be truly perfect and thus deserving, because of their absolute rectitude, to go straight to Heaven without paying in Purgatory any of the spiritual debts which they may have left unpaid in this world? Even those people whom *we* judge to be perfect, are really perfect only in *our* eyes and not necessarily in the eyes of God. The Saints say that very few indeed are truly perfect and able to go immediately from this life into the presence of God without passing through the purifying fires of Purgatory.

According to the Catholic teaching on Purgatory, the people detained there cannot help themselves in any way (though strange to say, they can and do help us here on earth, and we should call upon them for their assistance to us). Therefore, it is the greatest of charities to pray for the Poor Souls in Purgatory, to have Masses offered for them and to gain indulgences for their relief, especially plenary indulgences. The Book of Machabees tells us, "It is therefore a holy and wholesome thought to pray for the dead." (*2 Mac.* 12:46). In this regard we should always have before our minds the realization that we too shall die one day and that we may very well have to spend a long time in Purgatory. If during our own lives we were in the habit of praying for those in Purgatory, surely those in Heaven who, due to our prayers and suffrages, were released from or relieved of their sufferings in Purgatory while they were there, will pray for us when perhaps we in turn are in Purgatory. Too, God will surely have pity on us if we have had pity, while alive, on those in Purgatory; perhaps He will inspire some generous soul on earth to gain a plenary indulgence for us shortly after we die, and though otherwise we might have had to suffer many years in Purgatory because of what we owe to Divine Justice, yet because of our charity toward the Poor Souls while we were alive, perhaps we will receive the same sort of mercy at the hands of some other charitable person when we die, and we will thus be released from Purgatory's torments much earlier than we otherwise might have been.

With regard to Purgatory, we should always remember that the sufferings of that state, according to the teaching of the Church's Saints and learned Doctors, are the same as those of Hell, with the exception that the souls in Purgatory realize they have died in the state of grace and have saved their souls and that they will eventually be released from their sufferings and will spend eternity with God. What more powerful motivation could there be to pray for the poor suffering souls in Purgatory than the twofold realization that on the one hand they cannot help themselves and on the other hand that our charity toward them will surely be matched in our case, if and when we are in Purgatory.

The Corporal and Spiritual Works of Mercy, then, are a simplified or codified statement of our overall obligation to perform works of charity toward others. And charity (a word designating "supernatural love," or "Godlike love") constitutes the *positive* side of our efforts to avoid Hell and gain Heaven, where we take the initiative to do some *positive* thing. (Obeying the Commandments by avoiding sin we can say, is, in one respect, the *negative* or *combative* side of what is needed to avoid Hell—though not less important—where we mainly *fight* with temptations and conquer them as in a spiritual combat.)

Charity is a free giving to others what they need, and it is reflective of God's love toward man, for man needs *everything* from God, and God is the ultimate source of everything man has. Therefore, to fill, even partially, the physical and spiritual needs of others is a Godlike work, and it is the performance of these Godlike works that God requires of us to prove to Him we love Him. It will be recalled that at the Final Judgment, described by Our Lord in *Matthew* (25:35-37, 40), people are saved or condemned based on whether they practiced charity.

St. Peter says, "Charity covereth a multitude of sins." (*1 Peter* 4:8). The reason for this is twofold: Our charity helps repay the Divine Justice for our sins, and charity tends to destroy in us our propensities to pride, selfishness, greed, hatred, anger, etc.—even lust—for we cannot really harbor these evil sentiments and inclinations within ourselves when we enter fully into the performing of works of charity. For charity is a sort of "spiritual solvent" that tends, so to speak, to dissolve our hardened, ingrained and self-produced bad habits (habitual sins), and even our tendencies to sin (the Seven Capital Sins). It can almost safely be said that one cannot be Godlike in practicing charity and evil too at the same time. The two tend to be mutually contradictory. If one will continually and habitually practice charity, it is virtually assured that the evil habits and inclinations within him will eventually be eliminated.

Chapter IX

COMMON MORTAL SINS

In our effort to make a fair and candid assessment of the task of how to avoid Hell, we certainly must look at some of the "common mortal sins." Let us remember that moral sin is a grievous offense against God and His law which makes him who commits it deserving of Hell. Thus, it is the greatest of all evils. Let us also remember that mortal sin involves 1) a seriously sinful matter, or something we think is a seriously sinful matter, 2) that we know it is a serious matter and 3) that we fully consent to do it. Further let us also recall that, when a person commits a mortal sin, God's life (Sanctifying Grace) leaves his soul immediately; and if he dies in this state, without having repented according to God's requirements for forgiveness (see the chapter on Perfect and Imperfect Contrition), he will go to Hell. True repentance requires turning from and giving up *all* mortal sin. Therefore, it is of the utmost importance that we uproot every mortal sin from our lives. Eliminating mortal sin should be the number one priority for anyone who wants to save his soul—to be placed first, before pleasing ourselves, our spouses, our relatives or our friends.

We should also remember in regard to eliminating mortal sin that most of the sins which we commit are *habitual*, that is, we tend to commit the same types of sins over and over again, and because we are creatures of habit, we must focus upon those wrongful things which we do *habitually*—especially the mortally sinful ones—because these habitual mortal sins are the sins that most easily will cause us to lose our souls. Moreover, the *"common"* mortal sins are usually the most dangerous to our salvation because they often do not carry a social stigma; and since a person can rationalize that "everyone is doing it," the horror of these deadly sins is greatly lost on the person who commits them.

Not every person commits *all* the possible sins, and not all the sins that a person commits are mortal sins—some are mortal and some are venial. But since venial sins, by themselves, will not condemn us to Hell, we need to focus our attention first of all on the common mortal sins and seek diligently to eradicate them from our lives, or carefully avoid them if we are not now committing them. Concomitant to eliminating mortal sin from our lives, we should also concentrate on eliminating all *purposeful* venial sins, realizing that venial sin is also very displeasing to God and can lead us into mortal sin.

The following distinctions regarding the nature or "anatomy" of sin should be kept in mind and will generally prove helpful: Catholic moral theologians distinguish between *material* and *formal* sin. "Material sin" is the "act" itself, the "thing" we do, the sin considered *objectively;* sometimes this is called the "matter" of sin. ("Material sin" corresponds to the first of the three elements required to constitute a mortal sin.) "Formal sin" is the act committed with the knowledge or understanding in our minds of the deed's sinfulness and with our free consent. It involves the judgment in our minds, or the *idea* we have, of the wrong we commit. It is called "formal" because the word "form" refers to "idea" or "principle," i.e., the mental part of sin, that which concerns our *understanding* of and *consent* to its wrongfulness. (Therefore, a "formal" mortal sin is a *real* mortal sin; it consists of all three necessary elements: serious matter, the knowledge of sufficient reflection, and full consent of the will.) Still another way to state the case is this: We commit only a "material sin" if we violate God's law without knowing it; we commit a "formal sin" if, in addition to doing the wrong, we have knowledge that it is wrong and still give our consent to it. Thus, it is conceivable for a person to commit a *material sin* without consciously *knowing* it is a sin (though he will most likely have at least an "uneasy feeling" about it)—and even a material *mortal* sin, without realizing or knowing fully that this sin in the objective order is a mortal sin. (In such a case, he would not be guilty of committing a mortal sin.)

In order to commit sin at all, we must *know*

the thing we are doing *is* a sin, or at least we must *think* it is a sin; in other words, *for sin to be morally imputable to us, it has to be FOR-MAL sin, not just MATERIAL sin.* Consequently, a person's culpability in committing a material mortal sin without realizing its gravity will be less than it would be had he known such a thing is a mortal sin. We cannot determine how God will judge any given case of sin because often a person's understanding of a particular sin will be somewhat different from another's. But it is entirely conceivable that somebody might commit a "material" mortal sin while not knowing "formally" ("in his mind") its true moral import or gravity. We can presume that one's conscience would alert him to the fact that a material mortal sin is in fact at least a sin *of some sort*, but that he might not realize it is a *mortal* sin is entirely possible; therefore, it is possible that God might not impute a mortal sin to a person who had such faulty knowledge of the morality of what he is doing. (Such a case then depends upon a person's ability to find out the truth of the matter.) But on the other hand, God still might hold a person responsible for having committed a mortal sin, for a person has the obligation to *find out* what the law of God requires. Therefore, while it is *possible* that we could be doing something mortally sinful and yet not be guilty before God of mortal sin, it is most probable that in a case like this we will at least have a suspicion that what we are doing is something wrong, and should we fail to find out if what we are doing is a mortal sin, especially if we suspect that it is, God will surely hold us accountable for any mortal sin we might commit because we hid from the truth.

In considering these common mortal sins, we should keep in mind that these are mortal sins *materially speaking*, that is, in the *objective view* of the acts themselves. That they all are not always mortal sins *formally speaking*, that is, interiorly or within the conscience of the sinner, is obvious, for the person must know that his thought, word, deed or omission is a mortal sin, and he must fully consent to it in order for it to be imputed against him.

We must realize too that in discussing these sins we will likely touch upon some "raw nerves" and raise perhaps a good deal of controversy, *for often we do not want* to be awakened from our moral lethargy. However, if we are going to be honest and thorough in our efforts to avoid Hell, we have to evaluate *everything* in our lives, even if this includes some mortal sins that we or our friends and loved ones may be committing. If we truly wish to avoid Hell, it will not do to hide the truth from our minds, or to pretend that certain mortal sins are not mortal sins but only venial sins. If they are mortal sins, we have to know that they are and eliminate them from our lives, if we are to save our souls. After all, if because of blinding ourselves to the truth, we should go to Hell, what consolation shall we derive, during our eternal sufferings, from the memory that during life we enjoyed a bit more peacefully our sinful but still restless lives because we had fooled ourselves somewhat regarding our moral predicament.

Nor can we criticize the Catholic Church for maintaining that these "common" mortal sins are in fact mortal sins, despite what many, or even the majority of people might say to the contrary, or for her being very explicit about which sins are *always* mortally sinful, despite their circumstances, and which therefore one must certainly avoid in order not to go to Hell. Further, the non-Catholic reader must realize that in speaking of the Catholic Church we are not talking here about a man-made religion, but about the *True Faith*, about "The faith of God" (*Mk.* 11:22; *Rom.* 3:3; *James* 2:1; *Apoc.* 14:12), about God's revealed Religion, about the Religion over which the Holy Spirit, the Third Person of the Blessed Trinity, has kept constant watch and which He guides by His grace, so that it always continues to teach what Jesus Christ taught and what He sent His Apostles out into the world to teach. We must realize too that God, having created us and having established a Hell for the punishment of the perversely wicked, who refuse to repent of their mortal sins, and having Himself come into the world in the person of Jesus Christ—God made man—to teach us, among other truths, about the existence of Hell . . . that God would certainly also have taught us *how to avoid Hell!* And God, being perfectly just, obviously makes no law that is impossible for us to keep. Hear Scripture on this point. "This commandment, that I command thee this day is not above thee. . ." (*Deuteronomy* 30:11). "And Jesus saith to him. . .all things are possible to him that believeth." (*Mk.* 9:22). "For this is the charity of God, that we keep his commandments: and his commandments are not heavy." (*1 Jn.* 5:3). "My grace is sufficient for thee." (*2 Cor.* 12:9). "And God is faithful, who will not suffer you to be tempted above that which you are able: but will make also with temptation issue, that you may be able to bear it." (*1 Cor.* 10:13).

The mocker must be silenced with regard to Hell and mortal sin because Christ, who has the authority to teach and who has proved Himself to be God made man, taught of Hell; and also He gave us *the means whereby to avoid it,* that is, 1) *a true and certain knowledge* of the Commandments through the teachings of the Catholic Church and 2) the *Seven Sacraments,* which are the wellfonts of His grace, to *sanctify us and, to help us overcome our sins* and perform our duties in life. Therefore, when we begin to reflect upon those things which we as moral agents must do and must avoid in order to save our souls, we will recognize the fact that, all the other things Christ taught being true, then those common sins which His Church designates as mortal sins must in fact *be* mortal sins in the objective order, and as such, things strictly to be avoided if we would save our souls. For Christ, in a very real sense, is synonymous with His Church, and His Church simply carries on throughout the world the mission He gave it—a mission which includes teaching all that He taught. In this regard, let us recall His commission to the Apostles: "Going therefore, teach ye all nations; baptizing them in the name of the Father, and of the Son, and of the Holy Ghost. *Teaching them to observe all things whatsoever I have commanded you: and behold I am with you all days, even to the consummation of the world.*" (*Matt.* 28:19-20, emphasis added).

As we consider these common mortal sins committed in our society today, we should realize that many of them, if not most, are sins which have also been committed throughout the ages. Most of these "common mortal sins" are also explicitly condemned in the Bible; others are condemned by reason of logical consequences from categories of sin that are condemned in general. For example, if adultery and fornication are mortal sins, then incest is obviously a mortal sin also.

As we mention these sins, it must be realized that *they are not the only mortal sins human beings commit* and that *in some cases* they may not even be judged by the sinner to be mortal sins, that is, they are not "formal" mortal sins, i.e., mortal sins in the mind and heart of the sinner who commits them; whereas, they are in fact "material" mortal sins, or mortal sins in the *objective* order.

We must also realize that some potentially mortal sins, because of the particular circumstances surrounding them, may be only venial sins—though a change of circumstances could make them mortal sins. We must remember, too, the all-important point that a mortal sin cannot be committed unless the person *knows* he is committing a mortal sin and fully consents to do it. And further, if the sinner suspects an act might be mortally sinful and goes ahead and commits it without investigating to determine the truth, he is then *guilty* of a mortal sin.

Next we must realize that certain sins are *always* mortal sins; circumstances with regard to these sins simply never alter the case. Examples of such sins, as we have seen earlier (Chapter II), would be, *first*, sins directly against God (such as blasphemy, rejecting the gift of the Catholic Faith, apostasy from that Faith, heresy, and schism); *then*, all sins of impurity (adultery, fornication, masturbation, homosexual acts, willfully taking pleasure in impure thoughts, coveting someone's spouse, etc.); and *finally*, certain other serious sins, such as willful murder, suicide, abortion, tubal ligation and vasectomy (for birth control reasons) and artificial birth control. Many types of sins can be either mortal or venial depending on the degree of seriousness of the particular act in question; examples of such types of sin would be lying, stealing, anger and neglect of one's obligations.

And one final point must be covered: *There*

are degrees of seriousness even among mortal sins. Just one mortal sin, however "light" it might be, is sufficient, if unrepented when we die, to take us to Hell; yet among mortal sins there still remain degrees of seriousness. Stealing a hundred dollars from a person who earns fifty dollars a day would not be so serious as abortion-murder, though both are mortal sins. This much said, let us consider some of the most common mortal sins, applying traditional Catholic moral principles.

Idolatry: Leading off and far and away the most common sins are those against the First Commandment, which Commandment perforce we must violate in order to commit *any* sin, and particularly a mortal sin, because in consciously committing any sin we are thereby putting some person or thing or deed or ourselves before God; and it is in this respect that the object of the sin becomes to us an "idol" or a false god. No, it is obviously not a potbellied Buddha or some statue before which we offer incense or bow down. No. Rather, it is a very *subtle* idol, but it is an idol nonetheless; and idolatry is condemned by God in the First Commandment. Presumably, many people would sin only venially in this regard because their pursuing the "things of this world" would not be to the *utter* exclusion of the love and service of God, or even to exclude God to a very extensive degree. If it were, the sin would be mortal. And yet there are many who, in the service of self, neglect God

entirely or to such a large degree as to constitute a mortal sin. Such persons would commit
mortal sin in so acting.

*Failure to pursue the knowledge, love and
service of God:* In violation also of the First
Commandment of God, the complete failure on
our part to pursue, at least to some degree, the
knowledge, love and service of God, would constitute a mortal sin. In other words, if we are
living *only* for this world and *only* for the pleasures and comforts we can gain from this world,
we are living in mortal sin, because the first of
the two Great Commandments is, "Thou shalt
love the Lord thy God with thy whole heart, thy
whole soul, with thy whole strength and with
thy whole mind," which means that we should
seek *God* first. Not to seek Him *at all* would constitute a violation of our very nature and the
Creator-creature relationship which demands
that man exercise his mind in the search for
truth—which ultimately leads to the knowledge,
love and service of God. (Presumably, to pursue
the knowledge, love and service of God *to only
a small degree* would also constitute a mortal
sin, though a lesser one than complete failure,
because Scripture says we are to love God with
our *"whole"* "heart," "soul," "mind" and
"strength."—*Mark* 12:30.)

Living for this world: A corollary to "failure
to pursue the knowledge, love and service of
God" would be failure to orient one's life *at all*
toward God, choosing rather to orient it *com-*

pletely toward one's self and toward the world and one's pleasure here in this world. Let us remember in this regard the words of Our Lord from the parable: "And I [a rich man] will say to my soul: Soul, thou hast much goods laid up for many years; take thy rest; eat, drink, make good cheer. But God said to him: Thou fool, this night do they require thy soul of thee: and whose shall those things be which thou hast provided?" (*Luke* 12: 19-20). In this regard, again, many people presumably would sin only venially because their living for this world would not be 100%. (Pursuing, for example, one's career with a total commitment, *so long as one still fulfills his other basic religious obligations and the other obligations of his state in life*, is not a sin at all against God. Far be it. It is actually a virtue, and what God expects. For whatever we do wholeheartedly in our proper vocation becomes also a service to our fellow man and a great tribute to Almighty God.) Here too, even if one did not live *quite* 100% for this world, if he were living *primarily* for this world, presumably he would still be committing a mortal sin because, again, we are to strive seriously to love God with our *"whole"* mind, heart and will. God does not want us to love Him by parts. "I would thou wert cold, or hot." (*Apoc.* 3:15).

Failure to seek the True Faith: A further corollary to the two sins mentioned immediately above would be failure of a non-Catholic to seek out the True Faith, at least if he were to suspect

that there *is* a True Faith and/or if he were to
suspect that the Catholic Religion is the True
Faith. For those readers who are non-Catholic,
this very book is a challenge to investigate the
claims of the Catholic Church. For if we fail to
investigate the Catholic Faith, after having been
told by somebody in a very serious, very forth-
right manner that it *is* the True Faith and that
we have an obligation to investigate it or we will
sin directly against God and also be guilty of the
other sins we might commit for having failed to
investigate and join it, then we are guilty of not
obeying the First Commandment, in that we are
choosing not to pursue the knowledge and love
and service of God. So long as we *consciously*
and *willfully* fail to investigate the truth of the
Catholic Faith, if we are not Catholic and we
suspect this is God's revealed Religion, we would
automatically commit a mortal sin because this
sin involves the gravest of matters—namely our
duty to our Creator and our own eternal salvation, for without being a Catholic one cannot
save his soul. (See pp. 151 *ff.* for an explanation
of this matter.) In this regard the *degree* of our
sinfulness hinges upon the *degree of our suspicion or knowledge* that the Catholic Church is
the True Faith in which God wants us to be. If
we have a *strong* suspicion that God wants all
people to worship Him as Catholics, and yet we
fail to investigate the credentials of the Catholic
Church, then we are guilty of a mortal sin—and
a very serious one, too—because, as mentioned,

the "matter" of this sin involves the proper worship of God and our eternal salvation.

Missing Sunday Mass: For Catholics purposely to miss Mass on Sunday or a Holyday of Obligation is a very common mortal sin. The Third Commandment of God commands that we (all people) keep holy the Lord's Day. And even though the requirement for Catholics of Sunday Mass attendance under pain of mortal sin is a law made by the leaders of the Church, it is just as binding upon Catholics as if God Himself had personally commanded it. For Our Lord said to St. Peter, the first Pope, "And I will give to thee the keys of the kingdom of heaven. And whatsoever thou shalt bind upon earth, it shall be bound also in heaven: and whatsoever thou shalt loose on earth, it shall be loosed also in heaven." (*Matt.* 16:19).

It is essential for us as Catholics to understand why the Church obliges us to attend Mass on Sundays and Holydays of Obligation. The Mass is the re-enactment or re-presentation of the Sacrifice of Christ on the Cross—both the Cross and the Mass have the same victim (Christ) and the same chief priest (Christ). They are *the same sacrifice*—only the *manner* of sacrifice is different. In the Mass, the sacrifice is accomplished in an unbloody manner. But Christ is truly there present at the Mass—Body, Blood, Soul and Divinity—who said, "For without me you can do nothing." (*John* 15:5). It is at the Mass that we receive the Body and Blood of Jesus Christ, who in regard to receiving the Eucharist said: "Except you eat the flesh of the Son of man, and drink his blood, you shall not have life in you. He that eateth my flesh, and drinketh my blood, hath everlasting life: and I will raise him up in the last day." (*John* 6:54-55).

Therefore, we either receive the Eucharist, or we are not assured of having the Divine Life of Jesus Christ in our souls, according to Our Lord's own words, and without this Divine Life in our souls, we will not go to Heaven. But the Eucharist is given to Catholics in connection with their participation in the Holy Sacrifice of the Mass. Therefore, we can infer that we either go to Mass or we do not go to Heaven. Therefore, in the wisdom of the Church, we are commanded either to go to Mass on Sundays and Holydays of Obligation or we commit a mortal sin—and if we die with a mortal sin on our soul, we will go to Hell...But, one might say that by not going to Mass and receiving the Body and Blood of Jesus Christ (which is one of the necessary *means* of salvation) we were going to Hell anyway, we might as well know for sure that we are going to Hell for not attending Mass on Sundays and Holydays of Obligation.

This law looks severe when viewed from the outside by a non-Catholic. But it proceeds from pretty simple logic as applied by the Catholic Church, which understands Scripture and which possesses the living Tradition that goes back in an unbroken chain to the Apostles themselves.

(We are not saying that non-Catholics or Catholics in the state of mortal sin should go to Communion—far from it! Such would be a mortal sin of sacrilege. Non-Catholics must first go through the process of conversion, and Catholics with mortal sin on their souls must first be absolved through Confession before receiving Communion. "Therefore whosoever shall eat this bread, or drink the chalice of the Lord unworthily, shall be guilty of the body and blood of the Lord... For he that eateth and drinketh unworthily, eateth and drinketh judgment to himself, not discerning the body of the Lord."—*1 Cor.* 11:27 & 29.)

But in addition to this reason for the obligation of Mass attendance on Sundays and holydays "under pain of mortal sin," there is a second, and actually a more fundamental reason, though one perhaps not so easily explained or grasped. And that is that *the Mass is the specific homage (or worship) that God has designated man must offer Him.* For the Mass is actually the Sacrifice of the Cross re-enacted in an unbloody manner, a sacrifice wherein *God (Christ) offers to God (the Father)* the infinite worship and reparation for sin that Divine Justice requires. Man, being finite, cannot make this fundamental reparation, since it must possess an infinite quality; but in assisting at the offering of the Mass, man can join in the infinite offering of Christ. The priest who offers the Mass cooperates with Christ, the Principal Priest (or

"Offerer") of each Mass, by using the power given to him at his ordination to offer this Sacrifice. And the people join with the priest in a mystical sharing in the offering. Still, the Mass is principally God (Christ, the principal Priest at every Mass) offering to God (the Father) an infinitely meritorious offering, namely, His own (Christ's) death on the Cross.

Now our assisting at the Sacrifice of the Mass, the re-enactment of the Sacrifice of the Cross, is how God wants and requires man to worship Him. The Catholic Church in her wisdom knows this and therefore requires of her faithful members, under pain of mortal sin, attendance on Sundays and Holydays of Obligation at this one homage which God accepts as worthy to satisfy His justice. Further, the Church teaches that all our prayers, offerings, charities, etc. are acceptable by God only through and because of the Mass; and all the blessings and benefits we receive from God are received only through and because of the Mass—whether we be Catholic or non-Catholic! The Mass is of such *total importance* to man's eternal well-being that the Catholic Church simply requires, under pain of mortal sin, that her members attend each Sunday and Holyday of Obligation.

Unnecessary work on Sundays and Holydays of Obligation: Working on Sundays can be a mortal sin, *especially when the work is unnecessary and willfully habitual.* The most common and flagrant violation of this precept would be working at one's paid employment seven days a week. If the company one works for has so much work that its management thinks it needs to work on Sunday, then it should expand its workforce, buildings, equipment, etc., and *not* destroy its employees by making them attempt the impossible by working seven days a week. (If one is employed at a business that needs to be open on Sunday, such as a restaurant or a gasoline station, he must be sure to take one day off *during* the week and treat it as he would a Sunday.) Another common example of unnecessary work on Sunday would be working around the home and around the yard. (This might also involve a person in giving serious scandal to others, which may or may not be a mortal sin in itself). Many people enjoy gardening, yard work, washing the car, etc. on Sunday as a form of relaxation. Therefore, they can legitimately ask, "What is wrong with that?" The most obvious thing that is wrong is it is a scandal to others, if others see it, for others cannot look inside us and see that we are doing this work for enjoyment. They will just see us as working. *But further, it can very easily be harmful to ourselves—physically, mentally and spiritually—even though we may not be immediately aware of it.*

To use Sunday to catch up on our household chores and shopping is to profane the Lord's Day, which is a day to be set aside from our regular earthly pursuits. Such work and shopping, depending on its extent and frequency, can be a mortal sin. Obviously, some light work activity in the home is necessary every day, even on Sundays and Holydays of Obligation. Therefore, as a practical norm, the Church has regularly taught that any work around the house exceeding two hours would violate the prohibition against working on Sundays.

The Old Testament is quite clear about our not doing "any" work on the Sabbath, either by man or beast. "Remember that thou keep holy the sabbath day. Six days thou shalt labour, and shall do all thy works. But on the seventh day is the sabbath of the Lord thy God: *thou shalt do no work on it*, thou nor thy son, nor thy daughter, nor thy manservant, nor thy maidservant, nor thy beast, nor the stranger that is within thy gates. For in six days the Lord made heaven and earth, and the sea, and all things that are in them, and rested on the seventh day: therefore the Lord blessed the seventh day, and sanctified it." (*Exodus* 20:8-11, emphasis added). And that is God's *law*, not man's *choice! Nor is it just a nice old custom.* Sunday should be devoted to the worship of God, extra prayers, visiting the sick and one's relatives, rest and relaxation. It is intended as a day when we *stop pursuing earthly goals and pay special homage to God.* Whereas gardening, yardwork, etc. admittedly can be rehabilitative and enjoyable to the person doing them, they are done basically *in pursuit of earthly goals* and not for God. And if we do such activities on Sundays, rather than say extra prayers, visit the sick, rest, recreate, etc., are we thereby "keeping *holy*" the Sabbath day? Are we not rather just plain "serving ourselves," as little gods preferred before the one, true God?

The harder one works and the busier he or she is, the more that person needs Sunday as a "day of rest" in order to recuperate and be effective during the following week. The human body, mind and soul are constituted on a seven-day "clock" that is built into human nature by the Creator. Though some people may *appear* to be able to override this built-in seven-day cycle—whereby, on the seventh day a person needs rest—what actually happens is that the person who works seven days a week will be forced to take a break or will get sick during the following week (which the casual observer may never notice as connected to his Sunday work). And should he be able to keep going for a while, eventually something in his life breaks down—his health, his psychological well-being, his marriage, etc. Indeed, the blame may not be attributed to working seven days a week, but the cause is there nonetheless.

And finally, and most importantly, if we work seven days a week, when shall we ever "straighten our backs" and think of the eternal verities and study what it is that God expects of us to save our souls? We well might say to ourselves, "Oh, God does not begrudge us washing our cars, pulling some weeds or cutting the grass on Sunday." But what we do not realize is that doing these things means *we are not doing something else*, namely pursuing the knowledge of God. If we are perpetually busy with some type of earthly work, when shall we ever think deeply, pray, and devote time to God? Many of us need a nap on Sunday just to recuperate physically from the labor of our previous week. If the rest of Sunday is spent in work, when shall we think, pray, study, in order to grow in the knowledge and love of God? The bad physical, psychological and spiritual effects of working seven days a week may be too subtle for most people to discern in their lives, but they remain there nonetheless, exercising a baneful influence out of all proportion to what would *appear* to be a "small" offense.

Shopping on Sundays: Along this line, shopping on Sundays can be a mortal sin, especially depending on the amount of time spent at it and the frequency. Here again, moralists may debate one side or another of this particular action, but there should be nobody who has any doubts that routine shopping on Sunday is definitely a sin, and, at the very least, a very serious venial sin, for the Third Commandment of God states, "Remember thou keep *holy* the Lord's day" (emphasis added). Shopping is the conducting of a routine type of worldly business and the carrying on of our regular, "secular," Monday-through-Saturday occupations. How shall we justify to Our Lord on Judgment Day our shopping on Sunday in the face of so clear a Commandment? Obviously, buying a tank of gasoline during a trip on Sunday would not be a sin at all, or going into a restaurant to buy a meal, which we need for the nourishing of our bodies. But going to buy clothes or to buy a car or to buy something that can be purchased at any time during the week is going to be at least a venial sin, and very possibly a mortal sin, especially so if one shops on a regular basis on Sunday. Also we must remember that by shopping on Sundays we are, by our action, requiring other people to work unnecessarily on Sunday, and we are making it profitable for businesses, by our patronage, to stay open on Sunday, all in violation of keeping holy the Lord's day. (All this is not to mention giving scandal to others.)

Usurping the headship of the family: Under the Fourth Commandment, Catholic moral theologians have stated that for a wife *needlessly* to usurp the headship of the family from her husband is a mortal sin. People are all different, and it could very well happen that a woman is more intelligent, more decisive and stronger-willed than her husband, and she could find it very possible and maybe very easy to take over from him the leadership role in the family, especially if he is compliant in giving it up. But such a reversal of roles is not God's will, and, in fact, it is so contrary to God's will that some moral theologians consider it a mortal sin when done without a good reason. For it disorients the entire family—the wife, the husband and the children—

it makes the wife and husband miserable, and
it destroys the proper role models of father and
mother to their children, thus confusing them;
plus, it can lead to disastrous decisions for the
overall well-being of everyone in the family. Conversely, for a husband to tolerate this usurpa-
tion and not to take stringent action against it,
or to condone it, would be at least a serious venial
sin. In the event that the husband simply refuses
to take the headship of the family, or if he is
unable to (because of sickness, being away, etc.)
or if he is totally irresponsible, the wife would
have no other choice. Therefore, in this particular case, due to a change of circumstances, there
would be no sin at all, let alone a mortal sin.
*Conversely, for a husband to allow himself to
act so irresponsibly and childishly that his wife
must run the family, would therefore also be a
mortal sin.*

Many people today are confused regarding the
proper Christian role of headship and fatherhood
in the family—due in large part to the fact we
live in a secular society, one where the controllers
of the mass media have consistently projected
a pitiable image of manhood and authority, such
that practically speaking there is little in the way
of a role model for husbands to pattern themselves upon. But God created human beings
"male and female" (*Gen.* 1:27; 5:2; *Matt.* 19:4)
and in marriage He placed the man over the
woman to be her head. "But I would have you
to know, that the head of every man is Christ;

and the head of the woman is man...For the man is not of the woman, but the woman of the man. For the man was not created for the woman, but the woman for the man." (*1 Cor.* 11:3, 8, 9). Because men and women are equal before God as human beings, and because the special relationship of subordination of the wife to the husband in marriage should be well understood, therefore here we can do no better than cite a beautiful passage from the encyclical letter of Pope Pius XI to the entire Catholic world, entitled *Christian Marriage* (1930):

"There should flourish in it [the marriage relationship] that 'order of love,' as St. Augustine calls it. This order includes both the primacy of the husband with regard to the wife and children, the ready subjection of the wife and her willing obedience, which the Apostle commends in these words: 'Let women be subject to their husbands as to the Lord, because the husband is the head of the wife, as Christ is the head of the Church.' (*Eph.* 5:22-23).

"This subjection, however, does not deny or take away the liberty which fully belongs to the woman, both in view of her dignity as a human person, and in view of her most noble office as wife and mother and companion; nor does it bid her obey her husband's every request if not in harmony with right reason or with the dignity due to [the] wife; nor, in fine, does it imply that the wife should be put on a level with those persons who in law are called minors, to whom it is not customary to allow free exercise of their rights on account of their lack of mature judgment, or of their ignorance of human affairs. But it forbids that exaggerated liberty which cares not for the good of the family; it forbids that in this body which is the family, the heart be separated from the head to the great detriment of the whole body and the proximate danger of ruin. For if the man is the head, the woman is the heart, and as he occupies the chief place in ruling, so she may and ought to claim for herself the chief place in love.

"Again, this subjection of wife to husband in its degree and manner may vary according to the different conditions of persons, place and time. In fact, if the husband neglect his duty, it falls to the wife to take his place in directing the family. *But the structure of the family and its fundamental law, established and confirmed by God, must always and everywhere be maintained intact.* [Emphasis added.]

"With great wisdom Our Predecessor Leo XIII, of happy memory, in the Encyclical on *Christian Marriage* [1880] which We have already mentioned, speaking of this order to be maintained between man and wife, teaches: 'The man is the ruler of the family, and the head of the woman; but because she is flesh of his flesh and bone of his bone, let her be subject and obedient to the man, not as a servant but as a companion, so that nothing be lacking of honor or of dignity in the obedience which she pays. Let divine charity be the constant guide of their mutual relations, both in him who rules and in her who obeys, since each bears the image, the one of Christ, the other of the Church.' "

Suicide: In committing suicide a person chooses to die virtually in the very act of committing a mortal sin, and anyone who dies in this state will be damned for all eternity. Thus, suicide, the taking of our own life, is an especially dangerous mortal sin to our salvation because there is no guarantee that between the time of the fatal deed and the time our soul leaves the body we will have both the time and the grace needed to undergo a change of heart and make an act of perfect contrition and thus save our souls. (If we know someone who has committed suicide, we are always permitted to hope for his salvation because God's grace can work wonders, and there is no definite way of knowing just when the soul leaves the body. But in general we must admit it does not look good for the salvation of those who die by suicide.)

Suicide, being a form of murder, is obviously a mortal sin. But further, it is also a form of *blasphemy* against God because it implies that there is no good reason for our continued existence in this life. Now if this were true, then we are in effect calling into question God's wisdom and judgment in putting us here and/or in leaving us here. "See ye that I alone am, and there is no other God besides me: I will kill and I will make to live: I will strike, and I will heal, and there is none that can deliver out of my hand.'' (*Deuteronomy* 32:39).

The rate of suicide in the past three decades has grown to an alarming degree—which speaks louder than words that people do not have the True Faith. The Catholic religion teaches that *at any time* in our lives we can still lead a spiritually useful existence. At any time we can repent of our sins, and at any time we can still gain an increase in Sanctifying Grace (God's life in our souls)—i.e., we can gain merit for a higher place in Heaven. Also, the Church teaches that by our sufferings we can *expiate* or pay back to God the spiritual debt we have left over from our forgiven sins. Thus, it is exactly when we are most melancholy or depressed or in pain that we can best repay God's justice here on earth for the punishment due to the sins we have committed—by offering Him the sufferings we are undergoing because of our melancholy, depression or pain. The Catholic Church teaches us that we all have to satisfy God's justice for the spiritual debts due to our sins, either here on earth (by our sufferings, prayers, good deeds, almsgiving, etc.) or in Purgatory. Therefore, those painful states of mind that might lead a person without the Faith to commit suicide are themselves the very ''spiritual money'' we can use to ''pay the bills'' we owe to God—and even to ''pay the bills'' of the Poor Souls in Purgatory or to win the conversion of non-Catholic people or those in the state of mortal sin. Catholics are taught that suicide is *never* a legitimate answer to life's problems, for it will most likely earn a person a quick entrance into Hell because he will likely not have the time or receive the grace to make an act of Perfect Contrition for this sin before his soul leaves the body.

Birth Control: One of the most common mortal sins committed today is artificial birth control. It is committed by both the married and the single. This sin frustrates God's plan for new people to be brought into the world so that they can eventually go to Heaven. It is primarily a grievous offense against God, His law, and His Providence; but it also hurts society because it deprives society of new members, who are necessary to replace those who die; plus, it harms the people who practice it.

Birth control harms the unmarried because it allows them to continue in the mortal sin of fornication without the normal result of children. If artificial birth control were not available to sexually promiscuous single people, children would soon be born to their unholy alliance, which fact would very likely lead them to marriage or to discontinue their relationship. In either event, with a baby or babies on their hands, they would soon become ''other-oriented,'' and new life would have come into the world, fulfilling *at least* the first part of God's plan for the birth and rearing of children. But with artificial means of birth control being available, such sinners continue in their sin, oftentimes during the complete child-bearing years of the woman (and beyond), such that they never have the children God intended them to have, and they end up in middle and old age without a family to succor and support them and with only a well-entrenched vice as the byproduct of their sin, a vice that will surely take them to Hell if they do not renounce it with true repentance before they die.

Artificial birth control harms the married who practice it because the whole orientation of their marriage is shifted from accepting God's plan of love, self-sacrifice, babies, new people for society, new saints for Heaven, joy and peace for the couple, a contented old age, and prosperity for society. . .to their own miserable plan of "wealth" and "happiness" in this world, a piling up of luxuries and selfish pleasures and the very great risk of divorce. (After all, those who use the privilege of marriage but avoid children are basically living for their own pleasures, and when trouble arises in their marriage, as it does in almost all marriages, what is more logical to the self-indulgent than to continue to seek their own pleasure by getting divorced? Are not the facts of the present divorce rate—one out of two marriages here in the U.S.A.—proof of this claim?)

So bad is the sin of artificial birth control that God, in Old Testament times, slew Onan, the grandson of Jacob and the son of Juda, for practicing this sin. Let us read this episode as recorded in *Genesis:*

"At that time Juda went down from his brethren, and turned in to a certain Odollamite, named Hiras. And he saw there the daughter of a man of Chanaan, called Sue: and taking her to wife, he went in unto her. And she conceived, and bore a son, and called his name Her. And conceiving again, she bore a son, and called him Onan. She bore also a third: whom she called Sela. After whose birth, she ceased to bear any more. And Juda took a wife for Her his firstborn, whose name was Thamar. And Her, the firstborn of Juda, was wicked in the sight of the Lord: and was slain by him. Juda therefore said to Onan his son: Go in to thy brother's wife and marry her, that thou mayst raise seed to thy brother. He, knowing that the children should not be his, when he went in to his brother's wife, spilled his seed upon the ground, lest children should be born in his brother's name. And therefore the Lord slew him, because he did a detestable thing." —Genesis 38:1-10.

It is a common misconception among non-Catholics (and even among some Catholics) that the prohibition against artificial birth control is *a man-made Church REGULATION.* The fact, however, is that artificial birth control violates what is called in philosophy the "Natural Law," that is, the law which God built into nature when

He created it, and which man's mind can understand with his reason unaided by divine revelation. The Popes—Paul VI in *Human Life* (*Humanae Vitae*), 1969 and Pius XI in *Christian Marriage* (*Casti Canubii*), 1930—have pointed out this fact. The Catholic Church, in condemning artificial birth control, is simply upholding *God's law*, the Natural Law, as He incorporated it into the very nature of the things He created. It is extremely easy for the mind of man to understand that God created sexual relations in such a manner that when naturally performed and culminated this activity will produce babies (if one of the parties is not sterile) and that *the purpose of this activity, as God created it, is in fact to produce babies!* It is very easy for our minds to comprehend that when we perform the procreative act just to please ourselves and use some means to prevent the conception of a child (or its normal growth to term), we are by this artificial birth control committing an unnatural act and thereby *frustrating* the plan which God created for children to be born. We are going against God's will, opposing our wills to His! (Artificial birth control is analogous to the perverted practice of eating and then purposely disgorging the meal—thus seeking the pleasure, but rejecting the purpose of the act.)

With birth control so common a practice today, it may not occur to the minds of those who practice this sin that it is grievously (mortally) sinful in the eyes of God, but it is, as witnessed by

God's slaying Onan in the episode from *Genesis* cited above.

The pharisaical, in regard to this episode from *Genesis*, argue that the Lord slew Onan because he would not follow what is called the "Levirate law," a strictly *Hebrew custom* (requiring a man to raise up children in his brother's name if his brother died childless) and not because he "spilled his seed upon the ground" (a primitive form of birth control called *coitus interruptus*, or "withdrawal") and because he thereby violated *God's law*. The foolishness of this opinion is obvious: Would God slay a human being for failure to follow a strictly Hebrew law of custom? What kind of God would He be to behave in such a capricious manner? It is obvious that Onan was slain for violating *God's law* with regard to procreation; he was going through the motions of the procreative act, and yet he was not cooperating in God's plan for new people to be born, and therefore God slew him as an example to us.

It might well be asked, "Why is there only this *one* powerful condemnation of birth control in the Bible? Why are there not other passages in Scripture as well?" The answer to this objection is threefold: First, how many people does the Lord have to slay in order to get our attention and make us acknowledge the wrongfulness of this sin? Second, how would there be a "test" for us in this life if God made the obvious ridiculous in regard to this sin by killing many people who engage in this act. And third, the Bible *does* record other references to birth control, but more in the form of abortion and infanticide, for the refined techniques of birth control available to modern man were totally unknown in biblical times. Witness: "And it was not enough for them to err about the knowledge of God...for...they sacrifice their own children [infanticide]...so that now they neither keep life [abortion], nor marriage undefiled." (*Wis.* 14:22-24).

Abortion: Under the Fifth Commandment abortion-murder today is obviously a very common mortal sin. In the United States it is estimated that just over one million 500 thousand children are killed by abortion-murder every year. Worldwide, the figure is estimated at 25 million per year! Abortion-murder as it is practiced today flows directly out of the birth control mentality and is really a heinous form of birth control. That abortion is a common sin does not make it any the less serious for the persons committing it. That we call this sin "abortion" does not make it any the less a case of murder, which is specifically forbidden by the Fifth Commandment: *"Thou shalt not kill!"* (*Exodus* 20:13).

Tubal ligation and vasectomy: In the genre of birth control sins, tubal ligation and vasectomy for birth control purposes are also mortal sins. These are not only mortal sins of artificial birth control (and therefore in violation of the Sixth Commandment), but they are sins against the Fifth Commandment of God as well, which prohibits self-mutilation.

(With regard to the Sixth Commandment in general and the whole issue of sexuality and chastity, it is God who has provided us with the sexual faculty, and we are to utilize it only in the marital state. And only that use is legitimate which is done in a natural manner that will allow the conception of children to result. Any other use of the sexual faculty is a mortal sin, *"materially speaking"*; it is a mortal sin *"formally speaking"* if the person knows in his heart or has been informed that it is a mortal sin.)

Adultery: Sexual relations between a man and a woman who are not man and wife, and at least one of whom is married to someone else, is called adultery. This is the sin *expressly* forbidden by the Sixth Commandment. (By implication, of course, the Commandment also covers all sins against purity as well.) The evil of adultery is that it is a fundamental violation of the integrity of the marital relationship, is a grave act of injustice against one's spouse, jeopardizes the continuance of the family, leads to divorce, risks the birth of an illegitimate child, not infrequently leads to murder, and generally perpetuates itself until some additional dire consequence finally occurs. To the would-be adulterer the warning of Scripture surely fits: "He that troubleth his own house, shall inherit the winds." (*Prov.* 11:29). Further, adulterers have all the same problems as fornicators with regard to committing additional sins to keep their relationship secret and to try to avoid the birth of children. (See below, under "Fornication.") Adultery is always a mortal sin because it is always a grievous offense against the Law of God. Nor can the adulterer really plead ignorance of the Law as an excuse—if for no other reason than because he realizes all the severe repercussions that will occur if the offended mate discovers the adultery.

Fornication: Sexual relations between a man and woman who are not married is called fornication. This sin too is always mortal because it is a grievous offense against the law of God. Fornication without the additional sin of artificial birth control will usually lead fairly soon to the birth of a child out of wedlock, a child whom the sinning parents are usually not ready to receive. Children come into the world as helpless creatures, who for many years need the constant care of the mother and the financial support of the father, not to mention the early religious instruction and training in good character which are so necessary in a person's childhood. The fornicator has not thought this through, or if he has, he (or she) chooses to disregard these facts. But in our time, most people who commit fornication resort either to artificial birth control to avoid children—which is a worse sin than the fornication, because it is an unnatural act—or to abortion, which is a particularly heinous murder, as discussed earlier. Thus, fornicators (like adulterers) compound their sins. They often become liars besides, to conceal what they have done. And further, once this sin is committed, they generally continue to commit it, oftentimes with more than one partner. The end of it all is some combination of sorrow over losing their virginity, a feeling of being trapped, premature responsibilities, wounding their parents, the (at least partial) wasting of their lives, success and fortunes, and terrible regrets—a *high price* to pay in this world for a certain ticket to Hell in the next—if one lets this sin go unrepented.

Incest: Sexual relations between members of the same family is called incest. It is a particularly terrible type of adultery or fornication because it involves the breach of a most sacred trust by a father, brother, uncle, etc. This sin brings the child into intimate contact with moral corruption and takes away his or her most precious possessions, innocence and virginity. Plus, it generally corrupts the child, causes tremendous psychological damage, and gravely disorients him so that it is very difficult for him to come to proper maturity and an appreciation of chastity. Furthermore, the entire family where incest is carried on becomes disrupted. Those who practice this sin or who are tempted to it should recall Our Lord's words: "But he that shall scandalize one of these little ones that believe in me, it were better for him that a millstone should be hanged about his neck, and that he should be drowned in the depth of the sea." (*Matt.* 18:6). Of course God is infinitely merciful and can and will forgive any sin, including incest, but one should avoid it if tempted and cease immediately if involved in it. For the spiritual debt (temporal punishment) attendant to this sin will be very great.

Rape: Rape is sexual relations forced upon one person by another. Usually, this involves the natural form of sexual activity, and it is always mortally sinful because it involves *several* grave matters. Rape is also a serious crime in civil law, and a fairly common occurrence in our modern (now almost Godless) society. Usually, it involves a man forcing his evil desires upon a woman. Younger men in particular must be on guard against this sin, which is the byproduct of an unbridled nature in which impurity, self-will, violence and pride have overpowered right reason. This sin is very often fueled by pornographic books, magazines, movies and videos, which everyone has an obligation to avoid. But further, there even exists some rather well-known literature in which rape is mentioned and almost extolled, because it demonstrates (misguidedly, of course) what would parade as the virtues of masculinity, strength and decisiveness in our present social context where men have consistently been portrayed as weak and simpering.

But the reality is that rape is particularly wicked because it does great moral violence to the offended person and usually inflicts psychological damage that often lasts a lifetime. Plus, it often leads to physical injury and death for the victim. Rape might well be called the ultimate impurity, for the rapist lets nothing stand in the way of his determination to have satisfaction. Those tempted to this sin should realize that in the Old Testament, rape was punishable by death, so serious is this sin and crime.

Anyone tempted to this sin should realize that he has allowed himself to come to the brink of being totally out of control of himself, and he should seek the counsel of a holy priest on how to channel and bring into submission his sexual desires, for this dreadful sin—terribly grievous in itself—almost always leads very quickly to other tragedy.

Concubinage or "living together": People today often "live together" in a marital-type relationship with a friend of the opposite sex. The slang expressions for this sin are "shacking up," "living in," "living together." St. Paul calls it "chambering." "Let us walk honestly, as in the day: not in rioting and drunkenness, not in *chambering* and *impurities*, not in contention and envy: But put ye on the Lord Jesus Christ, and make not provision for the flesh and its concupiscences." (*Rom.* 13:13-14, emphasis added).

Were it not for the common practice of artificial birth control, such "living in" or living together would be called common-law marriage, for children would soon be the result of such relationships. But people today most often do not think of these "live-in" relationships as permanent, and therefore they are merely the mortal sin of fornication, usually with the added mortal sins of birth control and/or abortion and scandal to compound the guilt. Illicit sexual liaisons have been with man since the beginning of time, but they always have been mortally sinful, and they still are.

Those tempted to engage in the sinful sexual relationship of "living together" should realize they will be entering a moral quagmire, for soon many of the normal marital bonds develop in their relationship—physical, emotional and financial ties form; habits and interdependences take root; the relationship solidifies, binding the two people in some respects as though they *were* married and drastically weakening their ability to terminate their sinful union. *But still, the relationship is NOT marriage*, and it *is* a scandal to others.

"Live-in" fornication and adultery, even when they ape marriage by carrying many of the trappings of marriage, remain just that and will never be anything different in the eyes of God, whose law is being broken. People who enter such a relationship are just kidding themselves if they think it is not sinful. "No fornicator, or unclean, or covetous person (which is a serving of idols) hath inheritance in the kingdom of Christ and of God." (*Eph.* 5:5). Again, the passage on scandal: "And whoever shall scandalize one of these little ones that believe in me; it were better for him that a millstone were hanged about his neck, and he were cast into the sea." (*Mark* 9:41; also, cf. *Matt.* 18:6 and *Luke* 17:2). (To scandalize is to do something wrong that is likely to induce someone else to do something morally wrong. It is obvious that couples living together have caused widespread scandal to others, for this sin is now pretty much accepted in society; whereas, it used to be recognized as the serious sin it is.)

Masturbation: Covered also under the Sixth Commandment, masturbation (the sin of impurity committed with one's own body) is one of the most common of mortal sins. Yet because this sin *is* very common, especially in developing boys, many want to dismiss it as a venial sin at worst, and some would even say it is no sin at all. Psychologists, for example, will claim that it is simply a normal part of growing up. However, the Church has always taught that masturbation is gravely (mortally) sinful, and St. Thomas Aquinas, the greatest theologian in the history of the Catholic Church, tells us that masturbation is an even worse mortal sin than fornication, because masturbation is unnatural.

Homosexual acts: And if masturbation is worse than fornication because it is contrary to nature, then homosexual acts are even worse yet, because they are a far worse perversion and involve a second party; they are in one sense more difficult to overcome because there is a second party to tempt a person to sin again and again; and they steadily contaminate more and more victims, as homosexuals spread their perversion to those not previously infected.

Impure thoughts and desires: Among sexual sins, a very common mortal sin is willfully taking pleasure in impure thoughts and desires, that is, thoughts and desires of sexual actions other than those legitimate acts between one's self and one's marriage partner. (Even these latter thoughts and desires are dangerous, because they could lead to some kind of impure sexual act, alone or with another who is not one's marriage partner.) With regard to impure thoughts, we should always remember the warning of Our Lord: "Whosoever shall look on a woman to lust after her, hath already committed adultery with her in his heart." *(Matt.* 5:28). And with regard to married people's mentally dwelling upon the delights of their sexual activities, they should remember the advice of St. Paul: "That they also who have wives, be as if they had none." *(1 Cor.* 7:29).

Immodesty in dress: Anyone tempted to or engaging in immodesty of dress should ponder the following passages of Scripture and consider how they relate to the sin of immodesty: "But I say to you, that whosoever shall look on a woman to lust after her, hath already committed adultery with her in his heart." *(Matt.* 5:28). "Do not err: neither fornicators . . . nor adulterers . . . shall possess the Kingdom of God." *(1 Cor.* 6:9-10). "Am I my brother's keeper?" *(Gen.* 4:9). Modesty, especially in dress, is a virtue cultivated among Catholics knowledgeable in their faith because of the teaching of the Church that to take pleasure in impure thoughts is a mortal sin. Despite the fact that the current "Women's Liberation Movement" (promoted so universally by the mass media) would seem to want to blur the distinction between men and women, the Bible says, "And God created man to his own image: to the image of God he created him: *male and female he created them.*" (*Gen.* 1:27, emphasis added). Now the male is by nature the "aggressor," so to speak, the initiator, the forward one, in the male-female relationship. And a man is amorously attracted to a woman largely by sight in the initial stages; also, his initial sexual interest is triggered largely by *looking* at a woman. If, therefore, a woman is immodestly dressed, a man's amorous inclinations can quickly develop into thoughts of lust, and therefore, women have an especially grave obligation to dress modestly. By nature, a woman likes to adorn herself so that she is attractive, and it is this very fact that does attract men. But it is sinful for a woman to dress immodestly and merely say to herself that men do not have to look at her if they are going to be thinking evil thoughts. Of a given occasion a woman's immodesty may not bother some men (for a number of possible reasons), but in most cases, human nature being fallen as it is, the man *will* look at the woman's immodesty, *and the woman's immodesty* WILL *be a danger to his purity of thought*. Therefore, women who dress immodestly, or who are tempted to do so, should remember the murderer Cain's taunting question to God, "Am I my brother's keeper?" (*Gen.* 4:9).

If a man's willful impure thoughts toward a woman ("lusting after her") is a mortal sin because he "hath already committed adultery with her in his heart" (*Matt.* 5:28), then what sort of sin does the immodest woman commit who has been the occasion of these impure thoughts in a man by her immodesty, especially where it is purposeful and willful? Is she not also a murderer of sorts—one who at least helps to kill the life of grace in the soul of the man who lusts after her? The Church teaches that impure thoughts willfully taken pleasure in are mortal sins. Therefore, for a woman *purposefully* to dress immodestly where she will be seen by men is, *materially* speaking, a mortal sin, i.e., the deed itself is the matter of mortal sin. Of course, whether she actually commits a mortal sin (formally), i.e., in her heart, will surely depend upon her level of realization about the serious problems to purity her immodesty causes men. But surely too, God will to *some* degree at least hold her culpable for the impurity of thought, desire and even action that she helps to cause, and very possibly she will be committing a mortal sin, depending on the degree of her immodesty and the level of her awareness about the effects of her immodesty upon men.

As there are some realities about the feminine nature that men will never fully understand—because they never experience those things—so with impurity of thought in men induced by immodesty in women; it is something women will never fully appreciate because it is not within the realm of their experience. Therefore, women should take serious heed in this matter strictly on what they are told about it, because immodesty is something God will hold women accountable for.

The crucial question in any discussion of modesty, of course, is what exactly constitutes modesty for women. One can only speak in terms of general principles, and these will depend upon the occasion: whether it be normal daily activity, sports, swimming, etc. In general, the principles are these: 1) That clothing should tend to conceal rather than reveal; 2) that clothing should not be transparent; 3) that women's legs should be covered at least to just below the knees (this would apply in particular to normal daily activity); 4) that women should avoid sleeveless dresses and blouses; 5) that sheer, tight clothing should be avoided altogether; 6) that under most circumstances a woman should avoid wearing slacks and that when necessity may dictate their use that they should be loose-fitting rather than tight-fitting; and 7) that the neckline should not be less than two fingers' width below the pit of the throat.

By contemporary standards, such norms will be ludicrous to most women because our secular society makes immodesty in women a commonplace by the manufacture and promotion of immodest fashions. We must remember, however, that we are speaking here about true morality—about God's law and not man's customs or preferences. Yet if those parts of the female anatomy are to be covered and generally concealed which are most suggestive to men, then these principles need to be followed. (These guidelines follow those laid down by the Cardinal Vicar of Pope Pius XI in 1928.)

What about the beach, or sports or extremely hot weather. The general principles of modesty—especially with regard to concealing rather than revealing—still apply. A woman will have to use common sense in these cases and take some extra precautions, realizing she has a heavy responsibility in this regard. In hot weather a woman can wear a dress that is loose, light and cool and yet is still modest. At sport she can be innovative in order to be modest, depending on the activity. For the beach she can wear some type of pullover or cover-up garment save for the time she is actually swimming. Choice of a swimming suit for women today is extremely important. Most women's bathing suits are grossly immodest—due to being too skimpy, too tight or too sheer. A woman may have to make or provide her own combination that will be modest, but if that is what it takes to be modest she should do so.

When women are at sport or at the beach, men need to prepare themselves in advance by not going there to gawk, but they should realize they will be seeing women dressed for those occasions.

If they cannot avoid consenting to impure thoughts, they are duty-bound not to go to these places!

Lest this entire discussion of immodesty would appear to take no cognizance of immodesty in men and the problems it can cause to women, a word needs to be said about the man's obligations in this regard. Men should avoid even partial nudity where women will be present. They too should avoid tight clothing, especially tight pants. Men's shirts should be buttoned at least to within one button of the neck, and men should avoid wearing "muscle shirts" (undershirt style) and shirts that are tight and/or without sleeves.

People who wish to be moral in regard to modesty should realize that worldly fashions tend to take no cognizance of modesty or morality in dress. Therefore, any reference to "fashion" when it comes to the morality of modesty is simply futile. The norms for modesty must be Christian (Christlike) and based upon the reality of human frailty, not upon what is *a la mode* with the fashion world. (Modern fashions are often so immodest that one could well believe there is a conspiracy afoot to foster immodesty and therefore immorality.) The person who wants to obey God's law relative to modesty needs to realize that we all have a moral obligation with respect to our neighbor's purity of thought and therefore an obligation not to dress in any manner which would tend to lead him into sin.

Prolonged kissing, etc.: Any actions which give

venereal pleasure and/or arouse the sexual passions are mortal sins for those who are not married and also for those who are who might engage in such activities with someone other than their spouses. There are some actions which by their very nature tend to cause sexual arousal in the normal person. These are always to be avoided. Some people are unusually sensitive; such people also need to avoid *what for them* is the near occasion of sins of impurity, though the same thing might be no problem for most others.

Prolonged kisses and/or prolonged kissing is a mortal sin because it can easily arouse venereal pleasure and the sexual passions, which in turn can lead a person to commit fornication or adultery. This is particularly true of open-mouth kissing (sometimes called French kissing) wherein the participants touch tongues. This type of kissing is definitely a forerunner to sexual relations and is a mortal sin for those not married to each other, even if it does *not* of a given instance lead to intercourse. The same is true of fondling or petting, that is, caressing the sensitive parts of the other person's body. This too, is a preliminary to intercourse and is strictly forbidden to those not married to each other. The same is true of prolonged embraces and embracing, even though this might appear to cause only a very mild sexual-type pleasure and to be not very stimulating. Nonetheless, when done for more than a few seconds (as occurs in a hug from one's mother or father or a relative) it can lead to venereal pleasure and arousing of the passions and/or to other sexual foreplay and is therefore a mortal sin.

Also, dancing while holding the other person in contact with one's body is a mortal sin because it is nothing other than prolonged, intimate embracing, but it also has the added stimulus of rhythm, music and motion. Some may contend that it just gives them a "romantic feeling," but such a "romantic feeling" can easily develop into venereal pleasure; plus, what might be "romantic" to one of the dance partners may be a serious sin to the other. Dancing *per se* is not sinful, but this type of dancing is. Here again, we should recall the warning of Scripture, "He that loveth danger shall perish in it." (*Ecclesiasticus* 3:27).

Prolonged holding of hands could even be mortally sinful, *depending on whether or not it arouses those who do it*. For a reasonably short period of time it is generally no sin at all, *for most people, on most occasions*. For some, however, depending on their sensitivity and other factors, it may have to be avoided altogether. Here each person will have to have the honesty to judge the matter for himself. Let us repeat, for the sake of absolute clarity, *for most people, on most occasions*, there is no problem with holding hands for short periods of time, and the practice is merely a common and morally acceptable sign of love or affection. But for some it can be an occasion of sin and must be avoided; for others, it can *sometimes* be an occasion of sin and should therefore at that time be discontinued or avoided.

The principle involved in all the actions mentioned above is that one must strictly avoid seeking or accepting what is called "venereal pleasure," i.e., sexual pleasure (usually connected with the touching of bodies), which is strictly reserved to those who are married to each other. For sexual foreplay carries these pleasures with it, and as mentioned earlier, is essentially ordered to and in fact often leads to intercourse, which in its turn is essentially ordered to and soon (under normal circumstances) results in the conception of a child. And only the married are actually in a position to take on the responsibilities attendant to being parents. Sex, the Church maintains, and as can be seen from common-sense reasoning, is really all one activity; the preliminary actions are not isolated from the final act. Sexual activity is like a steep, slippery decline that leads swiftly to a sheer cliff, where the decline represents sexual foreplay and the cliff sexual intercourse. If one intends to avoid the latter, he must avoid the former. They are inexorably united.

Even if a person does not intend to engage in sexual intercourse, and even if he does not in fact engage in sexual intercourse, he still commits a mortal sin when he willfully takes any step toward sexual intercourse by engaging in any of the above-mentioned actions. Because sex is all one connected activity, to engage in any part of it with someone other than one's spouse is a mortal sin.

The immature, uninformed and naive may think that the Catholic position regarding sexual foreplay is Puritanical or prudish, but it is not. It is simply realistic. It is based upon an accurate understanding of God's law and of fallen human nature; the Catholic position comprehends what will almost certainly occur (if not right away, then in time) to people who flirt with danger by engaging in any of the sexual foreplay mentioned above.

No one will deny that such things are pleasant. God so constituted us to enjoy them in order to insure the propagation of the race, but He placed sex in the framework of love and marriage so that the immortal souls born to a man and woman will have the mother and father they need to rear and educate them. The sinful participants in such preliminary activities may *think* that they are not committing mortal sins and/or that they are not going to end up having intercourse, but invariably it will happen.

Avoiding the near occasion of this type of sin is essential to avoiding the sins themselves. (Again, the "near occasion of sin" is any person, place, thing or idea that is likely to lead one into sin.) Young couples in love have to be particularly careful not to fall into such sins. Double dating, not being alone together for very long (especially in a house or apartment), and avoiding in general all situations that can lead to these sins will help people avoid them. Prayer, the Sacraments and mutual cooperation to avoid these sins are essential to those who are dating with the serious intention of getting married, in order to help them be pure. To avoid sins of impurity, it is good not to have too long an engagement time before marriage. And it is definitely best to terminate a relationship with a member of the opposite sex when one is sure it will *not* lead to marriage.

The world does not see matters in this clear light but judges, rather, that all people have an inherent right to sexual pleasure and to do whatever is necessary to avoid the conception and/or birth of children. Such attitudes are exhibited openly in the movies and the mass media, but they are opposed to God's law, and they lead those who engage in promiscuous sexual activity to all manner of problems and profound unhappiness in this life and to the eternal misery of Hell, if they should die with these sins unrepented on their souls. Sinners live under the grand delusion that they can somehow fool God and avoid being penalized *even in this life* by the very sins they commit. But hear what Scripture has to say on this score: "Be not deceived, God is not mocked. For what things a man shall sow, those also shall he reap." (*Gal.* 6:7-8). "But the wicked shall be punished according to their own devices: who have neglected the just, and have revolted from the Lord." (*Wisdom* 3:10).

Pornography: The reading or viewing of pornographic materials would constitute the near occasion to sins of impurity and would therefore be in itself a mortal sin, since all sins of impurity are mortal sins if committed with knowledge and full consent. Nor can we claim in favor of our actions that the book, magazine or movie has other redeeming qualities that offset the pornographic part which is objectionable. For what possible redeeming quality can there be to offset the eternal loss of one's soul? And who can say that he will get past the indecent part of the book, magazine or motion picture without being moved to sin, and/or as a result, without becoming habitually corrupted? Again, even if one were able to avoid sins of impurity despite the near occasions of those sins that pornography carries with it, what about others who might read or view the pornographic materials we own? If they were to sin through viewing these materials, we would have contributed to their sin simply by our *owning* and making available such things to them. Further, if we buy pornography, we are to that extent supporting the pornographic publisher and thereby enabling him to that extent to subvert others as well.

Stealing: Under the Seventh Commandment, theft of an amount equal to the victim's daily earnings or more is considered by Catholic moral theologians to be a mortal sin. A very common form of serious theft is purposeful damage to one's rented quarters (house or apartment). In effect, a person who causes such damage is actually stealing from his landlord in a substantial way because repairs to buildings are *very* expensive. Even when the damage is done little by little yet cumulatively constitutes a large amount of damage, the sin is still mortal, for moral theologians recognize, as does our common sense, that a large (substantial) theft can be effected a little at a time. (Catholic theologians teach that this is not a case of a number of venial sins being added together to make one mortal sin, which is impossible; but rather, it is one continuous act that is mortally sinful, but which is comprised of a number of individual, related acts.) Remaining silent about a financial error made in one's favor could be a mortal sin, depending on the amount and the party being "stolen" from, as also could cheating an insurance company or other organization, even the government. For employees, theft from their employing company in the form of not putting in a full day's work for one's pay is a mortal sin if persisted in to the degree that the cumulative loss to the company is great. Also, any substantial stealing of the company's product, materials, tools or equipment, etc., could constitute a mortal sin, depending on the amount stolen. Also of a potentially serious nature (a mortal sin depending on the size) are those subtle forms of theft committed by business people which we have considered earlier under the Seventh Commandment. For generally these thefts involve considerable sums of money.

In regard to sins of theft, of whatever nature, we should remember the Biblical warnings, "Nor thieves. . . shall possess the kingdom of God." (*1 Cor.* 6:10). And, "Do not circumvent thy brother in business." It is often very easy for businessmen to bilk others out of their money because so much business is done on credit and on the good faith that the purchasing company will pay its bill. For a businessman to incur a substantial debt which he is not morally certain he can repay would constitute a mortal sin. "Deals" between a vendor to a large company on the one hand and the middle management personnel in the large firm on the other hand for contracts to the vendor often involve underhand payoffs to such middle management; in these contracts the large company often ends up paying much more for its goods and services than is necessary. Those who make such arrangements run the risk of committing mortal sin, where the losses to their company are substantial. Because theft can take many and very subtle forms, it is a sin we all should be especially careful of, lest we be guilty of something we give light consideration to; moreover, theft includes, besides taking physical property from another, such sins as calumny and slander, which steal another's reputation or good name. (Cf. Chapter II.)

Coveting someone's spouse: Any conscious and willful sin against the Ninth Commandment, that is, coveting someone else's spouse, is a mortal sin. And obviously, any actual attempt to steal someone else's spouse is also a mortal sin. It must be remembered that a "divorced" person is actually still married in the eyes of God, since the civil government has no power to dissolve a marriage. Therefore, one may not court or keep company with such a person unless there is proof the "marriage" was invalid.

Divorce: Among sins forbidden by the Sixth and Ninth Commandments, obtaining a "divorce" (which is only "separation" in the eyes of God) without a sufficiently good reason is a mortal sin. (Although God does not recognize divorce as dissolving the marriage bond, yet the Catholic Church sometimes allows a *civil* "divorce" for economic or other practical reasons. *Such a "divorced" person is in reality still married,* though separated from his or her spouse.) Valid reasons for separation (even including a legal "divorce") might be 1) adultery on the part of one's spouse, 2) danger to one's life or to the lives of one's children, 3) obstruction of the children's religious education, and 4) obstruction of one's practicing his religious duties toward God, or of the children's doing so. To "divorce" because one is no longer "in love," or because he wants to "marry" another, or because he is just tired of it all is mortally sinful and contrary to God's law. Married people should always bear in mind that God does not recognize divorce—to Him a "divorce" is really only "separation," with the marital bond remaining intact—even if the two persons *"FEEL"* that the bond is gone or that their marriage has "ended." "What therefore God hath joined together, let not man put asunder." (*Mark* 10:9). *Therefore, "remarriage" after "divorce" is always a mortal sin because it is simply adultery!* (Cf. Chapter II.)

Remarriage after divorce: "Remarriage" after "divorce," as seen above, is definitely a mortal sin. Our Lord said quite bluntly: "Every one that putteth away his wife, and marrieth another, committeth adultery: and he that marrieth her that is put away from her husband, committeth adultery." (*Luke* 16:18). And we know from the Bible that the adulterer will not enter the Kingdom of Heaven. (Cf. *1 Cor.* 6:9-10).

Wife abuse: Wife abuse (physical beating) will usually constitute a mortal sin. Moreover, it can easily result in murder, serious injury, and/or divorce, and it almost always leaves emotional scars on the wife—and the children too, if they should witness it. The causes of wife abuse are, of course, many and will vary depending upon the case. Nonetheless, no matter what the causes of wife abuse, one may never resort to evil that good may result—this is an accepted norm of morality. The main point to be made here, though, is that beating one's wife is a mortal sin and as such must be stopped if a man wants to avoid Hell. But conversely, it may be that the wife in such a case is also guilty of mortal sin by pursuing various kinds of provoking behavior. In general, most cases of this problem will be eliminated if both husband and wife understand well their basic roles in marriage, as explained in the Bible and as reinforced by the Church. However, beyond learning what are the basic roles for husband and wife in a Christian marriage, couples where wife abuse occurs should obtain marriage counselling from a wise Catholic person well grounded in the Catholic Faith. If both husband and wife then understand what God expects of them in marriage, and if they will study to learn some of the practical techniques to the art of being happily married, and if the husband and wife will strive to stay in the state of grace and will pray together (especially the family Rosary) most (if not indeed all) of the causes of wife abuse will have been neutralized. Concerning his conduct toward his wife, husbands should remember St. Paul's words: "Husbands, love your wives as Christ also loved the church, and delivered himself up for it . . . So also ought men to love their wives as their own bodies. He that loveth his wife, loveth himself. For no man ever hated his own flesh; but nourisheth and cherisheth it, as also Christ doth the church . . . Nevertheless let every one of you in particular love his wife as himself: and let the wife fear her husband." (*Ephesians* 5:25, 28-29, 33).

Child abuse: More and more, the sin of child abuse is becoming prevalent. This sin indicates that something has gone wrong with the parent's understanding of the institution of marriage and his or her vocation to the marriage state. Children, in God's plan, are the natural fruit of marriage, and are potential saints for Heaven. They challenge all the talent and wisdom of the parents to raise and educate them properly. Child abuse can be an easy sin for parents to fall into because the parent has a bona fide right to chastise the child corporally. The problem for the parent arises with regard to where to draw the line between what constitutes corrective punishment and what is just plain child abuse. The key lies in whether or not the parent's anger is out of control: whether the parent is acting out of righteous indignation and intends merely to punish a wrong and correct the behavior of the child or whether the parent is filled with personal pique and simply wants to get even. Child abuse also depends on how severely the child is treated by the angry parent. Whereas the physical harm done to the child may not constitute a mortal sin, the psychological damage may, because it could stay with the child for a lifetime. Children are a blessing from God, according to the Bible. And as such they represent a sacred trust from God, on loan, so to speak, to the parents. The parents' activity as educators is another acquired art connected with marriage—one which has to balance allowance of freedom with the possibility of chastisement for misbehavior, one which feeds the child continually on increased responsibility as he or she matures with the ever-present prospect of punishment for responsibility abused, one which balances love and warmth and friendship with authority and (when necessary) displeasure and righteous anger. Child abuse indicates that the parent needs guidance from a wise and learned Catholic person in how to be a good parent. Child abuse would indicate that the parent actually needs *practical* advice on the way to reduce stress in the home and how to handle children.

Child neglect: The Bible says, "Hast thou children? instruct them, and bow down their neck from their childhood." (*Ecclesiasticus* 7:25). Again, "Withhold not correction from a child: for if thou strike him with a rod, he shall not die." (*Proverbs* 23:13). Also, "It is a proverb: A young man according to his way, even when he is old he will not depart from it." (*Proverbs* 22:6). In other words, as the die is cast in youth, generally so shall the person be all his or her life. Parents may not realize the full extent of their responsibility toward their children with regard to their rearing. This responsibility (in an ascending order of importance) encompasses the *health* and *physical well-being* of the child, his *intellectual development*, and his *spiritual training* and formation. A book could be written on just this subject. But suffice it to say the following:

With regard to their *physical development*, children need wholesome food, daily exercise outdoors in the fresh air, and adequate sleep. To fulfill all these requirements the best tool is a regular daily and weekly family routine. Probably the most important aspect of the physical development of a child is to feed him *only* such food as will promote his health, *and to curtail all eating between meals*. Children tend to want to eat whenever they "feel" a little hungry, and if not schooled they will often eat foods that "taste" good but are not wholesome. They can easily have ruined their appetite when mealtime arrives by snacking and may thereby even ruin their health (or at least inhibit their development) if the habit goes on. Parents have a serious obligation not to be sentimental about satisfying their children's pre-meal hunger by allowing them to destroy their appetite for a proper meal. Too, parents should study to learn what foods are essential to healthful growth and well-being and then keep these in the house and work to eliminate all others. With so many foods being highly processed, it is conceivable that a person could consistently be eating a diet without much food value and/or that is positively harmful to health. There is no conceivable way that a child could reason through this problem. Therefore, his health care relating to diet is the parents' grave responsibility. Nutrition takes place little by little; a child does not *suddenly* become healthy or sickly. Both are the result of longterm habits. It is the parents' serious obligation to see that these longterm habits are good ones. *Probably, no one given point in the neglect of one's children's health would constitute a mortal sin, but a cumulative laissez-faire attitude of "let him eat what he wants when he wants and live how he wants"* could constitute a serious sin.

Concerning the *mental* or *intellectual development* of their children, probably the very best step that parents can take today is to get rid of the television set—or at the very least, monitor it strictly and allow it to be viewed only a few times per week or month, and that under strict supervision. The human mind is like a big mental stomach. If one allows the minds of one's children to be filled with ''garbage'' from the T.V., there will result, besides the bad information received, a mental nervousness and agitation that will upset their quiet absorbing of proper learning. Granted that television can be a powerful educator; conversely, it can be an equally terrible corruptor for a child—naive to the truth of many matters. A reading program should be set up for each child and discussions should be held at dinner time and other specific times. Parents should always try to answer their children's questions, be attentive to their intellectual needs, and whenever possible take them along on errands, during which time they can be constantly instructing them—while in the car, waiting in line at the store, walking, etc. This type of home background will promote the child's school education better than anything else, because it will prepare, cultivate and develop an inquiring mind. As with nutrition, a child's education does not come *suddenly*, but is built up little by little, through good habits. It is a serious obligation of the parents to attend to the sound intellectual formation of their children and not neglect it. Time passes quickly, and the child soon grows to adulthood—and will be well or ill-equipped intellectually, depending in large part on what time and interest the parents have taken in his mental formation. Helping one's child to learn on a regular, ongoing basis is the best manner to fulfill a person's moral obligation in this area. Neglecting to help the child with a *regular* program of learning at home, especially with a consistent reading program, is going to harm him irreparably the rest of his life. Again, as with neglect of the physical well-being of the child, probably no one given point of neglect of the child's intellectual development would constitute a mortal sin, *but the cumulative effect of general neglect very easily could*. Parents should realize that the intellectual preparation, help and development they give their children at home is the most important assist the children will ever receive in their intellectual development; and further, that this help will lay the foundation for their success in school and later in life. To neglect the intellectual development of one's children at home—especially when our technically complex society demands so much intellectually of everyone, on the job *or* at home—would be the matter of a mortal sin, when that neglect is considered in its entirety.

The *spiritual formation* and *development* of a child is the parents' most important parental obligation and therefore constitutes the area where it would be easiest for parents to commit a mortal sin of neglect. Religious instruction should be started as soon as the child can understand—even a little. Parents have a strict obligation to be excellent religious role models; they should lead the children in daily prayer; and they should teach them right from wrong and always require strict adherence to correct moral living. If proper formal religious training outside the home is available, the parents should see that their children attend, unless they themselves can do the job as well or better. Periodically, they must check this instruction to be sure that what is being taught in the name of Religion is really proper religious instruction, as well as insuring that their children are doing the assignments given.

Parents of children attending public schools have a grave obligation to see that their children are not corrupted by secular sex instruction, which in many ways is nothing more than an introduction to sin, a destroyer of innocence and an awakener of passion. Moreover, such sex education usually teaches that there are no moral norms, except ''What you feel is right for you.'' If parents judge they must send their children to public schools, they have a very grave obligation to do whatever is necessary to prevent the corruption of their children through such sex education programs. To neglect this obligation would be a mortal sin, especially since a child who is introduced to sexual sin at an early age will generally have a harder time breaking his bad habits and is that much more likely to lose his soul. In some cases parents may have no other moral alternative than to remove their children from public schools and teach them at home (a phenomenon, incidentally, which is increasing all the time and which is meeting with success).

A general failure by parents to perform their duties with regard to their children's physical, mental or spiritual development can easily constitute a mortal sin, and that is why so much emphasis is placed on this subject. Parents' obligations toward their children are so multifaceted and all-embracing that they constitute the parents' major obligation in life. Especially today do parents have to be extremely vigilant concerning the company their children keep and the moral influences that they are subject to. Parenting today is particularly difficult because society, far from reinforcing the sound moral development of the child, is allowing factors to undermine and even work powerfully *against* it. But as in every age, parenting can still be most rewarding, even today, especially when one considers that it is God's design for creating and preparing immortal souls who are intended to be with and glorify Him for all eternity.

Gambling to excess: Under normal circumstances, gambling is not a sin at all if we keep it within the realm of legitimate pleasure, using only such funds as we would normally budget for recreational use. But when in gambling we go beyond the use of such funds, gambling then becomes a sin. If moneys that are needed for the support of one's self and/or one's family are used, the sin could be mortal, depending on the *amount* and the seriousness of the loss to one's well-being or that of his family. For gambling away such moneys is in effect *stealing!* Even a wealthy person who gambles to excess might be guilty of the mortal sin of *profligacy* (wanton waste of one's means), even though he has not jeopardized his basic resources—for God places a heavy burden of responsibility upon the shoulders of the wealthy. ''It is easier for a camel to pass through the eye of a needle [small gate in a city's walls], than for a rich man to enter the kingdom of heaven.'' (*Matt.* 19:24).

Drunkenness: Drinking to intoxication is a common mortal sin; intoxication becomes a mortal sin when the person's ability to think and judge are seriously impaired. Moreover, it is one that is very easy to fall into. For the borderline between enough and too much to drink is often easily passed, because one's appetite for more alcohol often continues even after he has had enough; plus, a person may be thoroughly enjoying himself with the others he is drinking with, which is an added inducement to keep drinking even when one has had enough.

There are generally two types of drinker: those who can drink moderately and those who cannot drink moderately, because if they have one or two drinks, they continue until they have lost control of themselves. This latter type of drinker has a grave obligation to cease drinking altogether. Furthermore, drinking to excess—in our modern society—quite often involves also the moral problem of driving home with faculties impaired, thus endangering one's own life and that of others. This factor would add another mortal sin to that of becoming intoxicated.

As mentioned earlier, a person is culpable of whatever he does while under the influence of alcohol. The person prone to drunkenness, therefore, should be well aware of his limitations and should realize that alcoholic beverages, as with food or any type of drink, are to be taken in moderation, or he will be guilty of the sin of gluttony. But also, because drunkenness involves much more than mere gluttony, in addition to committing the sin of gluttony, the drunkard robs himself of the proper use of reason (that faculty which distinguishes man from beast) and leaves himself open to committing whatever sins he is prone to. The Bible warns us, "Woe to you that are mighty to drink wine, and stout men at drunkenness." (*Isaias* 5:22).

As mentioned in Chapter II, drinking can also lead to *alcoholism*, which is its own brand of moral problem. Oddly, one can develop into an alcoholic without necessarily drinking *to excess* at any one time (or even regularly). Although the root cause of alcoholism is still unknown, it usually develops from repeated, consistent (daily) drinking. Therefore, we are all duty-bound to avoid drinking in this manner, lest we "drift into" becoming alcoholic. Since the matter is serious, one could easily commit mortal sin simply by frequent, consistent (daily) drinking, even though the amount consumed would not necessarily be considered excessive or enough to produce drunkenness.

Drug-taking: If one perhaps might not commit a mortal sin the first time he tries "street drugs," surely with the second, third or fourth dose, a person would be stepping over the line from venial to mortal sin. It is common knowledge that these super powerful stimulants and depressants are extremely deleterious to the health of the body and thereby to the proper functioning of the mind, that they are taken largely *just* for the thrill of the experience or for the escape they provide, and that they very quickly become habit-forming. Most people know that taking these drugs carries the ultimate risk literally of destroying the user. Moreover, there is a chance of passing on the ill effects to one's future offspring. Therefore, in using illegal drugs there is no redeeming merit even remotely commensurate to all the risks and problems that attend this practice. Our bodies are a precious gift from God, the vehicle in which we are to work out our salvation. The use of illegal drugs can very quickly and very seriously jeopardize the user's health and well-being, and such use is therefore grievously wrong (a mortal sin); plus, it often leads to squandering one's money, which is an additional mortal sin. Use of drugs over a period of time can also render one dependent on others and unfit to work. Further, it means seriously breaking the civil law (another mortal sin), which God requires us to obey, causing the user to risk prosecution and imprisonment for his thrill. And it sometimes places the user squarely in the company of Class-A felons, the drug-pushers and those over them, people who will resort to intimidation, torture and murder to collect their fees. Just to consort with certain of these dangerous characters would be to risk one's safety, should a person fail to pay "when the bill is due," which would be a further mortal sin. The naïve may pooh-pooh the risk of associating with the drug ring, but the statistics prove them wrong. The potential drug-addict, before he takes that first "fix," would do well to imagine himself, having been murdered for non-payment of his drug bill, appearing before the Just Judge at his Particular Judgment. What possible defense shall he bring forward to acquit himself for having squandered his precious existence on such foolishness and for having committed four distinct mortal sins connected with the pure folly of his drug-taking? Shall he not more than likely hear the dreadful sentence, "Depart from me, you cursed, into everlasting fire which was prepared for the devil and his angels." (*Matt.* 25:41). Of all the moral "dead-ends" people enter, illegal drug use comes close to the ultimate in the human folly.

Wasting time: One may not realize it, but any gross wasting of one's time, such as just doing nothing for long periods, watching too much television, playing too much golf, frittering away great amounts of time on card games or pool games and/or any other sort of entertainment, could constitute a mortal sin, especially if this also leads to grave neglect of duty or becomes a near occasion of other mortal sins. Relaxing and diverting one's self, when done in proper proportion to the amount or intensity of one's work, would normally be no sin at all, but rather a virtue, because it restores the mind, the heart and the body. However, such diversions and recreations can easily be engaged in to excess or strictly for their own sake, and then, when engaged in excessively or as the principal activity of one's life, they could constitute a mortal sin; definitely they would then be at least venial sins. God has given us *time* in which to work out our salvation. No one knows how much time he has, and therefore a gross wasting of one's precious allotment of time could constitute a mortal sin. Here we should recall the sobering words from the book of *Wisdom:* "For his heart is ashes, and his hope vain earth, and his life more base than clay: Forasmuch as he knew not his maker and him that inspired into him the soul that worketh, and that breathed into him a living spirit. *Yea and they have counted our life a pastime,* and the business of life to be gain..." (*Wisdom*

15:10-12, emphasis added).

Profligacy: Another form of waste, profligacy, or gross waste of one's money and/or means, would constitute a mortal sin. We must remember here Our Lord's parable of the servants who were given the talents. Our Lord expects us to make good use of our time and *all the assets* He has provided us with.

Lack of charity, or selfishness: Under the general moral mandate that we do acts of charity, failure to help one's neighbor in his need, whether it be with food, drink, clothing, shelter or whatever it is he might need, could constitute a mortal sin. We need here only recall Our Lord's prediction about the Last Judgment, and we shall see that the sins for which those who go to Hell are condemned, in that passage of Scripture, *are sins of omission*; they are precisely the sins of omitting to help "Christ's little ones" in their needs. For Our Lord in Scripture identifies Himself with His "little ones," that is, the poor who are in need. (*Matt.* 25:35-37). We should remember too St. John's words: "He that hath the substance of this world, and shall see his brother's need, and shall shut up his bowels from him: how doth the charity of God abide in him?" (*1 Jn.* 3:17). (Here theologians distinguish among the levels of need by the poor: *extreme* need, *serious* need and *ordinary* need. For those in *extreme* need—water, food, clothing, shelter—we have to help them, even if doing so requires the use of our own goods superfluous to maintaining life.

For those in *serious* need—though not lacking the essentials of life—we must help them from our goods entirely superfluous to our state in life. For those with *ordinary* needs, we must help *some* of the poor *some* of the time, and from our goods superfluous to maintaining our state in life.)

Sacrilegious Communion: For Catholics to receive the Body and Blood of Jesus Christ in Holy Communion while in the state of mortal sin (having committed a mortal sin which has not been confessed and forgiven in Sacramental Confession) is itself a mortal sin—a mortal sin of sacrilege. St. Paul in *First Corinthians* expressly warns against this sin when he says: "Therefore whosoever shall eat this bread, or drink the chalice of the Lord unworthily, shall be guilty of the body and blood of the Lord. But let a man prove himself: and so let him eat of that bread, and drink of the chalice. For he that eateth and drinketh unworthily, eateth and drinketh judgment to himself, not discerning the body of the Lord." (*1 Cor.* 11:27-29). Today (1988), when most Catholics do not go to Confession from one end of the year to the next, and when in a sizeable parish it is not unusual for there to be under ten Confessions per week, and yet when it comes time for Communion at Sunday Mass, virtually everyone in attendance receives Communion, it can be presumed that many people—human nature being what it is—are receiving Holy Communion unworthily, i.e., while in the state of mortal sin. Prior to approximately 1960, it was the norm for practicing Catholics to go to the Sacrament of Confession once a week, or at least once every two or three weeks (whether or not they had a mortal sin to confess), and afterwards to receive Communion on Sunday. Prior to that time, the number of Confessions approximately equalled the number of Communions. About half of a parish would receive Communion on a given Sunday. Presently, however, there are hardly any Confessions, and the reception of Communion is almost universal. Granted, many of those weekly Confessions in previous years were probably Confessions of venial sins (not mortal sins), and thus they were not strictly necessary before Communion, yet we must admit that mortal sin has become far more commonplace today, and so it would only be a person wearing rose-colored glasses, one who wants to redefine the whole concept of sin, who would say that mortal sin has become so rare that only a handful of parishioners each week have need of Confession before receiving Holy Communion. (That handful who do go to Confession are likely to be the most devout and least sinful members of the whole parish.)

To insure that one is receiving Communion worthily, it is well to confess weekly and keep in mind at all times a "running examination of conscience." If one has the misfortune to commit a mortal sin, he should try to get to Confession immediately—that same day, if at all possible.

Weekly Confession helps one ward off mortal sin by the increased Sacramental grace received; plus, it helps a person to concentrate on his venial sins and begin to eliminate them also. (The Catechism warns that venial sin often leads to mortal sin. Therefore, he who would save his soul cannot tolerate purposeful venial sin in himself.) The Catholic Church tells us that man is basically good in his nature, but that he is *inclined* toward evil, due to Original Sin. When a person confesses often, he begins to see that as he overcomes one type of sin in his life, there seems to occur to his mind another type of sin that he was never before *aware* that he was committing. Going to Confession frequently forces a person to concentrate often on the sins he is committing. If one's frequent Confessions are sincerely and carefully prepared for, not only will mortal sin soon be overcome, but purposeful venial sin (as distinguished from venial sins we commit on the spur of the moment, or out of "frailty") will also be eliminated. From there, one then goes even further, to work on eliminating what are called "frailties," or venial sins committed hastily or out of the frailty of our fallen nature, and not with premeditated, complete consent of the will. When a person has begun to eliminate even his frailties, then he can say he is seriously on the way to perfection.

A person simply cannot be satisfied with just eliminating mortal sins from his life; he has to go all the way if he is to be and remain truly good and save his soul; he must eliminate especially his purposeful venial sins as well, and even his sins of frailty and peccadillos (tiny sins). Frequent (weekly) Confession serves as an essential aid to accomplishing this objective. The situation is comparable to the professional athlete who has to get his body into super condition in order to compete. He cannot be satisfied with just giving up smoking and drinking (which are the equivalent of "mortal sins to good health"); he also has to renounce inferior quality food, bad sleeping habits, and anything and everything else (the equivalent of "venial sins and peccadillos to good health") that hurts his conditioning in even the slightest manner. If athletes will so discipline themselves physically for a "corruptible crown," as St. Paul says (*1 Cor.* 9:25), should not we Catholics do so spiritually to gain "an incorruptible one" in the Kingdom of Heaven?

Heresy: Heresy is the abandoning by a baptized Catholic of belief in one or more of the articles of the Catholic Faith which all must believe to be Catholic (i.e., truly Christian, because one holds "all"—*katholikos*—of the teachings which Christ taught). A heretic says that he believes in Christ—maybe even that he believes in His Church, to the extent that he is still Catholic in name and "goes to church." But insofar as anyone—publicly or privately—withholds his assent from any of the dogmatic or moral teachings of the Church, that person is a *heretic;* he is not a Catholic, and in that respect he is not, strictly speaking, even a Christian.

Heresy is a mortal sin because thereby a person denies what Christ taught; he is most likely going to lose his soul because he allows himself to believe in error; and he can cause grave scandal to other people—who may also embrace the heresy and lose their souls. Entire nations have been lost to the Church because of heresy, and great wars have resulted from it (consider the Thirty Years War in Germany, 1618-1648, which historians estimate *required Germany 200 years to recuperate from!*).

Heresy might not seem to concern most Catholics, but such is definitely a wrong opinion. For many people, especially in our time, have adopted a "grocery-list" approach to religion, choosing to believe only what they want to. In effect, what such people are actually saying is that *God is wrong* on those points they choose to reject. At first sight, it is obvious that such people have not thought out their position because, if they had, they would see how foolish they make themselves. For insofar as they are Catholics, they are subscribing to a religion that says it was revealed to man by none other than God Himself and that there is no falsehood in it. For an individual, therefore, to start picking and choosing what he will and will not believe of this God-given religion, is tantamount to saying "God is wrong," or "I know better than God," or some other such foolish thing. But the heretic has not thought out his position anywhere nearly so thoroughly because, if he had, either he would reject the Church's teachings completely (become an apostate) or he would be forced to embrace them completely (which, again, is exactly what it means to be a "Catholic," that is, to accept *all* that Christ taught and *all* that His Church teaches in His name and by His commission.)

The average closet (quiet) heretic is generally not concerned at first with the doctrine of the Trinity or the way that grace operates in the soul, but usually he is concerned about the unflinching *moral* precepts of the Catholic Church, especially with regard to sexual morality: for example, no remarriage after "divorce," the immorality of artificial birth control, no abortion, no sex outside of legitimate marriage, etc. Surely there are some who begin their fall into heresy because they have difficulty believing in the Real Presence of Jesus Christ in the Eucharist, certainly a hard doctrinal tenet. But for the most part, the petty heretic will begin his drift into heresy mainly because he bridles over the strict *moral* teachings of the Church; nonetheless his heresy generally and rather quickly comes to include many of the Church's *doctrinal* teachings as well, for when a person once loses the Faith, his unbelief usually grows to include many of the Church's other teachings as well. The person of genuine Faith, however, when he or she has difficulty believing one tenet or another of the Church's teachings, considers the utter reasonableness and beauty and solace of the whole Faith and says with the man in Scripture, "I do believe, Lord: help my unbelief." (*Mark* 9:23).

Heresy stems from the capital sin of Pride, as Scripture maintains: "If any man teach otherwise, and consent not to the sound words of our Lord Jesus Christ, and to that doctrine which is according to godliness, he is *proud*, knowing nothing, but sick about questions and strifes of words; from which arise envies, contentions, blasphemies, evil suspicions, conflicts of men corrupted in mind, and who are destitute of the truth, supposing gain to be godliness." (*1 Tim.* 6:3-5, emphasis added).

Heresy soon leads to destruction, for people cannot live according to a lie or lies. Of such the Bible says, "A man that shall wander out of the way of doctrine, shall abide in the company of the giants." (*Prov.* 21:16). (The famous "giants" of the early history of man were destroyed by God because of their iniquity and are no more.) St. Paul warns against heretics when he says, "But though we, or an angel from heaven, preach a gospel to you besides that which we have preached to you, let him be anathema." (*Gal.* 1:8). And finally, Scripture tells us how to deal with heretics: "A man that is a heretic, after the first and second admonition, avoid. Knowing that he, that is such a one, is subverted, and sinneth, being condemned by his own judgment." (*Titus* 3:10-11).

Heresy is a mortal sin because it controverts what God has taught, leads a person to confusions in this life (because he is living by lies) and most likely to the loss of his soul, causes enmities and strife (and even war), and generally spreads to others and corrupts them—also with the same results. Of the Sixteen Great Heresies which have confronted the Catholic Church during the close to twenty centuries of her history, Protestantism (begun in 1517) is the only one which the Church has not yet overcome. (The Church has been able to defeat all the others by the grace of God and the influence of her preachers.) And Protestantism in our day, with its rationalism, naturalism, freedom of thought, voluptualism, and ultimate deification of man and man's judgment, has spread throughout the world and caused much of the social chaos which we witness today and which the world bemoans in its bewilderment over what to do to solve its problems.

Apostasy: The act or condition of abandoning the True Faith is called "apostasy" and constitutes a mortal sin because of the seriousness of the deed. Apostasy can stem from two sources: 1) living in mortal sin, which leads to a blinding of the spiritual understanding (a "reprobate sense" as St. Paul calls it), 2) failure to study the Faith and 3) failure to pray. With regard to the first, *living in mortal sin*, we all know that to save our souls from Hell we have to renounce

sin in general and lead a life *free* of serious (mor
tal) sin in particular. Sinners appear not to real
ize that sin carries consequences or results ever
in this life, one of which is the very likely possi
bility of loss of the Faith. In general, one canno
live in contradiction to the Truth and still *see
understand and believe in the Truth.* It is axio
matic that *living* in error will lead to *believing*
in error.

With regard to the second reason for apostasy
failure to study the Faith, the abandoning of be
lief in Catholicism for this reason often result:
from adults' not making an effort to develop ar
adult or educated understanding of their relig
ion, trying, rather, to function religiously witl
what they remember of religion from their child
hood. As adults, we go on to learn a great dea
about various fields, especially the one in whicl
we earn our livelihood. To this end we will ofter
study for years. But with regard to the knowl
edge we need to save our souls, we will ofter
adopt the disastrous intellectual position that w
already know enough. Meanwhile, many of u:
continue to operate in the spiritual and religiou:
realm with knowledge acquired as a child, knowl
edge which was probably but poorly learned an
is even less accurately remembered—and ye
upon which depends our eternal salvation.

True Religion involves some concepts that ma
for some be difficult to understand at first, plu
many concrete, practical applications based upor
these concepts. As a result, people often hav

questions regarding religion that need to be answered, and sometimes these questions—depending on the intelligence and education of the person—can become (to their thinking at least) complex and involved. But for anyone to think that there are no answers to his philosophical and moral questions with regard to religion or that the Catholic Church cannot satisfy him intellectually is an absurd supposition on his part—one that can easily lead to the calamitous result of apostasy (abandoning the Faith). If the Catholic Faith has been able to satisfy the minds and hearts of people like St. Paul and St. John the Evangelist, St. Augustine of Hippo and St. Thomas Aquinas, St. Thomas More (Chancellor of England) and Louis Pasteur, then surely it can also satisfy people today, if they will take the time and show the interest to ask informed Catholics for the answers to their questions.

As a rule, the average adult who is questioning aspects of the Faith does not really have very many or very difficult questions. But for that person not even to ask those questions of a priest or a knowledgeable Catholic or to search out the answers in books may well lead him to assume that the answers therefore do not exist and thus to adopt a state of disbelief and abandoning of the Faith. For anyone to assume that the Catholic Church, which is the religion revealed by God (as it openly maintains), is not able to satisfy him intellectually is extremely naïve and is disastrously mistaken with regard to his own eternal welfare. Scripture repeatedly admonishes us to receive instruction. Witness: "Cease not, O my son, to hear instruction, and be not ignorant of the words of knowledge." (*Prov.* 19:27). "Despise not the discourse of them that are ancient and wise, but acquaint thyself with their proverbs. For of them thou shalt learn wisdom, and instruction of understanding. . ." (*Ecclesiasticus* 8:9-10).

With regard to the third reason for apostasy, *failure to pray*, considerable attention has been given to this problem in Chapter XI. But let it at least be said here that if we fail to pray for the grace of salvation, we will not be saved. This is one of the requirements God makes of us for our salvation. Apostasy is one of the major pitfalls open to a person who fails to pray—which he might have avoided if he had prayed.

Actually, with human nature being weak as it is, apostasy usually stems from all three sources, *viz., sinfulness, failure to seek answers*, and *failure to pray*.

Agnosticism: The state of mind that considers the ultimate realities—the existence of God, the immortality of the human soul, how one should live his life, etc.—to be unknown to man or unknowable by man is called *agnosticism*, and the person who holds such a view is called an *agnostic.* (This word comes from two Greek words, *a*, meaning "not" and *gnostos*, meaning "known"; literally "not known.") Too, someone who says "There may be truth, but I don't know what it is" would also be considered an agnostic. Agnosticism, insofar as it is a *fixed* attitude of mind, is an absurdity, for the agnostic is saying, in effect, "There is no absolute, knowable truth, except the truth that there is no absolute knowable truth," which is of course a self-contradictory "principle." Agnosticism that is *temporary*, that reflects a state of suspended judgment about the truth, is not truly agnosticism, as the term is normally used, but rather a condition of "suspended judgment."

The crucial point in determining the moral guilt of an agnostic would be his *honesty* in adopting his position: If the agnostic state of mind is temporary, while the person searches for the truth, there is no sin. If it is a *confirmed* state of mind, one that refuses any acceptance of the eternal truths or any further serious consideration of them, then it would constitute a sin.

The non-Catholic agnostic would definitely commit a mortal sin if, when presented with the True Faith, he suspends his judgment and makes no decision about the truth of this matter—not even a decision to investigate the question further to determine the truth. For in the light of obvious truth, or a suspicion of where the truth lies, he would be saying, "I just don't know what is true." The non-Catholic agnostic commits a mortal sin at the point where he perceives a *grave obligation* to investigate the truth of the Catholic Faith and does not do so. In practice, a *"Catholic"* agnostic who loses his faith is very

unlikely to do so without having committed one
or more mortal sins along the way, because the
loss of one's Catholic faith is always a culpable
(blameworthy) matter. It is not sufficient for the
agnostic to say, "I just don't know," or "I don't
think man can know these things." For the
Church has the answers to any questions he
might have. Also, in the practical order everyone makes decisions every day based upon his
knowledge, and these decisions reflect the presence of truth in the mind. Therefore, each person can come to the practical determination that
the mind does know. And it also knows with regard at least to right and wrong and, according
to the teaching of the Church, that God exists
and the human soul is immortal.

Adopting the intellectual posture of *fixed* or
confirmed agnosticism would be to commit a
mortal sin. For Scripture again and again reiter-
ates the knowability of the ultimate truths. Witness: "The fool hath said in his heart: There is
no God." (*Ps.* 13:1). "Wherefore laying away all
malice, and all guile, and dissimulations. . .as
newborn babes, desire the *rational milk* without guile, that thereby you may grow unto salvation." (*1 Peter* 2:1-2, emphasis added). "And
whosoever shall not receive you, nor hear your
words: going forth out of that house or city shake
off the dust from your feet. Amen I say to you,
it shall be more tolerable for the land of Sodom
and Gomorrha in the day of judgment, than for
that city." (*Matt.* 10:14-15). "And when he drew

near, seeing the city [Jerusalem], he wept over it, saying: If thou hadst known, and that in this thy day, the things that are to thy peace; but now they are hidden from thy eyes. For the days shall come upon thee, and thy enemies shall cast a trench about thee, and compass thee round, and straiten thee on every side, and beat thee flat to the ground, and thy children who are in thee: and they shall not leave in thee a stone upon a stone: *because thou hast not known the time of thy visitation.*" (*Luke* 19:41-44, emphasis added).

The true or "confirmed" agnostic rejects the truth as not even knowable and thereby blasphemes his Maker by saying to God in effect, "Though I am made in Your image and likeness, You did not make me *well enough* to know these ultimate truths!" But what he is really saying, through his "malice," "guile" and "dissimulations" (*1 Peter* 2:1) is that he rejects the challenge which the Truth automatically imposes upon him because he is too lazy or too self-indulgent or too attached to his sins to accept that truth and make the changes in his life which the truth demands.

From the Scripture passages quoted above, we can see the attitude of Almighty God toward the agnostic: Through the sacred writer, He calls him a *"fool,"* probably the most derisive word in any language! Through the mouth of St. Peter, God admonishes all people to lay aside "malice," "guile" and "dissimulations" (in other words, the ruses used by the agnostic to avoid making the important decisions in life) and "desire the rational milk without guile," that is to say, "the easily received and digested *food of Faith*" which God has prepared for the minds and hearts of those who love Him and who love His Truth—which is no harder for us to receive (if we are humble and will accept the truth) than is its mother's milk for a little babe to drink in to its well-being—in order that we may thereby grow unto salvation.

From the passage of Luke, we see the attitude of our divine Saviour toward the agnostic and the unbelieving: Sodom and Gomorrha (which were destroyed by God with a hail of fire and brimstone) will be judged less harshly than those who have been presented with but have rejected the True Faith, which the Catholic Church possesses and teaches throughout the world and throughout all time. And as if these were not proof enough of the disdain the Almighty holds for agnosticism, we have the evidence of history itself to reinforce Our Lord's prophecy about the destruction soon to come upon Jerusalem because, as He says, she did not know the time of her "visitation," when the Saviour of the World, God Himself made man, taught and worked His miracles within her walls and inside her Temple. For the Roman general Titus in the year 70 A.D. brought her low and carried off all her inhabitants who were left after a most frightening two-year siege. Adopting the attitude of "fixed" agnosticism, therefore, in the face of the True Faith is a mortal sin because the matter involved is the most grave—ignoring or rejecting the truth whereby a person is to be saved—and includes a willful, fully conscious, non-concupiscential, absolutely and coldly rational decision on the part of the person who opts for this absurdity.

The near occasion of mortal sin: Any person, place, thing or thought that we know will easily lead us into mortal sin must be avoided, lest in fact it *does* lead us to commit a mortal sin. The Catholic Church calls such extrinsic and intrinsic situations which are likely to lead us to commit a sin the "near (or proximate) occasions of sin." Because mortal sin is absolutely the worst evil and because just one mortal sin is sufficient to condemn a person to Hell (if he dies with it unrepented upon his soul), *then for a person purposely to expose himself to the near occasion of any mortal sin is itself a mortal sin!* The only exception to this would be in case of a sufficiently grave necessity, e.g. a male doctor examining or operating on a beautiful woman.

Particularly common and extremely powerful and seductive are the near occasions to sins of impurity. This might be another person, a certain place, an immoral movie, a suggestive television program, an involuntary thought that just "popped" into the mind, etc.—anything that might lead us to commit sins of impurity (which are always mortal). But there are near occasions to other mortal sins as well. For example, for a person who often gambles to excess, it could be going to the game or the track, or maybe even associating with someone who wants him to go there. For the person prone to drunkenness, it might be the tavern or the night club where he likes to go with his friends, or even just being with the friends themselves who like to go there with him and will tempt him to do so.

We must avoid the near occasion of mortal sin if we are to be honest with God and with ourselves—especially if we have already fallen into certain mortal sins previously because a particular near occasion to those sins has led us into them. (Of course, we are actually obligated to avoid the near occasions of venial sin as well as mortal sin, but in this chapter we are concentrating on common mortal sins, that type of sin which will send us to Hell if we die with it unrepented on our soul.)

We must acknowledge that we are weak and that prudent precautions are essential to avoiding sin. With regard to the near occasion of mortal sin, we should keep ever before our minds the Scripture passages: "He that loveth danger shall perish in it." (*Ecclesiasticus* 3:27). And, "Pride goeth before destruction: and the spirit is lifted up before a fall." (*Proverbs* 16:18). If we will remain humble and sufficiently distrustful of ourselves, such that we sedulously avoid the near occasion of mortal sin, we shall have gone a great part of the way toward overcoming the mortal sins we are prone to commit. And by taking these precautions, we show God that we are *serious* when we ask for His forgiveness and promise to give up our sins.

This list of "common" mortal sins is not a complete list of all the mortal sins! It is intended to be only a review of the *principal* common mortal sins—mortal sins, or potential mortal sins—which are committed very regularly, each and every day, by many people in our society, even to the extent that some of these mortal sins are often "accepted" by society in general. (Many other mortal sins are easily discoverable by the unaided human intellect; for example, you may not throw a brick off the Empire State Building at noon on a workday because you very likely will kill someone below. That mortal sin is probably not in any other book discussing morality, or may never have been brought up for discussion anywhere prior to this. But the mind of man can quickly grasp that it involves a serious matter and is therefore a mortal sin.)

Applying the objective norms of morality, it is obvious that many adults commit mortal sin, perhaps even the majority (though, of course, in their consciences they may not be guilty of all their mortal sins because they do not always know the seriousness of their sinful actions). But it is potentially easy for an adult to commit a mortal sin if only because of the many serious obligations that an adult has and the many temptations that exist in the world, especially today with so many blatant temptations against purity. One must always be on guard lest he fall. (St. Peter says, "Be sober and watch: because your adversary the devil, as a roaring lion, goeth about seeking whom he may devour."—*1 Peter* 5:8.)

The person who is honest about avoiding Hell will not look at this listing (partial and incomplete as it may be) with an attitude of prideful fault-finding with the list, nor will he self-righteously feel that since specific sins mentioned here may not be a problem for him, that therefore he must already be a saint. Rather, he will humbly examine his conscience and try to determine whether he is committing any of the sins that are contained in this listing of the common mortal sins, based on traditional Catholic teaching, or if he could possibly be about to fall into them or even be just heading in their direction. For his mind will easily recognize them to be serious sins.

Our Lord told the Apostles: "He that heareth you [the Apostles, those whom He deputed to set up His Church], heareth me; and he that despiseth you, despiseth me; and he that despiseth me, despiseth him that sent me."(*Luke* 10:16). Therefore, if we do not hear and accept the teachings of the Catholic Church, we are refusing to hear and accept Christ. Plus, He also stated a powerful corollary to this when He said, "Amen, amen I say to you, he that receiveth *whomsoever* I send [i.e., any person or agent, this book, for example] receiveth me; and he that receiveth me, receiveth him that sent me." (*John* 13:20, emphasis added).

We have not given personal opinions here, but rather we have set forth the Catholic Church's traditional teaching as applied to today's situations. Anyone, therefore, who would controvert this traditional listing of mortal sins should examine his own conscience and ask himself why he is doing so. Is there perhaps some sin deep within his soul that he is trying to hide, or is there something sinful in his conduct that he needs to justify or rationalize? Rather than this traditional understanding of the common mortal sins being wrong, those who contest the traditional Catholic (Christian) morality are wrong.

Times may change, but right and wrong do not, for correct morality is based on God and His law, and we are all bound to obey the law of God or suffer the consequences of not doing so.

The mortal sinner who refuses to renounce his sin must battle continuously against his conscience and must continually tell himself that something is all right which is in fact a mortal sin. Therefore, he fights against and contests what the Catholic Church teaches and what people generally acknowledge, even if only to themselves, to be correct moral behavior. "For whereas wickedness is fearful, it beareth witness of its condemnation: for a troubled conscience always forcasteth grievous things. For fear is nothing else but a yielding up of the succours from thought."

(*Wisdom* 17:10-11).

For the most part, those who oppose traditional morality do so, not with regard to stealing or cursing or wife-beating, but with regard to the sexual sins and sins related to improper marriages and marriage-type arrangements. For such people have generally made an accommodation with their mortal sins of sexuality, and not being willing to root them out of their lives, and thus be happy and at peace and back on the road toward Heaven, they contest the very laws they are breaking and try to pretend they do not exist, or that they are not so serious as in fact they are. Such people need to reread the story of the woman at the well. (*John* 4). When Our Lord said to the woman, "Go call thy husband, and come hither. The woman answered, and said: I have no husband. Jesus said to her: Thou hast said well, I have no husband: For thou hast had five husbands: and he whom thou now hast, is not thy husband. This thou hast said truly." (*Jn.* 4:16-18). In other words, Our Lord showed her that her conscience was still telling her the truth (despite her five "marriages") and that the man she was living with was not her husband. The truth is always the truth, and our consciences, however "quieted" or blunted *by* sin to the seriousness *of* sin, can still see it; the question really is whether we are willing to acknowledge the truth or not.

So too with regard to *all* mortal sins, truth is truth, and God's Final Judgment will in the end settle everything. Then, however, it will be too late for the mortal sinner to change, and his earthly contestation of the moral code will turn to bitterest regret for his not having acknowledged while on earth the law of God in his life and in his actions—that law which his own conscience constantly reminded him of.

Chapter X

THE ROLE OF CONSCIENCE

Ultimately, man's eternal destiny—Heaven or Hell—is determined by whether or not he acts honestly in accordance with the dictates of his conscience and whether or not he has formed his conscience properly. Because we become confused over the nature and role of conscience, because we can become agnostic (professing not to know what is true) on the one extreme and scrupulous (thinking *everything* is a sin) on the other extreme, because *the way we act profoundly influences our perception of the seriousness of the evil we do,* because we can blunt our consciences with sin, because we think that we can lie to or ignore our consciences, because of all these reasons, it is imperative at this juncture to examine the nature and role of our conscience in the order of salvation and *how we can help it to function properly.*

The matter is really rather easy once a person sees how conscience functions and what are the three principal elements that join to comprise conscience, all as broken down in the common-sense and realistic philosophy and theology of the Catholic Church. But the reader will have to realize that a certain amount of philosophical discussion is necessary to our accurate understanding of the entire question of conscience and hopefully will indulge us during what might seem at times a rather tedious analysis.

There are three basic ingredients that coalesce to make up what we call conscience: 1) The moral knowledge that we have in our minds without being taught, in other words, what we know with the use of our unaided reason; 2) the moral principles we have learned (from parents, in school, etc.) and 3) the effects of our moral behavior (good or bad actions). The first two ingredients are easy to recognize, but the third is not so easy. All three of these elements combine to produce what we call our conscience. Now, moralists generally agree that conscience is not a *separate* faculty distinct from our mind, but simply a function *of* our mind.

In discussing the first of these three elements comprising conscience, the reader should realize that the treatment here is largely a description of *the anatomy of conscience*—that is, how the mechanism of conscience works within the processes of our minds. The purpose of entering into this rather technical discussion, which normally would be out of place in a popularly oriented book such as this, is to demonstrate as conclusively as possible the fact that the mechanism of our conscience always operates in its *basic* function in an *unerring* manner, that is, it always at least tells us fundamental right from wrong, though we may not always listen to it and though its "voice" may become weak by our frequently "overriding" what it tells us. It is, so to speak, a fail-safe mechanism, one that we cannot ever completely stifle or drown out. In many respects, the discussion about to follow is *pivotal* to our proper understanding of morality in general and how we can avoid Hell in particular. Once we grasp *how* conscience works, especially as pertains to our God-given faculty of being able to discern right from wrong, then we will understand *why* Almighty God can hold us accountable for all our actions and why, therefore, a person can be condemned to Hell for what he does.

1. The Knowledge in Our Minds

In the first place, many people through the centuries, and some even today, have been confused about the nature and function of the human conscience. For even now an erroneous idea is still fairly common that it is Almighty God who "writes" upon the human mind and in the human heart "the Law of God," such that we can never say we do not know the truth. In a sense this idea is correct, but the *way* that God "writes" upon our mind and heart is far more subtle than one might imagine or describe by this explanation.

Rather than act directly, God has created man in His own image and likeness, as the Bible tells us: "Let us make man to our image and likeness'' (*Gen.* 1:26), and being so created, *man's mind knows!* For God has created it to *know*. In fact the Sanskrit word for man is *"manas,"* which means "mind." The ancient great Greek philosopher Aristotle, for example, begins his philosophical work entitled *The Metaphysics* with the observation, "All men by nature desire to know."

For God created us to know, and He created us in His image and likeness. Now the revelation of Jesus Christ to the world is that God is not only One (as was revealed during the Old Testament to the Israelites) but that He is also at the same time *Triune* (threefold)—that there exists in Him *one* Nature but *three* Persons.

Ever since this revelation of Jesus Christ, the minds of Christian thinkers have struggled with the mystery of the Blessed Trinity, as the Triune God is referred to. The very greatest philosophers and theologians have tried to analyze just how it can be that there is but one God yet that He is comprised of Three Divine Persons, Each distinct, Each infinite, Each completely equal to the other Two, and Each completely God; and they conclude finally that it is a mystery which the human mind simply cannot fathom. But this does not mean to say, however, that the great minds of the Christian dispensation have not reached some very important conclusions about the Blessed Trinity and arrived at some very specific knowledge about the nature of God. Let us therefore examine some of the conclusions of the best thinking of the great Christian philosophers on this subject, and we must acknowledge here the first place to St. Thomas Aquinas, called the "Angelic Doctor" because of his soaring wisdom.

The three Persons in God are called God the Father, God the Son, and God the Holy Ghost (or Holy Spirit). From Aristotle, through St. Thomas, comes the philosophic concept that the nature of God is pure *Act*, that is to say, in God there is no *potency* to become something He is not; but rather, He already is *All-in-all* and *All-that-could-ever-be-of-true-existence*. It is said of God that God just IS. He *is* existence. He does not *have* existence, as we do and as do all created things.

Now with regard to the Blessed Trinity, Catholic philosophers and theologians have reasoned that the pure, unadulterated, complete *Act* of God (as the Father) is His *Thought* or His *Word* (*Logos*, to use the Greek word); and that *Thought*, being perfect and complete in Itself, is none other than God Himself again, and that *Thought* or *Word* that He thinks is what we call "God the Son," the "Word of God," who, we can see from this explanation, is "generated" from or "begotten" by the Father. Now when the Two look upon Each Other, what transpires between Them is again a *Pure Act*, an Act of Love, and that Pure and Complete and Perfect Act of Love is none other than God Himself again, and this Act of Love within the Godhead is what we call the Holy Spirit (or Holy Ghost), who in Catholic theology is said to "proceed from" the Father and the Son. (We must realize that there is no sequence, time-wise, in God, but all is an eternal *now*.)

What does this discussion about the Blessed Trinity have to do with us, and specifically with the question of our conscience? It has everything in the world to do with it, for without understanding at least something of the nature of the Blessed Trinity, we cannot really understand ourselves—for we are made in God's image and likeness—and therefore we cannot understand the nature and function of our conscience, nor really comprehend the role that it fulfills in our lives.

God reveals to us through Scripture that man is made in the image and likeness of God. But as God is Triune, so also man must have, in a certain respect, a triune characteristic—be a little Godlike creature. A human being is not three distinct persons, as God is, yet in man there is a certain threefold aspect in his essential being. And lo and behold, we find that man does display within his mind a little trinity. For do we not examine within our minds what we know, and do we not have a dialogue with ourselves over the matters under consideration in our thinking? And all the while, do we not sit in judgment over this dialogue or conversation that is going on within our minds over the subject under consideration? Of course we do! We take such activity for granted. But what we probably do not even consider is the fact that were our minds not of a triune nature, we could not really think at all, as we understand the process of thinking to be. We might have a certain type of knowledge, as the animals do, but we could not do anything to speak of with that knowledge because we could not judge, evaluate, analyze, compile, synthesize and reason—all of which functions we perform every day and on a continuing and routine basis, without ever thinking (for the most part) of how our minds work. We just use them. And they do indeed work quite well! Witness the cars and houses and huge buildings and bridges and complex machines we build and use. Witness the complex legal, social, political, moral structure we have built and live by, which we call by the general term "society."

But where in all this does conscience fit, and what is the role that conscience fills? We are approaching that answer. But first we must analyze a little further just how the mind knows.

Man has been described by philosophers as a "rational animal," where the *rational* refers to the mind (from "*ratio*" in Latin, meaning reason or mind), and *animal* referring to the body of man. We are this almost strange dual combination of mind and body, each of which part of us seems to function almost independently of the other, to say nothing of functioning in separate realms. Now, it is through our bodies that sense knowledge comes—"sensory data," as the philosophers call it. From this "sense information," the human mind receives basically all the knowledge that it has, for out of the sensory data we receive through our senses, we extract information with and build up in our minds all that we know about the exterior world.

If we prescind from that act of the mind whereby we compile the sensory data into a unified sensory whole, then the first act of the mind is one of LOOKING at this sensory data—to *see* it and to *see* what it is. In other words, the mind is like a powerful *eye* that *sees* the things it looks at and simply *knows* them. This first act of the mind is simple, singular, uncluttered, pure, automatic, fast, powerful and penetrating. With the analyzing, or what we might call the "thinking" part of our mind, we do not even know how deeply this *look* of the mind's *eye* goes into understanding the object it *looks* at, nor do we know how completely it penetrates what it *looks* at and *knows*. It just *looks*, and it *knows*—to some very considerable extent. The philosophers call this first act of the mind, in first looking at a thing, INSIGHT, that is, the LOOKING INTO the thing we know.

Now this first act of the mind (*insight*) in knowing some thing does not limit itself simply to single objects like people, trees, rocks, dogs, cars, etc., but it sees complex things also, such as relationships, judgments and other abstract ideas, including the moral rightness or wrongness of things. The human mind, when we analyze it, is subtle, quick and powerful, even in the "dumbest" person!

Further discussion about the first act of the mind (*insight*) is not necessary here to establish the truth of how the mind works in this its first function; a little self-analysis will suffice to reveal that the first act of the mind is simply to *see*. (The same and only information about the human mind which even the greatest philosopher has we ourselves also have, because each of us can only judge these matters by what we know goes on within our own minds. The analysis of others may be helpful to our understanding but the fundamental information about our minds and how they work is basically the same, and it comes from our own experience.)

What is important to grasp about *insight*—or the first act of the mind in knowing some thing— is that we get the knowledge NOW, immediately, without any reasoning of the "triune" part of our mind being involved. In this sense, therefore, we have the direct, simple, uncluttered, pure, penetrating, profound knowledge of things without any assistance from the rest of our mind, or from anyone else—from our education or from any outside influence. WE SIMPLY KNOW! *And that is how God "writes" upon our minds the truth of His Law.* He has created us in His image and likeness with a profound and powerful capacity to *see* and to *know* by our own power, a capacity that is amazingly accurate and complete, *and in front of which nothing can come—of ourselves or of other people. When we "look" at things with our minds, we simply HAVE the knowledge of* these things! And once we have that knowledge, nobody can take it away from us, nor can we deny to ourselves that we have it, that we know the truth.

Now INSIGHT *is the* BASIS *of conscience—that "voice" within us that cannot be lied to: God made our minds to function the way they do so that we would know the truth—immediately—without the assistance of education or of others or even of ourselves—so that we would* know the truth, one might say, without ever being able successfully to lie to ourselves. And it is partially on the basis of how we act in accordance with the knowledge of this "Godlike" mind which we possess that God will judge us on our judgment day. But we are going ahead of our discussion a little, for the analysis of *how* we know and *how* our conscience works is not quite finished.

After the first *look* of the mind at the object it perceives, that is, after the first original *insight* into the thing, the "triune" aspect of our mind comes into play; our mind *evaluates* what we have seen, and our mind even sits in *judgment* on this evaluation.

Now each of these steps involves an *insight*— an *insight* first into the object or relationship or issue or question itself that we are considering, an *insight* secondly into the evaluation we have made of our original insight into the thing itself, and thirdly a further *insight* into the judgment we have made of this evaluation. *But each insight is something we cannot influence or put anything in front of or lie to ourselves about—* for this first act of the mind (to repeat) is to *see* something directly and in an uncluttered manner, and once we have *seen* it, we know it for what it is, and we cannot later successfully lie to ourselves about the truth of the matter or ever really convince ourselves otherwise, for we already *know*, and nothing we can say to ourselves after the fact will ever take that knowledge away. (It is for this reason that our conscience will always "bother" us if we do something wrong, no matter how often we repeat the particular wrong.)

These acts of the mind, then—insight, evaluation and judgment—comprise what we call conscience. In general, we think of conscience as "the judgment of the mind about the truth of moral matters," which indeed it is! But what we generally do not realize is just what other factors work together to make up our conscience and why the first act of the mind, which forms the *basis* of the knowledge of conscience, is so very accurate, and therefore why we cannot, despite our very best efforts, really successfully lie to it (ourselves) when it comes to the truth of matters which we consider within ourselves.

To reiterate briefly, we have a "triune" mind, which is a reflection of the Blessed Trinity, in whose image and likeness we have been created. Unless we had a "triune" mind, we could not think, as we know human thinking to be. The first act of our mind in knowing a thing is a mental *look* called *insight*. By this *look* of the mind, we really *know* things—and we know them *profoundly*. With the "triune" part of our mind we can then analyze and evaluate our insights (knowledge), build up different ideas, reason with these ideas, and perform all the complex and abstract functions of the mind we normally just take for granted (including, of course, lying to ourselves when we act against the dictates of our conscience).

But each *look* of the mind's eye, each *insight*, at whatever level it may be within our mind— whether it be about a simple object (or a relationship or a judgment), about our evaluation of the object (or relationship or judgment), or about our judgment of our own evaluation of the object (or relationship or judgment)—each insight is an act of the mind that really grasps the truth, and the truth of this insight is held by the mind in a "failsafe" manner and is therefore something we cannot ever lie to ourselves about. We can easily and truthfully say: "Man's mind is made to know." And it does!

Conscience, then, is nothing more than that function of our mind that judges upon the moral truth of matters. And we can never truly lie to our conscience because, as we have seen, conscience is built up from and is based upon our insights into the truth of things, as well as into the truth of our evaluation of the truth of things, as well as into our judgment of our evaluation of the truth of things. We can just never get so abstract or so complex in our thinking nor can we ever introduce sufficiently cogent erroneous reasons to our minds that we are able to blur or override the truth of what our minds *see* with these insights—because God has made us this way, with an unfailing mechanism, so to speak, for knowing the truth, because nothing can come between our *insight* and the object it *sees*.

Now, since God has given us a mind with this wonderful power to see the truth, how does it happen that there is such a difference among people when it comes to conscience? To answer this question, we must now proceed in our analysis to the *second* of the three elements that contribute to the forming of our conscience. Concerning the *first* element, we have seen above that the first knowledge the mind possesses is built up from sensory data. From sensory data, our mind then makes a mental *look*, an *insight* into the nature of the objects it considers; plus it makes evaluations of its insights, and judgments about the evaluations it makes. All this concerns the *basic* knowledge of conscience and how knowledge is built up by the mind from objects *outside the mind* to ideas and evaluations and judgments *inside the mind*.

2. Moral Principles We Have Learned

At this point—and proceeding to the *second* of the three elements that contribute to forming conscience—we must now consider the knowledge we receive from "formal" education, that is, the learning we receive from books, from teaching and from the example of others—i.e., ideas we receive from *outside* the mind. (The word "form" corresponds to "idea." Therefore, any outside influence that produces an idea in us is "formal" education in the technical and strictest sense of the word—which is the meaning employed here, not just "school" education.)

Children when they are young are taught right from wrong in the home and at school. This "formal" education continues into adulthood—through reading, higher education and association with others. The type of knowledge we receive in this manner is in the form of abstract principles: e.g., "Lying is wrong," "Stealing is wrong," "Cursing is wrong." From "formal" education, therefore, *we have within our minds preformed moral principles that are pre-accepted by us as true* before we come up against a specific decision of conscience in a particular case where we must decide how to act.

What happens with regard to conscience, therefore, when we become involved in a practical moral decision, is that 1) our minds discern truth through our insight-evaluation-judgment process, but 2) *part of our evaluation and judgment includes our referring matters to pre-accepted moral principles we already have in our mind and which we consider as true*; these are the principles we have acquired through our "formal" education. In our specific moral judgments, therefore, we make use of 1) the raw data, so to speak, of the situation itself through our insight-evaluation-judgment mechanism and 2) the general principles of morality (hopefully, right morality) that we have learned beforehand. The human mind then goes into action and makes its final evaluations and judgments with the information before it from 1) insight and 2) the moral principles it already knows to be true.

(It is obvious, with regard to this second element of conscience, i.e., the prelearning of moral principles that these moral principles we learn must be *accurate* and *true*. Therefore, *the source and teaching authority from which we obtain our moral principles becomes a factor of absolutely the utmost importance in the forming of our conscience*. But more of this later.)

3. The Effect of Our Moral Behavior

There exists yet a *third* element, however, which contributes to the knowledge and judgment of our conscience—an element that is quite subtle in its influence compared to the first two. We have seen that 1) conscience is comprised in its basis from the *insight* of the mind (which is the first act of the mind) and 2) it is *informed* or influenced by our "formal" education, wherein we learn ethical principles ("Lying is wrong," etc.). The first element, *insight*, might be called the *basis* or foundation of conscience, for with the God-given faculty to know on our own without help from others, we thereby know the basic truth of things without having been taught. The second, *"formal" education*, is of the utmost importance, because through our "formal" education we *accept* certain norms as *true* before we ever encounter their specific applications to our own lives; e.g., we accept in our youth the idea that "adultery is wrong" long *before* we meet that attractive, desirable "divorced" person who wants to "marry" again; and we thereby know immediately it is wrong to "marry," or even to keep company with, such a person, who in the eyes of God is still married.

Now, as to the third element that contributes to the forming of our conscience, it too is very important, though not so pronouncedly obvious a contributor to our conscience as the other two elements. And because this element is *not* so obvious—but rather a very subtle, quiet, unnoticed contributor—it is all the more important that we understand the role it plays and how it influences the functioning of our conscience.

And that element is our own moral or immoral behavior.

The ancient pagan philosophers (such as Plato and Aristotle), even before the revelation of Christ, understood the principle that *in order to perceive the truth accurately, a person must be virtuous.* And to the saints this fact was obvious and axiomatic. We might express the principle in the following terms: *"You have to be good in order to know the truth!"*

The obvious objection to this principle would be the following: "How can a person 'be good' (perform good and true actions), if he does not know the truth beforehand? And if he does not know the truth beforehand, how can he 'be good'?" This question would appear to state an insolvable case of circuitous reasoning. However, the answer is really not very difficult after all. *If a person has a DESIRE to be good* (perform good actions and avoid evil ones), he will always do *only what he THINKS is correct*; that is, he will always act only in conformity with a subjectively *certain* conscience (one that is sincerely convinced of the truth). Plus, he will *seriously* study and inquire to know what is the *objective* truth of matters, so that he will soon also be acting with a *correct* conscience as well (a conscience in conformity with objective truth—what we call "God's law" or the Natural Law).

Such a person, who ardently *desires* to act according to the truth, who *prays* to know the truth, and who acts only in conformity with a subjectively *sincere* conscience, will soon come to know the *objective* truth and will thereafter be acting according to a *correct* (objectively accurate) conscience.

Our Lord indicated the functioning of this principle of "action-influencing-understanding-of-truth" when He said: "If you continue in my word, you shall be my disciples indeed. And you shall know the truth, and the truth shall make you free." (*John* 8:31-32). Expressing the negative side of the principle, St. Paul in Chapter 1 of *Romans* says of certain sinners, "And as they liked not to have God in their knowledge, God delivered them up to a reprobate sense." (*Rom.* 1:28). In other words, the sin of the sinner blunts or dulls his understanding of the truth, giving him a moral view of his actions which does not properly reveal the *depravity* of his actions, due to his conscience being "covered with the salve of sin," if we might coin a phrase to describe how sin mollifies the "prick" of conscience. "Reprobate" here means "abandoned" or "reprehensible," or "hardened." "Hardened" is precisely the word needed to express what happens to the sinner's conscience: It becomes *hard*, like a callus, because it has been abused and misused. It is still there, functioning, telling him right from wrong, but its reaction to the seriousness of sin is so hardend by the sinner's repeated sins and by his repeatedly lying to himself about the truth that it does not *bother* the sinner as much as the conscience of the righteous person would had he committed the same sins. Stated in another way, conscience has two spheres of knowing: 1) the right or wrong of our actions, 2) the seriousness of the wrong done; when we sin, the first goes on working, but the second type of knowing becomes faulty—we develop a reprobate sense and are as it were "abandoned" by God to our own confusion and error.

Every one of us takes it as axiomatic in the

physical and mental realms that "we *become* as we *do*." The person who adopts a regular exercise routine becomes strong—and he also *knows* thereby how to be strong. The person who diets consistently loses weight—and also he comes to know how to control his weight. Etc. In the mental order, it is no different: The person who goes to school and studies hard emerges with a brighter, more powerful mind—and he thereby also *knows* how to use his mind better than one who has not been to school and studied hard. He who practices memory exercises develops a better memory—and he also *knows* how to use his memory. The person who takes a speed-reading course ends up reading faster—and he also *knows* how to read faster. The one who daily keeps abreast of current events knows current events—and also he *knows* how to maintain his knowledge of current events.

Now the physical and the mental realms are analogous (similar) to the spiritual realm with regard to being good and knowing thereby *how* to be good and remain good. The person who works at it knows how it is done, and he *also* comes to know the truth of things better and better. In secular activities we say that a person "gets to know the ropes," that is, he becomes more and more familiar with his trade the more he works at it, and he thereby comes to *know* the facts connected with his business. No one would expect a carpenter or an electrician to be thoroughly competent at his trade after only his first day on the job. Because the spiritual realm is more subtle does not mean that the same type of principle is not in effect (even when supernatural Faith enters the picture). It is. Indeed it is! "If you continue in my word. . .you shall know the truth, and the truth shall make you free." (*John* 8:31-32). "Continue" implies we have to work at keeping Christ's word (commandments), and keep it over a period of time. *Then* we shall begin really to penetrate and to know the truth. We have Our Lord's word for it.

The key to growing in goodness, and thereby in spiritual understanding (even when, as mentioned, it includes the element of supernatural Faith), is to *DESIRE* this growth and this knowledge, because thereby we will cooperate with God's grace, do the good and work at acquiring the spiritual understanding. It is the same in learning any skill or trade. If we *desire* to know it, we will *learn* it and we will *know* it, and this knowledge will make us *"free"* to practice it.

To reiterate then, the practice of good repeated actions (virtue) will lead us into a deeper and deeper understanding of the truth; but the committing of evil actions (which we have to perform in contradiction to the knowledge of our conscience) will blunt our perception of the truth *because it causes our understanding of the MALICE of sin to be less than it would be if we did not sin.* Therefore, immoral actions will allow us to sink into a sort of moral blindness which, in turn, will allow us to sink *deeper* into sin.

Grasping this profound moral principle—of the direct relationship between our morality and our understanding of moral truth—will enable us to comprehend the otherwise mystifying statement of Our Lord: ''For to every one that hath shall be given, and he shall abound: but from him that hath not, that also which he seemeth to have shall be taken away.'' (*Matt.* 25:29).

Therefore, with regard to conscience, what all this discussion means—about how our actions influence our perception of the truth—is simply this: If a person wants to have a *correct* conscience (one in conformity with the objective truth), he has to make a practice of always acting in conformity with a subjectively *certain* (or sincere) conscience (a conscience in conformity at least with what he honestly *thinks* to be right). In other words, as we have seen, *''You have to be good in order to know the truth.''* If a person will proceed in this manner when he acts, all the while striving to gain a more and more accurate understanding of the truth through prayer and study, he will *grow* or progress in the *true* or *objective* knowledge of God's holy truth.

But if a person sins, he will ''develop a callus on his conscience,'' so to speak, so that it does not perceive the malice of sin so accurately or so sensitively as it should (though it still sees sin to be sin). Sinning blunts a person's conscience (by causing him not to understand the gravity of his sins) and thereby exposes him to fall more easily into further and graver sins. It is a self-

evident principle that *we become what we do.*
Therefore, when a person sins, he should realize
that he is thereby making any future attempt
to return to living by the truth that much harder,
for his return to correct behavior will be against
the grain of an evil habit and with a reprobated
(abandoned, hardened) conscience for a guide.

At this point, we are now prepared to see what
causes the diversity in the consciences of different people. (Actually, their consciences are probably pretty much the same, as we would note
if we could see them from God's perspective, but
the difference comes into play with regard to
the *level of awareness* that different people have
and the *honesty* with which they observe and
follow what their consciences are telling them.)

Moralists state that once we discuss conscience,
we have gone into the *subjective* realm of morality, that is, into "what the individual person sees
within his mind as true," as distinct from "what
is *objectively* true." It can readily be seen that
the only faculty each one of us has for making
moral decisions *is* our own conscience, for that
is what we all go by when making our moral
decisions. Therefore, *it is of paramount importance that our conscience be accurate and in accordance with objective truth.*

At this point it is important to examine some
specific technical terms with regard to our conscience: First of all, with regard to the nature
of conscience, it is acknowledged by Catholic

moralists that conscience is simply a name for "that aspect of our minds which makes moral evaluations"; conscience is not, therefore, a separate faculty distinct from our minds. (Conscience is also sometimes considered to be *the process which our intellects go through to reach such moral judgments.* It is also, and from still a different perspective, sometimes considered to be *the actual moral judgment or conclusion which the mind makes.*)

Secondly, our conscience can be said to be *correct* or *erroneous*, depending on whether the judgments it makes are in accord with the truth or contrary to the truth as it exists in the objective order. Obviously, we have an obligation to strive to have a correct conscience.

Next, our conscience can be *certain* or *doubtful*; now this distinction pertains strictly to *how we subjectively perceive a certain case*; that is, are we *certain* that we are right, or are we *doubtful* that we are right. Obviously, *we have a strict moral obligation to be as certain as we possibly can that we are right*. With regard to having a certain or doubtful conscience, it is obvious too that we might indeed have a *certain* conscience (that is, we think for sure that we are right), and yet we are in fact wrong (*erroneous* in the objective order). In other words, we can think, and even be *certain*, that we are judging correctly, and yet we can in fact be judging *erroneously*. (A very common example of this would concern the truth of one's religion; a person may *think* he is in the right religion to please God, when *in fact* he is not.)

Our conscience, moreover, can be *delicate* or *callous* (i.e., tender or tough, fine or blunt, etc.) depending on whether it is *sensitive* to the truth we discern, or whether it is *callous* and *insensitive* to the truth. (These conditions, as we have seen above, result from our practicing morality or immorality.) And finally, our conscience can be *perplexed* or even *scrupulous*: when our conscience is *perplexed*, we do not know which course of action is correct, or we fear that we will perform a moral evil no matter which way we act. A person with an habitually perplexed conscience is generally someone whose conscience is very delicate, but who has lost the ability to make practical decisions. A person with a scrupulous conscience is someone who sees small sins as big sins or innocent acts as sinful ones, or who is tormented by doubts and fears over moral decisions that have already been made and settled in the past, but which the person cannot let go of, etc. Scrupulosity has been described by moralists as more of a psychological problem than an ethical or moral one. The perplexed and scrupulous conscience are usually found together in the same person, and the entire syndrome is usually termed simply *scrupulosity*.

As we have seen above, part of what we call conscience involves our "formal" moral education—the process of *prefeeding* the mind with certain true moral principles whereby and upon which we base our actions, for example, the principles "Lying is wrong," "Stealing is wrong," "Cursing is wrong." *Now the proper and correct "formal" education of our conscience is one of the two most important factors in the entire notion of having a correct conscience, and it is so important that it is worth far more than whatever effort might have had to be made to struggle through this somewhat laborious dissection of the anatomy of conscience.* For if we do not have a properly informed and preformed conscience, we will not have the advantage of knowing *in advance* what is right and wrong; we will be left strictly to the natural workings of our conscience (the insight—evaluation—judgment apparatus), and we will be more easily subject to temptation and to fall into sin. It is obvious that accurate moral decisions will be that much harder. Therefore, *the moral obligation we have to form our conscience properly is of the very first magnitude.* And as a corollary to this, *it is of the very first magnitude to adopt as a teacher of right moral principles that authority which is unfailingly certain.* And as a further corollary, it is of equal importance that parents actually, and at the proper time, attend to the correct moral education of their children. Further, it can even be seen that therefore *we have an ongoing obligation to be sure that our conscience CONTINUES to be properly formed,* by means of sound reading and taking sound moral instruction, and that we continue to review our preformed moral precepts to be absolutely certain they are correct and we understand them.

The second of the two most important factors in having a correct *conscience is to avoid sin*! The habitual and purposeful sinner will never properly understand correct morality, for he is, so to speak, burying under a blanket of sin the element of his conscience that reacts to what his mind clearly sees to be wrong—thereby obscuring his perception of the gravity or moral import of his sins.

In order to please God in our moral actions, we must always act with at least a subjectively *certain* conscience (honestly accurate, as far as we are able to know), but we should also always be striving to have a *correct* conscience as well (one in conformity with the objective truth). The most important aspect about conscience is that we be *absolutely honest* with ourselves—that we act with complete integrity and that we always strive to learn the truth about a moral question. When we are in doubt, we should always inquire of the proper and unfailing Authority in matters of morality and thereafter follow sound advice. We must seek the truth honestly, rather than try to convince ourselves of what we *want* to believe or consult someone who we know will tell us what we want to hear.

God sees our *motives* in connection with every action we perform, and if our conscience is not sincere and at least subjectively *certain* (*true*, as we honestly see the matter), then He will hold us accountable for whatever evil we do. But we must realize too that we also have a strict obligation to be sure that our conscience is *accurate*, that is, that our moral judgments are in accord with the *objective* truth.

God does indeed expect us to be absolutely and totally honest in our moral decisions. Let us recall here two passages from Scripture: When the disciple Nathanael was first coming to meet Our Lord, Jesus seemingly could not help exclaiming, "Behold an Israelite indeed, in whom there is no guile" (*John* 1:47), which in other words was saying, "Behold a true believer in whom there is no deceit of soul." ("Israelite" means "true believer.") Our Lord's exclamation would seem to indicate that there are few people indeed who possess no guile or "deceit of soul." And the other passage is from the Old Testament, wherein the Prophet exclaims, "Woe to you that are deep of heart" (*Is.* 29:15), meaning, "Woe to you, the devious, dishonest, deep and crafty person who tries to lie to yourself and who blunts your conscience against seeing the true gravity of your sins."

To summarize the matter of conscience, God has created our minds to know, and they do know, and they know with an amazing accuracy and precision, without the assistance of "formal" education (outside help). Plus, our minds, of which the conscience is a function, operate in such a manner that they cannot ever be *successfully* lied to, nor can the truth about moral matters ever be *completely* obscured to ourselves by ourselves. However, every sinner to some degree or other does in fact *attempt* to lie to himself, either about the fact of his sin or about the degree of its seriousness. But he can never completely convince himself that a sin is not a sin, because God created his mind to work unerringly, and therefore he is unhappy, for his conscience keeps working as God created it to work, reminding him of his guilt, despite his having developed (by his sin) a "callus" on the reaction element of his conscience, whereby he no longer experiences the proper reaction to the gravity of his sins.

Unless we have *informed* our conscience in advance with TRUE moral principles, we will usually not make accurate judgments of conscience when it comes to specific cases requiring action, because we will not *in advance* possess within our minds the norms of *true* morality, which we can use as a guide. If we have not, so to speak, "advised" our conscience *in advance* with such *true* norms, we open ourselves more easily to commit sin (moral error); and to the extent that we could have learned the truth in advance but did not do so, to that extent we are guilty of whatever sins we may commit, even when acting sincerely (i.e., with a subjectively *certain* conscience), for by study in advance, we could have achieved a *correct* conscience (one in accord with objective truth).

Because the conscience of the sinner still works and always reminds him of his sin, yet because his very sin obscures to his mind the *gravity* or seriousness or exact *moral import* of his sin, we can actually say that *conscience has, as it were, "two visions,"* the one of what is good and evil (which never becomes obscured) and the other of the moral import or gravity or degree of wickedness of the good and evil we do. By sinning, we dull to some degree the sensitivity of "the second vision of our conscience"—that which reports correctly on the *gravity* of our sins. We then begin to see inaccurately the real perversity of our sins, for our view or understanding of them is weakened or obscured because of a sort of moral glaucoma on "the second vision of our conscience," the one that sees how bad our sins are. To a certain degree, then, our conscience becomes *blunt*, so that it is no longer sensitive, delicate and attuned to the seriousness of the sins we commit. This is what St. Paul refers to, as we saw, when he says about certain sinners that "God delivered them up to a reprobate sense" (*Rom.* 1:28), that is, to an inaccurate assessment of the seriousness of their sin. (Incidentally, the sin being discussed by St. Paul was homosexuality, but the general principle that *"sin blinds the sinner to the truth of the moral import of his sin"* remains true of all types of sin.)

On the other hand, by leading a virtuous life,

by praying to know the truth, by constantly striving to form our conscience correctly (by learning true moral principles from the authoritative and unfailing Source) and by always acting with a *certain* conscience, we can *help* our conscience to become a delicate instrument that will be not only *certain* (subjectively) but also *correct* or *accurate* (objectively speaking, that is, its judgments will correspond to the objective truth). Then, as we have seen above, it will be with us as Our Lord has said, "If you continue in my word, you shall be my disciples indeed. And you shall know the truth, and the truth shall make you free." (*John* 8:31-32).

Yes, if we form and inform our conscience with true moral principles from the proper, unfailing Source, and if we act according to it with proper certitude, we shall grow in the knowledge of the truth, we shall be free of our moral anxieties, and we shall achieve (if we pray to know the truth) a knowledge of the truth—even while on this earth—which will make us *"free," free* from doubt, *free* from feelings of guilt, and *free* from anxieties about going to Hell! "And you shall know the truth, and the truth shall make you free." (*John* 8:32).

Having gone through this somewhat technical analysis of the "anatomy of conscience" (what conscience is and how it works), we can now see why there is such a difference in the consciences of different people: The basic functioning of the mind (the insight apparatus) works unerringly to tell us at least what is right from what is wrong. But because many people have "advised" their consciences in advance with wrong principles and/or because they purposely lie to their consciences when they sin, there arises a great diversity of opinion about the truth in moral matters. And therefore the issue of morality becomes confused and controversial. Because sorting out the elements that contribute to true moral perception can be made so complicated (despite there being only three elements), the job becomes rather like untying the proverbial Gordian Knot, and people, in the interest of getting along with one another, tend to gloss over in society their real attitudes toward sin (especially mortal sin). The result is that in time we have developed a social condition where "just about anything goes," especially where it concerns the "common mortal sins." Because mortal sinners do not want to be roused out of their comfortable moral torpor, they will wrangle if anyone would suggest to them they are living in grievous (mortal) sin, a fact that only adds to the perception of a seeming great diversity among consciences. As mentioned earlier, if we had God's view, we would probably see that most *consciences* themselves are pretty much the same, but the diversity arises largely in the *honesty of heart* from person to person, whereby people acknowledge or refuse to acknowledge the truth in moral matters. Mortal sinners need to defend their error. If they did not, the constant knowledge of their dire predicament of imminently falling into Hell should they die would be more than they could bear. Thus, we have today the perception of great diversity of consciences; whereas, we have in fact *great diversity of honesty in the hearts of human beings.* As a reminder of the central importance of honesty in our moral actions, Our Lord gave us the beautiful Beatitude: "Blessed are the clean of heart, for they shall see God." (*Matt.* 5:8).

One final point now needs addressing: *What teacher shall we go to in order properly to inform our conscience with true moral principles*—the *second* of the three elements of conscience? We have seen the answer to this question earlier. It is to the Roman Catholic Church, to the One, Holy, Catholic and Apostolic Church founded by Jesus Christ upon the headship of St. Peter, the Rock (*Petros*) of the Church, that same historical St. Peter who went to Rome from Antioch to set up the seat of his bishopric. And we find St. Peter's See (diocese or patriarchal throne or seat) still at Rome after 266 successive Popes, all of whom have ruled the Universal Church established by Jesus Christ, the "city seated on a mountain [that] cannot be hid" (*Matt.* 5:14), whose leader, the Pope, is the greatest religious figure in the world, a hundred times (at least) over his nearest rival. Can there be any doubt where we should go to find accurate moral teaching? As Our Lord told the Apostles, "He that heareth you, heareth me; and he that despiseth you, despiseth me; and he that despiseth me, despiseth him who sent me." (*Luke* 10:16). In other words, the truth of the Master's voice will always be recognized, speaking down through the ages, whenever it is presented by His true disciples—whether they teach using His exact words from the Gospel, or whether they present His doctrine in the words of the Roman Catholic Church, the Mystical Body of Christ on earth.

This strong endorsement for the Catholic Church is not uttered from a triumphalist attitude. No, for as a Catholic, one realizes that he must "with fear and trembling work out his salvation." (*Phil.* 2:12). Rather, it is stated from a firm conviction of the truth and from an anguish at seeing so many people wallow in mortal sin and in the error, confusion and unhappiness which it inevitably brings in its train, with seemingly no knowledge of how to extricate themselves from their difficulties. For the evil fruits of sin—namely, unhappiness and misery—do indeed begin right here in this world. In an effort to wake people from their moral error, God often sends them "warnings," in the form of accidents, damage to property, wasted time, disappointments, confusion, poverty, sickness and even the death of their loved ones. (This is not to say, of course, that these things are *always* "warnings" from God, for they also happen to people who are good.) The point is that *when the mortal sin-ner encounters a SERIES of these "problems,"* he should look to his behavior as the very likely cause of possible "warnings" from God. For God does not necessarily wait for the misery of Hell in the next life to alert people to their moral predicament, but in His tender mercy, He often tries to spare the mortal sinner eternal damna-tion by sending certain painful "reminders" to him that he is going astray and that he should return to obeying God's law, lest in the end he suffer the loss of his immortal soul.

If, after all the warnings the mortal sinner receives, he still does not repent and do pen-ance for his sins, surely on the Particular Judg-ment Day of that person God will remind him that He made him "in His own image and like-ness," with a mind fully equipped to know. And God will accuse that sinner of not following the true dictates of his conscience, either because that person acted directly against what he knew to be true or because he acted without bother-ing to ascertain the truth in advance of acting; whereas, he could have come to a knowledge of the truth by investigating to know the truth where he suspected it to be. No one will be able to say to Almighty God on Judgment Day, "I did not know." For God has created us so that we *do* know and in such a way that we can never truly and completely lie to ourselves successfully.

If we die in the state of mortal sin, therefore, and go to Hell, we will have only ourselves to blame, because God has equipped us to know the truth with our natural reason, plus He has given us His divine Revelation through the teaching authority of the Catholic Church, which He has established to act as our guide. Through this Church He has provided us with His grace, by the means of the Seven Sacraments, to overcome sin and to do good. Overcoming sin and practicing charity through the help of His grace is the way we are to save our souls from Hell and enjoy the happiness of Heaven forever.

A brief restatement of the principles outlined in this chapter goes as follows: God has created our minds to know things, which they truly do know, through the processes of the unaided reason; the insights we have of things are accurate and cannot really be obscured by our lying to ourselves. To aid and assist our minds to know the truth of moral actions, we learn moral principles ("Stealing is wrong," "Cursing is wrong," etc.) from our parents, elders, schools, *et al.*, which our minds know and accept as true *in advance* of our practical moral decisions and by which our minds measure our actions. But we can confuse our moral judgments to some degree by trying to lie to ourselves about the moral truth of matters and also by committing sin (acting contrary to what we know is the truth), which dulls our perception of the seriousness of our sins and makes it that much easier for us to continue to live in serious sin.

It can be seen from all of the above that two elements in the formation of our consciences are most important: First, *we must receive our formal moral principles from an unfailingly true source.* (The only claimant to this title is the Catholic Church.) And second, *we must be morally good in order not to dull the perception of our conscience about the truth of the moral gravity of our sins.* In order to have a correct conscience (one in accordance with the objective order, i.e., the facts) *it is imperative that we be sincere, open, humble and honest* in our attempt to know the truth, and *pray for God's grace* to know it. By this method we can unfailingly come to know the truth because we will have working in our favor 1) the natural faculties of our mind, which God created to know, 2) the divine Revelation of Jesus Christ, which is taught by the Catholic Church and which aids and assists the natural mental faculties, and 3) true moral living, which opens the moral perceptions of our minds to a deeper understanding of the truth of moral matters.

A final few thoughts need to be appended to this chapter on ''The Role of Conscience.'' The first has to do with the knowability of things in the objective order (the ''real world''). Philosophers distinguish two basic or fundamental principles within everything that exists: 1) its *essence* or *nature* or *''form''* (this last is a technical word, meaning ''essence''), and 2) its existence. Of the things which God has created, and also which man makes, there is an essence or nature—the knowable aspect of the thing. (And closely linked with an object's *essence* is its *purpose*.) It is this essence of things which the mind of man grasps in its effort to know things. The mind quickly knows that the "essence" (or purpose) of a house (a man-made thing) is primarily to give shelter, of a baseball bat to hit a ball. Without going to school to learn this and without having to have someone else tell him so (inform his conscience), a person knows with his unaided reason that houses and bats, under normal circumstances, are not intended for kindling wood; and therefore the making of fires with them, under normal circumstances, is wrong. The essence or knowability of these objects (which includes the purpose for which they were created) can be grasped by the mind of man without assistance from someone else. Therefore, the mind of man realizes it is wrong (i.e., a sin) under normal circumstances to use houses or baseball bats to build fires with.

It is the essence or nature or knowability of things in the objective order which man's mind grasps through the apparatus of sense perception and insight, discussed at the beginning of this chapter. Thus, the knowability (essence or nature) of things can be picked up by man's mind from the world outside—what is called the "objective order." Because all things that exist have their own particular values—(goodness)—

which values are determined by their nature—
to use them contrary to their nature is morally
wrong (a sin).

The basic fact that the wrong use of things
is a sin is easily grasped by the mind of man
through his insight. And man's conscience will
always remind him of the fact that he is doing
wrong when he sins. Yet, the *degree of the seriousness* of the sins man commits cannot always
be fully grasped by just the use of his mind—i.e.,
by using only his unaided reason.

And this is where the Revelation of Jesus Christ
enters the picture; Revelation fills out the
understanding that man has of the true seriousness of sin (which, philosophically speaking,
amounts to "acting against the values or goodness inherent within and deriving from the nature or essence of things").

Because the eternity and the level of suffering in Hell are beyond human comprehension,
man, without the assistance of divine Revelation, and using only his unaided reason, could
not arrive at a true view of this state of punishment. Human beings can with their unaided reason figure out that there is a God, that man's
soul is immortal, and that there will be some
sort of punishment for sin. But it is beyond the
pale of unassisted human reasoning to figure out
that certain evil actions are mortal sins and will
(if the person dies with them unrepented on his
soul) condemn his soul to Hell for all eternity;
whereas, certain other evil actions (venial sins)

will not. In other words, without the help of
Revelation, man, as we know him, could not figure out by himself the clear distinction between
mortal and venial sin, let alone their ramifications in the next world. Nevertheless, this distinction, though *beyond* man's unaided reason,
is in harmony *with* reason. But this cannot be
said of the Protestant error which says, "Sin is
sin," which means that all sin is equally serious
and equally deserving of punishment.

At this point in our discussion, the absurdity
of a position which disregards the difference between mortal and venial sin should be obvious
to all. To steal a penny from a millionaire would
be no worse, using the "sin-is-sin" reasoning, than
to steal a thousand dollars from a poor widow
with small children to support. Granted both *are*
sins—and in this respect they *are* the same—but
the degree of seriousness is profoundly different!

But, though we *can* figure out certain basic
guidelines, such as those set forth in this example, still it is not possible for a person to say that
he can figure out on his own the true moral implications and ramifications of human actions,
and that he has therefore no need of God to tell
him for sure what is right and wrong and just
how serious certain actions are.

When Jesus Christ appeared on earth and
began His Public Ministry, people recognized the
truth of what He was telling them. Their minds
already knew basic right from wrong without
any outside help. Those who first heard Our Lord

the Jews, were in the True Faith of the Old Testament, and therefore from two sources (their own unaided reason and the revelation of God through Moses and the prophets) they could tell that Jesus Christ spoke the truth, that "never did man speak like this man" (*John* 7:46), and they noted that "he was teaching them as one having power." (*Matt.* 7:29).

Further, when the Apostles went out into the Gentile (non-Jewish) world to spread the Gospel, they simply resorted to using the very words of Our Lord to give the message He had commissioned them to spread. And the Gentile peoples, too, recognized the truth of Our Lord's words. Their minds did not have the advantage of the Old Testament Revelation, but by their unaided reason they already knew the basics of moral truth as built into nature, and the divine Revelation of Christ (in the New Testament) could simply be ingrafted upon what they already knew of that natural truth. Thus it is that Our Lord could say, "Every one who is of the truth, heareth my voice." (*John* 18:37).

We can conclude here by saying that the "law of God" is written by the Creator in the nature of things—i.e., it is within the essence of everything that God creates, and even everything that man "creates." And the essence within things, making them what they are, determines how these things are to be used by man. We can say that man's mind, unassisted by Revelation, knows the basic goodness or evil of actions (because his mind—through insight—grasps the nature of various things and therefore how they should be used). But Revelation sharpens and hones to a fine edge *man's understanding of the exact import of his evil actions*—an understanding that includes the difference between mortal and venial sin and that spells out the nature of true contrition for sin, the necessity of having (or regaining) Sanctifying Grace (the divine life of God) in our souls, and the need for reparation for sins already forgiven but unatoned for. That man's mind, *without divine Revelation,* could fully understand all these implications to moral actions is beyond imagination. And this is why we need the Revelation of Christ to guide us with unfailing sureness.

Now this Revelation is presented to the world by the Catholic Church. *Thus, it is to the Catholic Church that we all must go to inform our consciences with true moral principles*—principles that will aid and assist and guide us in our practical day-to-day moral decisions. *Much* indeed of what we need to know about sin— what to do and what to avoid—comes from the natural processes of our minds. But an essential element must be supplied by God, through the Church, if we are to save our souls and avoid Hell, *because we simply cannot on our own know the full dimension of sin and its true import.* Therefore, simply in the interest of knowing the Truth, we are morally bound to apply to this great official Teacher of Christ's Revelation for the true and accurate "formal" moral guidance (the moral principles) we must have in order to sharpen our natural understanding gained by the unaided mind through the process of insight. If we will add to this mix *prayer to know the truth* and *honesty in acknowledging the truth*, we shall have present all the ingredients for a properly formed and accurate or correct conscience, one that will aid us unfailingly to save our souls and avoid Hell.

Chapter XI

THE NECESSITY OF PRAYER

St. Alphonsus Liguori (1696-1787), when he founded the Redemptorist Order and sent his priests out to give missions to the people living in the countryside, instructed them to teach the people the simple principle: "He who prays will be saved, and he who does not will be lost." Why is this so, and how could St. Alphonsus be so certain?

First, it must be remembered that he was one of the most learned Doctors of the Church who ever lived—one might say, a gift from God to the Church and to the world. He was a profoundly and vastly intelligent man, who was as pure as an angel and who had gone back through the great writers of the Church and had read everything he could find. Just to read him reveals an erudition that is staggering. And the Popes have repeatedly urged the widespread dissemination of his writings, which number 111 in all; on May 18, 1803 Pope Pius VII ratified the investigation of a pontifical committee commissioned to review all of the Saint's writings: That committee found that "no proposition deserving of censure has been found in the writings of Alphonsus de' Liguori." Thereafter it is wrong to apply a note of censure to any of his writings.

Why is it true, then, that if we pray for our salvation, we shall be saved; and if we do not, we will not be saved? There are two basic reasons: The *first* is that it is the certain will of God that we save our souls. For this is the very reason He created us. Now we know by our reason, unaided by Revelation, that God is absolute truth, that He cannot contradict Himself or His decisions. He made man in His image and likeness, "to know, love and serve Him in this world and to be happy with Him forever in the next," as the Catholic Catechism says, and thus it is God's will that each and every person be saved and come to live with Him eternally. Therefore, when we pray for our own salvation, it is certain that God will grant our prayer (if we pray with humility, confidence, perseverance, etc.) because it is exactly and most importantly what He wants for us.

The *second* basic reason why we will be saved if we pray for our salvation is a bit more difficult to understand, but yet it is still not really difficult at all. We know by Faith, and the Bible tells us, that the supernatural virtue of Faith is a free gift of God and that Sanctifying Grace, which we receive through the Sacrament of Baptism, is also a free gift of God, which the receiving person does not earn or merit on his own, but which God freely gives. As He says in the book of *Exodus*, "I will have mercy on whom I will, and I will be merciful to whom it shall please me." (*Exodus* 33:19). Also, "But to every one of us is given grace, according to the measure of the giving of Christ." (*Ephesians* 4:7).

We have seen too that "actual grace," which is the supernatural "*help*" from God which prompts us and enables us to do whatever supernatural good we do, each and every time we perform a good act, is also a free gift of God. *But the actual grace necessary for us to CON-TINUE in a morally good life (that is, "in the State of Grace) and therefore to save our souls is a gift that God normally gives only if we ask for it!* Now we know that God wills our salvation, and therefore if we pray for the graces necessary for us to save our souls, God will give us those actual graces we need, day to day, in order that we might do the things we have to do to gain our salvation.

St. Alphonsus cites St. Augustine as an authority for this position: "And St. Augustine teaches that, except the first graces of vocation to the faith and to repentance, all other graces, and particularly the grace of perseverance, are granted to those only who ask them. 'It is evident that God gives some graces, such as the beginning of faith, without prayer, and that He has prepared other graces, such as perseverance to the end, only for those who pray' (*de Dono Persev.*, c. xvi). And in another place he writes that 'God wishes to bestow His favours; but He gives them only to those who ask.' (*In Ps.*, c.)." (*Sunday Sermon* xxxix, par. 4). St. Alphonsus goes on to say, "Hence, theologians commonly teach, after St. Basil, St. John Chrysostom, St. Augustine, Clement of Alexandria, and others, that, for adults prayer is necessary *as a means* of salvation; that is, that without prayer it is impossible for them to be saved." (*Sunday Sermon* xxxix, par. 5). He proceeds to cite several scriptural passages to support his point: "We ought always to pray." (*Luke* 18:1). "Ask, and you shall receive." (*John* 16:24). "Pray without ceasing." (*1 Thess.* 5:17). St. Alphonsus continues, "The words *we ought, ask, pray,* according to St. Thomas (3 *Part, qu.* 39, *art.* 5) and the generality of theologians, imply a precept, which obliges, under grievous sin, particularly in three cases. First, when a man is in the state of sin; secondly, when he is in great danger of falling into sin; and, thirdly, when he is in danger of death. Theologians teach that he who, at other times, neglects prayer for a month, or at most for two months, cannot be excused from mortal sin; because, without prayer we cannot procure the helps necessary for the observance of the law of God. St. Chrysostom teaches, that as water is necessary to prevent trees from withering, so prayer is necessary to save us from perdition." (*Sunday Sermon* xxxix, par. 5).

St. Alphonsus cites several Scripture passages that prove that God hears and answers our prayers: "Call upon me in the day of trouble: I will deliver thee, and thou shalt glorify me." (*Ps.* 49:15). "He shall cry to me and I will hear him." (*Ps.* 90:15). "Cry to me, and I will hear thee." (*Jer.* 33:3). "You shall ask whatever you will, and it shall be done unto you." (*John* 15:7). "Ask, and it shall be given you; seek, and you shall find; knock, and it shall be opened to you." (*Matt.* 7:7). God, who is Goodness Itself, desires to shower His blessings upon us—if we will but ask...and ask in the right manner. If we will ask, and do so with the correct dispositions, His answers will be unfailing. For, as St. Paul says, God is "rich unto all that call upon him." (*Rom.* 10:12).

Now, what are the proper dispositions for prayer in general, that when we pray for our salvation, we can have assurance that our prayers will be answered? The Catechism teaches that when we pray, we must do so 1) with *humility*, 2) with *confidence*, 3) with *perseverance*, 4) with *attention*, and 5) with *penitence*. (These five "qualities" for effective prayer are summed up simply by saying we must pray with *sincerity*.)

Before continuing this discussion on prayer, an important distinction must be made *with regard to WHAT we pray for*. If we pray for our own salvation, with the above-mentioned five conditions attending our prayer, the Catholic Church teaches that we will be infallibly heard and will obtain what we pray for, because it is pre-eminently God's holy will that we save our souls. *If we pray for anything else*, no matter how selfless and noble a cause it might be, and no matter that our prayer be perfect, i.e., having the five

necessary qualities for prayer to be truly acceptable to God, there is no *absolute* guarantee that
God will grant what we pray for because, for
example, it may not be good for us or the answer may depend upon another person's being
worthy to receive it, etc. Yet *morally speaking*,
the Bible assures us that God will hear the prayer
of the "just"—i.e., the morally good (him who
is in the State of Grace)—and grant him what
he prays for.

We must pray with *humility* because "God
resisteth the proud, and giveth grace to the humble." (*James* 4:6). "The prayer of him that hum-
bleth himself, shall pierce the clouds. . .and he
will not depart till the most High behold." (*Ecclesiasticus* 35:21). "He [the Lord] hath had regard to the prayer of the humble." (*Ps.* 101:18).
"A contrite and humbled heart, O God, thou wilt
not despise." (*Ps.* 50:19). Humility is pleasing to
God because the primary aspect of the virtue
of humility is acknowledgment of the truth—
and the truth about ourselves in relation to God
is that we are as virtually nothing and God is
virtually everything. Humility is the virtue which
recognizes this basic fact.

We must pray with *confidence* because, as
Scripture says, "All things, whatsoever you ask
when ye pray, believe that you shall receive; and
they shall come unto you." (*Mark* 11:24). And
again, "No one hath hoped in the Lord, and hath
been confounded." (*Ecclus.* 2:11). And further,
St. James says, "Let him ask of God, who giveth

to all men abundantly. . . but let him ask in faith, nothing wavering." (*James* 1:5, 6). And St. John states, "And this is the confidence we have towards him: That whatsoever we shall ask according to his will, he heareth us." (*1 John* 5:14). God grants our petitions according to the degree of our confidence in asking.

We must also pray with *perseverance*, that is, we should pray regularly, every day, and we should not cease to pray. The Bible tells us, "Pray without ceasing." (*1 Thess.* 5:17). "Let nothing hinder thee from praying always." (*Ecclus.* 18:22). "Watch ye, therefore, praying at all times." (*Luke* 21:36). "We ought always to pray." (*Luke* 18:1). And Our Lord, in *Luke* 11, gives us the example of a man who goes in the night and knocks on the door of his friend, asking for bread, because an acquaintance has come and he has nothing to feed him. The friend does not want to get up and give it to him because he is already in bed, but because of the man's importunity, or annoying persistence, in *continuing* to knock, the friend gets up and gives him whatever he wants—*because of his importunity!* Our Lord's point is that if a friend will give just because he is importuned (pestered), how much more readily will God give, who *desires* to give. We know that we should persevere in prayer because of the assurance of the above parable and Our Lord's words: "*Ask*, and it shall be given you: *seek*, and you shall find: *knock*, and it shall be opened to you." (*Matt.* 7:7, emphasis added).

Thus, by saying, "ask . . . seek . . . knock," Our Lord is *inviting* us to be importunate in our prayer requests and to keep up the asking until the favor be granted.

We must pray with *attention*, that our prayers may have power. St. Louis De Montfort (1673-1716) says, "It is not so much the length of a prayer, but the fervour with which it is said which pleases Almighty God and touches His heart." St. Bernard (1221-1274) has observed, "When we pray, the voice of the heart must be heard more than that proceeding from the mouth." St. Thomas (1225-1274) says, "Purposely to allow one's mind to wander in prayer is sinful and hinders the prayer from having fruit." And finally, St. Frances Xavier Cabrini (1850-1917) has noted, "One whose soul is in disorder, whose mind is wandering with vain, useless thoughts, cannot pray. To pray, we must unite the flesh and its feelings to the soul with its imagination, memory and will." No one would even think of asking another person for a favor and all the while not pay attention to the person from whom he asks the favor, nor pay attention to what he is asking. It would be absurd to do so. The same is true with prayer. God says in the Book of *Isaias*, "This people draw near me with their mouth, and with their lips glorify me, but their heart is far from me." (*Isaias* 29:13). (Almost everyone, however, suffers from distractions in prayer, which are no sin, according to the great spiritual writers, so long as we do not intend them or encourage them. A good habit for those distracted at prayer is to intend to concentrate and to offer up as a penance the very distractions themselves. Also, spiritual writers tell us we should not go back and repeat our prayers when we realize we have let our attention be distracted. Concentration at prayer, of course, is much better than distraction, but God sees our intention and effort, and those are what count most. We can still derive *great* fruit from prayer, even though suffering distractions. For it is "infinitely" better to pray though distracted than because of distractions not to pray at all.)

And finally we must pray *with true penitence*, that is, with sorrow for our sins. (We should pray even though our sorrow may as yet be imperfect and even though we may not yet have actually renounced our sins.) For, true repentance of soul is absolutely essential to having our prayers for our own salvation unfailingly answered by Almighty God. With regard to having our prayers answered by Almighty God for requests *other than* for our own salvation, the Bible makes the matter abundantly clear that such requests will be heard if they come from a morally good person (the "just"), what the Catholic Church calls a person "in the state of grace" (i.e., having Sanctifying Grace in his soul, which is a sharing in the life of God). Let us recall what was discussed above, that "whosoever shall keep the whole law, but offend in one point, is become guilty of all." (*James* 2:10). If we have set ourselves against

Almighty God by committing mortal sin—even just one kind of mortal sin, or just *one* mortal sin—for which we are unrepentant, why should the Lord hear our prayer for something other than our own salvation, for then is not our prayer a lie; are we not then asking of God—when we pray for such a thing in a state of unrepentant mortal sin—to confirm the lie of our sin? Could the all-just and all-true God do that?

The Psalmist says, "Fear the Lord, all ye his saints: for there is no want to them that fear him." (*Ps.* 33:10). And again, "Behold the eyes of the Lord are on them that fear him: and on them that hope in his mercy." (*Ps.* 32:18). And again, "O love the Lord, all ye his saints: for the Lord will require truth, and will repay them abundantly that act proudly." (*Ps.* 30:24). But probably no lines of Scripture tell the story so well as these, "And the Lord will reward me according to my justice; and according to the cleanness of my hands before his eyes. With the holy, thou wilt be holy; and with the innocent man, thou wilt be innocent. And with the elect thou wilt be elect: and with the perverse thou wilt be perverted." (*Ps.* 17:25-27).

No, we cannot fool God, nor can we expect Him to confirm our mortal sins when we pray to Him in a state of unrepentant mortal sin for something other than our own salvation. But the consoling fact is that, despite our past sins, despite the fact that we may still be habituated to sin (even to mortal sin), if we will have at least *a* sincere heart to change, to try to overcome our sins, if we will be sorry for them, if we will repent of them—even if, all the while we are still steeped in them and still not successful in overcoming them, but if we sincerely *want* to be free of them and become virtuous—*then* God will hear our prayer for our own salvation and will help us come to true repentance if we ask Him. For— and let us remember always—God wants nothing more than that the sinner repent and be saved. In fact, He wants our salvation even more than we want it for ourselves.

(Truly, there is *no one* who should not pray for his own salvation. *Even if a person can only say that he WANTS TO WANT TO REPENT*, this is at least a beginning and will open the door for God to help him advance further toward true repentance if he will pray perseveringly as best he can.)

In order that the entire discussion about "prayer for our own salvation" not go without some sort of reference to prayer in general, it will be good at this time to make a brief general overview of prayer, that we might see where in this entire picture our "prayer for our own salvation" fits into the picture.

In general, prayer is defined in the Catholic Catechism as "a raising of the mind and heart to God." Now this activity can and does take many different legitimate forms. The two principal kinds of prayer are *mental prayer* and *vocal prayer*. In *mental prayer* we generally meditate upon the truths of Holy Religion, either as found in the Bible or as we learn them from the lives of the Saints or from the Catechism. Here there is no vocalization with words, but rather a mental pondering of God's holy truths and their meaning for our lives.

With *vocal prayer*, we are actually speaking words, at least with our minds, but maybe also with our lips at the same time. Vocal prayer can take a number of forms: There is 1) *repetitive prayer*, such as saying several *Our Father's*, *Hail Mary's* or *Glory Be's*; then there is the Rosary (which consists of a *number* of repetitive prayers together, plus meditations). Vocal prayer can also consist of 2) *prayers read out of a prayerbook, a breviary, or a missal.* And again vocal prayer can be 3) just *speaking with God* in a free and extemporaneous manner.

What should be remembered is that all these forms of prayer are legitimate and that we should engage in all of them at various times—though from person to person, one form will predominate in his prayerlife over the others.

Actually, there is still a third form of prayer other than mental and vocal prayer, one whereby we offer all our actions to God as sort of a "living sacrifice," as St. Paul calls it in *Romans* 12:1, where he says, "I beseech you therefore, brethren, by the mercy of God, that you present your bodies a living sacrifice, holy, pleasing unto God." This type of sacrificial prayer could really be either mental prayer or vocal prayer, depending upon how we make our offering. What is valuable about offering our sufferings or even our entire life to God is that this type of prayer goes on working for us even when we are busily engaged in our daily activities and do not have the time for mental or vocal prayer. However, *it should never be considered a substitute for mental or vocal prayer*, which are prayer more properly and formally speaking.

The reasons *why we pray* are 1) to *adore* God, 2) to *thank* Him for His many favors, 3) to *petition* Him for our many needs, and 4) to *ask pardon for* and *expiate* (make up for) our sins. Regarding the reasons why we pray, we can see that our prayer for our own salvation comes under the third reason, to *petition*, and at that it is only one of the many reasons for praying in petition to God, since there are many other legitimate things to pray for as well, though none other is so important.

We pray to *adore* God because His majesty demands it, since He is the Author of all that is, ourselves included, and since He alone is truly good and perfect. We pray to God in *thanksgiving*, because ultimately He is the source of all things we have, and our prayer of thanksgiving is simply an acknowledgment on our part of this fundamental spiritual truth. Prayer of thanksgiving keeps our minds and hearts continuously aware of our debt to God. We pray to God in *petition* for our own many needs (not just for our salvation) and the needs of others because

He wants us to ask Him for everything we need, and He wants us to pray for others, too. Granted that God knows in advance what we need, and granted—except for special favors—that He already provides us with most of what we need without our even asking Him for these things, nonetheless, He still wants us to ask Him for our particular needs, especially *because this forces us to acknowledge Him as the source of these things and of all favors we receive and because it keeps us close to Him.* And finally, we pray to God to ask pardon for our sins and to expiate them (make atonement for them) because we are all sinners and we all need God's forgiveness, plus we need to pay back the spiritual debts that we have incurred through our sins.

If each day we will recall our obligation to pray in this fourfold manner—in *adoration,* in *petition,* in *thanksgiving,* and in *pardon* and *expiation*—and if we will always pray for others as well (including the Poor Souls in Purgatory), our prayers will become much more effective, and certainly God will be that much more receptive to our prayers for our own salvation.

We have already considered *how* we should pray, and we have seen that we should pray with 1) *humility,* 2) *confidence,* 3) *perseverance,* 4) *attention,* and 5) *penitence* (i.e., with sorrow for our sins).

At this point, let us now consider *whom we should pray for.* The Catechism tells us that we have a duty to pray for 1) ourselves (our salvation, etc.), 2) our parents, 3) our relatives, 4) our friends, 5) our enemies, 6) sinners, 7) the Poor Souls in Purgatory, especially those who are related to us or who were our friends or whom we may have injured or scandalized, 8) the Pope, bishops, priests, missionaries, religious, etc., 9) our government officials, especially the President, our legislators and judges and 10) anyone we may have injured or scandalized by our sins. (We do not have to pray for all of these people specifically each time we pray. Sometimes we can simply offer prayers "for all those for whom we are obliged to pray.")

And now it is important to consider *some general aspects* about prayer, for example: Why is it that our prayers sometimes do not seem to get answered? What are some very effective ways to pray? How much should a person pray? To whom or through whose intercession should we pray? How much should we thank God when He has answered our prayers? When should we pray? With what method should we pray? What should we do when we do not feel like praying or when we get no consolation from it? These questions all need to be addressed because the basic reason we all should pray and should want to pray is to avoid Hell and to go to Heaven.

Probably the most common question asked relative to prayer is, *"Why do my prayers go unanswered?"* The answer to this question is best summed up by a quote from St. Basil the Great (329-379): "The reason why sometimes thou hast asked and not received, is that thou hast asked amiss, either inconsistently, or lightly, or because thou hast asked for what was not good for thee, or because thou hast ceased asking.'' (*Voice of the Saints*, p. 43). God will not give what is harmful, or what is asked for flippantly, or without constancy and perseverance. St. Vincent de Paul observes in his *Thoughts* (May 10) that one of the most important things that we can do spiritually is to *be consistent in saying our prayers*. And St. Thomas Aquinas says, ''For prayer to be effective, our petitions should be for benefits worthily to be expected from God.'' (*Voice of the Saints*, p. 41). With regard to praying for our own salvation, however, the petition is indeed worthy to be expected from God, and it is something that is God's will to give. But since we will not really know for sure whether we have received the answer to this particular prayer until we shall have died and been judged, we need to gain familiarity with prayer in general and how it works so that we will be sure that we pray every day and as much as we should, in keeping with our duties and our state in life.

Some very *effective ways to pray* are the following: As regards *mental prayer*, we should choose a scriptural passage to be meditated on, and read it at night before retiring. In the early morning, before becoming involved in any routine activity and before talking with anyone, we should read and reread carefully this passage for its profound meanings, and then meditate on them. This is, generally speaking, the method outlined by St. Ignatius Loyola (1491-1556) in his *Spiritual Exercises.*

With regard to *vocal prayer,* every Catholic (and even non-Catholics too) should say the Rosary every day, at least five decades. There is something about the Rosary which transforms a person's life. Many private promises are attached to praying the Rosary, but perhaps a person must experience using this devotion before he will realize its power. Another excellent method of praying is to have a set routine of prayers to be said from one's prayerbook, missal or breviary; the more one says these routine "printed" prayers, the more familiar they become and, if we will just concentrate on them when we pray them, the more effective they become as well, sort of like a familiar tool we use all the time. The most powerful prayer one can offer is the Mass (in union with the priest), and probably second to the Mass would be our private prayers just after Holy Communion. At this time we are intimately united with our Redeemer, and we have just made a powerful act of faith by receiving Him in this Sacrament, where all we perceive are the characteristics of bread. Anyone who wants to make swift advancement in holiness should go to Mass and Communion often, even daily! Making a holy hour (praying for an hour) in church after Mass and Communion, or at least making a holy hour before the Blessed Sacrament at some other time during the day, is a particularly powerful method of prayer and one whose efficacy the generality of Catholics do not sufficiently appreciate.

How much a person should pray depends entirely upon his state in life and the demands of his duties, plus it also should take into account his disposition to pray. In general, however, it can safely be said that *everyone should devote a substantial amount of time to prayer each day*, and by this is meant a minimum of 15 minutes each morning and evening. Now some people, because of their duties on certain days, may not be able to do even this much or do it all the time. But in general, most people can do much more. (One should budget time for prayer, just as we budget time for any important business, since prayer is a necessity and not a "frill.") Something between one-half hour and two hours of prayer should be well within the capability of the average lay person. Priests and religious should generally do even more yet, depending upon their religious rule and their duties. In general it can be said of religious and consecrated souls that the more difficult and important their vocation becomes, the more they should pray. (When one compares this to the time he spends watching T.V., these norms will not appear excessive.) Let us consider for a moment Our Lord's words to St. Peter, "What? Could you not watch one hour with me?" (*Matt.* 26:40; *Mk.* 14:37). In light of this passage, where Our Lord seems to be asking for one hour, it does not seem excessive to dedicate at least 15 minutes morning and evening to prayer. For we all should realize, with regard to prayer, that this is the practice that will win for us the graces necessary to save our souls. Therefore, no one should be stingy in this activity. The longer one prays, the longer one is able to pray, and usually the more benefit he derives from prayer and the more he looks forward to it—also, the more he will feel a need to pray, if only to satisfy his longings for contact with God.

To whom, or through whose intercession should we pray? Prayer may be offered *directly to God*— or specifically to God the Father, to God the Son, to God the Holy Spirit. Our Lord has particularly asked us to pray to the Father through *Him*; "Amen, amen I say to you: if you ask the Father any thing in my name, he will give it you." (*John* 16:23). Also, prayer may be offered *through the intercession of* one of God's friends. Now the closest and dearest friend God has is His Mother, the Blessed Virgin Mary. Consequently, our prayers should most often be offered through her intercession. It is an excellent practice to end our prayers to God with the words, "I ask this through the Sacred Heart of Jesus and the Immaculate Heart of Mary," thus involving Heaven's two greatest intercessors (though, of course, Our Lord is infinitely greater, and all of the Blessed Virgin Mary's intercessory power comes from Him.) (Strictly speaking, we do not pray *to* the Blessed Mother and the Saints and angels, but *through* them, asking for their intercessory power with Almighty God on our behalf.)

There is a branch of Catholic theology called Mariology (the study of Mary), and one of the points in Mariology is that the Blessed Mother is the "Mediatrix of all Graces," that is to say, that all graces flow from God to us and all our prayers ascend to God from us, *only through Mary.* Most Catholics believe this to be the case; in fact, most Catholics think this will some day become a defined doctrine of the Catholic Faith, since it is already universally believed by Catholics as one of our traditions. But whatever may be the truth in this matter, it is certain that Mary is far and away the most powerful intercessor with God. Nay, so powerful is she that a priest once said in a sermon: "It is as if God had a weakness, and that weakness is Mary, so that if you cannot obtain a favor in any other way, you can do so through Mary." In this writer's experience, it can almost be said that if one does not want something badly enough to ask the Blessed Virgin Mary for her loving assistance in obtaining it, he probably will just have to do without it. For it would seem that Almighty God has decreed that the unique role of the Blessed Mother in our salvation be acknowledged by and before all mankind, so that her greatness and her wonderful role in our Redemption will become universally known and accepted.

It would seem, moreover, that He has reserved certain prayer intentions to her intercession alone, intentions such as the conversion of Russia and peace in the modern world. So powerful is she that the great St. Bernard of Clairvaux composed the incomparable prayer, the *Memorare* in her honor, which all instructed Catholics know by heart:

THE MEMORARE

Remember, O most gracious Virgin Mary, that never was it known that anyone who fled to thy protection, implored thy help or sought thy intercession was left unaided. Inspired with this confidence, I fly unto thee, O Virgin of virgins, my Mother. To thee I come, before thee I stand, sinful and sorrowful. O Mother of the Word Incarnate, despise not my petitions, but in thy mercy hear and answer me. Amen.

After the Blessed Virgin Mary, who has the pre-eminent place among the Saints as a powerful intercessor with God, there come St. Joseph, St. Michael the Archangel, our Guardian Angel, the saint after whom we have been named, the patron saint of our parish or religious order or pious association, and particularly—though most people may have no cognizance of this whatever—*the saint whose feast is celebrated on that day!* After all, the True Religion has set aside a particular day in that saint's honor, and even Heaven acknowledges it through this means. (It is to the Venerable Anne Catherine Emmerich—

1774-1824—that we owe this beautiful and most beneficial revelation.)

And finally, there is a number of truly powerful and popular saints, whose intercession is virtually unfailing, saints such as (again) St. Joseph (Patron of Workers, of a Happy Death, of the Universal Church, etc.); St. Jude the Apostle (Patron of Impossible Cases); St. Ann (mother of the Blessed Virgin Mary); St. Rita of Cascia (Patroness of Impossible Cases); St. Anthony of Padua (Patron of Lost Objects); St. Martin de Porres; St. Therese the Little Flower (Patroness of Missionaries—who promised to spend her Heaven doing good on earth); St. Philomena (known as "Powerful with God"); St. Francis of Paola (a great miracle-worker); St. Lutgarde; St. Aloysius Gonzaga (Patron of Youth); St. Gerard Magella (Patron of Expectant Mothers); etc. Each of these saintly intercessors is usually famous for various types of help, and some are renowned for helping in *any* type of need. Nor are these the only "great" intercessors; there are many others besides. Truly, God is rich in His saints!

When we have received a favorable answer to our prayers, *we should thank God* profusely for the benefits He has showered upon us. If possible, we should thank Him as much as we spent time in praying for the blessing, but often this is impractical, as for example, a wife praying for the conversion of her husband, which may take an entire lifetime; obviously, she could not spend as much time in thanking God as she spent in her prayer of petition. But a good rule is each day to call to mind during one's prayer of thanksgiving all the many answers to prayer received over the preceding week and month and year. That way, we will always say our prayers in a spirit of thanksgiving, so that we are continually aware of all that God has done for us.

As to *when we should pray,* St. Paul tells us, "Pray without ceasing." (*1 Thess.* 5:17). And St. Peter says, "Be sober and watch: because your adversary the devil, as a roaring lion, goeth about seeking whom he may devour." (*1 Peter* 5:8). Consequently, we should pray on a continuing and on-going basis. From a practical point of view, the Catholic Church recommends that we say at least morning and evening prayers. Included in the morning prayers, we should say a "morning offering" and consecrate our day's activities to Almighty God and offer Him all our prayers, works, joys and sufferings, through the intercession of the Immaculate Heart of Mary, the Mother of God. And in the evening, we should especially include an "act of contrition" for all the sins we may have had the misfortune to commit that day, plus we should say other prayers of our own choosing. But especially, we should say the Holy Rosary every day.

It has also long been a custom for Catholics to go to a noonday Mass during their lunch hour from work, if they have the time, or to go to make a visit and say some prayers before the Blessed Sacrament at that time. These too are beautiful customs. Throughout the day, we can continually raise our minds and hearts to God in supplication, in adoration, in thanksgiving or in expiation. And for this purpose it is good to say what Catholics call "ejaculations" or "aspirations," i.e., very short prayers, such as, "O Mary, conceived without sin, pray for us who have recourse to thee," or, "My Jesus, mercy," or, "Most Sacred Heart of Jesus, have mercy on us," (to be said three times in succession while striking the breast each time).

How and when one prays is very much up to each person, but the main thing is that we *do* pray and that at least twice a day we set aside some time *just* for prayer, when we are not distracted by anything else in our lives; we should dedicate this time to God alone as an offering strictly to Him.

Regarding which method we should use when we pray, as we have seen, it is very much up to each person—with the exception that we should all, if we are Catholics, pray and offer with the priest the Holy Sacrifice of the Mass as often as we can, plus pray the Rosary (five decades) every day. As to the other prayer devotions which we employ, these are our own choice. We should try to cultivate mental prayer as a routine part of our prayerlife because it fulfills the role of deepening our understanding of and appreciation for the truths of Religion better than anything else. A good book on the subject will help us understand how to make this practice, and thereafter we need only to fit it into our daily prayers.

With regard to our entire daily prayer routine, we should recall the words of St. Vincent de Paul about being consistent in our prayers and devotions: "There is one thing which will do much to bring down the blessing of God on yourselves and on your work, and that is the observance of your devotional exercises." (*Thoughts*, May 10). As to the *power* of prayer, the same saint has boldly stated: "Give me a man of prayer, and he will be capable of doing all things; he can say with the Apostle: 'I can do all things in Him that strengtheneth me.'" (*Thoughts*, May 22).

What can we do when we do not feel like praying? The best advice is to pray anyway and ask God for the grace to overcome our fatigue, boredom, indifference, dryness, distraction, anxiety or whatever else is bothering us at the time, remembering all the while Our Lord's words to St. Paul, "My grace is sufficient for thee" (*2 Cor.* 12:9), as well as the verse from the Old Testament, "Thy youth shall be renewed like the eagle's." (*Ps.* 102:5). Oddly enough, through prayer, we can often actually gain back our physical and psychological freshness and be ready once more to carry on with our daily activities. We can pray for this special grace whenever we find prayer difficult. In any event, there is always a host of reasons presenting themselves to our minds as to why we should not pray or why we should quit praying, but we should always have before our minds the realization that *prayer is the means of obtaining God's grace* in our lives and ultimately thereby *it is the instrument of our salvation.* This is a powerful incentive to override the fatigue or dryness or other problems we encounter in connection with saying our prayers regularly.

Once a person really becomes involved in a regular and serious prayerlife, he begins to realize that we live in a universe governed by spiritual power, and that *if we are to enter into the real world and play an active part in what goes on, as well as in our own destiny, especially in the job of working out our salvation, then we definitely have to make prayer the central part of our lives.* Let us remember always the words of St. Alphonsus de Liguori, "If we would be saved and become saints, we ought always to stand at the gates of the Divine mercy to beg and pray for, as an alms, all that we need," as well as those of St. John Chrysostom (347-407), "It is simply impossible to lead, without the aid of prayer, a virtuous life." (*Voice of the Saints,* p. 35).

He who prays shall be saved, and he who does not shall be lost. Let us begin *now* the job of praying regularly, and with all the right dispositions, so that God can favorably answer our prayers and we can avoid Hell and gain Heaven for all eternity.

Chapter XII

THE FUNDAMENTAL
OPTION THEORY

There is circulating today a popular—albeit false—theory called the Fundamental Option Theory, which unfortunately is being espoused by many Catholics today, even if they are not familiar with the term as such. This theory is seriously in error and is extremely dangerous to any who embrace it because it lulls them to sleep about what is required to avoid Hell and gain salvation. Under the Fundamental Option Theory, the presumption is made that so long as a person has made the fundamental option (or basic choice) for God and for goodness and for virtue, then God does not condemn that soul for an occasional mortal sin which he might commit here and there, so long as the fundamental thrust of his life is in the direction of God and of salvation. The idea behind this error is that God sees the overall intent of the person and the overall thrust of his life, and He considers *these* rather than the occasional "slip-ups" (traditionally called "mortal sins") that the person might have.

This theory is *not* the teaching of the Catholic Church and is definitely condemned by the Bible. The basic error of the "Fundamental Option

Theory'' comes from its failure to see exactly what occurs each time the person who has ''fundamentally opted for God'' has a ''slip-up'' (mortal sin). The person who commits a mortal sin has actually already made, by reason of that very choice, a ''fundamental option'' for evil and for himself, and against God, against God's law, against goodness and against virtue. For, by committing a mortal sin, a person has chosen to do a grievous wrong, which he fully and consciously knows to be wrong, and which he fully consents to do anyway. In so acting, he has placed before the true God an idol of his own choosing, the deed he prefers to God. *This choice is so fundamentally wrong that it constitutes all by itself a ''fundamental option'' or a ''fundamental choice'' for evil and against God.* And the person committing such a deed has set himself upon the road to Hell, no matter that the rest of his actions are fundamentally good. For, as the Bible says, and as we have quoted several times, ''And whosoever shall keep the whole law, but offend in one point, is become guilty of all. For he that said, 'Thou shalt not commit adultery,' said also, 'Thou shalt not kill.' Now if thou do not commit adultery, but shalt kill, thou art become a transgressor of the law.'' (*James* 2:10-11). The point is very simple: By choosing to disobey seriously His laws, the person who willfully sins grievously (commits mortal sin) has implicitly denied the authority of the Lawgiver, who in this case, obviously, is none other than God Himself. If the mortal sinner repents, of course, he can receive God's forgiveness and grace and can reorient himself toward God. However, we must realize here that it is the choice of the will that constitutes whether or not a baptized person will continue to live in God's grace or whether he will live in the state of mortal sin.

From this it can be seen that the "Fundamental Option Theory" is entirely wrong—that once a person consciously commits a mortal sin, he has made his "fundamental option" for evil; and until he renounces his sin, even though it is only one type of mortal sin, or just *one* mortal sin, and even though in all other respects the person is leading a virtuous life, he has still violated the whole law, as the quote from *James* 2:10-11 indicates, and all his good deeds will not help him toward gaining Heaven, until he repents of his mortal sin and turns back to God.

Further, the Catholic Church has always taught that one unrepented mortal sin is all it takes to condemn a soul to Hell. In this regard it would be good at this point to consider the following: Many people attempt to outguess God when it comes to trying to analyze why certain people die very young, whereas others are allowed to live out a full life. It may very well be that the person who dies young may have been in the state of grace, and God sees that, if he were allowed to live, he may have fallen into mortal sin and lost his soul. Or, it may be that God sees that the young person has begun to live a life committed to mortal sin and if allowed to continue to live, would have gone from bad to worse and would have ended up in a much deeper place in Hell, to say nothing of taking others there with him. As an act of mercy, therefore, God may allow that person to die earlier rather than later in life, in order to lessen his suffering in Hell and possibly also to spare others the same fate. "For who among men is he that can know the counsel of God? Or who can think what the will of God is?" (*Wisdom* 9:13).

One cannot gainsay or outguess God, of course, and there is no way of knowing why any one given person dies at an early age and why another person is allowed to live a long life. Nonetheless, the entire concept of our eternal destiny's being based upon "a general, fundamental option toward God or toward evil" is an error which is running current today and needs to be exposed for the error it is.

If a person were to analyze the motive behind the proposal of the Fundamental Option Theory, the truth would probably come out that those who suggest this idea cannot come to grips with the plain fact that so many "good" or "nice" people are doing things which, objectively speaking, are mortal sins, and therefore that these otherwise "good people" are on the way to Hell for violating the Law of God, *even though perhaps in just one specific matter.* As quoted above, the Scripture says, "And whosoever shall keep the whole law, but offend in one point, is become guilty of all." (*James* 2:10). Because the human mind cannot grasp the heinousness of mortal sin, nor see the true perverseness of heart of the mortal sinner, and because the mind cannot actually see that mortal sinners are very likely committing *more* than one type of mortal sin, a person can understandably be led to propound this novel and erroneous "Fundamental Option Theory." And the mortal sinners who learn of it grasp it and cling to it, not unlike the drowning man to a straw, in an effort to salve their guilty consciences and think themselves to be safe when indeed they are on the very brink of perishing eternally.

Therefore, as to those who propound this theory, theirs would appear to be a misguided effort to soften the Law of God in the face of so many obvious mortal sins being committed today; and on the part of the mortal sinners who embrace the Fundamental Option Theory, such acceptance would appear to be an effort to ease their guilty consciences, which ever sit in that interior tribunal of truth to accuse them of their sins. Both the proponents and the adherents of this error need to meditate on Our Lord's words: "Be you therefore perfect, as also your heavenly Father is perfect." (*Matt.* 5:48).

Chapter XIII

INDICATIONS THAT ONE IS ON THE WAY TO SALVATION

Are there any indications that a person is on the road to salvation? This might at first seem to be a difficult question to answer because the Bible assures us that "man knoweth not whether he be worthy of love, or hatred." (*Ecclesiastes* 9:1). And, "Who can say: my heart is clean, I am pure from sin?" (*Prov.* 20:9). And again, "Blessed is the man that is always fearful." (*Prov.* 28:14). Even St. Paul says, "But I chastize my body, and bring it into subjection: lest perhaps, when I have preached to others, I myself should become a castaway." (*1 Cor.* 9:27).

However, St. Paul in another passage displays a confident attitude about arriving at salvation: "I have fought a good fight, I have finished my course, I have kept the faith. As to the rest, *there is laid up for me a crown of justice*, which the Lord the just judge will render to me in that day; and not only to me, but to them also that love his coming." (*2 Tim.* 4:7-8, emphasis added).

Therefore, Catholic spiritual writers tell us that there are certain signs that we are on the road to Heaven. Some of these are the following (Now these indications are not intended to be all-inclusive, or infallibly necessary; they represent merely the human wisdom of the Church in her holy members and as rephrased by the present writer):

1. *A love of prayer.* The Christian begins to see that prayer is an essential part of his life each day and spends substantial time at prayer. Also, he begins to derive great fruit from his prayer and sees answers to his prayers.

2. *A sense of dedicating one's life entirely to God.* Here the lover of God often turns his entire life and being over to God, asking for His direction, and more and more he finds himself interested in the things of God and of Holy Religion.

3. *A love for the Holy Sacrifice of the Mass* and a desire to go to Holy Communion often, even daily.

4. *A serious effort to examine one's conscience daily and go often to Confession.* "Often" today is considered once a month, but "often" in the practice of the Church means *at least once a week*. Many saints went several times a week, and some every day. St. Philip Neri required the members of the Oratory to go every day, and the great St. Vincent Ferrer, a prodigious miracle-worker, confessed every day.

5. *A love of charity.* As a person progresses in the love of God, he begins to lose the normal human selfishness and finds great joy in helping others, and he also discovers himself performing works of charity on a more and more regular basis.

6. *A life of penance and sacrifice.* As a person grows in the love of God and as he comes to realize the role of sacrifice and penance to help gain for poor sinners the grace of conversion, he begins to practice penance and sacrifice on a routine basis and comes to love doing so. St. Margaret Mary was such an ''efficient worker,'' so to speak, in the realm of penance, that she needed continually to search out new ways to mortify her life, or she was just not happy.

7. *Devotion to the Blessed Virgin Mary.* This wonderful devotion goes back to the time of the Apostles themselves, who *knew* Mary personally and loved her and were devoted to her themselves. It is *they* who have imparted to the Catholic Church *throughout the world* this unique Catholic devotion that marks all true believers. Once heretics break from the Apostolic Tradition of the Catholic Church, they quickly lose this devotion. Catholics know by experience the power of Mary. That Catholics believe devotion to Mary is a sign that one will be saved was beautifully stated by Pope Pius XI on February 2, 1923: ''. . .nor would he incur eternal death whom the Most Blessed Virgin assists, especially at his last hour. This opinion of the Doctors of the Church, in harmony with the sentiments of Christian people, and supported by the experience of all times, depends especially on this reason, the fact that the Sorrowful Virgin shared in the work of the Redemption with Jesus Christ.'' (*AAS* 15.104). As mentioned earlier, one

priest has called Mary "God's one weakness," as it were, for through Mary we can obtain answers to prayer that seemingly are possible in no other way. God wishes to honor His Blessed Mother, and the answer to several specific prayer requests are, according to certain private revelations, reserved to her intercession—and consequently will add to her glory. One of these is world peace; another is the conversion of Russia.

8. *Devotion to the Most Holy Rosary.* This devotion was given by the Blessed Virgin Mary to St. Dominic (1170-1221), according to legend within the Church. It has become a universal devotion in the Church and one by which we will often obtain favors and spiritual progress which we seem able to obtain by no other method of prayer. Non-Catholics often think the Rosary is a bland, simplistic, mindless repetition of prayers; whereas, it is probably the most complex, varied and overall richest form of prayer that exists (except for the Mass and Divine Office). For its 15 Mysteries are a recollection of principal historical events connected with our Redemption; it is directed to the greatest, the closest and most powerful friend of God who exists, the Blessed Virgin Mary; it helps a person to keep his mind focused on his prayer during 15 to 20 minutes, by continually bringing the mind back to the object it should be focused on (whereas man's normal attention span is very brief, but a few seconds at best); and it employs the four greatest prayers we have—the *Our*

Father, Hail Mary, Glory Be and the *Apostles'
Creed*. In praying the Rosary, the mind can legitimately focus upon 1) the mystery being meditated on, 2) the person to whom the prayer is
directed (Mary), 3) the intention for which one
prays, and/or 4) the meaning of the prayer itself
which is being said. The mind, being restless by
nature, can move from one to another of these
four legitimate objects of focus and yet can still
be concentrated on the overall prayer of the
Rosary.

Despite our fulfilling all of what we may think
are our basic moral obligations, and despite our
seeing in our life many or even most of the above
"typical signs" that we are on the road to salvation, we should never become complacent about,
or even take for granted, our eternal salvation,
lest we fall into serious sin and lose our soul.
Especially do we have to guard against sins of
omission, which can easily be mortal sins if they
involve serious neglect of our fundamental obligations in life.

The overall thrust of the Gospel of Jesus Christ
is positive, is joyful, because it is "good news"
about how we can *definitely* save our souls—
"gospel" *means* "good news." The message of
Christ bears the name "good news" because Our
Lord has taken the *doubt* out of the task of salvation. Granted that the attainment of one's salvation is a big job, the biggest job any of us will
ever undertake, it is nonetheless within our capa-

bilities. This book for some may appear to pose of salvation an overwhelming task, but it really does not. The job of salvation is most assuredly a *limited* task...when we have done what is necessary for salvation, we have done what is necessary, *and* we will be saved. Therefore, we should approach the whole matter with 1) full knowledge of what must be done, 2) prayer that we shall succeed, 3) and a firm resolution to do whatever is necessary *to* succeed.

Chapter XIV

SOME WORDS OF CAUTION

During the nearly 2,000 years of Catholic Church history there have been some 16 Ecumenical Councils, that is, great councils of the whole Church, comprised of the bishops of the world who are in union with the Pope in Rome. Generally, the purpose of these Councils of the Church is to settle doctrinal and moral disputes and questions and/or establish disciplinary rules and regulations to govern the Church. Some of these Councils, such as the Council of Trent, have been very comprehensive in their treatment of doctrinal matters.

But always two factors have been present at all these major councils. The *first* is that they have all been held with the approval and ratification of the Pope—the visible head of the Catholic Church, who is the supreme governing authority in the Church. And the *second* is that, as far as faith and morals are concerned, they did not propose anything new, but rather, were held in order to explicate, confirm and define those beliefs of Catholics that have been believed by the faithful throughout the world and during all of her history as part of Sacred Tradition.

Whether we are already Catholic or whether

we might be a prospective convert, it is vital to our adhering successfully to the True Faith that we recognize the plain fact that during most of Church History there has been on-going at least one virulent heresy (major doctrinal error) which tended to confuse some of the Christians. As mentioned earlier, there have been 16 *major* heresies in the history of the Catholic Church, and numerous minor ones too, most of which the Catholic Church has been able to overcome. We are all familiar with Protestantism, whose main tenet is salvation by faith alone without good works, but which also denies four of the seven Sacraments, the doctrine of Purgatory, the Real Presence of Jesus Christ in the Sacrament of the Eucharist, that the Holy Sacrifice of the Mass is the re-enactment or re-presentation of the Sacrifice of the Cross, etc. Few today realize, however, that during the 4th and 5th centuries there developed a heresy called Arianism, after its proponent, Arius (256-326), a priest of Alexandria, Egypt. This heresy denied, among other things, the divinity of Jesus Christ. In many respects Arianism was a greater heresy than Protestantism in that it was more widespread and deceived a larger percentage of Christians. Historians estimate that some three-fourths of the world's bishops at one time held this heresy. It was so widespread that St. Jerome (342-420) commented, "The world groaned to find itself Arian." Besides the 16 major heresies, however, there have been numerous "minor" ones also, such as (and these are mentioned as examples only), Quietism and Jansenism in the 17th and 18th centuries, both confined mainly to France.

Our own age is no different. During roughly the past 100 years, starting in the late 19th century, there has arisen a heresy called "Modernism," which is somewhat indefinite in its beliefs—because it allows people to believe, really, whatever they want, "whatever is meaningful" to them. One of the principal tenets of Modernism is the idea that "doctrine evolves" and that what was once held by Christians in former times might not necessarily be true today. In this respect, Modernism is really *"relativism,"* that is, the notion that truth is relative to the mind, rather than an objective fact which the mind knows and which is always and everywhere true, whether people acknowledge it to be true or not.

Modernism was formally condemned in 1907 by Pope St. Pius X (1903-1914) in his encyclical letter to the entire Catholic world entitled *Pascendi Dominici Gregis* (*On Modernism,* September 7, 1907). Therefore, anyone who holds to the tenets of Modernism is not and cannot be at the same time a Catholic, because the two belief systems are antithetical (opposed to each other, contradictory).

Let us take as an example a person who has been a lax Catholic and has not studied or practiced his Faith, or even a non-Catholic who has become interested in becoming a Catholic. During, say, the reading of this book or some other thorough exposition of the Catholic Faith, or by association with some knowledgeable Catholic, he then comes to learn what the Catholic Church really teaches. Later, in discussing these traditional Catholic teachings with others who call themselves "Catholic" (but are really Modernists), he hears something like, "Oh, that old stuff! The Church doesn't teach *that* anymore." Or another variation of the same idea, "The Church *used* to teach that, but she doesn't anymore."

As soon as one hears this type of comment, he should realize he is in the company of a Modernist, a person who holds to a heresy formally condemned by the Catholic Church in this very century. Such a comment should be an immediate warning signal that this person does not believe correctly and is therefore not a Catholic.

The errors of such people might be even more subtle and difficult to detect than the example given above because they may be expressed, not as formally wrong statements on doctrinal matters, but concerning the moral teachings of the Church. Thus, one might hear something like the following: "You just have to follow your own conscience with regard to birth control." Or, "Nobody has a right to tell you what you have to do; if you think you should get an abortion, that's up to you. It's strictly between you and God, and nobody has a right to decide for you." In such cases, the implied error of "moral relativism" contained in Modernism is still involved.

As will be recalled from Chapter X, "The Role of Conscience," we all have a serious obligation to "inform" our consciences with correct moral principles, *in advance* of our encountering specific applications of these principles. And as we have seen, the only authority in the world that boldly states to the whole world that SHE is that authority is the Catholic Church.

The Modernist error can crop up in yet a *second* very subtle way, as when someone will say of traditional Catholic doctrine or morals something like, "That's *one* 'approach' to these things. But I have another 'approach.' " The other "approach," of course, is a Modernist (erroneous) one.

Still a *third* ruse of Modernism is to speak in terms of "liberal" and "conservative." "Liberal" and "conservative" have nothing to do with being *"Catholic,"* the meaning of which word is *"all."* Catholics are to believe *all* that Christ taught about salvation—not more, not less—*all* and *only* what He taught. For, with regard to being right or wrong concerning the truths of that Faith revealed to man by God, there is no room possible for being "liberal" and "conservative." Either one is a Catholic and accepts all that Christ taught, or he is not and does not accept all that Christ taught. We cannot have a situation of "more or less" with regard to what one must believe and do in order to save his soul. We might as well speak about liberal and conservative mathematicians. "There just ain't no such thing."

St. Paul in several places warns us about error (heresy), and though we have cited these passages previously, it is good to quote them again in this connection: "But though we, or an angel from heaven, preach a gospel to you besides that which we have preached to you, let him be anathema [excommunicated]." (*Gal.* 1:8). "Preach the word: be instant in season, out of season: reprove, entreat, rebuke in all patience and doctrine. For there shall come a time, when they will not endure sound doctrine; but, according to their own desires, they will heap to themselves teachers, having itching ears: and will indeed turn away their hearing from the truth, but will be turned unto fables." (*2 Tim.* 4:2-4). Also there is the solemn warning of Our Lord, "For amen I say unto you, till heaven and earth pass, one jot, or one tittle shall not pass of the law, till all be fulfilled." (*Matt.* 5:18). In other words, we are to avoid deviating from the teaching of Christ and we are to realize that the *full* teaching of Christ must remain, as it always was, until the End of Time! It does not undergo mutations or become relative to man's thinking and/or his behavior, as the Modernists would have it. We should, therefore, be on guard against Modernism, the heresy that is current—and even widespread—today. In his condemnation of Modernism, Pope St. Pius X called it "the synthesis of all heresies," largely, it would seem, because it condones or allows one to hold as true whatever he wants to. Heretics can be very convincing; therefore, those weak in the Faith and/or those just studying the Faith for the first time must be especially careful of people tainted with Modernist thinking. These may even be people who have been "Catholic" all their lives, and who do not even realize they are in error. Such people are even more dangerous because they *are* convinced of their position and because they can cite the fact that they were born and raised as Catholics. It does not matter. They are espousing error, and if anyone would adhere to the Truth taught by Jesus Christ, he must shun these Modernists and their beliefs. They even use much of the traditional Catholic terminology, but what they mean and understand by the words they use is not what the Catholic Church means and understands by them.

If one is to be a Catholic, he must believe all the doctrines which Christ has taught and which He teaches still through the Roman Catholic Church and which have always been held by the Church as true and "of faith." And these traditional teachings are found in what the Catholic Church calls her "Magisterium," that is, the teaching authority of the Church, which consists of the Popes and the universal (ecumenical) councils of the Church in union with the Pope. Even if a priest or bishop were to teach a doctrine other than that which is taught by the official Magisterium of the Catholic Church, we must not believe him, but rather, we must look to the Official Teaching Authority of the Church for our certain guide.

(This book has been written in keeping with the Traditional Faith of the Catholic Church as it has come down to us from the Popes and official Ecumenical Councils of the Church. What is presented in this book is not new doctrine or "just the opinion of one person." Rather it is an honest attempt to state clearly, in outline form, what people must do and avoid in order to save their souls. Therefore, if anyone were to take exception to these teachings, the reader should be careful to avoid him.)

Chapter XV

ADOPTING A CATHOLIC ATTITUDE

Let us consider a man who likes to hike in the mountains and who decides without any extensive preliminary study to travel to Mount Ararat in Eastern Turkey to climb in search of Noah's Ark. Arriving there during the evening hours, he anxiously awaits the dawn when he can get started. But when morning comes, the mountain is enshrouded with clouds so that there is little to be seen. Consequently, he waits for the weather to clear. And he waits, and he waits. . .while days pass into weeks. But finally there comes a clear day, and he can see the entire mountain in all its colossal splendor. But when he does, he realizes that he had been mistaken about the job of climbing Ararat in search of the Ark, that it is not a task to be accomplished in a single day, but rather, one which will take weeks, and that further, it is definitely not a task to be undertaken alone, but with the help of others—of experienced people, well-equipped, and employing guides for the journey. Therefore, he goes away in order the better to prepare for an attempt that is considerably greater than he had at first naively imagined, an attempt that will take all the strength and all the resources that he can muster.

So it is with many people who, without sufficient information, consider the job of attaining their salvation. They naively imagine that it is not so hard a job, that many before them have achieved it, and that they too will "have a go at it." Or perhaps they even have the absurd idea that almost everyone is saved, that only terrible criminals go to Hell, and that a person will automatically go to Heaven unless he practically *works at* going to Hell. Others, accepting the Protestant heresy, may imagine that attaining salvation is the work of a moment, rather than the project of a lifetime. Thus, when presented with the true scope of the task, they are often incredulous and sometimes discouraged, or they become angry with the person who reveals to them the truth. ("Am I then become your enemy, because I tell you the truth?"—*Gal.* 4:16). But the truth, nonetheless, is still the truth. The Bible does not lie. And we have Our Lord's solemn word about the difficulty of the task. But it definitely is *not* an impossible one. It is just that salvation will yield itself only to the resolute. "No man putting his hand to the plough, and looking back, is fit for the kingdom of God." (*Luke* 9:62). And it is a job that requires help from others, for a knowledge of the way, and spiritual assistance, so that in time of difficulties we may do the good rather than fall into evil.

Let us consider now some passages from Sacred Scripture on this point and then proceed to determine what it will take to be successful in the job of salvation. First we have the very sobering words of St. Peter: "If the just man shall scarcely be saved, where shall the ungodly and the sinner appear?" (*1 Peter* 4:18). "Be you therefore perfect, as also your heavenly Father is perfect." (*Matt.* 5:48). "For amen I say unto you, till heaven and earth pass, one jot, or one tittle shall not pass of the law, till all be fulfilled." (*Matt.* 5:48). "Do not think that I am come to destroy the law, or the prophets. I am not come to destroy, but to fulfill." (*Matt.* 5:17). "And whosoever shall keep the whole law, but offend in one point, is become guilty of all." (*James* 2:10). "With fear and trembling work out your salvation." (*Philippians* 2:12).

In other words, St. Peter is telling us that it is so difficult even for the just (those in the state of Sanctifying Grace) to persevere in that state and thus be saved that they shall scarcely make it. Our Lord is telling us to be as perfect as our heavenly Father in order to *assure* to ourselves that we attain salvation—hopefully to go directly to Heaven rather than having to go first to Purgatory—an achievement we all recognize to be very difficult because of the difficulty of being perfect. (Perfection would be necessary for us to go straight to Heaven; whereas, departing this life in the "state of Sanctifying Grace" is the minimum necessary requirement to avoid Hell. We would go to Purgatory if we died without being perfect but in the State of Grace, and thus we would *still* save our soul.) Further, Our Lord is saying that He did not come to do away with any of the law of God with regard to what all men must do to be saved, but rather to fulfill it (make it fully known and understood), and that not one jot nor one tittle (diacritical marks in writing comparable to the dots over our *"i's"* and the crossings of our *"t's"*) of God's law shall pass till the End of the World—in other words, the *whole* law of God (the Natural Law, built by God into the structure of creation, plus the Revelation He has given us) is in effect, right to the End of Time. Therefore, there can never be a "modern" or "enlightened" era, one in which the laws of God change or are suspended, as mortal sinners are so often wont to presume of their own period in history. St. James is saying that he who offends against the law in one thing (one mortal sin) violates the entire law, and he will go to Hell as surely for one unrepented mortal sin as for ten different kinds of unrepented mortal sins (though the guilt, of course, would be less). And finally, St. Paul is saying we should work out our salvation with a healthy fear of offending God and a certain "healthy nervousness" about whether we are satisfying God's justice. In other words, we need constantly to be reviewing and examining our moral lives and constantly to be perfecting them.

Indeed, the job of salvation is not so easy as many imagine—such that one can simply lolly through this life and waltz into a comfortable place in Heaven. No, Our Lord is very definite about its taking all of our mind and heart and will and effort to achieve salvation. This is really to say that we must make a *fundamental, entire* and *fully committed* orientation toward gaining our salvation. Hear what He told His followers: "If any man will come after me, let him deny himself, and take up his cross, and follow me. For he that will save his life, shall lose it: and he that shall lose his life for my sake shall find it. For what doth it profit a man, if he gain the whole world, and suffer the loss of his own soul? Or what exchange shall a man give for his soul? For the Son of man shall come in the glory of his Father with his angels: and then will he render to every man according to his works." (*Matt.* 16:24-29). (Protestant readers should note here that Our Lord says He will render to us according to our *works*, and not according to our *faith*, a point reminiscent of *Psalm* 60:13, ". . . for thou wilt render to every man according to his works.") Our Lord is telling us that we have to deny our nature, and take up our cross and follow Him. Now, when you take up your cross and follow Jesus, where are you going. . . but to a crucifixion! *Your own crucifixion!*. . .where the old man, the natural man, who seeks all and only the comforts of life, is going to be put to death. (In a very real sense, the human condition is a crucifixion and a misery anyway, whether we accept it as such or not. The true Christian merely *embraces* his cross—be it light or heavy—

whereas the non-Christian soul tries to avoid his. However, both still carry their cross.) Our Lord goes on to say that he who would save his life (the natural man with his self-seeking) shall lose his life (his soul for all eternity), but he who would sacrifice the life of the natural man—including, when necessary, the comforts, luxuries and self-fulfillment that we naturally seek for ourselves—shall find the life of the spirit (the supernaturalized man) and shall save his soul for all eternity.

But Our Lord goes even further than telling us we must *deny* ourselves. Hear what He has to say in *Luke* 14—and we shall take this passage as the keynote of this chapter on adopting a proper Catholic attitude toward our salvation:

"If any man come to me, and hate not his father, and mother, and wife, and children, and brethren, and sisters, yea and his own life also, he cannot be my disciple. And whosoever doth not carry his cross and come after me, cannot be my disciple. For which of you having a mind to build a tower, doth not first sit down, and reckon the charges that are necessary, whether he have wherewithal to finish it: Lest, after he hath laid the foundation, and is not able to finish it, all that see it begin to mock him, saying: This man began to build, and was not able to finish. Or what king, about to go to make war against another king, doth not first sit down, and think whether he be able, with ten thousand,

*to meet him that, with twenty thousand, cometh
against him? Or else, whilst the other is yet afar
off, sending an embassy, he desireth conditions
of peace. So likewise every one of you that doth
not renounce all that he possesseth, cannot be
my disciple.''* —Luke 14:26-33

Our Lord is obviously not telling us that we
literally have to "hate" our father, mother, wife,
etc., but He is telling us that they must all be
put aside if they stand in the way of our salvation—yes, even our very life must be considered as nothing when it comes to doing what
is necessary for salvation. Witness the tens of
thousands, and millions even, who have been
martyred (murdered because of their Christian
belief) rather than renounce Christ and His Faith.

Within this passage is the mysterious, almost
anomalous part about the person about to build
a tower, how he should reckon before starting
if he have the means to finish, and about the
king going to war with ten thousand against a
king having twenty thousand, who should consider first if he can win, or whether he should
sue for peace before the battle commences. Now
we know that these two examples are an integral
part of the whole passage because Our Lord ends
by saying, "So likewise every one of you that
doth not renounce all that he possesseth, cannot be my disciple." (*Luke* 14:33). This last statement corresponds to verses 26 and 27, where
He says we must "hate" our father, mother, wife,

etc.—even our very *life*—and carry our cross and come after Him, or we cannot be His disciples.

What is the meaning of this seemingly incredible passage from *Luke*? What in the world is Our Divine Saviour telling us? Is this really what the Bible says? Or have the texts of Scripture somehow become jumbled in this passage?

Our Lord is saying quite simply that the job of salvation can very easily entail renouncing everything we have—our relatives, our possessions, our very lives—if it comes to a test of our faith. He is saying, in effect, that we have to prepare ourselves interiorly, in advance, by becoming detached in spirit from even those things we hold most dear in this world, so that we shall be ready to make even the ultimate sacrifice, that of our lives, should this be necessary as a testimony to His truth and our faith in Him and His Holy Religion. And if we do not consider and weigh well what it will require to save our souls *and then give it our all(!)*, we shall be like the person who starts to build a tower with insufficient materials and cannot finish because he did not first seriously consider how much it would require and see beforehand that he had not secured the means to finish what he planned to start; or we shall be like the king going into battle with ten thousand men against a king with twenty thousand, who loses because he did not first evaluate the magnitude of the job he had set out upon.

Yes, we shall also be like the hiker who intended to conquer Mount Ararat on his own—without climbing gear, without the assistance of others, and without a guide.

Those who criticize this book because of the large scope it presents of the job of salvation must contend in their objections against Our Divine Saviour Himself, *who says it will take all we have and all we are!*...that it *may* require the sacrifice of our loved ones, our possessions, or even our very lives. Far from presenting the task of salvation as more difficult than it is, this book probably comes up on the shy side. For Our Lord in other passages supports completely what we have just read from *Luke* 14. Consider, for example, the following passage from St. Matthew:

"Do not think that I came to send peace upon earth: I came not to send peace, but the sword. For I came to set a man at variance against his father, and the daughter against her mother, and the daughter in law against her mother in law. And a man's enemies shall be they of his own household. He that loveth father or mother more than me, is not worthy of me; and he that loveth son or daughter more than me, is not worthy of me. And he that taketh not up his cross, and followeth me, is not worthy of me. He that findeth his life, shall lose it: and he that shall lose his life for me, shall find it."

—Matthew 10:34-39

For our purposes here, this quotation is a perfect explanation in Our Lord's own words of *Luke* 14:26-33, quoted earlier, for it shows how deadly serious Our Lord is about the reality of the job of salvation. From His own words we can see that it is a *tough* job, *one that will for certain be achieved only by absolutely resolute souls*, people who set their aim at Heaven and will let *nothing* stand in their way—who do not look back at the "joys of the world," who do not long for the "flesh-pots of Egypt" (a biblical symbol of sinful worldly pleasures), as many of the Israelites did who left that country and crossed the desert (a symbol of the Christian life in this "vale of tears") to the "Promised Land" (a symbol of Heaven).

Nor can it be said that the battle is all grim and gruesome, and nothing but a sterile, thankless, drudging chore. *Indeed not*. There is, in fact, a strange paradox about the true Christian or Catholic way of life. It is like the life of the soldier or the athlete; it is a burden, yes, but it is in a certain sense delightful, and delightfully achievable. It is hard, yes; but strangely, it is also a great joy. Our Lord tells us: "Take up my yoke upon you, and learn of me, because I am meek and humble of heart: and you will find rest to your souls. For my yoke is *sweet* and my burden *light*." (*Matt.* 11:29-30, emphasis added). That is the paradox: Our Lord, if we are to be His followers, is giving us a cross to bear, a yoke to carry. But if we will just accept it, if we will just take it up willingly, lovingly, joyfully, and do what we are supposed to do, we will find His burden is not so very hard after all, that in fact it is a delight, especially if done out of love for Him, who, out of an incomparable and incomprehensible love, has done all for us.

God is not some ogre or cruel and unreasonable judge. Indeed not! For speaking through Solomon, He says in the Old Testament: "For God made not death, neither hath he pleasure in the destruction of the living. For he created all things that they might be: and he made the nations of the earth for health: and there is no poison of destruction in them, nor kingdom of hell upon earth." (*Wisdom* 1:13-14). Also, as we saw earlier, God, speaking through Ezechiel the prophet, proclaims: "Is it my will that a sinner should die [i.e., go to Hell], saith the Lord God, and not that he should be converted from his ways and live [i.e., return to justice and living in the state of Sanctifying Grace]?" (*Ezechiel* 18:23). But God does want us to know the magnitude of the task of salvation, and that is part of the reason why Our Lord suffered His cruel and bitter Passion, dying the most excruciating death imaginable—crucifixion! Why?...if not to show us what sin cost Him and to show us that we too will have to go through a certain "agony" and a "death-by-crucifixion" of sorts as we crucify the "old man" with his concupiscences and inclinations to evil in order to let the "new Christian man" be born in us out of his death. Let us recall Our Lord's words to Nicodemus as recorded in *John*: "Amen, amen I say to thee, unless a man be born again of water and the Holy Ghost, he cannot enter into the kingdom of God. That which is born of the flesh, is flesh [the old man, the natural man]; and that which is born of the Spirit, is spirit [the new man, the supernaturalized Christian man, born of the Sacrament of Baptism]." (*John* 3:5-6).

If we will but accept Christ and all He taught, the job of salvation will become relatively easy, for we will have all the "tools" and aids and assists that Our Lord has built into His Holy Religion. This is a sign of God's love. As Our Lord told Nicodemus further on, "For God so loved the world, as to give his only begotten Son; that whosoever believeth in him, may not perish, but may have life everlasting. For God sent not his Son into the world, to judge the world, but that the world may be saved by him. He that believeth in him [and does all which that faith entails] is not judged [condemned to Hell]. But he that doth not believe, is *already* judged [condemned]; because he believeth not in the name of the only begotten Son of God. And this is the judgment: because the light [Christ] is come into the world, and men loved darkness [their sins] rather than the light [Christ and His truth]: for their works were evil." (*John* 3:16-19, emphasis added).

If, therefore, we will accept Our Lord *and ALL He taught*, we will not be condemned, for He has provided in His Religion the relatively easy means of salvation: 1) the truth, whereby we are to live the true Christian way of life, and 2) the Sacraments of His Church, to give us His divine life and to help us be good, through the sacramental graces they bring. But if we do not accept Christ and the obvious truth which He teaches, we shall be condemned. "Every one that is of the truth, heareth my voice." (*John* 18:37).

Adopting a Catholic attitude, therefore, entails humbly accepting ALL (*katholikos*) that Christ taught, taking up our cross daily and following Him, i.e., performing our daily duties (to perfection, if we would avoid Purgatory) and avoiding all mortal sin, at the very least (and all venial sin if, again, we would avoid Purgatory), and being prepared to sacrifice *all* (father, mother, wife, possessions. . .self) rather than deny or forsake (by sin, by silence or by outright apostasy) the truth which Christ taught and which He makes synonymous with Himself. "*I* am the way, and the truth, and the life. No man cometh to the Father, but by me." (*John* 14:6).

Such an attitude of life, dear Reader, entails being a Catholic—in order to tap into the Living Vine that is Christ and to learn what it takes to save our souls from the Apostolic Tradition that has come down to us from the Apostles themselves, which is still as present in the world today as it was when Sts. Peter and Andrew, James and John, and the rest of the Apostles went out into all the known world, preaching Christ, and Him crucified. And such an attitude also entails being a Catholic in order to tap into the Seven Sacraments instituted by Christ which impart the divine life of God to our souls and give us the grace necessary to avoid sin and faithfully perform our duties.

If we are to be Our Lord's disciples, let us follow His prescriptions: Let us deny ourselves, take up our cross daily and follow Him. Let us crucify the "old man," in order that the new, the Christian man might be born within us, that we might say with St. Paul: "as dying, and behold we live; as chastised, and not killed; as sorrowful, yet always rejoicing; as needy, yet enriching many; as having nothing, and possessing all things." (*2 Cor.* 6:9-10).

Then shall we enjoy the *fruit* of the true Christian life while yet in this world: "But the fruit of the spirit is charity, joy, peace, patience, benignity, goodness, longanimity, mildness, faith, modesty, continency, chastity" (*Gal.* 5:22): and in the next world we shall enjoy the *fruit* of eternal happiness with God in Heaven, where we shall have all knowledge, see all beauty, and experience every joy we could possibly desire or conceivably imagine.

These, then, are the fruits of the true Christian attitude toward life—of adopting the proper Catholic attitude toward our salvation. But without this Catholic attitude, which stems from True Faith in Christ, we cannot achieve the goal of salvation, yet with it, we can say with St. Paul, "I can do all things in him who strengtheneth me." (*Philippians* 4:13).

Chapter XVI

CONCLUSION

We have considered in Part II of this book the question "How to avoid Hell." To the well-instructed Catholic there is no real problem of *what* to do, but rather of *doing* it and doing it *well*. For, the instructed Catholic is well-versed in what God requires for salvation—what He requires by His Commandments and what He expects of us in charity.

But the uninstructed Catholic and those outside the Catholic Faith (which, let us remember, is none other than God's own Religion) generally have only a vague notion at best of what is entailed in the task of saving one's soul. And when one probes their thinking, he usually finds a personal religious philosophy that has been haphazardly assembled from various sources—a partial understanding of the Bible, early (and rather incomplete and poorly remembered) religious instruction, personal experience, the example of others, worldly "wisdom," and so forth—but yet their personal moral philosophy (as exemplified by their actions) almost always condones and/or accepts things which are directly at variance with what Our Lord Himself has said will lead a person to Hell. Whether such people are sincere we cannot judge, for we cannot see inside their consciences. That they are confused and living by a patchwork quilt of pieced-together moral philosophy, and that their philosophy contradicts in some points what Christ explicitly taught (e.g., "He that shall marry her that is put away committeth adultery"—*Matt.* 5:32) is obvious. Here we should recall once more the words of Scripture, "And whosoever shall keep the whole law, but offend in one point, is become guilty of all." (*James* 2:10).

We have considered Our Lord's words: "Go ye forth into the whole world and make disciples of all nations, teaching them to observe whatsoever I have commanded you. He that believeth and is baptized shall be saved: but he that believeth not shall be condemned." (*Matt.* 28:19; *Mark* 16:15, 16). We have seen that by this commission to His Apostles and by His words to St. Peter—"Thou art Peter; and upon this rock I will build my Church, and the gates of hell shall not prevail against it. And I will give to thee the keys of the kingdom of heaven. And whatsoever thou shalt bind upon earth, it shall be bound also in heaven: and whatsoever thou shalt loose on earth, it shall be loosed also in heaven" (*Matt.* 16:18-19)—that Our Lord spoke clearly of establishing a church, His Church, and that it would be founded upon Peter, the Prince of the Apostles, and that the Gates of Hell would not prevail against it, that is, it would last for all time. Elsewhere He called it "a city seated on a mountain [that] cannot be hid.'' (*Matt.* 5:14). He said it would be persecuted and His followers persecuted as well, just as He was, and that they would be put to death, just as He was. And these things have all come to pass.

We saw that only the Roman Catholic Church has all the hallmarks of the Church of Christ: We have seen how it alone is *one, holy, Catholic* (universal) and *apostolic.* We have seen that there is no other organization like it in the world, that it is a true government (though its kingdom is not of this world), that it is the largest of the major religions in the world (whether they be highly organized or loosely federated), that it is by far the most highly organized religion in the world (one might even say, the *only* really governmentally organized religion), that it is bigger than all Protestant Christianity put together (according to some statistics, as much as triple the size), that it is the only religion truly spread *universally* throughout the world, that it everywhere teaches *one* doctrine and is everywhere governed by *one* head and everywhere worships in *one* manner, that it goes back uninterrupted in time to the *Apostles* themselves, that its doctrine and worship have never changed (it still has the same Mass and the same Seven Sacraments), that it has produced *holy* people in every age (the prodigies connected with the lives of Catholic saints are unique in the world).

We have seen that the Catholic Church maintains that all men must join her ranks in order to achieve salvation, which requirement is merely a restatement of what Our Lord said, "He that believeth and is baptized, shall be saved: but he that believeth not shall be condemned." (*Mark* 16:16). We have seen that no other religion makes this bold, flat-footed claim or even presumes to arrogate to itself such authority; that none other is so bold as to say *it ALONE is the "True Faith,"* the Faith revealed by God Himself, outside of which there is no salvation. We have seen a thorough, albeit short, presentation of the Commandments of God and what they cover, which we *all* must obey in order to gain eternal life. ("Good Master, what shall I do that I may receive life everlasting?...Thou knowest the commandments: Do not commit adultery, do not kill, do not steal..." —*Mark* 10:17, 19). We have seen the Precepts of the Roman Catholic Church elucidated and how they are merely logical extensions of the Ten Commandments of God and of Our Lord's commission to the Apostles and St. Peter. We have considered the Seven Capital Sins (which non-Catholics probably have never heard of, as such); we have seen that they are the *principal sins* we fall into and the *sources of sin* within us—those *inclinations* which cause us to sin (though as inclinations only they are not themselves sin). We have seen what is required for true contrition for our sins before God will forgive us; we have also seen that when one combines the Catholic Sacrament of Confession with properly motivated contrition, there exists an unfailing combination for the forgiveness of our sins—and we have considered what is the accompanying heavenly peace of soul which results from one's repenting and confessing in this manner. We have considered the Corporal and Spiritual Works of Mercy, which are none other than a codification of what the Bible says is required of us in order to have proper charity (God-like love) toward our neighbor—which all stems from statements in Scripture such as, "If any man say, I love God, and hateth his brother; he is a liar. For he that loveth not his brother, whom he seeth, how can he love God, whom he seeth not?" (*1 John* 4:20); as well as from the Two Great Commandments: "Thou shalt love the Lord thy God with thy whole heart, and with thy whole soul, and with thy whole mind . . .and . . . thou shalt love thy neighbour as thyself" (*Matt.* 22:37, 39); as also from innumerable other passages from both the Old and New Testaments. From all such Scriptural passages we see that charity toward our neighbor, as called for in the Gospels and as codified by the Roman Catholic Church in the Corporal and Spiritual Works of Mercy, constitutes basically one-half of the true Christian life, the *active side*, so to speak, with obedience to the Commandments comprising the other half, or what one might call the *side of combat*.

We have considered statements from Our Lord, such as, "Except you eat the flesh of the Son of man, and drink his blood, you shall not have life in you. He that eateth my flesh, and drinketh my blood, hath everlasting life: and I will raise him up in the last day." (*John* 6:54-55). "Without me you can do nothing" (*John* 15:5), "I will not leave you orphans" (*John* 14:18), and "Behold, I am with you all days, even to the consummation of the world." (*Matt.* 28:20). All such statements show that Christ intended to found a church, a church exactly like what the Catholic Church is, a church which possesses the Real Presence of Jesus Christ, the God-man, in its "temples," as the Old Testament Hebrew religion possessed the Shekinah Presence of God dwelling in the Holy of Holies of the Old Testament Temple in Jerusalem, and which dispenses the actual, real Body and Blood of Jesus Christ as true spiritual food for its members.

And Christ did not leave us orphans. Indeed not. He left us His Church, His Mystical Body extended in time, the Roman Catholic Church, to which He sent the Holy Spirit to be with it and keep it from any error, and in which He dwells—by Sanctifying Grace in its members and by His Sacramental Presence in the Holy Eucharist, where, in His total Godhead and humanity, He daily awaits His faithful servants.

He is in a very real sense to be found in the "temples" of the True Religion, the Catholic Church, even today, as of yore when Mary and Joseph searched for Him during three days, only to find Him in the Temple of the True Religion of the Old Testament. Those who want to know and love Jesus Christ can still find Him out. And they will find Him just like Mary and Joseph did—dwelling in the "temples" of the True Religion of the New Testament. He is so close and so real that His divine presence in the flesh will doubtlessly come as a shock to those who discover Him. Indeed, we need Him to save our souls; and yes, He gives Himself to the world most liberally; but yet He makes certain requirements. We have to have Faith, His Faith (*Apoc.* 2:13; 14:12; *Gal.* 2:16; *et al.*); we have to believe in Him; we have to, as it were, stretch ourselves that little bit to accept on faith those things about His teaching we cannot fully comprehend, but which we take as true, nonetheless, because God is the Author of the revelation, who cannot deceive us. In making our act of faith, we can say (if we have to) with the man in the Gospel, "I do believe, Lord: help my unbelief." (*Mark* 9:23). Then, having faith, will we be able to be baptized and receive Him in Holy Communion. Then will we fulfill His requirements: "He that believeth and is baptized shall be saved: he that believeth not shall be condemned" (*Mark* 16:15, 16); "Except you eat the flesh of the Son of man, and drink his blood, you shall not have life in you" (*John* 6:54-55); and so forth. From all the Bible quotes above, it becomes quite obvious that we must, in a completely real sense, join ourselves to Jesus Christ, to His Body, to His Mystical Body, to the Catholic Church, in order to be saved, in order to avoid Hell and gain Heaven,

where we shall be happy with Him for all
eternity.

That in essence is what we must do to avoid
Hell: Join the Roman Catholic Church (Christ
Himself), observe the Commandments, receive
the Sacraments, pray regularly, practice charity
(do good works, support the Church, give alms),
root out our sins and the evil inclinations within
our souls and substitute for them the Christian
virtues (good habits), do penance for our sins,
and live our lives in the State of Sanctifying
Grace, that when the Bridegroom of our souls
shall come with the wedding party, we shall be
ready and waiting with our lamps burning (souls
in the State of Grace) and be able thereby to
enter joyfully into His glory with Him. (Cf. *Matt.*
25:1-13).

"If you continue in my word," said Our Lord,
"you shall be my disciples indeed. And you shall
know the truth, and the truth shall make you
free." (*John* 8:31-32). Notice from these words
of Our Lord that we must first *be good* and *then*
we shall know the truth. If we sin, our minds
are clouded to the truth, and we begin to lie
to ourselves in order to cover up our sins and
hide them from ourselves. But God knows our
inmost hearts. He knows when we are lying to
ourselves and to Him, on the one hand, and
when, on the other hand, we are possessed of
a pure heart—when we are like the disciple
Nathanael, "an Israelite [true believer] indeed,
in whom there is no guile." (*John* 1:47).

We all know with our natural reason, unaided by Revelation, that there is an afterlife. We all know (however deeply and inchoately within ourselves it may be) that a final reckoning is coming at the end of our lives, a Day of Judgment, when all will be put right and when final justice will be done. We know, too, within our heart of hearts, that our own eternal destiny will be determined by how we live and what we do here in this world. We all know that when we commit mortal sin, we must either accept the fact we are thereby on the road to Hell, or we have to lie to ourselves and say, "It isn't a sin." Or, "It isn't that bad." Or, "But God understands. He will have mercy."

Yes, He does indeed understand, and He surely will have mercy *on the truly repentant* (otherwise, who among us would ever be saved); but He is also just, in fact He is Justice Itself, and it is His very justice that will condemn us if we do not repent of our mortal sins—all of them—if we do not do penance and amend our lives once and for all before we die.

People wait and wait while they live on and on in the state of mortal sin, thinking always within themselves: "I must change. I must correct my life. . .soon!" But for many mortal sinners "soon" never comes, as months drift into years, and as they continue to defer the time of their conversion—many until it is too late, and they are cut off by an accident or a heart attack while still in the fullness of their powers, or until they have grown old and become sick or senile and have not the mental strength anymore to focus on the eternal questions of Heaven or Hell and just what God requires us to do to satisfy His justice in order to be saved.

But the certain way to avoid Hell is to start *now*, from wherever we might be, and turn to God, asking of Him the gift of Faith, true repentance, the forgiveness of our sins, a spirit of penance (to make up to Him for our lost years spent in sin and self-indulgence) and the virtue of charity—a Godlike love of God and of our fellow man. If we are Catholic, we must go to Confession with the proper dispositions—at least of imperfect contrition for all the mortal sins we may have committed and with a firm resolve to commit mortal sin no more. And if we are not Catholic, we should approach the Catholic Church for instruction, that we might gain entrance to the Mystical Body of Christ, to His Church, which is none other than Christ Himself extended in time and presented to the world.

At that point we shall THEN *have entered upon the field of battle and* THEN *we can begin in earnest the job of our salvation.* "Stand, therefore, having your loins girt about with truth, and having on the breastplate of justice, and your feet shod with the preparation of the gospel of peace: In all things taking the shield of faith, wherewith you may be able to extinguish all the fiery darts of the most wicked one." (*Eph.* 6:14-16).

It is not until we become truly Catholic that

we *begin* to live the life of Christ here in this
world, that we *begin* to prepare ourselves for
Heaven by living a life of virtue—a life wherein
we start to observe meticulously all the Commandments, root out the Seven Capital Sins, practice virtue seriously, pray, receive the Sacraments
instituted by Christ to help us with His grace,
live a life of true Christian charity, and start on
the road to being perfect as our Heavenly Father
is perfect. (*Matt.* 5:48).

Short of doing all these things, we will not have
the true hope of saving our souls. But if we do
them, we have the promise of eternal life with
God in Heaven. "He that eateth my flesh, and
drinketh my blood, hath everlasting life: and I
will raise him up in the last day." (*John* 6:54-55).
But if we are not Catholics, how can we receive
the Body and Blood of Christ in Holy Communion, upon which, in great part, and according
to Our Lord's very own words, depends our eternal salvation?

Let us consider, finally, a passage from St. Matthew's Gospel wherein Our Lord compares the
Kingdom of Heaven to a treasure hidden in a
field, to a pearl of great price, and to a net cast
into the sea, and let us draw from this reading
some of the lessons Our Lord wishes to convey
to us about attaining our salvation.

" *"The kingdom of heaven is like unto a treasure hidden in a field. Which a man having
found, hid it, and for joy thereof, goeth and*

*selleth all that he hath, and buyeth that field.
Again the kingdom of heaven is like to a mer-
chant seeking good pearls. Who when he had
found one pearl of great price, went his way,
and sold all that he had, and bought it. Again
the kingdom of heaven is like to a net cast into
the sea, and gathering together of all kind of
fishes. Which, when it was filled, they drew out,
and sitting by the shore, they chose out the good
into vessels, but the bad they cast forth. So shall
it be at the end of the world. The angels shall
go out, and shall separate the wicked from
among the just. And shall cast them into the
furnace of fire: there shall be weeping and
gnashing of teeth. Have ye understood all these
things?' They say to Him: 'Yes.' He said unto
them: 'Therefore every scribe instructed in the
kingdom of heaven, is like to a man that is a
householder, who bringeth forth out of his treasure new things and old.'"*

—Matthew 13:44-52

The Catholic Church is the Kingdom of Heaven
already begun on earth by Jesus Christ. Now the
Kingdom of Heaven (the Catholic Church) is like
a treasure hidden in a field because, though of
inestimable value, few people (proportionally
speaking) realize it is there, and fewer still truly
appreciate it. But to those who have found it,
the Kingdom of Heaven, the Catholic Faith, is
an inexhaustible treasure of grace and knowledge about the way to salvation, and those who

find it willingly sacrifice everything for it. The Kingdom of Heaven (the Catholic Church) is like a pearl of great price because there is only one like it, and it is worth all we own and all we hold dear in order to possess it. And once having found it, the true believer will sacrifice everything to own it.

Again, the Kingdom of Heaven (the Catholic Church) is like a heavenly net cast into the sea of this world, which "catches" both the good and the bad (the virtuous and sinners, those who join His Church and those who outright reject it, those who cooperate with the graces of Christ given through His Church and those who do not); the good will be taken to Heaven, but the wicked will be cast into Hell, where "there shall be weeping and gnashing of teeth" (*Matt.* 8:12), for then it will be too late to rectify our lives.

But *now* it is not! *Now* we still have time to change our lives—to join ourselves to Christ, to repent of and confess our sins, to do penance, to pray and to honor God, to do good in the world, to work out our salvation.

Let us therefore begin the task. Let us set about the work of our salvation. Let us buy the field wherein is hidden the "Treasure," that we may possess it. Let us become true Catholics, who believe, with St. Ignatius of Antioch, "*katholikos*," *all* that Christ taught! Let us join the Church if we are not yet members, or let us live up to our Holy Religion if we already have the gift of Faith. Then shall we *possess* the "Pearl of Great Price''; then shall we be ready, as the net of the Lord is cast into the sea of this life, to be taken by the holy angels to Heaven, there to live with God forever.

Let us become, each one of us, a ''scribe instructed in the kingdom of Heaven'' (i.e., a supernaturally enlightened person of Faith), that we may draw forth out of the treasure of the deposit of the Faith, new inspirations and old, that we may continue *steadily* and *with certainty* upon the path to Heaven, so that when finally we meet our Heavenly Judge, we shall hear with joy those blessed words: ''Well done, good and faithful servant, because thou hast been faithful over a few things, I will place thee over many things: enter thou into the joy of thy lord.'' (*Matt.* 25:21).

God be with you, dear Reader.

The End

***If you have enjoyed this book, consider making your next
selection from among the following . . .***

Prices guaranteed through June 30, 1991.

Prices guaranteed through June 30, 1991.

Secular Saints: 250 Lay Men & Women. Cruz. HB 40.00
Imitation of Christ. à Kempis. Trans. Challoner 9.00
Stories from The Catechist. Howe 13.50
Confession Quizzes. Radio Replies Press 60
Purgatory and Heaven. J. P. Arendzen 2.50
What Is Liberalism? Sarda y Salvany 4.00
The Creator and the Creature. Fr. Frederick Faber 12.00
Radio Replies. 3 Vols. Frs. Rumble and Carty 33.00
Convert's Catechism of Catholic Doctrine. Geiermann . . . 2.00
Light and Peace. Fr. R. P. Quadrupani 4.00
The Evolution Hoax Exposed. A. N. Field 4.00
Christ Denied. Fr. Paul Wickens 1.25
Birth Prevention Quizzes. Radio Replies Press 60
Marriage Quizzes. Radio Replies Press 60
True Church Quizzes. Radio Replies Press 60
The Happiness of Heaven. Fr. J. Boudreau 6.00
How Christ Said the First Mass. Fr. Meagher 13.50
Too Busy for God? Think Again! D'Angelo 2.50
St. Bernadette Soubirous. Trochu 15.00
Passion and Death of Jesus Christ. Liguori 5.00
Treatise on the Love of God. 2 Vols. de Sales 13.50
St. Philip Neri. Fr. V. J. Matthews 3.50
St. Louise de Marillac. Sr. Vincent Regnault 3.50
The Old World and America. Rev. Philip Furlong 12.50
Prophecy for Today. Edward Connor 3.50
Bethlehem. Fr. Faber 13.50
The Book of Infinite Love. Mother de la Touche 3.50
The Church Teaches. Church Documents 12.50
Conversation with Christ. Peter T. Rohrbach 7.00
Spiritual Legacy/Sr. Mary of Trinity. van den Broek 8.00
Incarnation, Birth, Infancy of Jesus Christ. Liguori 5.00
Dogmatic Canons & Decrees of Trent, Vat. I 6.50
The Primitive Church. Fr. D. I. Lanslots 7.00
The Priesthood. Bishop Stockums 8.50
A Tour of the Summa. Msgr. Paul Glenn 12.50
Spiritual Conferences. Fr. Frederick Faber 11.00
Bible Quizzes. Radio Replies Press 60
Mary, Mother of the Church. Church Documents 2.00
The Sacred Heart and the Priesthood. de la Touche 6.00
Blessed Sacrament. Fr. Faber 13.50
Revelations of St. Bridget. St. Bridget of Sweden 2.50
Magnificent Prayers. St. Bridget of Sweden 1.50
The Glories of Mary. St. Alphonsus Liguori 13.50
The Glories of Mary. (pocket, unabr.). St. Alphonsus . . . 5.00

Prices guaranteed through June 30, 1991.

The Spiritual Doctrine/St. Cath. of Genoa............. 8.00
Three Ages of Interior Life. 2 Vol. Gar.-Lagrange. HB...48.00
Characters of the Inquisition. Wm. T. Walsh...........10.00
Heliotropium—Conformity of Human Will to Divine.... 9.00
Fundamentals of Catholic Dogma. Ott.................16.50
Clean Love in Courtship. Fr. Lawrence Lovasik........ 2.00
Where We Got the Bible. Fr. Henry Graham.......... 4.00
The Two Divine Promises. Fr. Hoppe................. 1.25
St. Teresa of Ávila. William Thomas Walsh...........16.50
Isabella of Spain—The Last Crusader. Wm. T. Walsh....16.50
Philip II. William Thomas Walsh. H.B................37.50
Blood-Drenched Altars—Cath. Comment. Hist. Mexico..16.50
Self-Abandonment to Divine Providence. de Caussade...15.00
Way of the Cross. Liguorian...................... .75
Way of the Cross. Franciscan..................... .75
Modern Saints—Their Lives & Faces. Ann Ball........15.00
Saint Michael and the Angels. Approved Sources....... 4.50
Dolorous Passion of Our Lord. Anne C. Emmerich.....12.50
Our Lady of Fatima's Peace Plan from Heaven. Booklet. .40
Divine Favors Granted to St. Joseph. Pere Binet........ 3.50
St. Joseph Cafasso—Priest of the Gallows. St. J. Bosco.. 2.00
Catechism of the Council of Trent. McHugh/Callan.....20.00
Padre Pio—The Stigmatist. Fr. Charles Carty..........11.00
Why Squander Illness? Frs. Rumble & Carty.......... 1.50
Fatima—The Great Sign. Francis Johnston............. 6.00
Charity for the Suffering Souls. Fr. John Nageleisen....12.50
Religious Liberty. Michael Davies................... 1.00
Sermons on Prayer. St. Francis de Sales.............. 3.00
Sermons on Our Lady. St. Francis de Sales........... 8.00
Sermons for Lent. St. Francis de Sales............... 8.00
Litany of the Blessed Virgin Mary. (100 cards)......... 4.00
Who Is Padre Pio? Radio Replies Press............... 1.00
Child's Bible History. Knecht..................... 2.50
The Life of Christ. 4 Vols. H.B. Anne C. Emmerich....50.00
St. Anthony—The Wonder Worker of Padua. Stoddard... 2.50
The Precious Blood. Fr. Faber..................... 9.00
The Holy Shroud & Four Visions. Fr. O'Connell....... 1.50
The Prophecies of St. Malachy. Peter Bander.......... 3.50
The Secret of the Rosary. St. Louis De Montfort....... 3.00
The History of Antichrist. Rev. P. Huchede........... 2.00
Hidden Treasure—Holy Mass. St. Leonard............ 3.00
The Life & Glories of St. Joseph. Edward Thompson...11.00

At your bookdealer or direct from the publisher.

Prices guaranteed through June 30, 1991.

GIVE COPIES OF THIS BOOK

Give copies of this book to friends and relatives, to Catholics and non-Catholics, to young adults and to those who are confused. Many people today are searching for the truth and need the direction in their lives that this book has to offer. Many, too, are confused and yet of a good heart; this book will help them understand what they must do to save their souls. Some people may even think they do not care where they go when they die; such people also need to read this book. Others, too, have gone astray and think that the way they are living is all right because so many are living the same way; they need to read this book to understand what is really required of salvation. In short, *everyone* needs to read this book because it says uncompromisingly what needs to be said about the job we all face in saving our souls, and it is probably the only book written for people today that is so complete and so powerful.

Through the agency of this book you can become an army of one, working for Christ and the salvation of souls. If you prefer not to give this book personally, simply send your order to the Publisher along with the addresses of those you would like to have receive it, and these can be sent with or without any indication that you are the donor; just spell out your choice.

This book was written to help you help others save their souls. It can only achieve that end if you will give copies to those who need to read it.

ORDER FORM

HELL and HOW TO AVOID HELL

1 copy	$10.00	
5 copies	6.00 each	30.00 total
10 copies	5.00 each	50.00 total

Postage and handling on each order—$2.00

Gentlemen:

Please send me _____ copy (copies) of **Hell and How To Avoid Hell.**

☐ Enclosed is my payment in the amount of _____ .

☐ Please bill my credit card: ☐ VISA ☐ MasterCard

Credit Card No. _____

4-Digit No. (MasterCard only) _____

My Credit Card expires _____

Name _____

Street _____

City _____

State _____ Zip _____

TAN BOOKS AND PUBLISHERS, INC.
P.O. Box 424 Rockford, Illinois 61105

Tel. 815-987-1800. FAX 815-987-1833. For fastest service, phone or FAX your order. VISA and MasterCard welcome. Give all numbers on your card, plus the expiration date.